5758444

7/12

Please renew/return this item by the last date shown.

So that your telephone call is charged at local rate, please call the numbers as set out below:

	From Area codes 01923 or 0208:	From the rest of Herts:
Renewals:	01923 471373	01438 737373
Enquiries:	01923 471333	01438 737333
Minicom:	01923 471599	01438 737599

L32b

24 OCT 2002

21 JUL 2006

22 JUL 1994

19 MAR 1997   **16 AUG 1999**

16 SEP.

=7 OCT 1997   - 6 MAY 2003

29 OCT   **6 JAN 2004**

23 NOV 1998
2 DEZ 1998

SOMERSET

THE KING'S ENGLAND

Edited by Arthur Mee

In 41 Volumes

ENCHANTED LAND (INTRODUCTORY VOLUME)

Bedfordshire and
  Huntingdonshire
Berkshire
Buckinghamshire
Cambridgeshire
Cheshire
Cornwall
Derbyshire
Devon
Dorset
Durham
Essex
Gloucestershire
Hampshire with the
  Isle of Wight
Herefordshire
Hertfordshire
Kent
Lake Counties
Lancashire
Leicestershire and
  Rutland

Lincolnshire
London
Middlesex
Monmouthshire
Norfolk
Northamptonshire
Northumberland
Nottinghamshire
Oxfordshire
Shropshire
Somerset
Staffordshire
Suffolk
Surrey
Sussex
Warwickshire
Wiltshire
Worcestershire
Yorkshire—East Riding
Yorkshire—North Riding
Yorkshire—West Riding

THE KING'S ENGLAND

SOMERSET

By
ARTHUR MEE

fully revised and edited by
E. T. LONG

Illustrated with new photographs by
A. F. KERSTING

HODDER AND STOUGHTON

Printed in Great Britain
for Hodder and Stoughton Ltd.,
St Paul's House, Warwick Lane, London, E.C.4,
by Richard Clay (The Chaucer Press), Ltd,
Bungay, Suffolk

INTRODUCTION TO REVISED EDITION

In preparing the new edition of THE KING'S ENGLAND care has been taken to bring the books up to date as far as possible within the changes which have taken place since the series was originally planned. In addition the editor has made his revisions both in text and illustrations with a view to keeping the price of the books within reasonable limits, in spite of greatly increased production costs. But throughout the book, it has been the editor's special care to preserve Mr Arthur Mee's original intention of providing something more than just another guide book giving archaeological, ecclesiastical and topographical information.

In the case of every town and village mentioned in the King's England Series, it has been the intention not only to indicate its position on the map, but to convey something of its atmosphere. And the biographical selections about people who are ever associated with that part of the country in which they lived, or who are commemorated in the parish church—which was such a popular feature of the former edition—have been retained and in some cases supplemented.

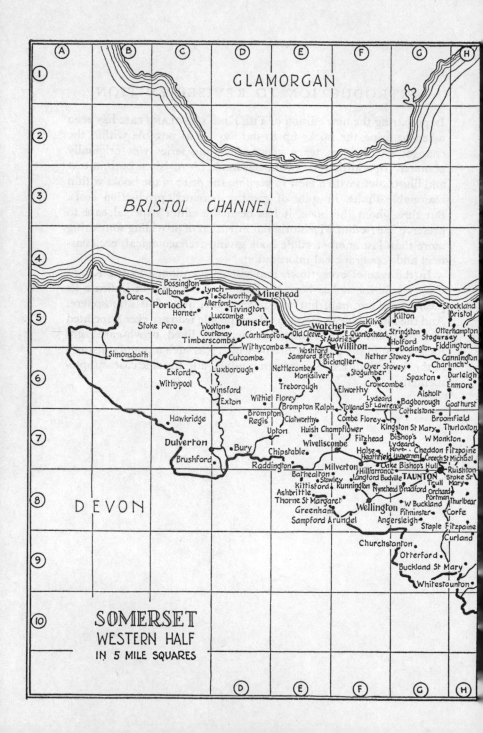

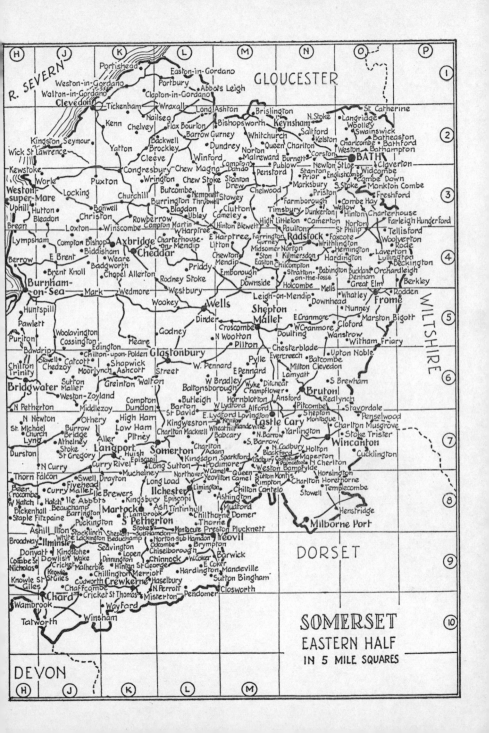

SOMERSET
EASTERN HALF
IN 5 MILE SQUARES

LIST OF ILLUSTRATIONS

SOMERSET

INTRODUCTION

IT is impossible to imagine the pilgrim who can be disappointed in Somerset, the Crescent County of the West. Surely its million acres have everything that is wanted by the traveller in search of delight.

It is romantic and historic. It has vast landscapes and impressive heights. It has deep solitudes far away from men and busy ways along which life has thronged for centuries. It has spectacles to stir the wildest imagination. It has been the scene of one of the noblest and one of the ignoblest struggles for the English throne. It has one of the most remarkable monuments of the Roman Empire set in one of the most beautiful of English cities. It has the sacred soil of Glastonbury and the matchless glory of Wells, the very heart of our English Romance and a unique mediaeval city. It has the finest towers in England and a dazzling splendour of architecture in its churches. It has some of the most attractive little towns in England and hundreds of delightful villages.

It dips its shores into the Bristol Channel, down which the Cabots sailed to find the Empire's oldest colony, and from one of its heights it can look over Devon to the Channel, down which the great ships of the world go out from London and Southampton. It has 60 rivers running through it, four groups of great and little hills, and Exmoor and Sedgemoor—Sedgemoor with its melancholy tale of a broken dream, Exmoor with the incomparable glory of nature on the heights and in the hollows. It has Athelney, the scene of Alfred's wanderings as a fugitive, and the lovely Vale of Avalon to which tradition brought Joseph of Arimathea and where it laid King Arthur. It has the remnants of lake villages older than history, with the mounds on which the ancient Britons set their huts, and great houses in which life has gone on like an unbroken thread from century to century. It has ruined walls that echo with the feet of monks and pilgrims, and one of the noblest churches of our own century.

Three magic names leap to any mind that thinks of Somerset: Bath, Wells, and Glastonbury. Bath is like no other place in England. Before it came down in the world it must have been a spectacle of dazzling splendour. It has been the delight of generations of famous folk, and it comes into the writings of Fielding, Smollett, Jane Austen, Thackeray, Dickens, Macaulay, and unnumbered smaller folk. It has been the centre of fashion and a magnet to scores of famous people who have done a great life's work and longed for quiet and beauty in the evening of their days.

I

It has had a continuous story since Roman times. We know of nothing in the history of England more incredible than that in the 18th century, when the genius of the Woods and the generosity of Ralph Allen and the dandyism of Beau Nash were making Bath the City Beautiful, laying it out anew to attract the travelling world, nobody realised that a few feet below these streets was something of the Roman Empire unique on this side of the Alps.

We are drawn to Glastonbury by the sight of Glastonbury Tor, which is seen for miles around, and, though new Glastonbury depresses us, all that is old is beautiful to see. We may like to think there is something in the story that the man who laid Jesus in the Holy Sepulchre wandered to England and planted the Thorn which has come down to us. We may like to think that he was laid in the beautiful stone coffin now in the church.

As for Wells, its magic is indoors and out. Who would not like to spend a week in its cathedral? Who would not walk about for hours in its old narrow ways, up and down its Vicars' Close, round the bishop's moated walls? Who has not stood spellbound at the marvellous craftsmanship on the capitals of those great cathedral columns?

Indeed Somerset is rich beyond the dreams of many counties in its mediaeval churches. It is not her towers alone that give her architectural fame. She has wonderful interiors, and churches rich with treasure. Only about a dozen of her churches have Saxon work in them, but if Saxon is rare there is Norman work in abundance. We find it in scores of arches and doorways, and at least 150 churches still have Norman fonts, those at Langridge, Lullington, Compton Martin, Portbury, South Stoke, and Glastonbury being proud examples.

Somerset has about 400 ancient fonts; two notable 15th century ones are those at Crowcombe and Minehead. It has more mediaeval stone pulpits than any other county in the land—20 out of about 60 in all England; everyone should see the pulpit at Shepton Mallet. It has also grand mediaeval wooden pulpits, one at Trull with five statues; and with the pulpits go the pews, for Somerset is famous for bench-ends. We should look for them at Trull, Crowcombe, Cheddar, Bishop's Hull, Bishop's Lydeard, and Brent Knoll on its lonely hill. As for roodscreens, though Somerset cannot equal Norfolk or Devon she has more than 70 from mediaeval England, and they are lovely to look upon; we see them at Dunster, Minehead, Withycombe, and Queen Camel.

The roofs are splendid when we come to Shepton Mallet, Mar-

tock, Selworthy, and Somerton, and, as for the towers that soar towards heaven, where can we beat those of Taunton, Huish Episcopi,
Kingsbury Episcopi, Batcombe, Buckland Denham, Cheddar,
Glastonbury, Wrington, Ile Abbots, Ilminster—a long list which
should be longer, for these towers are superb?

If we want lovely villages with lovely names (scores of them named
after Norman lords), or views of our countryside with something unforgettable in them, Somerset will not disappoint us.

Of great houses, Somerset has the incomparable Montacute, set
in its wonderful garden; the splendid Tudor Sutton Court behind
its battlemented walls near Stowey; Brympton House with its long
Tudor front and its grey-gold walls; and Barrington Court with its
glorious gardens in the care of the National Trust, as Montacute is.

Abbots Leigh. It lies amid the glory of the wooded hills which draw the eyes of all who cross the great suspension bridge at Clifton, high above the gorge in which the Avon flows. They are the Leigh Woods and Nightingale Valley, with an ancient camp belonging to the National Trust. There is an old inn which was once a church house, with a fishpond near it in which monks would keep their fish for Friday.

It was at his house in these woods that Sir George Norton sheltered Charles II after his flight from the Battle of Worcester. He had ridden pillion with Jane Lane for three days, disguised as her servant, and after a rest in Warwickshire had come to Abbots Leigh, arriving at Leigh Court to find its owner willing to entertain a stranger in distress. They entertained him unawares, but the king was recognised by the butler, who had served him as a boy at Richmond. At the Restoration Charles made his host a knight, and here in the chancel is the knight's elaborate monument set up by his wife, whose sculptured portrait shows her in curls reaching to her shoulders, matching the medallion of her lord, who has the curly wig of his day.

The chancel walls may be Norman, though they have been much transformed. It is all very charming now, the roof panelled with stone tracery, 18 panels painted blue and picked out with stars. The walls are lined with oak, and in the chancel is an attractive high-back chair. The Norton monument reaches to the ceiling. Next to it is a tablet to Robert Hippisley Trenchard, a forgotten man of 1787 whose fame has gone astray, for his epitaph tells that he will be remembered for all time. There is a richly carved oak pulpit. In one of the aisles is the magnificent canopied tomb of other Nortons, which may be thought to be now at rest, for it has been moved once from the chancel to the tower and again from the tower to where it stands. It is charming, the deep canopy resting on slender columns and the whole tomb delicately carved. The home of the Nortons was rebuilt in 1814 and is now an institution; only a fragment of the ancient wall of the house is left.

Set in one of the walls of the church tower is a sculptured monument of two women weeping for Philip John Miles; it is by the famous Bristol sculptor E. H. Baily, who set Nelson on his column in Trafalgar Square.

Aisholt. One of the shining poets in our own time loved this place and the beautiful country round; he was Sir Henry Newbolt,

5

whose wife drew up the list of Aisholt's heroes on the parchment in the church. Proud Lady Newbolt must have been to do so, for this is one of the Thankful Villages, one of a group of eight that we have come upon in Somerset where all the men came back from the Great War.

The little 15th century church clings to the side of a hill so steep that the top of the churchyard is level with the belfry. Here is a lovely view over the trees to the moorland where Will's Neck touches the highest point of the Quantocks, about 1300 feet up. The church has a chest with iron bands worn deep into the crumbling oak, and a peephole is cut eight feet through a wall to give a glimpse of the lovely chancel.

Alford. Its church is in the park which belonged to the man who built it 500 years ago. His house has changed, but the church is much as he saw it, the same font, the same screen, and the solid oak seats he sat in, with curious designs on the ends. On one is a young man, on another a pelican, and a third has a dragon with its eyes fixed on a gruesome meal—a man's head dangling before it in space. Painted on old glass is another dragon on a shield, with four angels and a girl. The year 1625 is cut on the back of the oak pulpit. The chalice was made in Elizabethan days, and a splendid churchyard cross has (like the mass dial on the wall) lasted out the centuries. All it has needed after 600 years is a new head.

The River Brue flows by the church through the park, having been joined by the Altham, over which steps a pack-horse bridge.

Aller. Its great day was 11 centuries ago, when Guthrum the Dane was baptised here with 30 of his men, King Alfred standing sponsor for the man he had defeated at Aethandune. The Peace of Wedmore followed, and Alfred, trusting these new Christians to keep their word, allowed them part of the country as vassals.

We should like to think that it was round this simple font the warriors stood, but authority is against us, for it is Norman. At one time no one cared for it, and it was thrown into the vicarage pond. Near it today is a font with a curiously twisted pedestal, which took its place in 1663. A doorway with zigzag and several round pillars is a survival from the Norman church for which the old font was made. About as old is the scratch dial which told the time of mass. The oak pulpit is Jacobean.

Under a stone canopy a weary knight lies in armour on his tomb, thought to be John de Clyvedon, builder of the chancel, a great man of the 14th century. He rallied the men of Somerset to make a stand against the Scots invading England after Bannockburn. He led them against Lancaster and the Barons, and as a justice of the peace he had the odd duty of going to Bristol to stop people crowding round the gallows where two of Lancaster's men were hanged. Another knight lies cross-legged here after spending years in the churchyard, probably Sir John Aller, who took his name from this lovely bit of Somerset at the foot of High Ham Hill.

Side by side with the church is a mediaeval house which has been refashioned but has kept its late 15th century barns and stables.

Allerford. A hundred years ago children in these cottages would wake to hear the clatter of hoofs on the cobbled pack-horse bridge seen from their windows. A Dutch boat had dropped its cargo in the bay, the barrels had been hauled ashore, and now the Gentlemen were off on their rounds. The name of a lane leading out of the hamlet has a suspicious sound—Brandish Street, as if it might have been christened by the smugglers themselves with the brandy from a broken bottle.

The narrow bridge, with its two low arches, still spans the hurrying stream, and grouped round it are little cottages and great walnut trees, a delightful picture against the background of the wooded hills.

Angersleigh. The friendly little church, standing among the fields, guards for its scattered villagers their heritage of ancient art. The beautiful oak carvings of the reading desk and the lectern are worthy of a pilgrimage. The church, made new 500 years ago, has still the small rough-hewn font of the Normans.

Ansford. With Castle Cary so close, and new houses advancing in all directions, it is amazing how well Ansford manages to keep its village character. Small and compact, we may recognise in it still the home of Parson Woodforde, whose delightful diary makes us intimate with the folk who lived here then. He was born at the Parsonage in 1740, and, after riding to and fro for his terms at Oxford, served as curate to his father, who was rector for 50 years. We may almost live through those days with the kindly simple diarist, going off to Ansford Inn to read the news in the morning or for a ball in the evening, playing fives against the church tower, noting the games of cards, the deaths, the births, the marriages, the worry over Brother John so constantly coming home drunk and so successfully cadging the diarist's last guinea, the visits to friends and relations, the proud lending of a new spyglass to see the tower which Mr Hoare the Banker was raising in memory of King Alfred,

7

the bear-baiting, the loaded meals, the brandy smuggled into the Parsonage, the last games of backgammon with the father who died in 1771, and the vexation when a cousin was given the living the diarist was hoping for.

Parson Woodforde's father and mother, and the Nancy whose pertness was a constant worry, all lie here in the family vault, but the church has been rebuilt since the diarist records marrying his first couple here, an 80-year-old farmer and a widow of 70. Only the tower with its gargoyles is left, the round font which may be Norman, and the neatly carved oak pulpit from which Parson Woodforde preached. On the chancel wall is the Latin epitaph he wrote for his father and mother.

Ash. This is the only village we know in Somerset (and perhaps in England) where a church tower has been built as a War Memorial. It is a thin little tower, but in it is enshrined the memory of the heroes of this small place, and it gives a dignity to the 19th century church.

Ashbrittle. It is a long steep climb to this place perched on the border between Somerset and Devon. All round are wooded hills and valleys, and in the churchyard an ancient hollow yew grows on a tumulus more ancient still.

Ashcott. It has a splendid view from its perch on the Polden Hills, but its church has been badly used; all that is left of the old place is the 15th century tower with an abbot's mitre and staff cut on one of its stones, a plain Norman font, a few carved bench-ends, and a poor old wooden pulpit.

Ashill. Rather it might be called Yewhill, for the sake of the twins in the churchyard. They are magnificent, tall, and more than 25 feet round the trunk, though one is solid no more. The church (with a mass dial on its walls) is delightful, having a Norman doorway north and south, both with carved capitals, and a triple Norman arch to the chancel, the central arch adorned with chevron moulding but the side openings now closed. In two recesses in the wall lie a nameless 14th century knight in armour and the figure of a nameless 14th century lady. She has a heart-case in her hands to show that only her heart is here, but she has a stone canopy over her head and two angels at her pillow. Three dragons are running round the top of the Jacobean pulpit, the font is carved with Tudor roses, and the sanctuary has two carved chairs and an old oak table.

Ashington. Where a few homes cluster near the River Yeo stands the manor house with the fine archway and the pinnacled gable, built 400 years ago by the St Barbes, the last of whose family now lies in the church beside it. Two sundials to mark the times of mass centuries ago are scratched on the buttresses. A bellcot balances on the gable at one end of the nave, and at the other is a recess with a tiny group so worn that we can scarcely make out the man with the bound hands, thought to be St Vincent with the two companions who sorrowfully watched him tortured 1700 years ago.

The nave, with its fine windows, is 16th century; the chancel, with little pointed windows carved inside the arches and with stone heads outside, is 200 years older. Two box-pews (a reading desk fitted to one) and six other pews with doors, all decorated with Jacobean carving, are the only seats, enough for this small place. The oak pulpit, its back panels supporting a canopy, has 1637 and several Tudor roses carved on it. On a wall is a drawing of a missing stone which bore the rough outline of a knight in chain mail cut as though with a chisel.

Athelney. It is an island no more, but in its hollow plain are reed and osier beds and in floodtime Athelney becomes an island as in Alfred's day. Well he knew this place which has now so little for us to see that is worth while. We may walk where he walked, may stand where he stood as he looked out over the scene of his campaign against the Danes, and may wander by the riverside where, we shall be told, stood the peasant's cottage in which Alfred hid himself and received the housewife's scolding for allowing her cakes to burn. It was all somewhere about, and we have two witnesses. One is a common stone set up in the first year of last century, telling us that Alfred was here but giving us the wrong date (879 for 878); the other is the hill across the marshes with the round church on top—St Michael's Church on Burrow Mump. Burrow Bridge is close by and what is called the Mump, near the bridge, is a little hill which was probably Alfred's fort.

Axbridge. All the life of the town meets in its wide square; houses jostle round it with overhanging storeys; every narrow street hurries to it; while the towering ridge of the Mendips turns it into a sun-trap.

The town hall stands at one corner guarding three things from the past life of the old square—the stocks, a money-changer's table of 1627, and a sort of anchor to which the bull was tied when the square was filled with folk and yapping dogs for the bull-baiting.

At another corner, up three rounded tiers of stone steps, the church reigns like a queen on her throne, a reign which has lasted 500 years.

The tower has a crowned figure and John the Baptist under triple belfry windows, and pinnacles round pierced parapets and doorways, and the porch is rich with carvings in canopy and niche, and in its lovely stone roof. Inside are four more splendid roofs, two of panelled oak, one fan-traceried, and a plaster roof above the nave with massive pendants and a moulded pattern of the Crown of Thorns. It is one of the best roofs in Somerset, made by an Axbridge man in 1636, held up on many stone heads.

Eight angels spread their wings round the 15th century font. There is a bit of a 14th century painted screen, four new oak screens from last century, a scrap of wall-painting in the south aisle, and a tiny peephole giving us a view of the altar from the old sacristy. A giant chest has three locks.

The Prowse family has made the church its own with numerous memorials; even the old nurse is here. William Prowse of 1670 is sculptured with a skull in his hand, and Ann, whose father was four times mayor, kneels behind an altar, a dainty lady in bonnet and kerchief. A few years after Ann's death in 1668 another Mrs Prowse, Abigail by name, started to stitch the tapestry for this altar. For seven years she worked at this quaint design of a communion table spread with goblets, plates, and red-bound books under a velvet canopy, with the arms of Axbridge on one side and of her father's bishopric on the other. Roger Harper, a 15th century merchant, has his portrait in brass, kneeling with his wife.

By the west porch is a quaint house with a garden reaching down to the square as a background for the War Memorial.

The Old Manor House, which dates from the 17th century, is open to the public once a week during the summer.

Babcary. It lies among the elms of Caryland, as peaceful as the little river flowing by. The church, filled with the scent of the limes on summer days, has a 15th century tower, a font of the same age, and a Jacobean pulpit. On a window recess near the piscina is a carving of a little flower done by a craftsman of long ago. There is a mass dial on the wall.

On a January morning in 1764 the new curate of Babcary came riding from his home at Ansford, and that night duly entered in a diary which is now famous that he dined here "on a sheep's heart which I carried in my pocket". It is our old friend Parson Woodforde, who was officially rung into the parish the following Sunday, the ringers receiving a pail of cider from the churchwarden and half-a-crown from the new curate. The next time he came to put up at the parsonage here he brought with him "three dozen and nine bottles of cider and eight bottles of strong beer, with a little jar of pickled oysters, some cheese, and some cold tongue, all which were given by my father". Soon he is busy planting peas and beans and radishes in the parsonage garden, and he records how he won 2s 9d betting on a game of fives played against the church tower.

Babington. An avenue of elms and beeches brings us to its great house and its little church; we imagine that the church could be put into one of the rooms of the manor and it is reputed to have been designed by Sir Christopher Wren. The two doors face, the 17th century manor house door having a charming hood, the church door bringing us into a little porch with a great stone of John Fricker which has been saying for 200 years to all who come this variant of familiar lines:

> Prepare to follow, for be sure you must,
> One day, as well as I, be changed to dust.

The church has a small octagonal turret built by Elizabeth Long in 1750, and the east end has an apse under a domelike roof. Where the east window should be is a queer piece of plaster work with cherubs and oddly winged angels. On one side of the apse is a double-decker pulpit into which a preacher can just creep, and on the other side is a wall-monument with a 17th century cherub.

The manor house, with a yew hedge like a solid green wall, has a gold watch believed to have been left here by Charles II. With it is preserved a velvet saddle with a gold cloth which Elizabeth Long's father probably bought for the royal visit.

Backwell. It stands on a ridge looking towards the Bristol Channel, with woods behind it and three enchanting combes close by. Builders of five or six centuries, from the 12th to the 17th, have had a hand in the church, and a magnificent place they made of it, except when they repaired the top of the tower so oddly. Luckily, they have not spoiled the pinnacled bellcot.

For years the beauty spot in the church was half hidden by a wall which has now been cleared away as litter, so that we clearly see Sir Walter Rodney lying with a host of angels round his tomb in the exquisite chapel his wife made for him. He died in 1460, and Elizabeth married another, but in the end she was brought back to lie at his side. The stone-ribbed roof and the miniature stone screen make this shrine as beautiful as love could build it. On one of the walls is a pathetic inscription to two other Elizabeths, a mother and her little one five days old.

The chapel looks to the altar through a tiny window framed in Norman carving, and there is another peephole in a small chamber next to it, whereby hangs a tale. This is no other than an anchorite's cell, with a peep through a quatrefoil to the altar. In this little cell lived (and no doubt died) a hermit immured for life within stone walls, the nearest approach we have in our history to the strange eastern fakirs who spend their lives sitting on pillars or torturing themselves in weird and fearful ways.

We come into the church through a stalwart door in the horseshoe porch, a veteran of the ages, but the oldest possession is the Norman font, pieced together again after lying broken and buried in the churchyard. Across the nave and the aisle stretches a fine mediaeval screen. The brass chandelier is approaching its 200th birthday, and the brass portrait of a 17th century family remains, long after the names have been forgotten.

Badgworth. Straight to the church we must go, pushing open the old oak door carved with Tudor roses, for here is all that Badgworth has to show. Queer worn-out stone figures hold up a wooden pulpit finely carved with Jacobean lilies and thistles. The font is 13th century; the stalwart oak seats are 16th. In the tower hang two bells older than the Reformation. This is the only church in England dedicated to St Congar, though the neighbouring village of Congresbury owes its name to this Celtic saint of 1400 years ago.

Bagborough. Has any village a lovelier setting for its church, standing in the garden and parkland of the great house beside it? Flowering shrubs, bright borders, and stretches of smooth lawn lead up the slope to this temple 500 years old, yet with a spirit vital and living, for it has fine modern glass by Sir Ninian Comper, and a tower screen carved by its own village folk, who put into it figures of the Crucifixion and the names of five of their comrades who fell in the Great War.

The processional cross and the carved bench-ends are treasures from the prosperous farming days of 500 years ago. Standing under great sycamores we may look for miles over what is still one of our most fertile valleys, while a climb up the hill brings us to a delightful wilderness of bracken and woods and hidden places with a sudden view of the sea.

Baltonsborough. This is St Dunstan's village. Here he was born, it is said, and he it was who diverted the River Brue, sending it along the course of the little Southwood stream that his village might have more power for its mill.

The Brue flows by St Dunstan's, a transformation of the 15th century church, still keeping the old stone pulpit and oak pews. A bench-end near the pulpit holds the hourglass stand, another has one of the old flap seats sometimes added by a pew-owner for a servant, who thus found himself sitting conspicuously in the aisle. There is also a fine chair made in 1667. The roofs are old, the repainted chancel one having round it a richly carved and coloured oak cornice with wooden angels holding books. Even the piscina is painted to match. The traceried south door has a fine old knocker ring, and on a doorway stone is a scratch dial. The fine wooden screen is modern, and so is the churchyard cross, though it proudly bears its ancient head, which has been dug up among the tombs.

In a tomb in the tower lies an old Sweet William of Baltonsborough who was laid to rest here in 1638; we remember his epitaph for its mention of a flower growing in these cottage gardens:

> *Would you know whom this tombe covers,*
> *Tis the nonparell of lovers?*
> *It's a sweet william, sweeter far*
> *Than the flowers that so stiled are.*

Banwell. It is a place of great antiquity, with a cave which has contributed much to our knowledge of ancient man, a round earthwork of 20 acres crowning a hill, and a mysterious cross which has puzzled people for many generations.

If we have been in Taunton Museum in our Somerset tour, we shall remember the great collection of William Beard and the story of his cave. There was an old tradition that Banwell Hill enclosed a cavern, and William Beard, as he wandered about his father's farm, thought much of it. In 1824, halfway through his long life, he sank a shaft 100 feet deep in the hill and found a stalactite cave, the burial-place of long-extinct creatures. He drove an approach to it from the face of the hill, and from that day till his death the cave was his interest and hobby in life. It had a marvellous store of prehistoric treasure, and yielded the finest skull of a great cave lion ever found in England. The cave is closed today, but what William Beard found in it may be seen by all at Taunton. Beard lies in Banwell churchyard.

The mysterious cross which puzzles the traveller is about 120 yards north of the Roman road, and about 150 yards from Banwell Castle, a mediaeval-looking house built by a bishop of the early 19th century on the top of a hill. The cross is in the castle wood, and is a ridge of earth surrounded by a ditch and rampart, with an entrance at the east end. The cross is raised two feet high and is about ten feet wide, and the arms are of unequal length, varying from 56 feet to 72. At the point where the arms meet a Wellingtonia is growing. It has been held that the cross had some connection with the Roman system of surveying, but authoritative belief is against this theory. Nor does it follow that the cross has any religious significance, or even that it goes back to Roman days. There is no actual knowledge on the subject.

Banwell is proud of having preserved the old manor house of the Bishops of Wells, which keeps company with the church and is called the Abbey. It is a curious home with towers and turrets, pinnacled buttresses, a great east window to a chapel, and low cloisters, the whole having grown from the 15th century palace of Bishop Beckington, who helped to make this church so beautiful and left his heraldry in the window.

The church is 14th century, with a tower rising over 100 feet and its turret higher still. It has a pierced parapet, gargoyles, stone faces, and two dainty rood stair turrets with a sculptured Madonna in one recess and the angel bringing her the good news in another. A finely carved doorway, resting on stones engraved in Tudor days with the mason's compasses and square, brings us to the rich interior, in which the eye is caught by a superb chancel seen through a carved and gilded screen. The painted roofs, the stone angels with painted shields, the gilded frieze, and the altar rails make up a perfect whole; even the roofs and the bands of carving round the columns are painted to match this colour scheme. The two doors of the screen were cut in 1521 from a single block of oak.

There are massive old seats with poppyheads, and one of that group of mediaeval stone pulpits which numbers about 60 for all England. This is one of the finest in the Mendips, most beautifully carved with an oak canopy of 1620, probably by the men who made the cover for the Norman font. The decoration of the font is by 15th century carvers, who gave it lilies to match the lily of the Madonna on the tower—where, by the way, we noticed that Gabriel also has a lily.

The church has a western gallery, carved and gilded, made from the great 16th century pew of Bishop Godwin, who had a summer

14

resort here called Tower Head Farm, still with his arms and motto over the door, *Wyn God, win all.*

The lord of the manor is here in brass; he was the physician-parson John Martok, with the pattern of his cope picked out in red. He died in the manor house in 1503, and the famous Bishop King, who made Bath Abbey new, died in the same house while Martok lay in his coffin. There are other brasses, one of John Blandon of 1554 and nameless ones of a 15th century couple.

In the room over the porch we found a rough old altar table, a lectern, and a quaintly shaped almsbox, all 400 years old, and there is glass of about the same period in the nave and clerestory windows. The finest old glass is in the vestry windows, put there by a 19th century vicar who used the vestry for nearly 60 years and enriched it with roundels showing stories from the Apocrypha and the Bible. The glass is Flemish and over 400 years old.

Barrington. An old door in a charming porch leads us into a church with the work of many centuries in its walls; on one of them is a scratch dial. Its chief beauty is a 13th century piscina, a benign human head supporting the bowl, while a dog and a monkey hold a canopy over it. The central tower is octagonal.

The great house, Barrington Court, is held by the National Trust. It represents the very height of Tudor beauty, standing like a symbol of its builder, Henry Daubeney, first Earl of Bridgewater, the most extravagant nobleman of an extravagant age, a man whose band of minstrels ranked with the king's. He came of a family famous for its zeal as crusaders, and it is said that a Daubeney still lies outside the church of the Holy Sepulchre in Jerusalem. It stands on the site of an earlier house of which traces were found in 1920.

The Court does not reveal its beauty to the traveller on the road, but from the E-shaped front its mellow stone rises in a host of tall gables, twisted chimneys, and pinnacles, while great transomed windows look out on to a wide stretch of turf. Only a few years ago it was an empty shell, but its first tenant under the National Trust brought back its former glory, with linenfold panelling, carved beams, a minstrel's gallery, and furnishings which seem to bring the past to life again. Nowhere have we seen a room lovelier than the smaller dining-room, with its traceried screen and its 16th century ceiling like a wooden honeycomb. Much that is old has been brought from other houses, but there are two magnificent fireplaces put here in the 17th century, one with the Judgment of Solomon in plaster above it. By the big kitchen fireplace are the nooks which gave shelter from the heat to the boys turning the spit. By the old front door is something which must have surprised Lord Daubeney's guests, a stone basin where they could wash their hands. In the attics a gallery runs the whole length of the house, similar to the gallery Wolsey made at Hampton Court to walk in during bad weather. What the luxurious Wolsey had the extravagant Daubeney wanted, and so these galleries, the first of their kind, are almost the same age.

The gardens, too, are like a miniature Hampton Court. On the lawns a sundial with ten faces tells the time to within five minutes. Past the water garden we come on a curious building of many arches, each with its old gate. It is a very interesting 17th century stable, its 12 stalls each divided for a cow and a calf for what we know as buss-beef, a very popular dish in those days.

In the 17th century the Court passed to the Strodes, who built the stables now turned into a house. Architects of our own time have added a little village of houses and charming thatched cottages grouped round the Court as homes for its workers, and so it comes about that the best period of Tudor, the period of Wren, and fine work of our own day are all represented here in a perfect whole, a veritable school of harmony for architects.

Barrow Gurney. From their windows the villagers look out on to three Bristol reservoirs; but the church and the big house have something better, for they stand together in a glorious garden. The Court, a great Elizabethan house, has a Jacobean porch and a tithe barn with a curiously high-pitched roof needing whole trees for tiebeams.

Two heraldic lions stretched against a rose tree bar our way into the church; they are on an excellent 19th century door copied from a 17th century one. It is to the south aisle that we turn on coming in, attracted by the rich colouring and gilding. Once a nun's chapel attached to a small Benedictine Priory, it is the only bit of the old church which escaped the builders of last century. High on the wall Francis James, Chancellor of Wells 300 years ago, kneels with his wife and children, 11 little alabaster figures. Rich tapestry hangs on the chancel wall. Wooden angels stand before the nun's altar, and in recesses are the Madonna and the Archangel Gabriel, all brought from Oberammergau. More modern carving in wood and stone is in the font, the pulpit, the screens, and the reredos. An old stone altar has been raised on new ebony pillars and marked with an ivory cross. On the floor is an ancient bell, cracked at last after 500 years.

16

Barton St David. Glastonbury Tor raises its head above the trees of Caryland for Barton St David to look at, and down by the River Brue is a bridge with something mediaeval in it, including two recesses in which the saints once stood to guard the village folk. Still on the shaft of the 500-year-old cross is Barton's saint, wearing a bishop's mitre and carrying a pilgrim's wallet. A Norman doorway with a carved arch leads into the church, which has an octagonal tower, an old mass dial, and 13th century transept arches. A plain old pulpit matches the old door, and on a wall hangs a crude painting of David with his harp, one of many we found hereabouts.

Barwick. The road from Yeovil cuts deep through the rock to get to this village, whose charming church turns its best face to the road, its 15th century north aisle with decorated battlements. The tower, oddly placed at the east end of the aisle, is older, and there is ancient history in all four walls, a scratch dial on a chancel buttress, seven consecration crosses, and half another cross on the gravestone used to make a doorway up to where hang two mediaeval bells. Within is a rich array of mediaeval seats, marked with the axe which shaped them, and carved everywhere with men and birds, animals and shields. Here a seagull preens its feathers, here are lilies in a bowl, a fox trots off with a goose in its mouth, an archer aims at a bird busy with some berries, and another man holds up the date 1533 to show when all this fine work was finished. There are choir-stalls to match, and an old chest. Shallower carving decorates the pulpit, on which are the initials of a rector and the date 1619; and cable moulding proclaims the font to be Norman. The north aisle has panelled arches and the original oak roof.

Batcombe. Its 15th century tower looked to us like a piece of hanging lace. Its elegant buttresses creep to the top. Its lovely canopied niches are like a lady's mirror, with the handle for holding it. Above the tower's west window stands Christ on a globe borne by an angel, with angels on the wall around Him carrying censers and the symbols of His suffering. There are charming quatrefoils and shields in the parapet round the nave and aisles, and pinnacles and gargoyles everywhere.

The whole exterior is charming; even the modern vestry is tucked away like a little house with an old stone roof. The Normans replaced the Saxon fane with a church that disappeared. A fragment of Norman carving is preserved on the south wall. The chancel is of 14th century origin, and the tower and the nave are late mediaeval.

17

The south doorway has charming spandrels, and the roof of the porch is panelled in lovely old oak. The tower arch is panelled and the roof fan-vaulted; a row of angels looks down from the spring of the arch at each side.

There are glowing bits of mediaeval glass in the chancel. There are a curious quatrefoil piscina, Jacobean altar rails, and an oak chest and a chandelier of the same time.

Bath. All travellers come to it, for it is beyond compare. Like most of the world it has fallen upon hard times and something has gone out of it, but the traveller who would rest and be tranquil need no farther go. Here he will find a piece of England like no other, with a piece of Roman Britain matchless in these islands.

It has been the delight of famous people for a hundred years and more; writers, artists, musicians, scientists, have all found here something like their paradise. It is set in a hollow of the hills with noble country everywhere about it, with crescents and terraces and gardens laid out to face the sun, with a river running through it, trees in rich profusion, and all the West of England radiating about it. And it has, to crown all, a noble church and a Roman bath.

It begins far back in legend with the story of King Bladud, the royal magician who lived at the time of Elijah and was father of King Lear; the Bath he knew would be on the 22-acre hilltop called Little Solsbury Hill. His memory would be fading when the Romans came and made a sort of Rome from Rome, called Aquae Sulis. There the greatest builders of the ancient world set up a city with no parallel this side of the Alps, with a temple, a forum, immense baths, and noble houses. Four hundred years they were here. Saxon fire and sword overthrew their city at the end of the sixth century, but in 775 a college of secular canons was founded here which became a Benedictine monastery about 970.

The Saxons built their abbey and buried their dead over the rubbish which had accumulated through the centuries above the most magnificent ruins in England, 20 feet below. Complete oblivion had fallen over the centre of light and learning. Saxon Bath succeeded Roman Bath, Norman Bath succeeded Saxon Bath, and at last the Norman abbey fell in ruin; the abbey built in the 16th century incorporated merely a small part of the Norman. The history of Bath is a continuous story for 1900 years; the beauty of its abbey is a continuous story from the 16th century up to our own time.

It was not until the 18th century that Bath revived with the enthusiasm of Ralph Allen the Cornishman, who had made a fortune out of Bath stone and by carrying mails, and spent it in Bath by giving the Woods (the architect father and his son) the opportunity to lay out a City Beautiful in one of Nature's favourite places. They took this wondrous site that Nature had prepared for them in the hollow of the hills and laid it out with squares and circuses and terraces, building charming houses which from then till now have never ceased to delight the eye with their quiet dignity and their great simplicity. It was the first fine piece of planning any English town had seen, and Bath had its reward by becoming for generations the fashionable home of musical and artistic and intellectual England. Everybody went to Bath, and everybody either stayed or wished they could stay.

Yet nothing did these builders know and nothing could they dream of the unparalleled opportunity that lay so near their picks and spades. They set their houses creeping up this fine hillside but realised nothing of the wondrous things that lay 15 feet below the surface. It was about 200 years ago, some time in 1755, that the voice of the past caught a listening ear. In the rebuilding of Bath the old priory buildings by the abbey were being pulled down when an incredible thing happened. Men came upon Saxon coffins, and as they brought them to light of day *hot springs came rushing out from Roman masonry*. It is almost unbelievable to us in these days, when the past is so enthralling to us, that nothing was done for about 100 years; but it is true.

It was not until the second half of the last century that the site was slowly uncovered, and what was revealed is now before all eyes in this fine city of the West.

There was nothing like it anywhere else in England. It is the richest collection we have of Roman sculpture, masonry, jewels, and ceramics. We walk where the Romans walked. We see the running waters by which they stood, in which they bathed. We see the lovely things they looked upon. Nowhere do we feel the spell of Roman Britain as we feel it here. What we see is wonderful enough, for all about us is the visible city of the 18th century crowned with a central glory of its 16th century abbey, and in the midst is this wonder made by men whose fathers may have heard of a man named Paul walking captive in the streets of Rome. What we do not see no man knows, for no man can imagine what still lies buried under the streets of Bath.

What we see are baths made by the Romans, with hot water pouring out of the earth straight into them, a curious sight in England, yet it has been going on for generation after generation, century after century. It is one of the most astonishing experiences an Englishman can have at home to stand inside the bronze doors where these waters come gushing up; these waters are actually the overflow from the King's bath above, and flow from here to the Roman bath.

They flow into one bath 80 feet long and half as wide, with a platform running round it, six steps down to the water, and seat recesses with stumps of the stone piers which supported the elliptical roof which covered the whole area. The Roman duct which conveys all unused water to the River Avon is still in use. The floors of the baths are still covered with lead from Roman mines in the Mendips.

Set all round the baths are the wonderful and beautiful and curious things that have been found. There are carved cornices, capitals of columns, pediments of temples, heads and figures and fragments of sculpture.

In the 18th century Bath had the good fortune to have among its benefactors the rich Ralph Allen and the capable John Woods, John the father and John the son, architects of genius and imagination who stamped their character on the face of Bath. Even then, before their Roman origins were known, the waters of Bath attracted to the city all who were in search of health from nature's healing springs, and these waters were the centre of the new city that rose on the ruins of the old. In the great transformation the ruins of Roman Bath were tapped, but nobody cared and they were left alone. The Pump Room and the fashionable Assembly Rooms came into being while still the Roman Bath below lay hidden, all unrealised, for it was not until 1869 that the city architect began a proper survey of the ruins, and it was not until 1881 that the great bath was discovered.

Through all this time the city has never ceased to foster the development of Bath as a modern spa. We may think of this wonderful city as a historic monument without a rival, but it is more; it is one of the best equipped spas in the world, with a fine tradition of long service in healing, and in these days especially a place of great repute in the treatment of rheumatic diseases, for which it has founded a National Hospital.

In the fine halls and rooms built about these Roman baths in the 18th century is enshrined the memory of Bath's great days as the social centre of fashionable England. The story of the Assembly Rooms covers 230 years, and the original rooms in which Beau Nash held sway have disappeared; they stood across the street from the abbey in the gardens by the river. The grander rooms, the finest

Bath: the Abbey and Roman baths.

Bath Abbey: the nave.

secular building in the city, were built on the hillside near the Circus in 1771 by the young Wood. Unhappily, they were destroyed by fire in a raid in April 1942, but they have now been restored, and are the property of the National Trust.

From the beginning of the 18th century to the beginning of the Great War Bath had a Master of Ceremonies who looked after its pleasures, its entertainings, and its hospitalities. In his best days he ruled as if he were a king, and even today the name of Beau Nash, the most famous master of them all, is spoken with a sort of awe in the shadow of these walls. He was a nobody who made himself a great somebody, for he was lord of the city to which all the fashionable world was coming, and he laid down laws of precedence as if he had been the Lord Great Chamberlain. Some of the doings in the Assembly Rooms in those days were hardly reputable, for the dissolute days of Charles II had left their mark, and it was a vulgar age of drinking and gambling as well as an elegant age of gaiety and pageantry. Here came all who would, and chose their own way of pleasure. John Wood and his son John, with Ralph Allen's big pocket behind them, laid out the new city on the side of the hill, with terraces and crescents and streets and squares delightful to see, and Richard Nash brought into his Assembly Rooms kings and queens and fashionable folk, rich merchants and poor writers, poets and artists, dandies and noodles, until Bath was like a magnet, drawing to itself the whole of the travelling world.

The German air-raid of 1942 wrought much havoc in this noble city but most of the worst damage has now been made good, though we must deplore the wanton destruction of the stately 18th century campanile of St James's Church, torn down a few years ago in the name of progress. The church had been wrecked in the air-raid but the lofty campanile was virtually unscathed and was a prominent feature in most views of the city.

Walking about these streets, living in these houses, visiting the Assembly Rooms, have been such celebrities as Edmund Burke, Jane Austen, Mrs Siddons, Bulwer Lytton, Oliver Goldsmith, Fanny Burney, Mrs Thrale, Henry Fielding, Lord Chesterfield, Lord Chatham, Lord Clive, the Arctic explorer Sir William Parry, Wolfe of Quebec, the immortal Gainsborough, Macaulay, David Livingstone, and an uncounted host of names that come into a thousand books. We may be glad to think that, in the words of a great friend of the city, these rooms are filled no more with the "wastrels, half-wits, gamblers, drunkards, and simpering misses who kowtowed to Beau Nash and his successors", but who would not be thankful for

B

the chance of seeing the elegant throngs of decent people passing through these rooms and the Pump Room down below? In the Pump Room, built in the classical style at the end of the 18th century, is the statue of Beau Nash they would look upon in the later days, and below him the Tompion clock given by Tompion himself, and mentioned in Pickwick. There are Chippendale seats with graceful carved backs in which are inlaid the arms of Bath. There are glass cases filled with such costumes as were worn in the early 18th and 19th centuries, the Bath chairs and sedan chairs they sat in then, and on the walls of the small gallery connecting the Pump Room with the Roman promenade are portraits of notables.

It was towards the end of last century, when Roman Bath was being brought to light at last, that the ancient abbey was restored and made the wondrous place we see. It is old and new together, and its long, strange tale covers more than 1000 years. Here was a Saxon church swept away in Norman times, but the Norman structure that succeeded it was destroyed by fire in 15 years, another Norman church rising from its ruins. Below ground we may see Norman stones, above ground we may see a Norman arch remaining from those days. The Norman church stood 300 years, but it fell into ruin like the rest of this ancient city and was a pitiful sight when Bishop Oliver King came to it to install Prior Byrde into office at the end of the 15th century. The story goes that the bishop dreamed a dream in which he saw a ladder with angels ascending and descending, and heard a voice crying, "Let an Olive establish the crown, and let a King restore the church." At the foot of the ladder grew an olive tree supporting a crown, and there was no mistaking the meaning of the dream. The bishop set to work, and in the next few years the abbey rose much as we see it, with the famous west front on which the angels are mounting and descending the ladders. Alas, the rapacious hands of Thomas Cromwell and his imperious master could not be kept from this majestic place. The abbey was stripped of its lead and glass, its iron and bells, which were sold to enrich the coffers of the king, and its ruined walls passed into private possession.

It is right that the chief monument here today should be the tomb of Bishop Montagu, for he it was who saved the abbey from the wind and rain. He was bishop here in Shakespeare's day, and was walking with Elizabeth I's godson, Sir John Harington, when the rain drove them into the abbey. However, they found the rain pouring here too, and the witty Sir John wondered "how, if the church does not save us from water above, how shall it save us from fire below?" The bishop took the hint, and obtained the help of the knight in repairing the roof, the whole building being at last made good. Even then, however, Bath had not come to realise the glory of this place, for the town allowed building leases close to its walls, and even allowed the north aisle to be used as a public thoroughfare.

The abbey church is, of course, the most beautiful thing in this most beautiful town, a veritable delight to every passer-by, for it stands like a majestic jewel in the heart of the town, with the great windows that fill it with light, the rich pinnacles and the elegant turrets that rise above the open parapets, and the noble tower in all its 16th century splendour. The windows have won the abbey fame as the Lantern of England; but the west front is the glory of the town. It looks down on the original abbey churchyard where all travellers saunter outside the Roman baths, and the great west door-way, the great west window, and the ladders soaring on each side of them, up to the turrets with three tiers of richness, make a unique group. It is one of the most interesting of all our cathedral-like fronts. The west door itself is heavily carved with heraldic shields set in a triple arch with richly carved spandrels, and on each side are wonderful stone canopies, covering ancient figures of St Peter and St Paul and of Osric and Offa, the Saxon kings, the latter of whom founded the college.

We are entranced as we come into this place and allow our eyes to rest on its exquisite beauty. The aisles, the nave, and the choir are all fan-vaulted, the woodwork is dignified and beautiful, the bench-ends are fascinating, and the lofty interior, unbroken by a screen, is filled with light from 52 magnificent windows. It is enriched like a miniature cathedral, and stands after its long adventurous story as an impressive oasis of silence in the midst of our whirling world. It was on this spot now crowned with such great glory that an event of supreme importance for the unity of our race took place. Here nearly 1000 years ago King Edgar was crowned by Dunstan, Arch-bishop of Canterbury, and Oswald, Archbishop of York, their union proclaiming the final unity of the English people under the crown.

Whether we look at the old or the new, the roofs are magnificent. The vaulting of the choir and the north transept are original; the nave and south transept are modern copies of it. It is thrilling to sit in this great place, more than 200 feet long, 70 feet high, and 70 feet wide, and gaze on its richness in colour and superbness in detail. The 52 windows are crowded with figures, 100 from the Old Testament in the west window alone, and the east window with 56 incidents in the life of Our Lord. Only a little glass is old.

23

One of the loveliest corners of the abbey is the Chantry of Prior Byrde on the right of the chancel. It is one of the gems of English architecture, built in 1515, 16 feet long, its walls richly carved with canopied niches. Its fan-vaulted roof is a delight to see. On the other side of its south wall is a fine Norman arch, the only part remaining of the Norman church; it is in the small chapel with the War Memorial cross in memory of the men of the Great War. We come in by an oak screen. The Norman arch has been here since the abbey was rebuilt in 1122, and is the oldest part of the abbey above ground. The Norman stones are in the foundations of the opposite corner near the south aisle door.

The abbey is a model to all churches in the manner of its treatment of hundreds of tablets that have been fixed here through the centuries. There are still too many, but Sir Gilbert Scott had 600 of them neatly arranged along the walls so that we can miss them if we like. Some of them are notable, some are beautiful, one or two are by such sculptors as Flaxman, Nollekens, and Chantrey, and there are epitaphs that have found their way into literature.

The most beautiful monument is in the nave, where Bishop Montagu lies between two pairs of columns crowned with sculptured heraldry and enclosed in fine railings. He wears the mantle and badge of the Order of the Garter, and his hands are clasped in prayer, a figure of great dignity, with a skull cap on his head and a ruff round his neck. The most elaborate tomb is that in which lies the wife of Sir William Waller, who commanded the army for Parliament in the Battle of Lansdown on the hills above Bath. It was the battle in which Sir Bevil Grenville died in the hour of his victory. On the tomb reclines the defeated General, leaning on his elbow and looking at his wife; and their two children are sitting in chairs beside them.

The streets of Bath are delightful to wander in on a summer's day, for we feel that we are in a dream town that has been properly made. Especially delightful is the space about the abbey, the west window of which looks into the square outside the Roman Bath, the east window looking towards the lovely gardens on which we look down from a stone balustrade to see the river flowing past green lawns, having come through the three arches of Pulteney Bridge to fall over the weir like foam with a roar that never ceases and never fails to thrill.

If we climb only halfway up the hills to the north we can walk round the cleverly planned Circus or about the marvellous Crescent, 600 feet long and as fine a domestic group as any piece of England.

The Circus and the Crescent, with the noble Queen Square down below, have been the home of scores of famous people; the Circus was built by John Wood the father, and the Crescent by John Wood the son in the 18th century, when Ralph Allen was lavishing his fortune on Bath and building his own great house, Prior Park, a little way out at Widcombe but one of the remarkable remains of the city's great days, with a frontage of 1300 feet. The house is now a school.

Down in the town itself, across the street from the abbey, stands the 18th century block of municipal buildings, the guildhall with a banqueting room decorated by Robert Adam, the Art Gallery with a small collection of pictures and a museum collection of great interest, and the Library with a rare collection of Napoleon literature.

The Holburne Art Museum, which is the principal museum in Bath, is nobly housed in a handsome Adam building closing the vista of the long and lovely Pulteney Street to which we come over Pulteney Bridge, which the great Robert Adam built.

It is one of the few bridges still left in England covered with shops, and if we follow Pulteney Street round, past the Holburne Museum, and climb up towards the London Road, we come in half a mile to the most delightful of all the Bath bridges, the Cleveland Bridge high above the Avon, with something like a little Greek temple at each end. It has a span of 100 feet. It was built in 1927 and links Walcot with Bathwick. Twenty-one coins of Constantine were found in the foundations. The little model temples at the ends were toll houses; we find them also on the North Parade Bridge.

We may come to Pulteney Street for the sheer delight of seeing the 18th century house which is now the home of the Holburne Museum, but if we are here in one of its few opening hours we shall wish to see its collections, for it is the only purely art museum in the West Country, and has a wide reputation beyond the limits of Bath. The miniatures and porcelain and the gallery of Old Masters are more varied and comprehensive than any other collection in the West; the antique silver is unrivalled outside London, and the Apostle spoons are almost unequalled; the bronzes are known to all connoisseurs.

If we should tire (as is not likely) of walking about in the streets of Bath, the city is rich in green spaces. On the slope of one of the hills have been laid out the beautiful 50 acres of Victoria Park, with three acres of botanical gardens in one corner filled with rich and rare plants. The park has oak trees planted for royal anniversaries in the Victorian era, a small shrine set up to celebrate the 300th year of Shakespeare, two vases of Carrara marble sculptured by Canova and given by Napoleon to Josephine, and an immense statue of Jupiter seven feet high cut out of a block of stone weighing six tons. It is the work of a self-taught artist named John Osborne, who is said to have died in poverty. The Parade Gardens by the river and near the Abbey are delightful. Henrietta Park, north of Pulteney Street, has seven acres which have grown out of two meadows. Sydney Gardens are laid out with lovely walks and a little Roman temple. Hedgemead Park is a beauty spot which the city owes to a landslip that ruined many shops and houses, and Alexandra Park, up on Beechen Cliff 500 feet above the sea, has one of the noblest views in the west of England. On one side the city lies hundreds of feet below at the foot of Beechen Cliff, the crescents of 18th century Bath climbing up the opposite slopes of Lansdown. The valley of the Avon runs down to Bristol on one hand and up towards Bathford on the other. Hampton Down, with Sham Castle on its edge, is to the right, and farther round are the combes of Widcombe and Horse-combe, the fields, the orchards, and the copses; Widcombe Manor (once the home of Horace Annesley Vachell); the old Widcombe Church of St Thomas; near are the fishponds of Prior Park, Ralph Allen's great house, at the top of this shallow open combe.

Such glory has Bath all about it out of doors. If it should rain Bath has a delightful arcade of shops close by the guildhall; it is known as the Corridor, and is an altogether attractive place to saunter in or to shop in, whether we want Bath Buns, Bath Olivers, or Bath Chairs.

On one of the hills is the village of Twerton which Bath has swallowed up; it looks across the valley to the curious tower built on the opposite hill by William Beckford, who lies at the foot of it. Twerton's church has a Norman doorway with an arch on zigzag and twisted columns, decorated with chevron moulding and wrinkled faces of men showing their teeth. The font is also Norman. The tower is 15th century.

At Walcot, a suburb of Bath, is an 18th century church which has a nave and apse, and a tower with one bell. It is to many travellers the most interesting of this group of churches, for Fanny Burney used to worship here. Known to history as Madame D'Arblay because she married a refugee French general of that name, she was one of the remarkable women of the 18th century, though indeed she lived till nearly halfway through the 19th. It was her good fortune as a girl to hear the drawing-room talk of such men as Edmund Burke, Sir Joshua Reynolds, and Dr Johnson, but she had not been suspected of genius till her novel *Evelina* appeared anonymously and made a sensation. It tells of a young lady's entrance into the world, and was a best-seller. Sir Joshua had to be fed while reading it, for he would not stop, and Burke sat up with it all night. The famous Mrs Delany introduced Fanny to Court, and she was made unhappy by her life as keeper of the robes to Queen Charlotte, living the wearisome life of a lady's maid. She gave it up and settled at Mickleham, where she met some refugees and married one—General D'Arblay, who took her to France in due course. When he died soon after Waterloo Madame D'Arblay came back to England, and lived quietly till she died at Bath in 1840. There is a memorial tablet to her, and she lies with her husband and son in the little graveyard close by.

St Michael's has an elegant spire of 182 feet, and St Mary's, Bathwick, with a chancel by G. E. Street, has a tower of 125 feet. The conspicuous pinnacled tower at the top of Lansdown crowns St Stephen's Church, whose pride is in the high oak canopy of its font. St Mary Magdalene Chapel (in Holloway) was transformed last century from the old structure built in 1495 by Prior Cantlow; it is a small place 46 feet by 14, with fragments of old glass in the west window and five damaged tabernacles in the porch, where an inscription records the building of the chapel. Overhanging the porch is a beautiful Judas tree. In the Vineyards is Vineyards Chapel, where John Wesley preached with Horace Walpole in the pew.

The pioneer town of the West, inspiration of so much that is beautiful, has seen the birth and development of an idea that other towns might copy with profit to the nation. It has turned one of its 18th century houses (home of the Dukes of Buckingham) into what is known as Citizen House, the centre of a far-reaching organisation for the study and encouragement of drama. It was the first Little Theatre in this country, and the first Little Theatre wired for broadcasting. It is equipped with a wealth of material for the help of all dramatic students and companies. It has a library containing every published play, an advisory bureau available for all who need it, stage curtains of all sizes, colours, and textures available for all, thousands of costumes of all periods, and furniture and properties to furnish almost any play one could think of. As a museum of the drama Citizen House is full of interest, with a big collection of costumes worn by Ellen Terry and Sir Henry Irving, relics of Mrs Siddons (who called herself "a child of Bath") and the finest known collection of theatre playbills in this country. The Mrs Siddons collection has a very beautiful mirror made for her by three Bath apprentices, bearing the inscription: "Like its mistress, to reflect naught but truth and beauty." Horace Walpole once lived in Citizen House.

High up on Lansdown Hill is the Beckford Tower, at the top of which we can stand 930 feet above the Avon and look across to the mountains of Wales, with the hills and valleys of six counties before us. The tower was built by that astounding man William Beckford of Fonthill, of whom we read in our Wiltshire volume. He was one of the most extraordinary men who ever lived. Rich beyond all dreams, he built himself the marvellous Fonthill Abbey, planting a million trees in one year on seven natural terraces three miles long. His house was the talk of Europe. He collected art treasures in great profusion; all the catalogues of the art dealers of Europe were handed in at Fonthill gates. Yet he ate simply, dressed simply, and lived almost like a poor man in his palace of dreams. Suddenly he crashed. His West Indian estates had failed, and he sold Fonthill and came to Bath, where he built this tower from which he could see Fonthill.

Dressed in green coat and breeches, a buff waistcoat, and brown top boots, he would ride through Bath on an Arab steed with a groom at his heels and a dwarf on a great pony, and would terrify his guests by trotting them up and down Bath streets at terrific speed. The time came when his three houses were not enough for him, and he bought a piece of land running up to the top of Lansdown Hill, with an abandoned quarry and a farmhouse, and amused himself for 20 years in laying it out. He turned the quarry into dark mysterious caverns, the farmhouse into an Italian summerhouse, and what was bare hillside he transformed into a miniature forest. In the first year of the Victorian era he built this great tower, 130 feet high, surrounding it with exquisite plants and flowering trees.

He lies under a sarcophagus made in his lifetime, hewn out of a block of granite. A small trench runs round it, and on one side are a few words from the last pages of his book:

Enjoy humbly the most precious gift of Heaven to man—Hope;

and on the other side are two lines from a poem he wrote on Fonthill:

Eternal Power, grant me through obvious clouds one transient gleam
Of Thy bright essence in my dying hour.

Bathampton. It lies just over the Avon from Bath, set in a lovely dip, its church standing between a fine yew and a Wellingtonia higher than the tower.

28

The churchyard is full of ancient tombs, round one of which we found a border bright with forget-me-nots. In one tomb lies a general of the East India Company, in another the father of Sir Roderick Murchison, the famous geologist of last century who surveyed the Russian Empire and predicted the discovery of gold in Australia. In the chancel lies one of the pioneers of Australia, Admiral Phillip, first Governor of New South Wales, whom they laid to rest here in the year before Waterloo. Here lies also Sir Alexander Mackenzie, who was Senior General of the British Army when he died at 83.

The church has three monuments from mediaeval England, a 14th century lady lying on a windowsill, her knight broken and battered on another, and in a recess under the east window of three lancets, where the rain of centuries has fallen on him, an old bishop with a face worn out of recognition but still grasping his crozier, and with the pleats of the sleeves of his flowing robes still visible. In the south aisle are many tablets to the family of Ralph Allen, the extraordinary man who made the first fortune ever made out of the Post Office and spent it in building up Bath. He lies at Claverton near by. The poet Pope used to stay with him at Prior Park, and once ventured to ask Allen to lend the manor house of Bathampton to a friend of his. Allen refused, whereupon Pope made in his will a note leaving the rich man £150 to cover the cost of his hospitality. Allen accepted the legacy and gave it to Bath Hospital. The corner of the church in which the Allens lie has still its ancient roof, with one oak angel looking down.

Bathealton. Sometimes the cottages gather round their church as if to shield it; sometimes, as here, it is the church that seems to stand protecting them. A fine old yew hangs over the churchyard gate, but the church itself is mostly new. Nor is there much to be seen of the ancient fortified camp on the hill above. The Court is a grand old farm, preserving the work of 17th century builders.

Batheaston. Has any churchyard a nobler group of firs than this, with a splendid yew to keep them company? From his niche in the 13th century tower St Swithin looks down on them; seeming a little weary with the centuries and with a canopy taller than himself. His tower has a fine turret with a pretty arcaded cap and an open parapet with great gargoyles looking down. The south porch, with the old village stocks beside it, has an angel and the Good Shepherd above the doorway. In the porch are two windows with four queens, and standing by the door are two small coffin stones.

29

There is an old font and a new one, the new one being carved with scenes from the life of Christ. There is a neat oak pulpit and a modern oak screen to the tower, and on the chancel wall is a brass tablet in memory of the commander of a submarine who perished with his crew off Gibraltar.

Bathford. It has one of the most charming shingle lychgates we have seen hereabouts, carved with roses. The patron saint of the church stands in a niche of the tower, and through a Norman doorway we come into a spacious nave with two great possessions, a Norman font and a Jacobean oak pulpit. The pulpit is delicately carved with six upright panels and six small square ones, the stone base having niches with the Four Evangelists in them and a sculptured group of shepherds with their sheep huddled together, listening to the song of the angels at Bethlehem.

Bawdrip. It is the village of two brides, the memory of one living in the ruin of a tower, the other in a ballad known to millions of our children.

The ruin is all that is left of a sham castle built by Benjamin Greenhill for the bride he brought from France to Knowle Hall in the middle of last century. She was homesick, and he hoped it would cheer her to see the towers from her window and imagine she was looking at her chateau. Perhaps she sometimes climbed the spiral staircase still jutting out at the top of one of the crumbling towers, to sit in the little room up there gazing towards the Mendips.

Yet the bride they will tell you of here was the bride of the Mistletoe Bough, Eleanor Lovell. She was the rector's daughter and lived in this rectory, with walls six feet thick and a veritable maze of rooms. She was married in this church, the charming 13th and 14th century building shaped like a cross, still much as she would see it on her tragic wedding day. Two pairs of corbel heads under the arches of the tower show the changing fashions of mediaeval England, the headdress of the lady to the north being years later than that of the lady on the west. Four faces keep watch over the stone figure of a knight who has been here 600 years, his shield on his arm and a heart in his hands, a mediaeval way of saying that only a heart was buried here. There is an ancient statue of the Madonna, a precious fragment guarded in the aumbry, and there are still three of the original piscinae, one having been broken to form a peephole to the altar, another tapering up and becoming a king's head.

What will probably attract most pilgrims is a panel of oak

carved with Tudor roses looking like the front of an ancient chest, for it will set the pilgrim thinking of the story. It is not, however, the chest into which the rector's daughter crept to hide on her wedding day and found herself a prisoner. That chest has vanished, but its story lives, for in it the bride lay while all around the search went on, and no one heard her cries. The tragedy was complete, and not for years, when the old chest was opened by another generation, was the missing bride discovered.

A stone behind the altar in the chancel tells her story, and there is a copy of it in the porch, where we may read of the "daughter and heiress of the family honour and estates who died June 14, 1681, taken away by a sudden and untimely fate at the very time of the marriage celebrations".

Beckington. Noble sheaves has it garnered from the past, for it has a castle and an abbey, an ancient farm, and a legacy from the Normans. Also it is the birthplace of Bishop Beckington, who added so much beauty to Wells and built so many churches, and won the tribute from old Thomas Fuller that he was a good statesman, a good churchman, a good townsman, a good kinsman, a good master, and a good man.

The ancient castle has been transformed into a small mansion and stands on the street, making a picturesque corner with its battlements, its three steep gables, and its two rounded towers. The so-called abbey is a 17th century building also in the street, with a plastered ceiling in one of its rooms and marks of Norman arches all over it. Seymour Court Farm, a little way out, was the home of Protector Somerset's brother, who married the widow of Henry VIII.

The noblest possession of Beckington is the fine Norman tower of the church, with gargoyles above its windows. We do not remember any windows quite like them for the capitals in their zigzag arches. The capital is just a face. Inside, the tower has a deeply vaulted roof with four heads at the corners, and outside are gargoyles looking down. On one of the walls is a mass dial.

The interior of the nave, a little gloomy with its rough stone walls, is crowned with a heavily timbered roof above the clerestory windows, and the walls are relieved with many stone figures. There are corbel heads in the aisles, two tiny faces with eyes closed in a canopied niche, and two splendid heads peeping down from corners. Looking down from over the aisle windows are three crouching animals, all rather terrifying. On one of the walls are monuments

31

of weeping figures, and a bust in memory of Samuel Daniel, whom Shakespeare's friend Ben Jonson called a good honest man but no poet. He died at a farm called Beckington Ridge and lies in the churchyard. In one of the aisles is a heavy oak screen with a finely carved top centuries old.

There are two peepholes into the chancel, and well it is worth two peeps, for it has a splendid roof with 144 panels, each with a cross in a quatrefoil, and three mediaeval sculptures of a knight and two ladies who lived in the castle. Side by side are John Erleigh and his wife; he wearing a deep mail collar, she with a wimple with little angels looking at her, their feet on two small creeping creatures. They have been here since 1380. Close by is an Erleigh lady of the next generation, wearing a square headdress with a neat cap under it; she is a shapely figure.

In the floor of the chancel are 15th century brass portraits of John St Maur and his wife; he has with him his sword and his dog. John was a wool merchant and must have known the merchant John Compton, who is with his wife in brass in the floor of the chapel.

It was the famous Countess of Pembroke (Sidney's sister, Pembroke's mother) who encouraged Samuel Daniel, the poet who lies in Beckington churchyard; and nearly thirty of his sonnets were printed at the back of Sir Philip Sidney's *Astrophel and Stella.*

When Edmund Spenser died Samuel Daniel took his place as leader of English poetry, and his was the poem of welcome which reached James I at Burleigh, where he stopped on his way from Scotland to take the English throne. Then came his hour of glory. His plays were performed at Court and Inigo Jones designed the scenery for one. However, the tide of fortune turned for him at 41, when he left London to live near Bristol and take charge of a company of the child players so much disliked by Shakespeare. Soon he left such things to younger men, and retired to a farm, where he wrote this most pathetic epitaph:

> *Years hath done this wrong,*
> *To make me write too much and live too long.*

Beer Crocombe. First there is the village to find and then the church, which is still more secluded up a narrow grassy lane, with the old rectory for company. The 14th century tower is charming, and supporting its arch are two extraordinary little stone men. Vastly uncomfortable they look as they crouch there, one with his hands on his knees, the other pushing up against the arch as if to relieve his head from the intolerable weight, yet all the time grimacing back at his companion, who is scorning him with a tongue put out. The slight tower screen, simply but effectively carved, was probably once between the chancel and the aisle. Some of the old rough-hewn benches are here, near the 15th century font with a drain-stop like a water lily. The pulpit is Jacobean, and has a row of dragons creeping round the top. The massive wooden lock of the door has been guarding the lonely church for centuries.

Berkley. It is just one of our English groups—the great house, the farm, the school, and the church huddled together. The yew is higher than the little tower and its branches sweep the ground. An ash is weeping over broken tombs. Inside it is all surprising, for here is a classical church of the 18th century, with a domed roof copied from a London church, decorated with white plaster scrolls on a green ground and crowned with a small glass cupola. On the wall is a proud boast of the Newboroughs, of whom we are told that they came down from a cousin of the Conqueror and went on and on till 1680, when they died out; the last one lies in this place.

Berrow. The sand blows from the beach over the churchyard wall, for its mediaeval church lies nearly in the Bristol Channel. The richly carved head of the old cross has been brought indoors for protection, but it is too late; the little figures worn by sea mists, sun, and rain are fading away. So are the garoyles, and the two old figures lying near the porch. The old door still swings on its hinges as it has swung open for seven generations of Berrow folk, and in the niche of the wall are two small stone figures, battered and broken, but with their hands clasped in prayer. The preacher preaches from the Jacobean pulpit with its two tiers of arcades, still reads the lessons from a desk of 1651, still uses the odd little piscina carved with a band of foliage; and there is sheltered in the nave a carved beam of an old gallery which tells us, "I was set up right and even in 1637". There are two old chairs in the sanctuary, and two fonts, one with an elegant band of flowers round the stem, the other a massive bowl 600 years old shaped like a quatrefoil, still with the hinges of the lid that used to guard the holy water.

Bickenhall. The Norman church has been pulled down, its oak screen has gone to Staple Fitzpaine, and the village is scattered. Only the 500-year-old font is left, with a bit of ancient carving on the pulpit, and the figure of Rachel Portman, a daughter of the manor, in her red and black robes. She kneels in prayer before the altar of the new church as she used to kneel 300 years ago.

Bicknoller. The lane can climb no farther, blocked by the ridge of the Quantocks, which Wordsworth and Coleridge used to climb from the other side, striding through heather and bracken past the burial mounds of our ancestors and the remains of a prehistoric fort, Trendle Camp.

They must often have looked down on this quiet village, where we found a house covered a foot deep in winter jasmine, with only its windows peeping through. An exasperated cry breaks into the quiet of the place, for we read these lines on a worn gravestone in the wall of the church porch:

> *O who would trust this world or prize what's in it,*
> *That gives and takes and chops and changes every minit.*

Yet it seems that nothing much has changed here. The ancient stocks still shelter under an immense split yew in the churchyard, where a stone seat runs outside the east wall of the chancel facing the almost perfect 14th century cross. As for the church and tower, they are about as the 15th century builders left them, with unique stone angels spreading their wings at corners and impossible animals poking out their heads round the walls. The gable crosses, the parapet, and the handsome transomed windows are all daintily carved, the leafy capitals of the arcade are all different, and one pictures a man escaping from a most realistic coiling snake. The mediaeval woodcarvers must have enjoyed themselves as much as the stonemasons in making the delicate fan-vaulted chancel screen and the magnificent benches, some with carved fronts, some with carved backs, and all with handsome ends, one showing a bird singing among the branches growing from a grinning face.

The pillar piscina is the only bit left of the church of Norman days. Two side windows of the chancel, with ornamented recesses below them, contain fragments of old glass, and one has a spirited modern picture of Saul's conversion. Another mediaeval window found blocked in the wall has been opened out in our own time. A mediaeval bell rings in the tower, and a plain chest of 1699 is in the vestry, which was once the Thorncombe chapel. Sir John de Sweeting Thorncombe, who died in 1688, has on his memorial two angels with golden hair reclining among roses and skulls.

Biddisham. The new village grows along the motor road, and keeps its narrow 13th century church hidden up a lane. It need not be ashamed that the tower is not as straight as it should be, but it may be proud of its Norman font, with scallops below the bowl. There is a carved oak Jacobean pulpit, and two mediaeval heads outside a chancel window. By the ancient churchyard cross we see Brent Knoll rising suddenly out of the meadows of the plain; and on the walls is a scratch dial from the days before clocks.

Bishop's Hull. A gaunt Elizabethan house looks across the road to where its builder lies with his wife and children round him; he was Sir George Farwell, who lies in the chancel of the church. Generations after him brought other Farwells to keep him company, till last of all came three in swaddling clothes. Here they laid another child in other days, and we read his famous name on a stone in the wall; he was little John Shelley, nine years old, Shelley's nephew.

The 15th century church has an odd eight-sided tower two centuries older, and the spoiling of the ancient structure has happily left for us some of the old bench-ends. On one we noticed a familiar figure of the 15th century, the night watchman with his lantern; and on another is a vivid carving of Christ rising from the tomb with three soldiers asleep. One of the bells was ringing in the tower when the bench-ends were made.

In the churchyard lies a remarkable man in the history of music, William Crotch, who died here while on a visit to his son, headmaster of Taunton Grammar School. It is said that when he was little more than a baby he could strike the keynote of favourite tunes on the organ his musical father had made, and by the time he was two he had taught himself to play God Save the King. Someone read a paper on young William to the Royal Society, and in 1779 an advertisement appeared stating that "Mrs Crotch is arrived in town with her son, the Musical Child, who will perform every day from one o'clock to three, at Mrs Hart's, milliner, Piccadilly." That was his first London performance; his last was when he played the organ in Westminster Abbey at the Handel Festival in 1834. Hosts of people would come to concerts to hear him play the piano or the organ sitting on his mother's knee. At eleven he went to Cambridge for his first music lessons, but two years later went to Oxford to study for the Church, though he ended with the degree of a Bachelor of Music. All this time he was composing and giving concerts, and for ten years he was lecturing at Oxford. As a hobby he sketched its colleges. In 1812 came the London performance of his greatest work, the oratorio *Palestine*. It was never printed, but he used to lend the score for 200 guineas provided he was allowed to conduct. His other oratorio, *The Captivity of Judah*, was performed for the first time when the Duke of Wellington was installed as Chancellor of Oxford. When the Royal Academy of Music was founded he was its first Principal.

Bishop's Lydeard. It is as red as the soil of its fields, its church and houses all made of the sandstone from its quarries. High above them all rises its lovely tower, a 15th century masterpiece. A narrow door, heavily clamped and plated, indicates that it was a tower of refuge as well as a storehouse for the arms of Sir John Stawell, the Royalist against whom the redoubtable Blake was sent with his army.

The noble tower looks down on one of the finest churchyard crosses left in England. It was here before the tower, and was then a centenarian. One of the steps is hollowed out like a bowl, perhaps for alms or holy water, and round the base are sculptured the Twelve Disciples, with Christ risen and enthroned. Above stands John the Baptist with two smaller figures in a niche on the shaft. Close by is the village cross, old and broken.

The church has a wonderful fan-vaulted screen of the 16th century, and a magnificent set of 16th century bench-ends. Their bold carvings, against a painted background, have characteristic Somerset scenes, a stag on a hill, a miller, and a ship under sail. The backs of the pews are beautifully carved, probably by the craftsmen who did the fine carving in the pulpit, with the rose and thistle and a row of cherubs.

By the great studded south door, with its immense lock, is Nicholas Grobham engraved in brass; he has his wife and five children with him. In one corner of the brass the artist has engraved an angel trumpeting, and in another a boy blowing bubbles. A man's life, says the moral, is as a blown bubble, and then the Judgment; and we are grimly warned that we must all become "a prey unto the silly worm". Nicholas died in 1585, but his name lives on in this curious brass and in the almshouses founded by his descendant Sir Richard, of the 17th century.

Bishopsworth. It is one of the villages high up round Bristol, and has a fine copy of a church the Normans built in their homeland at Caen. It is a noble-looking place, with an apse, and a low tower with something like the strength of castle walls.

Its nave has ten lofty bays, and very impressive is the view of the chancel through two noble arches, rough and clean in white stone and with three high windows in dazzling colour. The great corbels at the entrance of the chancel are finely sculptured, two with angels on them. Two carved lions look down from the sanctuary walls, on which is a tribute to a chorister who sang in the choir for 61 years.

This church has two fine treasures, one of them a precious possession indeed, a museum-piece. Both are paintings of St Elizabeth and the Madonna. One shows the visitation of Mary to Elizabeth by Alexander Guvenet; the other ranks among the pictures of the world, showing Elizabeth with Mary and the Child in an original painting by Nicholas Poussin, one of the creators of French art in the 17th century. It represents the Madonna with the Little One on her knee, in a homely scene.

Blackford. There are two Somerset Blackfords, one near Wedmore with little to show, and this one near Wincanton with a gem of a Norman doorway and a Norman font in its simple church. From the old stone seats of the porch we may admire this carved doorway and marvel how lightly it carries its 800 years. By another doorway is a head so extraordinary it might inspire an Epstein monster. There is also a scratch dial. Our own day gave the church the fine screen and the chancel panelling, with seats to match; the oak pulpit is Jacobean. Aumbry and piscina combine to guard a fragmentary but still beautiful figure, with a cloak draped over mail and shield. He is St Michael, once part of an alabaster reredos, and found with a figure of Christ built up in the roodloft stairs.

Blagdon. It is a noble spectacle as we look to it from afar, wondering at the high tower across the vast lake which gives Bristol its water. The tower has dominated this landscape since the 15th century, and the 20th century has crowned its hilltop with one of the noblest churches of our time. For hundreds of years it will stand as a witness of the genius of our age. We seem to see here something of the gracious dignity of Bristol's university, for which the builder of this church gave part of his fortune.

He was William Henry Wills, one of the famous family which has turned such tiny things as cigarettes into such noble things as universities and picture galleries. He found an ugly church at Blagdon and left a lovely one, and in the shadow of its tower he lies, under a granite cross. He was the first and last Lord Winterstoke.

The church is great in its simplicity, with no intricate beauty, no richness of decoration, no hundred-and-one things to draw the eye. It is fine for its stone, the splendour of its oak, and the beauty of its glass. The windows are unequalled in any modern church for many miles around, and the woodwork is impressive everywhere. The great piers rise in clustered columns, with small carved capitals bearing up spacious roofs arranged in over 500 panels. The chancel roof rests on four stone heads, a king and queen, a monk and a nun. The screens have splendid cresting, the pulpit has finely carved panels, the pews are rich with tracery, and the choir-stalls have poppyheads, the front ones enriched with figures of the Four Evangelists.

Looking down on it all from above the tower arch is St Andrew with his cross, his canopied niche resting on two lions. The tower roof has a fine piece of fan-vaulting and the glowing windows are filled with majestic figures of saints, prophets, kings, and martyrs. It is a feast of colour and a gallery of art.

The chancel has two fine possessions, treasures of art with 800 years of time between them. One is a very lovely reredos, one of the few altarpieces we can look at again and again. It is by Oswald Moser, a painting of the Last Supper by flickering candlelight, the faces fascinating and the grouping unusual. The other treasure of the chancel is the oldest possession of the church, a Norman stone at the base of the piscina. It is as quaint a sculpture as we have seen, with four heads under arches, the kind of heads small children draw. There are two old heads of a king and queen under a window in the vestry close by; and three mediaeval figures much worn by time are let into the tower outside.

Bleadon. Like many Mendip villages, it has a cave, but more attractive for most of us is the scene in which the high tower looks down on the 600-year-old church, the cross that has kept it company all the time, and the old house close by. The cross has suffered through the ages, for the shaft was long used as a tethering post for horses, was once found by a rector propping up a hen-roost, and was once without a head. It is believed that the original head is the canopied relief now in the church porch, showing a man and woman kneeling before a dainty Madonna and Child. The present head of the cross was made new last century.

The church has many quaint gargoyles, one of a little fellow sitting cross-legged playing bagpipes, and two humorous faces near the buttress on which is an old mass dial. An angel and an old stone head have found a new home in the blocked-up arches of a chapel which was begun but never finished. The chancel has changed since it was dedicated in 1713, a canopied tomb serves as a seat for the priests, and on the floor lie two men from the 14th century, both with satchel purses, and one wearing a very early hat, low-crowned and narrow-brimmed; this once fashionable figure lay with his companion for

200 years in the churchyard, and both are much worn and battered. The font is Norman, and there is a very old chest with a curious lock. The pulpit is one of that small group of mediaeval stone pulpits left in England, and has a wonderful bit of carving with Tudor flowers.

Bossington. In this western land of walnut trees the Bossington walnut reigns, a king among them all, each spreading branch as big as a tree itself. Down by the stream are more of these magnificent trees, but none to compare with the famous walnut in the heart of the hamlet, over five yards round the trunk. Here are cottages covered with creeper and ivy, sometimes to the chimney. An outward curve in a cottage wall tells of a bread oven within, and there are more soft curves in the thatched roofs waving up and down over tiny windows. Behind them all a hill rises steeply to the beacon a thousand feet high. Ten minutes walk and we are on the pebble beach; or climb through the woods to the top of Hurlstone Point and we look over Exmoor and the coast to Lynton. For its church Bossington has the ancient chapel of Lynch long used as a barn.

Bradford. Late summer is the time of Bradford's glory, for then the church is clothed in a glowing mantle of red and gold. The leaves creep up to the very battlements of the tower, where hang six bells, five of them old and mellow. The tenor, which has been ringing since 1520, is one of the finest in Somerset. The church has Norman work in its walls and in the base of the font, but most of it belongs to the 14th and 15th centuries. The broken stone figure of a patron of that time lies in a recess, an armoured man thought to be John de Meriet. It was about this time also that the beautiful bridge across the Tone was built at the end of the village street. Both Bradford's bridges were repaired sometime in the 17th century, and one of them was built in the 14th.

Brean. It has grown into a straggling collection of bungalows with a long narrow green jutting a mile into the sea, but 200 feet above, overgrown with grass and wild flowers, is a sanctuary for wild birds. They have another sanctuary on Steep Holm, the island a little way out at sea, with Flat Holm beyond it. In the days before history men built a camp on this high stretch of land, and in the century before ours it was made a fort again. Now the fort has been dismantled and there is hardly a sign of either of these defences. The church of St Bridget has survived the passing of camp and fort. It has had its adventure in its 700 years, for lightning struck the tower and it has never been repaired. For years the north side

39

of the churchyard was set apart for sailors drowned on the treacherous Brean Sands when Bristol's ships were constantly passing this way. The stump of the ruined tower was roofed over with gables, and in it still hang three bells that have been ringing for 400 years. In the tower is an oak seat shaped with an axe 500 years ago, and from it the new pews have been copied; the same high bench-ends with elaborate carvings are in the chancel seats. The pulpit has a shallow carving of Jacobean days, and we read on a panel that George Gudrid gave it in 1620. The font is 13th century and has flowers carved round the bowl, fading with time. Looking down from the chancel arch are the heads of a man and a woman of Richard II's day.

Brent Knoll. It has taken the name of a solitary hill which every motorist in Somerset knows, rising 450 feet above the pastures. It was to the shelter of the earthworks crowning the hill that the Saxons hurried their women and children and flocks when the Danes came raiding. From these ramparts the women would look down on the battle, first with terror and then with joy, for Bishop Ealhstan of Sherborne, he who taught Alfred much battlecraft, taught the Danes also a lesson that day.

From the height is one of the finest views in Somerset, over sea and marsh, the flat land broken here and there by a streak of white road, the smoke of a train, and the moving cattle on a little farm. We see for nearly 20 miles along the coast, from the high point of Brean Down above Burnham as far as Minehead. We see the island bird sanctuaries of Steep Holm and Flat Holm, and to the north is the long line of the Mendips with Glastonbury Tor jutting up as an afterthought, then the Poldens and the Quantocks.

It is a Norman doorway with a chevron arch and a wonderful old door that brings us into the 15th century church. There is a small Norman pillar still left and a row of 13th century heads along a wall. The magnificently carved oak roof borne by angels is crowned outside by a lovely pierced parapet running round it and the tower, and in the tower the clock of a Glastonbury monk still ticks the hours away.

It was in mediaeval days that the church received its chief glory from the famous woodcarvers of Somerset. Every one of these high bench-ends has its own pattern, and three have a story. It seems that the Abbot of Glastonbury tried to seize the revenues from the parish priest, but the parson won, and the three bench-ends were carved to celebrate his victory. They tell the story of what happened.

In the first sits a greedy fox in abbot's robes, a mitre on his head, a crook in his hand, a bit of fleece sticking from it to show that his flock was not shepherded for nothing. Looking up to him are three pigs with cowls, a crane, an owl, a cock, a hen, and a few geese victims of the greedy fox. The second picture shows the rebellion of the geese, led by an ape with a stick. The fox is stripped of its robes, shackled, and put in the stocks, his mitre tantalisingly hung before him. In the third picture he himself is hung, the geese all pulling the rope, two watch-dogs barking triumphantly.

The font is about 600 years old, twice as old as the pulpit, which was new when they set up here a colossal monument on the wall gorgeous with all the flamboyance of the 17th century. In the middle, delightful in red, white, and blue, is John Somerset with a wife each side of him, one in a high-crowned hat painted red under the brim, the other a sombre figure with a black scarf round her head, and below her a picture of her resurrection, a small shrouded figure sitting up in a coffin as an angel blows the Last Trump from the clouds. Below the first wife her children kneel and pray, one poor child in swaddling clothes having a skull to play with. We are told that the Almighty found John Somerset fit for bliss in 1663.

Bridgwater. Somerset is rich in its towns, for it has Bath and Taunton, Glastonbury and Wells, and fine little places like Bruton and Frome. Bridgwater, however, has a pride of its own, for it is Robert Blake's town, and it has on one side the heights that lead us to Glastonbury, and on the other the vast plain in which lies Sedgemoor with its poignant memories. It stands on the River Parret, notable for its Bore, which comes up twice a day with the tidal waters, bringing a tang of sea air from the Bristol Channel.

Still the chief port of the county, Bridgwater after Bristol is the only seaport with any distinction on its side of the Channel. It received the first news in England of the Spanish Armada (said to have been made known by Humphrey Blake, the Admiral's seafaring father), and it was important enough for Charles I to lose all hope when its castle fell. All that is left of the castle today, 700 years after its building, is a stone archway on West Quay, part of the old water gate; one of the last memories of the castle is that the Duke of Monmouth was crowned here and proclaimed king by the mayor and corporation. Fifteen days later the duke climbed to the top of St Mary's Tower and viewed the field of Sedgemoor before he left to battle for the kingdom; the lane down which he went is still War Lane.

Bridgwater still has the house in which Robert Blake was born. It is down a narrow street not far from where he stands magnificent in bronze, watching the traffic at the meeting of the streets. He is the work of Mr F. W. Pomeroy, who has shown him with his sword in one hand and his right hand outstretched, pointing his finger as if to the sea, a stern man, looking rather like Cromwell himself. Round the pedestal are three bronze plaques showing two of his battles off Portland and Santa Cruz, and another of the bringing of his body into Plymouth Sound. On this is engraved this quotation from Edmund Spenser (whose name is unhappily wrongly spelt):

Sleep after toyle, port after stormy seas, ease after war,
death after life, doth greatly please.

Blake was born in this town in 1598 and died at sea in 1657. His house is now a museum and has four rooms filled with historical and curious things. There are fragments of the ancient Franciscan house of which the doorway still exists in a street close by. There is a hollowed-out trunk of a tree used in the old days as a water-pipe. There is a piece of timber believed to have been the name-board of the famous American ship *Alabama*, sunk in the Channel during the Civil War, an event famous in history because it led, under the guiding influence of Mr Gladstone, to the first great example of arbitration between nations. There are relics of Sedgemoor—flint pistols used in that tragic battle, and a skull with a bullet hole through it. On the wall hangs a document signed by Blake asking for more men from the Parliament, and near it is his original will.

We may wish the admiral could have lain in his own church, for at its font he was baptised. The font was in its second century when they brought Blake to it; but its cover has been made new and on it is the curious Greek inscription which spells the same words both ways and means: Cleanse my sins, not my face only.

Often the 12 Blake boys must have been brought to this fine church by Humphrey Blake, the merchant of Bridgwater, for his father was mayor and must have sat in the chapel set apart for the mayor and corporation; he would sit in this very chair with the little image of the castle set in the back of it. It is like all the oak of this great place, magnificent.

There can be no doubt concerning the finest possession of this famous town; it is the collection of screens in the nave and chancel of St Mary's. The whole nave is filled with pews to match, but they are modern like the screens to two of the chapels. The rest of the screens are among the finest craftsmanship of the 15th century;

42

Sir Gilbert Scott said he knew of no screen finer than the screen round the corporation pew. It is 16th century; the rest of the old ones are 1420 and 1480. They are all in black oak, all nobly carved, and are a truly impressive spectacle.

The screen surrounding the civic pew, the newest of the old ones, is an enchantment. It has two doorways and 14 bays, the bays divided by round columns neatly carved with a crest running along the top, crowned by silhouette carving in many quaint shapes. At the base of each column is a finely carved face; at the top is a small complete figure sitting; and below and above the bays is a band of rich carving crowded with fascinating figures of fancy and reality such as ancient carvers loved to put on their screens and ancient masons on their corbels.

The oldest screens of all are in the chancel, where the handsome choir-stalls are richly carved to match the screens dividing the chancel from the chapels. Perhaps the best single piece of this mass of carving is the superb bench-end of the sedilia on the right of the altar. The fine oak sedilia have been here 600 years, and the bench-end facing us has been called by a high authority the finest in Somerset—a tribute indeed, remembering that Somerset is perhaps unsurpassed in England for this kind of carving. Facing the sedilia across the sanctuary is a desk made from the ancient bench-ends and a piece of the old beam from the belfry on which the bells hung for 500 years. The altar, which dominates this chancel so rich with black oak, is worthy of it all, for it is one of the finest Jacobean altars in the country. The roofs looking down on this fine craftsmanship are modern but have great dignity, the nave and chancel roofs being a variety of hammerbeam. The great beams rest on stone angels, the roofs are arranged in hundreds of panels; at the four corners of the nave roof are stone figures of the Four Evangelists.

During the recent restoration of the church, when the walls were whitened and greatly brightened the interior, a remarkable discovery was made concerning a piece of 14th century woodwork used as the base of a lectern. It is a fragment of a richly traceried canopy something like a font cover and it is believed that it may have been a cover for the hanging pyx in which the sacrament was reserved before the Reformation. Should this be so, the canopy has a special interest, for such things are rare survivals, and one of the few known to exist is in the crypt at Wells.

Yet all the glory of this woodwork is not told, for standing out among it, drawing every eye from every part of this great nave, is the marvellous pulpit of black oak. It is a veritable masterpiece of the 15th century craftsmen. Its panels, all crowded with delicate carving, are divided by pinnacled buttresses with dainty window tracery between them. The pulpit is linked with the screens, seeming to crown a perfect whole.

So rich a church should have a treasure at its altar, and the altarpiece of St Mary's is a treasure indeed. It is a great French master's conception of the Descent from the Cross, so big that it covers up the east window as far as the tracery, and so fine that it is said Sir Joshua Reynolds broke his long coach journeys between London and Plymouth to sit and look at it. Nobody knows who the artist is, but the picture is apparently 17th century.

Perhaps we may not feel that the 15th century church, with its red stone tower and its octagonal spire, is fine enough for the richness within, but the spire has looked down on life in these streets for six centuries, and the weathercock looks down on the marshland about it from a height of 175 feet. The church has traces of Norman and mediaeval architecture. There are two porches with heads wearing papal tiaras greeting us at one of them, and both have galleries over them. The rose window above the north door is flanked with canopied niches, and in its tracery we noticed four emblems of hearts, diamonds, clubs, and spades. It is at this door that loaves are given every Sunday to poor people. There are some carved heads on the walls inside, one of a crusader in chain mail and one of a pouting woman to keep him company.

In the chancel is a wall-monument on which an Irishman named Francis Kingsmill lies in the pompous manner of the 17th century, with two sons kneeling above him; and there are in the nave 13th century recesses with richly carved stone balls hanging from the cusps. In two recesses in the outside walls by the north porch lie stone figures worn almost to nothingness by the wind and rain of about 600 years. A little way off, under a magnificent cedar, is a circular stone about ten feet round, the base of the old Pig Cross.

One of the oldest doorways in Somerset stands by the church in Silver Street; its ancient timbers are shaped from the solid trunk of a tree, and are believed to have been the gateway to a college of Greyfriars built in 1220, the only house in the county of the followers of St Francis. The house in which Judge Jeffreys stayed on his Assize, when he sentenced 300 rebels of Monmouth's insurrection to death, has its carved oak front looking on to the church. The handsome market hall has Ionic columns, a dome, and a lantern, and the town hall and municipal buildings have a fine and dignified front in Italian style. Among the treasured possessions here are three

44

rich silver maces, made in London about 300 years ago, and portraits of mayors, as well as one supposed to be of Blake. In the richly decorated council chamber are tapestries which once hung in Enmore Castle, one showing Alexander bidding farewell to Philip of Macedon and again mourning the death of Darius. There are many old houses and fascinating walks along the quay, where some of the vaulted cellars of the castle still remain. Up in King Street, not far off, is the Great War memorial sculpture by John Angel. The Library, with its pillared porch, reminds us that Bridgwater was the pioneer of free libraries.

Brislington. Bristol will soon enfold it in its wings, and it will give that great city of churches a 15th century church that has been much changed, with a Norman font and a neat Jacobean pulpit, a deep arch panelled all round, and two epitaphs we remember. One is from the 18th century and is in the porch:

A heap of dust alone remains of thee,
Tis all thou art and all the proud shall be.

The other is by the altar, and these are its fine words:

Those who knew him best loved him most, and for the applause of the stranger, what availeth it?

Broadway. It stands on an ancient track cut through a royal forest, leading straight as an arrow to the fortified hill of Castle Neroche; it is said that the wide verges of this old road were for preventing robbers from hiding close enough to spring out on the unwary traveller.

By the road stands the 13th century church, with a scratch dial on the wall, and an interior rich with old oak—solid bench-ends with poppyheads, a black pulpit with delicately carved panels showing the five wounds of Our Lord, and carved beams and bosses in the chancel roof. There are eight 15th century figures of saints niched round the font, still fine after all these years, and the churchyard cross still has its statues on the shafts after 500 years of sun and rain.

We noticed that some Americans, proud of their ancestry from this village of charming cottages and gardens ringed in by tree-covered hills, have put a tablet in memory of it on the walls of the church. A little way off is a link with another continent, the house called Jordans, home of John Hanning Speke, who found the source of the Nile and died by an accident on the very day he was to tell of his discovery to the British Association at Bath. He lies at Dowlish

Wake. The Spekes lived in this neighbourhood for three centuries, owning Jordans and the lovely farm at Horton Cross, a low spreading mediaeval building with the original staircase and many ancient windows.

Brockley. Samuel Taylor Coleridge, climbing the combe cut through this wooded hillside, could not refrain from ending a poem with the sigh, "Enchanting spot! O, were my Sara here!" The church has found an enchanting spot too, for it stands in the park of Brockley Court, with one of the earliest chimneys in England in the farm behind it. Made entirely of flat stones, the chimney is believed to be 700 years old.

The church itself is mainly 13th century, with a modest Norman doorway, a Norman font, a charming mediaeval black-and-white roof, and one of a score of 15th century stone pulpits in Somerset richly carved and with a rare stone canopy. So high it stands that it is reached through the rood stairs doorway.

The Court pew has an elaborate stone fireplace with the Pigott arms, with above it a Chantrey sculpture of a woman weeping, in memory of a rector, Wadham Pigott. In the window are Edward I and Nicholas and Dorothy Wadham, founders of Wadham College, Oxford, from whom the Pigott family descended. From the same family of benefactors the church received in 1821 its carved organ and the striking picture over the altar, a 17th century copy by Nicholas Poussin of Volterra's fresco in a church in Rome. Magnificently it portrays the taking down of Our Lord from the Cross.

Brompton Ralph. Once more the ancient screen stands in the church, fitted together from fragments found in the manor and round about. It was a fortunate day for Brompton Ralph when Mr Toms left America to search for his family records. He came to this small place on the edge of the Brendon Hills, where his great grandfather had lived, and found the villagers delighted to have discovered fragments of their lost screen, but with no money to set it up. He happily had the money and the will to do it, and the screen now stands to the glory of the church and the memory of Mr Toms. The pews and the font are from the 15th century, the chalice is Elizabethan, and there are four old bells, one a mediaeval Angelus bell made by the famous Robert Norton, which says in beautiful lettering, *Gabriel is my name: In me find no blame.*

Brompton Regis. We stand at its church porch and look over the hills and fields to Haddon Hill, marvelling at this sturdy village defying the storms that sweep over Exmoor, with only steep and stony roads leading to its few lonely neighbours. The church has lost its fine fan-vaulted screen, for it threw it away last century, when it was sold and carried off to Tiverton, to what new destiny nobody knows. The restorers gave the 13th century tower a new arch and a new west window, but happily did not pull down the fine arcade of clustered pillars which have stood 400 years. What we thought most interesting here was a brass to the Dykes of Stuart days, which remembers a young woman of 19 with these lines:

> Reader, it is worth thy pains to know
> Who was interred here below.
> Here lies good nature, pity, wit,
> Though small in volume yet most fairly writ.
> She died young, and so oft-times tis seen
> The fruit God loves He's pleased to pluck it green.

Broomfield. Great beeches shelter the road to this Quantock village, and far below is spread the pastel coloured vale of Taunton Deane. The church has an early 14th century chancel, the rest is mainly early 16th century. There is a fine array of carved Tudor bench-ends. The name of the man who made them, Simon Werman, stands out clearly on one, and another shows a graceful vine with a bird pecking at the grapes. There is a patchwork of mediaeval glass, two old Bibles, a long chest with enormous locks, and a fine holy table of 1677, while little wooden angels wearing crowns look down from the delicately panelled roofs. One of the four old bells prays that we will let its sound move us to God's glory.

The Romans may have used the ancient Ruborough Camp now grown over with fir trees, for their coins have been found in a field close by. In 1800 Holwell Cave was discovered in a limestone quarry. It is 140 feet long and in places 20 feet wide. Stalactites hang from the roof, which is at one end encrusted with crystals, their pattern spreading like coral, exquisitely white with flushes of rosy pink.

Broomfield was the home of an electrician whose experiments created something of a sensation in the first year of the Victorian era. He was Andrew Crosse, who was born in 1784 at Fyne Court on the Quantocks, and died in the same room in 1855. He lived most of his life alone in this quiet place, absorbed in his experiments and seeing few people. He was almost an intellectual hermit.

Brushford. By the church porch stands a noble tree, spoken of even in Shakespeare's day as the old oak. It cannot be less than six and is probably eight centuries old. A few of its branches rest on crutches, but it is strong and green and should outlive many more of man's short generations.

The church pews were cut from another oak 500 years ago, when the massive screen was also made, beautiful with fan-vaulting. The marble font has a Norman design of arcades often used in the 12th and 13th centuries, and near it is a mediaeval chest hollowed from the trunk of a tree. *Peace and good neighbourhood* says one of the bells, bringing down the centuries the lovely West-of-England greeting.

Through the amber windows of a chapel designed by Sir Edwin Lutyens a warm glow like sunshine lights up an altar tomb. The stone figure lying on it is no courtier in his elaborate robes, no knight in armour, but the simple figure of a man in shirt and riding breeches, yet a soldier nevertheless, his sword hanging above him. It is a beautiful reminder of one of the rare men of our century, Colonel Aubrey Herbert, diplomatist, traveller, poet, with an amazing knowledge of Eastern languages. He fought for Turks against Albanians, but when taken prisoner he learned so much about Albania, and so completely won the people's confidence, that during the Great War he was offered the command of an Albanian regiment raised in America.

Bruton. It is one of the gems of Somerset, a small town of heights and depths and lovely views across the valley. It still keeps the pack-horse bridge, about three feet wide, over which men and horses tramped for centuries when this was the only way. Over it walked William Dampier, the Bruton schoolboy who saw Robinson Crusoe, for he grew up to be a pirate and was on the ship which found Alexander Selkirk, whose story Daniel Defoe made into the greatest boy's story in the world. We come upon Dampier at his birthplace near Yeovil, East Coker.

There is a fine view of the town from this little bridge, showing the weir and Hugh Sexey's ancient hospital, the magnificent church tower, a bit of the ancient school, the end of the mediaeval wall of the priory, a lovely cedar in the churchyard, and the old red roofs of the rambling streets on each side of the valley.

If we walk down from the pack-horse bridge we find ourselves in narrow passage-ways which bring us to the High Street, and, passing the old Court House with its painted shields and its carved stone corbels of queer animals, we reach an ancient gateway tempting us in. It is Hugh Sexey's Hospital, the Jacobean corner of Bruton, bequeathed to his old village by this Bruton ostler's boy who went up to London and became auditor to Elizabeth I and James I. Here he is in a niche above the doorway of the courtyard, looking like Shakespeare with a painted shield and two goats about him.

There is a gallery running round to the comfortable little homes in which the old folk live. Opening off the courtyard is a hall and a chapel, both charming interiors. The hall has an oak screen with six pillars and fanlike carving, and a chest which we believe is a marvel of mediaeval craftsmanship, one key fastening 12 locks by a complicated mechanism which shone like silver. The chapel has Jacobean panelling, a fine canopied pulpit tucked in a corner above the stalls, and a speck of ancient glass.

The charming exterior of Sexey's Hospital is crowned with lovely gables and gives us one of the best views of the town from across the valley. One of the loveliest laburnums we have seen was in full bloom in the master's garden when we called. It would thrill the warm heart of Hugh Sexey to see that his corner of Bruton is so bright today, a comfortable and a beautiful place.

We stood in Hugh Sexey's Chapel and looked out through the windows at one of the rarest little sights that Bruton has, a fine two-storeyed dovecot of the ancient priory, high up on a green hill with a wall a mile long running round it. The dovecot is in the possession of the National Trust; the wall enclosed the 12th century monastery. Much of the wall is broken down but it is magnificent at the end by the church, where 14 of its buttresses are still intact. Facing the wall is what is left of the old grammar school, which has a new hall with a fine hammerbeam roof.

The spectacular glory of Bruton is the great 15th century tower of its church, which has a little tower to keep it company. It is one of the fine sentinels of Somerset, enriched with canopied niches, some of which rest in angels' wings.

The spacious 15th century church, its clerestory resting on clustered columns, is impressive. The roofs are magnificent, oak panelled with tracery above the beams. The chancel is in the classical style of the 18th century. The roof is painted, and the east wall has, instead of a window, two great columns and a pediment. There is a beautiful pair of silver candlesticks on the altar.

The chancel was built in the middle of the 18th century by a great family whose tombs are in the vault below; their names are known to all who know London, for they are the Berkeleys of Berkeley Square, and they gave the name of Bruton to that Bruton Street which links the square with Bond Street. One of them lies here in a noble tomb older than the chancel; he is Sir Maurice Berkeley, a splendid figure between two wives, standard-bearer to Henry VIII and Elizabeth I. It was Henry who gave him Bruton Abbey as his reward for being Keeper of the Tower. They buried him at midnight, as all the Berkeleys here were buried, and the little black lamps by whose flickering light they were laid to rest are hanging on the wall.

In a great altar tomb at the west end of the church lies William Gilbert, Abbot of Bruton in 1510. He lived behind this great wall when it was a marvellous abbey, and when this lovely dovecot was alive with doves. He finished the work Prior Henton laid down in 1494 and completed the church in the first years of the 16th century. Hanging on the wall near his tomb is a piece of 15th century embroidery.

There is a 13th century chest about seven feet long, some Jacobean benches among the modern ones, two chained books, and a fascinating painted oak carving of the arms of Charles II; these lay in a builder's yard until a few years before we called, when a local craftsman found them, restored them, painted them, and set them up again. The fine oak screen in the tower is Jacobean, with heads running along the crest. The reredos in the grammar school chapel has four little sculptured figures of St George, St Aldhelm, Edward VI, and Richard FitzJames, the Bishop of London who founded the school. The only old glass in Bruton is in the border of two clerestory windows.

Brympton d'Evercy. A long oak avenue and a drive lined with shrubs lead to its church—and to a little paradise. We turn a corner and, lo, there is something not of the everyday world, for here, by the church, is one of the surprises of Somerset, unexpected and unforgettable, a group of private buildings round a green forecourt, stables, dower house, and the manor house itself, one of the most beautiful of Somerset's country homes.

It is all there is of Brympton d'Evercy, but it is enough. We feel we are back in the days before the world was spoiled by the madding crowd, the days when the lord of the manor was lord indeed of the countryside, and his domain was unspoiled. This great house, with its exquisite Tudor front, sculptured and battlemented and 130 feet long, is England at her best, serene and something like a dream. Its grey-gold walls are set in a lovely park with grand old yews and a lake like a mirror for all the beauty round about. It has work attributed to Inigo Jones on its garden front, which was added about

1680. Indoors little has been changed since then. The porch was added in 1722.

The tiny dower house has a charming turret, a carved stone fireplace 400 years old, and a plaster ceiling of the 17th century. It is a self-contained little place, built for Dame Sydenham in early Tudor times, a retreat where she could be quiet in her old age but never nervous, so close to her young people in the great house.

By the dower house is the delightful church with a quaint top-heavy bellcot. Here sleep those who knew and loved this place. There is Thomas d'Evercy, a 13th century knight, and near him a grand lady of the 15th century with two puppies at her feet, one lying on its side with its feet stretched out, as every puppy lies on the rug. In the transept are the figures of a lady and a priest under canopies carved with vivid scenes of the Annunciation and the Adoration, the Passion and the Crucifixion. One of the canopies is mediaeval, the other is a splendid imitation by John Edward Carew, sculptor of the panels round Nelson's Column in Trafalgar Square. He restored the figures, also, for they had lain for years in the churchyard. Both are 15th century, and the face of the priest is haunting in its serene beauty. The lady looks towards the altar through a peephole.

Dividing the chapel from the chancel is a striking painted canopy, with black rams bearing the heraldic arms of John Sydenham. Under his chequered tomb lies a gaunt skeleton, a little horrifying until we realise that it is carved in stone, like the three skulls lying by it. The skeleton is all we have to see of good John Sydenham, but a verse tells us that he died in 1626, and adds:

Report it, Sir, he died an honest man.

There is a charming 15th century stone screen, with the roodbeam on the top of it painted red and blue and gold. It bears the coat-of-arms of John Stourton, who bought the manor house 500 years ago and gave it to his daughter Joan on her wedding day. The screen has quaintly carved spandrels, foliage and faces on one side and dragons on the other, and something we do not remember seeing before—stone seats running along each side, believed to be for the lords of the manor on the west and for the priests on the east.

There are two fine old chairs in the chancel and a little ancient glass with fragments of figures. The pulpit is Jacobean and the font is 14th century. Out in the churchyard, with the base and steps of the ancient cross, are two other fonts far older, perhaps older than anything else here.

51

Buckland Denham. Its tower has seen five centuries, standing proudly as if conscious that it is one of the loveliest of all the towers of Somerset. It looks down on a lychgate and two old yews, and has gargoyles to guard it and stones about it older than itself, for something is here from Norman England—fragments of the doorway, two windows, and a font with two styles of carving running round it in a band. There is a mass dial.

The beautiful porch came with the tower and is worthy of that lovely structure, its stately windows and their charming tracery. The porch roof is richly vaulted with four fans meeting in a circle deeply carved in eight sections.

On the floor of his chantry Sir John Denham lies in stone, his wife at his side; they have been here 600 years, he with his long hair and she in a wimple with a scarf on her shoulders. The chantry has ten stone corbels all neat and fine, and an arch with two stone faces. In the wall of an aisle is a ledge of stone projecting on which Sir John may have seen the candles burning; here are still the holes the candles stood in. Here, too, are the old brass candle-brackets on the walls, now adapted for a brighter light.

Through a hole in the wall the vicar climbs into his Jacobean pulpit, and by the altar is a Queen Anne chair; they saw the coming and the going of the Stuarts. The priest's seat has a little old oak panelling let into it.

Buckland St Mary. Seven hundred feet up the Blackdown Hills, its Victorian church cost the life of a man who helped to build it. He was carting material when his horses ran away; the wagon overturned, and the man was crushed beneath the stones. His story is on a stone with this quaint warning: *May all carters who read this take warning and never get in their wagons.*

It is a massive church for so small a place, and is decorated with great skill. The reredos, the roof, and the font have all rich carving of saints, apostles, and angels. Many niches with sculptured figures run round the splendid roof made from oaks which grew on the Blackdown Hills.

Burnett. It is a little world of its own among the green hills on the banks of the River Chew, with an old manor house, gabled farms, and a 15th century church with 15 pews to hold 60 people. A bishop and a king greet us at the door, which has Tudor roses round its arch. The porch has a charming canopied niche with two queer faces and a tiny ceiling with foliage ending in a rose.

Its finest possession is a brass two feet square on the chancel wall.

52

Bath Abbey: the west front.

Bath: Lansdown Crescent.

Bath: Pulteney Bridge and the River Avon.

Barrington Court.

Bridgwater Church.

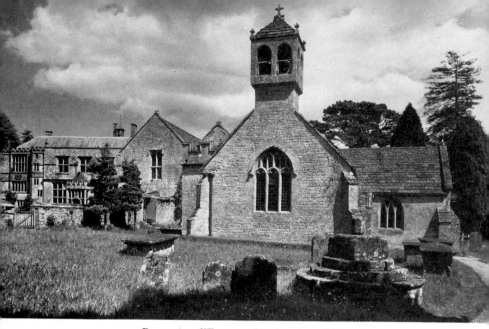

Brympton d'Evercy: the church and house.

Brympton d'Evercy: the house.

On it kneels a man who was Mayor of Bristol before the Spanish Armada, and with him are his wife and their 12 children. He is John Cutte, his wife is Joan, and we know the names of all his children, for they are with their portraits. John and Joan kneel at a desk with books, and on the desk is lying a pair of gloves. Near the brass is a square old stone deeply carved with two arches, in one of which we read of the death of a son and in the other of the death of a daughter at the rectory in Cromwell's time.

Burnham-on-Sea. Its tower is leaning in the sinking sands, for its 15th century church stands almost on the shore of this bright little seaside town. There is a lighthouse which flashes a white light to warn ships from Gore Sands.

The church has three things to attract the traveller. One is a fine brass chandelier of 1773, with three tiers and about 20 lights. The second is a pair of thanksgiving windows, both charming, both showing Christ in white and gold, once as a young man kneeling in a red cloak, and again with His mother in glowing blue and purple, after the Resurrection. There is also a little old heraldic glass.

The third notable possession of the church is something Inigo Jones designed for the chapel of Whitehall Palace, an altarpiece set up there and saved from the fire. It was then put in Westminster Abbey, where it was found too big and altogether out of place, being thrown out when the Abbey was prepared for the coronation of George IV. Then the vicar of Burnham begged it for his church and here it is, split into many parts. It fills the east wall of the chancel with its marble cherubs, its mosaic centrepiece hidden by the altar. The rest is under the tower, two winged angels with a group of lovely little cherubs, like soft wings circling round baby heads. They are the best fragments of this gigantic work which has seen so much adventure, and they are altogether charming.

Burrington. We come down to it from the tops of the Mendips, through a gorge with rocky heights climbing 250 feet each side, not so grand as Cheddar a little way behind yet with a fame of its own in science and in story; for here are natural caves, in one of which was found a company of 50 men long dead, and here is a cleft in the rock which in a marvellous way has woven itself into the spiritual life of mankind.

For it is the Rock of Ages. A great storm was blowing from these Mendip heights, and the thunder was rolling down the gorge, when a curate from Blagdon, Augustus Toplady, passed by. He sheltered in a cleft of the rock till the storm was passed, and while the thunder rolled he thought out the lines of that hymn which has been sung around the world.

The church is magnificent with a rich exterior of parapets and pinnacles, turrets and battlements, lovely faces at the windows, and queer creatures creeping down. Here we patted a gargoyle on the back, for he was very low on a windowsill. Among his 40 companions we noticed a man with a barrel, a little animal holding a big one's mouth open, and a host of laughing and melancholy creatures.

The old door, packed at the top with window and quatrefoiled tracery, brings us into an interior enriched with modern oak worthy of the 15th century church: carved bench-ends, linenfold choir-stalls, and screens with panelled vaulting and gold stars. The roofs are borne by stone angels with painted shields on which are the emblems of the Passion; the nave roof has painted and gilded bosses. We found in the tower an odd fragment of timber from the ancient roof with a small piece of metal set in it from one of the old bells, engraved with a ship some centuries ago. The tower has a fine fan-vaulted roof.

The oldest possession of the church is perhaps a stone in the sanctuary wall, sculptured with five figures. It is supposed to represent Christ with angels on each side and two figures kneeling, and to have been part of a mediaeval Easter sepulchre. One of the windows is rich with a mosaic of ancient glass, showing the Madonna with two children on her knee. There are other fragments in the tracery.

In a chapel is an epitaph to one of a vicar's 20 children, drowned at sea; she was Albina Jackson, and her epitaph was written by her friend Hannah More, beginning

Fair joy and hope, loving and beloved,
A daughter cherished and a wife approved.

There are two fine yews in the churchyard, one a hollow giant probably older than Magna Carta, for he is eight yards round his trunk. Hidden behind a wall a mile away is Langford Court, a great house altered and added to since Elizabeth's day, when someone wrote over one of its doors in Latin:

Christ enter Thou my house with me
Until I enter heaven with Thee.

Burrow Bridge. Men may come and men may go over this bridge where the Tone joins the River Parret, but still one name rules here: it is Alfred's kingdom, the Isle of Athelney where he

sought refuge in a peasant's hut and planned the defeat of the
Danes. Burrow Mump, the hill beside the bridge, was probably his
fort. Alfred himself marked the spot by an abbey, but its stones have
gone.

Today there stands at the foot of the Mump, the conical hill with
the comical name, a little church of 1836, and on the top of the hill
are the ruins of another church, looking as if it had been caught
unaware and carried up. The ruin is of St Michael's Church,
broken walls of a nave and tower through whose doorless arches the
cattle wander at will. It is worth a climb up the steep turf to stand
by the ruin and see Glastonbury Tor rising like a miniature Fuji-
yama above the hills that break the plain.

Bury. A narrow mediaeval bridge spans the River Haddeo a
mile before it flows into the Exe. Here is the hamlet of Bury, set
against the lovely line of Haddon Hill, with the fortified height of
Bury Castle an outpost between it and the road.

Butcombe. It has a fine old yew and a noble fir, and a new
Crucifixion cross on ancient steps in memory of eight men who
died for England. Its charming 15th century tower is battlemented
and has gargoyles with canopied niches at the corners and buttresses
climbing to the top. The nave is no bigger than the chancel, which
has a charming roof painted red, white, blue, and gold, with a
central boss of the Madonna and Child. The chancel screen is made
up in memory of a young captain who fell in Mesopotamia and his
brother who fell in France; it is mostly old carving worked into a
central doorway and four bays with rich tracery and three bands of
cresting. There is a tiny piscina and three stone seats for priests.
The east window has about a dozen fragments of old glass, in which
is a gold-crowned Madonna, a pilgrim with his staff, and a woman
with golden hair. The pulpit has some old panelling, and an old
niche in the chapel has a new Madonna.

Butleigh. We are here on the top of the world. It is charming
in itself, but its high woodland, solitary, and rich in almost every
kind of English tree, is one of those green places where memory
may take sanctuary in a city's din. Could any lovelier spot have been
found than the grassy knoll on Windmill Hill for the great column
to Samuel Hood? From one side of the column we look down on
typical Somerset, a wide plain heaving up with cone-shaped heights;
on the other side the beeches are cut to frame a view of Glastonbury
Tor so delightful that we accept the green seat made for us by nature,

55

and sit and gaze. For miles around the Hood Column draws the traveller's eye, and well is he rewarded as he sits here on the height and sees the world below him.

Sir Samuel Hood shares a memorial in the church with his two sailor brothers, their long epitaph written by Robert Southey, whose young brother was killed with Alexander Hood. The eldest Hood was drowned as a young man; Alexander went with Captain Cook on his second journey round the world; and Samuel, the youngest, was with Nelson when his arm was shot off at Teneriffe. One incident in his life is pictured in relief on his memorial here. He had ordered a boat to put out to rescue three men on a wreck, and his men hesitated to set out in the raging sea, whereupn he leaped into the boat saying, "I never gave an order to a sailor which I was not ready to execute myself."

Facing the memorial to the brothers is one to their kinsman Samuel, who was vicar here for 38 years and whose two sons made even greater names for themselves in the navy, one becoming Viscount Hood and the other Viscount Bridport. They were the greatest of all the Hoods, and were both born in this vicarage.

Well would they know this pleasant church, partly 14th century, though the pillars of the south doorway are possibly Saxon and may be part of the old chancel arch. There is a mass dial from the days before clocks. In the west window is a little old glass, four tiny figures in red and blue. The 15th century font is carved with the lamb and eagle of two St Johns. One of the windows has been turned into a memorial to James Grenville and his two sons, General Richard Grenville and Lord Glastonbury, all of the 18th century. Their names are in brass, and the splay of the window is filled with their tree of life in stone and an array of shields. Three black-robed Jacobean figures, Thomas Symcocks with his wife and child, kneel on this windowsill, their rightful tomb having been destroyed. They were at Butleigh Court before the Grenvilles, but the old home has gone and its Victorian successor is in ruins.

Its trees are the pride of Butleigh, and in the garden of the Court are some that are truly magnificent: a great cedar of Lebanon, a Judas tree, a mighty beech, and a vigorous growing thorn which puts forth its white flowers at Christmas like its parent tree, St Joseph's Thorn at Glastonbury. A long and thick yew hedge, in one place over 20 feet high, divides the Court from the church, and a little distance from the house are the foundations of a far older manor, with a few feet of a round niched wall left of its mediaeval dovecot.

56

In Nelson's day the naval records bristled with the name of Hood, and Butleigh was the birthplace of the two most famous, Samuel, Viscount Hood, and Alexander, Viscount Bridport; while at the same time there were the three fighting brothers from Kingsland in Dorset. All the Hoods were cast in heroic mould, and their deeds created such problems of identity for the Admiralty that we find Bridport writing to ask if my Lords do not mean his brother Samuel when they offer him the captaincy of a ship.

Cameley. Alone with a farm it stands, on a hill with a wide view across the valley, and we wonder if the centuries have left us an odder little place. We come into it through a Norman porch, having first been attracted by a flight of steps outside. They lead us to a gallery which was built at the west end in 1711. Even then this place was short of room for those who came to it, and in 1819 they ran a gallery along the south wall "for the free use of the inhabitants". Here are the pegs on which they hung their hats.

The porch has more than the Saxon gravestone to hold us for a moment; it has a tiny battlemented cornice black with age, and a doorway with an arch of twisted rope work by Norman masons, the arch resting on two shafts with carved capitals. It leads us into as quaint an interior as we have seen, white from floor to ceiling, with benches hewn from solid trees 500 years ago, the marks of the axe still on them—uncomfortable seats of the days when we were not supposed to fall asleep in church. The pulpit is a two-decker with a neat canopy over it; its carved oak is 300 years old. The roof is white-washed—oak panelling, carved bosses, and all. Three of the bosses have carved heads, a remarkable mitred bishop at one end, and at the other a charming face set in a neat band of tiny tracery.

Twenty-five generations of Cameley children have been baptised at this font, which has a band of rope carved round it and an old timber cover over it. Here would be christened in the 17th century Cadwallader Jones, who lies under the nave with a curious stone above him on which is a little moral advice for his parents. Here also would be christened many of the proud Hippisleys of Tudor days, who owned the manor. Here they would bring the children from the hamlet with the lovely name of Temple Cloud, said to be so called because the Romans built a temple there to Claudius Caesar.

Camerton. We can recommend it for a lovely hour of Somerset, for it is a charming place, and the traveller who can find its church will find much to entertain him. We found the church and lost it;

57

we lost it even in the churchyard, for it disappears at the gate. It lies in a dip on the edge of a park, with the great house looking down and a fragment of the chantry of the monks of Glastonbury near it, serving the useful purpose of a water tank.

It has an extraordinary little sculpture gallery that catches our eye as we come, mediaeval fancies creeping over the 13th century porch and the 15th century tower—a woman telling her beads and another playing a guitar, a grinning cat and a snarling dog, a rhinoceros and a baby pig; there is even an elephant, a very rare thing on a church.

The porch, on which we found pilgrim's crosses, has two niches older than itself, and a magnificent door four inches thick, arcaded and with quatrefoil tracery. It brings us into a truly noble village church, spacious and light, with barrel roofs, a 15th century font with a 17th century cover, a pulpit of Cromwell's time, and, let into the wall of the nave, the door which led to the roodloft stairs.

The great possession is the chapel of the proud Carews, where Sir John lies with his Dame Elizabeth on one great tomb, and his son John with his Dame Dorothy on another. Father John has curly hair and is in ruff and armour with red trunk hose; Elizabeth has a stiff lace cap under her wide headdress and wears a black gown tied with a sash and with nine looped buttons. Their three sons and four daughters kneel at green desks round the tomb, the sons with swords, the daughters with hair tied back and wearing veils. With the daughters is a poor shrouded baby lying across two skulls. Hanging by these tombs is a dainty silver lamp 300 years old.

Cannington. Time comes and goes and its changes never end. Away in the church at Combe Florey lies the heart of Maude de Meriett, a lady of Cannington long ago. She lived in the days of Magna Carta at a nunnery which stood where now stands a 17th century house with an earlier core and charming mullioned windows incorporating older work. The wheel of time went round and once again the 19th century brought the Benedictine nuns to this great house; they came and went, and the hallowed ground of the nuns is now an agricultural college.

Close to the college is the church, impressive with its great height. Its tower is 14th century and still has in it stones from the Norman church which stood beside the nunnery. Its ancient gargoyles would look down on the 15th century builders building the nave, the chancel, and the aisles. One tremendous old roof covers all, panelled with oak bosses and painted with gold stars; it rests on angels with shields and the cornice has fine tracery. Round the outside walls is a remarkable series of 17 consecration crosses marking the place where the bishop touched the walls with holy oil on consecration day. It is a surprising collection, one of the best and biggest we have seen, and it is good that such a possession should have a splendid setting. The churchyard has four stately yews trimmed like round tables; we walked round one of them and found it 20 yards. In a niche of the tower stands St Boniface and over the west door is a delightful Madonna and Child. They look down on a pair of iron gates which have been buried in the earth and found again.

The interior of the church is worthy of its splendid setting. There is a Tudor screen across the nave, finely carved, and a pulpit which has seen prouder days but has lost none of its beauty. It was once a three-decker and stood in the middle of the nave at the entrance to the chancel, the clerk's seat below, the reading desk above, and high above all the pulpit as we see it, the mediaeval craftsman's carving all unspoiled. The oak from the lower parts has been used for the front pews of the nave. There is an elegant 15th century font carved with Tudor roses, and a Bible of 1617 finely bound and with cunning clasps. In the chancel is a beautiful iron screen in black and gold with painted heraldry.

Looking down on the village is a hill that looks down on the Channel, and on the hill is Cynwit Castle, with the earthwork defences from which Alfred's men crept out and fell upon the Danes. Here in those days they slew a Danish king. Hereabouts is Old Gurney Street Farm with much in it of the long ago—a room over the porch, stone stairs, and a tiny chapel a few feet square; it has a Gothic window over the altar and a piscina still in the wall.

Carhampton. It has a church with a magnificent screen, bright with greens and blues as in the 15th century. Its colours are repeated in the fine east window with its picture of the Last Supper. The church has a long Peter's Pence chest, a carved frieze of oak leaves round the aisle, and a chalice made in Germany 300 years ago.

Between Carhampton and the sea is the hillock where Turner sat to paint his picture of Dunster Castle, and near by is an ancient and lovely place called Marshwood Farm. The walls of this house at the back are about seven hundred years old; a front room has a good Elizabethan ceiling; and in the porch by the old oak door is plaster work which has been removed from the rooms above.

Castle Cary. Its houses are in a hollow, where we noticed two swans swimming round the War Memorial cross set in a stretch of water by the street; but there is a steep little hill to climb for a view over Caryland and the narrow river Cary on its way to join the Parret.

The most curious of all the town's buildings is its miniature prison, a tiny round place with a dome, dark and airless, with only a couple of gratings for ventilation—the lock-up where many a rowdy has repented since it was built in 1779. Nothing is left of the castle above ground and little of the ancient church, but the little includes one of the most perfect 15th century oak pulpits in Somerset, niched with statues of the disciples, as well as a 14th century font with leaves curling above the panelled pedestal, an old stone statue, and a collection of fat gargoyles. The new spire is good, but the rest of the rebuilding is commonplace.

As we passed out of the town on our way to Ansford we thought of the lady who came riding into it with her postilion one September evening in 1651, to spend a night at the manor house long since tumbled down. She was Jane Lane, and her servant was her king, whom she was helping to escape after the Battle of Worcester.

Catcott. Very pleasant are its stone houses, with the ridge of the Poldens behind them and the Mendips afar off, and very quaint is the 13th century church, long and narrow, with neither aisles nor chancel arch. Only two feet of passage-way separates the rows of solid white oak seats, slotted at the ends for the stools (some still here) which pulled out to form an extra seat for a servant. A modern box-pew with curtained windows adds to the general quaintness. There are Tudor roses and a woman's face on the oak bosses of the chancel roof. The plain font is 13th century. The pulpit and altar rails are 17th century. On the wall is painted the Lord's Prayer, and in older lettering, embellished with crude figures, is this sermon from Titus for women of the village:

> *The aged women likewise that they be in behaviour as becometh holiness, not false accusers; teachers of good things, that they may teach the young women to be sober, to be chaste, keepers at home, to love their husbands.*

On the opposite wall is a similar one for men.

Chaffcombe. It hides its charms among hills wooded with oak and larch, with a paved way up one of them through a tiny orchard to the church. We found it in apple-blossom time, and saw the creeper-covered tower between pink trees, a lovely memory. When this tower was new 500 years ago a bell was made for it which hangs there still, and in the church hangs this verse by Sir Matthew Hale, the judge who so loved bell-ringing that he would hasten ahead when on his circuit and help to ring the bells that were to welcome him:

> *A Sunday well spent*
> *Brings a week of content*
> *And health for the toils of tomorrow.*
> *But a Sabbath profaned,*
> *Whatever be gained,*
> *Is a certain forerunner of sorrow.*

Oldest of all here is the Norman font.

Chapel Allerton. It has the tower of a windmill built into a house and a fine view of the white tower and lovely broad sails of the windmill at Ashton, the last to be worked in Somerset. Though it has now joined the unemployed, it is a fine sight. An ancient crippled yew, so hollow that it is supported with stones, is outside the 13th century church, which has been rebuilt and enlarged till there is little of the 13th century left. The new font has still the Norman font to keep it company, with a carved cover by a Jacobean craftsman. In those days the village folk loved to see on the altar the mediaeval embroidery of the Madonna with angels about her against a background of pomegranates; but the church has given this ancient treasure into the keeping of the museum at Taunton.

Chard. The Romans gave it its straight wide street, the Saxons gave it its first name, but Nature gave it the most surprising thing it has—a stream running down each side of the street and dividing at the foot to go two ways, one going south to pour itself into the English Channel, the other going north to the Bristol Channel. Odd it is to think of the great parting of these tiny waters, to meet again in the wide Atlantic. Charles I's men marched down the street between them, Monmouth rallied his men here, and Judge Jeffreys hung a round dozen of the rebels.

There is a Tudor inn at the top of the hill and a Stuart Court House at the foot, with two magnificent mullioned windows of 20 lights and quaint figures in the plaster walls and ceiling. Daniel is here in doublet and hose with two lions; Solomon delivers his

61

famous judgment; Shadrach, Meshach, and Abednego walk through the fiery furnace; and over the grand fireplace are the arms of Chard. Lower down the road is the grammar school, a school to be proud of with 1583 on a rainwater-pipe, though it was not founded till 1671.

The church was begun and finished in the 15th century, perfectly proportioned, with a pleasant parapet and pinnacled porches. The font is carved with a Tudor rose. Two slits cut in the chancel piers give a view of the altar, and the chapel, with a mighty oak roof, has another peephole for the little stone figures of the Brewers in a Jacobean monument on its wall. William Brewer, a Chard doctor, and his wife are here with their family of 11, *all men and women grown and all comforts to them*. On the tombstone of William Hitchcock, who died in 1793, we read that the world is full of crooked streets and Death is the marketplace:

> *If life were merchandise that men could buy,*
> *The rich would always live, none but the poor would die.*

He sounds a disappointed man, and so was John Stringfellow, a Chard man who made an aeroplane to fly in 1847 but reaped little glory from it. At an Aeronautical Exhibition in 1868 one of his machines flew the length of the Crystal Palace, lifting several feet in the air the wire which anchored it. The engine was heated by methylated spirit, and that was its undoing, for in the air the flame kept blowing out. The monoplane he made in 1848 is engraved on the British Silver Medal for air feats; his models are in the Science Museum today; but the old man died at 84 knowing little but ridicule and not guessing the high place he would be awarded on the roll of pioneers. He ended his days making brass bobbins for Chard's net industry.

A happier man was James Gillingham, who succeeded. He was only a Chard cobbler, but, hearing that a man had his arm accidentally shot off during the rejoicings over Edward VII's marriage, he made for him an artificial limb which was so successful that he left off cobbling and started making arms and legs. His son and his grandson carried on his work, and during the Great War Chard had the only VAD hospital where limbless patients could be fitted, all due to this Chard man James Gillingham of long ago.

Charlcombe. It stands amid the natural glory all round the marvellous city of Bath, and the stone floor of its little church has been worn down by a multitude of pilgrims. We do not remember another floor so worn. We push open a door that has been swinging on its hinges for centuries in a plain Norman doorway, and come into an interior 20 feet wide and barely 50 feet long, with a narrow chancel arch across which is an elegant iron screen in memory of a girl, the best bit of workmanship in the church.

The north wall of the church is still as the Normans left it, with another round doorway leading into a new vestry. Near this doorway a sad cherub with huge wings has been greeting all who come for 200 years. The fine font is the legacy of the Normans and has a Norman mason's lilies on its base. The pulpit is big enough to hold half a dozen preachers, nine feet round inside, with stone walls a foot thick. The south wall of the nave is so thick that the stairway to the tower runs up through it. Inside the tower is a monument to Henry Fielding's sister Sarah, of whom we read that she was worthy of a nobler monument but her name will be written in the Book of Life. By the tower arch is a peephole to the altar, a very unusual position for it.

Two other remembrances we came upon here, one to John Taylour, a rector for 54 years, from the 17th century into the 18th, and a shrouded and cloaked lady at a desk in the tower to Lady Barbara Montagu, daughter of Earl Halifax, in memory of her manifold virtues *and the height to which they carried her*. There is a rectors' list going back to 1312.

Charlinch. It has a lovely view of the Quantocks and a glimpse of the Welsh mountains across the Bristol Channel. Its church was made in several centuries, with a Norman doorway and a Norman font, a 13th century arch, a 14th century east window, and a 15th century chapel. The tower and two of its bells are 500 years old. There is a mass dial from the days before clocks, and in one of the windows is a small figure of St Osyth in ancient glass.

There was a priest here much beloved in ages past, for a stone in his memory declares that his passing *merits rivers of tears, though the tide were pearls dissolved or crystal liquefied*. A brass set in the floor is to Jasper Bourne, who lived at Gothelney House, a fine building with something still left of its minstrel gallery. Blackmore Farm close by keeps a chapel with a great Gothic window flanked by niches.

Charlton Adam. It twists itself about in a square, and round it are set pretty cottages, a fine old stone house called the Abbey, and a church beautiful in its simplicity. It is 15th century. Over the door in a niche is a quaint figure with a book, looking as if it might have been carved long ago but actually the work of a villager of our time.

63

The Norman font has gaps in the rim where the hinge and lock of the lid used to be when the font was locked.

Near the Jacobean oak pulpit are the roodstairs, with the tiniest trefoiled window imaginable, and there is a canopied tomb of 1592 and a memorial of 1638 to Anne Strangways, mother of 16 children. A new cross crowns the old stone steps outside.

Charlton Horethorne. Round it on the map are such pretty names as Golden Valley, Silver Knap, Dark Harbour, Windmill Hill; and it is all as pleasant as it sounds. Three round barrows hereabouts have been opened, and a dark coffin, a bronze dagger, skeletons, ashes, and flints have been found, some of which are to be seen in Taunton Museum, where are also the stone figures from the top of the churchyard cross. The north aisle is nearly all that is left of the original church, and has its own tiny bellcot, an east window with lovely tracery, canopied niches, and a beautiful stone head of a woman with horned headdress, two other tiny heads above her. The strongly buttressed tower is 15th century, but oldest of all is the curious Norman font, like a wide stone pipe on a flat base.

Charlton Mackrell. It was the home of a man who has come curiously into ancient books, for he wrote what is still remembered as *Lyte's Herbal*, and it is told of him that he stopped Elizabeth I on her way to St Paul's to present her with one of his works. He must have been a daring man who stopped the queen that day, for she was on her way to give thanks to God for sending the great wind that scattered the Armada. The work of which the poet begged the queen's acceptance was his eulogy of the queen as the Light of Britayne.

Here for centuries lived and died the Lytes of Lyte's Cary, yet nowhere in the church or round about it is their name today. All, all are gone, the old familiar faces. Only two broken stone figures remain, thrown out of the church in the long ago and now under a yew for the rain to fall on.

Most of the old church has gone too, though we may still peep through the hole cut in its central tower to give a glimpse of the altar, another of the peepholes in this rare position which we find in Somerset. There is a beautiful window from the 14th century in the north transept, but all the old glass is gone. The Norman font remains, side by side with the new one, and there are old benchends carved with tracery, except one which has a quaint satyr dancing along it, an odd figure to find in a Christian church. The oak roof of the chancel has angels curiously placed above the corbels so that they lie full-length along the hammerbeams as if peering down at the choir boys.

The old churchyard cross has been given new statues under a canopy, and four figures stand once more at the pedestal corners.

Henry Lyte, who sleeps here, proved to his own satisfaction that his ancestors reached Britain after the fall of Troy. The Lytes were an ancient and scholarly family, and Henry, whose long life came to an end in 1607, was the 11th of his line settled on the patrimonial estate. At a time when English botany could hardly be said to have a literature he made a valuable contribution to the subject by translating the work of a famous Dutch naturalist, in which Lyte wrote: "If perchaunce any list to picke a quarrell to my translation, as not being either proper or not ful, I will not much strive: for I seek not after vayne glorie, but how to benefite and profite my countrie."

The work met a public need, for three editions were called for in a few years. Henry Lyte's other literary production was one of those in which his age delighted. He accepts Geoffrey of Monmouth's legend as to the origin of the British race. Not only do we derive from Venus and the father of Aeneas, but Brut on his voyage here was accompanied by a Lyte of that prehistoric period! Even James I came into the ancient pedigree, and was delighted with his family tree, rewarding its compiler with a portrait of himself framed in gold and diamonds.

Charlton Musgrove. It has four fine old yews, and a sundial which has told the time for many generations. The tower of the 15th century church is rich with gargoyles. The porch has a charming barrel roof of oak and plaster and over the door one of the neatest little niches we have seen. The roof of the nave has painted red and blue beams with gold bosses. The choir-stalls are Jacobean, and so is the chair in the sanctuary. What seemed to us the best possession of the village is a little door behind the neat panelled pulpit; it leads to the mediaeval roodloft, and has the original ironwork and studs, looking as old as anything we can imagine. There is a panelled chancel arch and a very unusual font.

Charterhouse-on-Mendip. In this vast lonely place high up above the busy world, we liked the first thing we saw that men have set up, a cross in memory of all those who have lived and worked on Mendip and lie in God's Acre. It strikes the right note for this vast

65

solitude. It is a wild and lonely scene, where dead men lie in barrows on the skyline, where Romans came after them and left their mark in lead mines strewn about. A desolate world it is on which the cock on its steeple looks down.

It is a fine little place on which the cock rises above its shingled oak spire, a church of almost primitive simplicity yet with touches of beauty and excellent craftsmanship; it dates only from 1908. It has oak everywhere, in the roof beams with their tiny bosses, in the panelling of the walls, in the dignified reredos with King Arthur and St Hugh in canopied niches, and in the elegant chancel screen with delicate tracery and miniature fan-vaulting under the cross. The screen is set in an arch panelled with oak and encased in dainty tracery.

A touch of utility and of beauty we found in this place so far away; it is so remote that it has its own domestic quarters. It is the only church in which we have discovered two fireplaces and a scullery with a copper and a sink.

Cheddar. Its caves are as famous as its cheese but it has something better than either, the Grand Canyon cut out of the rock 10,000 centuries ago and a church set up five centuries ago.

The Cheddar Gorge is one of the amazing sights of our country-side, a grand canyon a mile long into which we could drop St Paul's so that the dome would be lost 100 feet below the peaks. It is one of the mighty things of our little island, and if we can come to Cheddar when the trippers are away, when the streets are free from litterers and shouters and the noise of charabancs, there are few things more impressive than these gigantic walls rising from the twisting road in tier on tier, with ledges carpeted and green all the way up, with birds nesting here, flowers hanging there, and Nature's own pinnacles piercing the clouds.

Inside these rocks is a wonderful world, for the trickle of water that runs into the hills has shaped out caves with room to hold 100,000 people, with architecture of fantastic shapes and gorgeous colours, with stalactites creeping down from the roof and stalagmites growing up from the floor, growing up and growing down 1000 years, 10,000 years, 100,000 years, until they meet.

The caves have been made attractive for whoever likes to visit them. From one of them (known as King Solomon's Temple) 2000 tons of earth have been removed in our time to make a spacious entrance, and 200 Roman coins of bronze and silver and gold were found. Bronze axe-heads and flint scrapers have been dug up, and in another cave a skeleton of one of the early inhabitants of England was found in the first years of our century. It was a dramatic discovery, for the skeleton was encased in a stalagmite and it is believed that the man may have been drowned in the cave 50,000 years ago when the river flowed at a higher level. As down the ages the water wore away the earth his bed was deepened and he was wrapped in a crystal winding-sheet which preserved his frame till our time.

Always there is a sound of running water in the caves, and an eerie feeling everywhere, but on we go, up steps and down steps, switching on lights to illumine domes and turrets and walls and crevices, until we tire of so much that is weird and strange and are relieved to come out into the common world again.

We walk down through Cheddar, past its 15th century market cross with heads all round it fading away, to find a church magnificent. The tower rises 110 feet high and ends in a beautiful parapet; pinnacles crown the buttresses, and ancient statues adorn the walls. Queer gargoyles look down on its charming churchyard, shaded by an old yew and three great sycamores; all that we could see of one of these strange stone faces was a broad grin.

The church was gay with colour when we called, even the delicately carved 15th century stone pulpit was covered with paint. The 200-year-old oak panels of the nave roof were painted; the angels bearing up the roof were painted. Under a painted canopy of a painted tomb is the brass portrait of Sir Thomas Cheddar, a Bristol merchant who died in 1442, whose wife's portrait is with his.

Cheddar is rich in woodwork. There must be 100 old bench-ends, all carved 500 years ago, mostly with tracery, and some with little faces peeping out, picturing sins as the mediaeval artist loved to picture them. Two women with twisted tongues are for Gossip, Deceit is three-faced, Bitter Words dart as arrows from an asp's mouth. One bench-end is more friendly with a graceful hand holding out a rosary. There are oak screens to the aisles made by the same 15th century craftsmen, one having holes for children to see the altar through. The old roodscreen has been made into panels for choir-stalls and reading desk, and the chancel has been panelled to match with modern linenfold.

Above the 17th century altar table is an oil-painting of the Supper at Emmaus by a 17th century Dutch artist. Under the tower are two crude paintings almost as old as the Reformation, one showing Death as a skeleton, the other Father Time. More charming are the paintings in some of the windows. In old glass in the 15th century chapel is St Catherine with her tower, angels and faces, roses and shields, and in the middle a horseshoe. In the splay of this window is a canopied niche with a 15th century statue of the sailor's saint, Erasmus. Other canopied niches here have tiny modern figures of Stephen, Augustine, and John the Baptist.

There is a pillar piscina and another double one, an ancient font with a quaint frieze of pomegranates round its cover, and a grand old ironbound chest with three locks and a slot for coins.

Cheddon Fitzpaine. The beautiful stone lychgate lets no one pass by without remembering the heroes of Cheddon Fitzpaine. Their cenotaph lies in the centre of the way, a table tomb with a cross. A wonderful old door opens into the church, with a handle nearly a foot long and a key to match. The ancient gargoyles grimace below the open parapet. On one of the capitals inside is a lovely 15th century angel with sweeping wings, and eight angels look down from the nave arcade. The bench-ends have much beautiful carving of the 17th century.

Chedzoy. On the sandstone buttresses of its church the men of the village would sharpen their scythes and axes before tying them to long poles and marching off to fight in the last great battle fought in England. Back to this churchyard they were brought for burial after being deserted by Monmouth at Sedgemoor.

Now noble trees are growing above them, two splendid beeches and some enormous elms, five of them 17 feet round the trunk, and a hollow one bigger still. We found white roses climbing over the 16th century porch, and little carved roses in four consecration crosses where the holy oil touched the walls 700 years ago, when the round pillars of the nave were set up. Two Norman pillars have been built into these old walls. The pleasant tower with a high panelled arch is 500 years old.

A curious key opens the great carved door, a fitting entrance to this church full of old oak. Every seat of the nave and the aisles was made 400 years ago, and each ends in a different design. Here is a rampant dragon circled by a leather belt, here the letter W with a snake coiling through it, here a crowned M between a thistle and a rose. A Jacobean craftsman made the arcading of the organ seat (sadly spoiled); another fashioned the reading desk with carved and gilded ends. The handsome pulpit has Tudor linenfold, one of the few pulpits left from the reign of Edward VI, and the font, though it has been recut and given eight sides, was originally made by the Normans.

Bareheaded in his 15th century armour, with a greyhound at his feet, is an unknown warrior, lying so near the unknown soldiers of Sedgemoor outside. He may be a Sydenham. It was a Sydenham who left some land to be sold every 21 years to pay for church repairs, and ever since 1490 the sale had taken place by candlelight. Half-an-inch of candle is lit and the last bidder before it goes out has the property.

The altar frontals have a touch of romantic history in them, for they were made from a cope which lay hidden here about 300 years.

Chelvey. Here is the old group of church and court, rectory and buttressed barn; but gone are the cottages which once gathered round them.

The church of St Bridget has a beautiful pierced parapet to crown her small tower, but all is worn and forlorn inside, yet with a charm of its own. It has a plain Norman doorway, a Norman font, fragments of mediaeval glass like golden stars, a patchwork of dainty Tudor roses and fleurs-de-lis found hidden by plaster above the altar, a bit of a fresco or a consecration cross, and an old hourglass in its bracket. A 700-year-old stone bears a few words in French praying God's mercy on someone whose name is lost.

There are remarkable pews both for the squire and the people. The squire's is in the 15th century Tyntes chapel, an elaborate Jacobean stall with high carved seats and front and still higher panelling at the back. The people's seats are some of the oldest and shabbiest in England, roughly hewn with poppyheads probably over 600 years ago. Under the fine Jacobean altar table in the squire's chapel is a stone bearing the outline of a 13th century soldier, six feet tall. He grasps his spear in one hand, the scabbard of his sword in the other, and the mail covering has slipped from his head and left it bare.

Edward Tynte, who is buried with his wife in the church, built the extraordinary manor house soon after 1600. It is rather like a fortress, a grey mass three storeys high, with no windows on one side, only a few on the other, and with a deep drop all round, so that we can only reach the porch across a tiny earthen bridge. This porch has saved a little from its former grandeur, but no one uses it now, and we must go round to another door if we would see the wonderful Jacobean staircase with horseshoes nailed to the bottom stair to stop witches from walking up. In the kitchen are trestle tables said to be 200 years older than the house itself, black and worn with age.

69

Chelwood. It lies in the superb country round Bath, and its tiny church has watched its people come and go about 700 years. One small angel looks down from above the chancel arch, and two of the loveliest little faces we have seen hang from the richly carved brackets at the ends of the nave arcade. The brackets are carved with vine leaves and the women's heads are neatly dressed in the fashion of the 13th and 14th centuries.

The church is light and white, and three of its south windows glow with the rich colours of ancient glass, probably 16th century and from the Continent. It is in three groups, and among the fragments are many attractive faces: women with fair hair, a golden lion, a hand with an orb, men with spikes and torches, feathered angels, the stoning of Stephen, and the nailing on the three crosses at Calvary. There is more old glass in the west window of the tower, where a lovely head of Christ is set in a mosaic of glowing fragments. On the tower wall is a tablet to a 17th century Sheriff of Somerset, with winged cherubs in black and gold at the corners. The big Norman font has still the marks of the staples which locked it.

Chesterblade. It has a small church, charming on its own little hill, and the stem of an old cross under an ancient yew 13 feet round the trunk. Dawn breaks on the village behind the steep Small Down, where Roman coins and pottery have been found; we have seen them in Taunton Museum.

We left the haymakers just over the churchyard wall and came into this lovely place through outer doors like a barn's and through an inner doorway which has welcomed 25 generations of village folk, for it was fashioned by the Normans. The arch has a row of beading round it ending in a wolf and a hare, the round supporting shafts having fine capitals, on one of which is a face with great beaded eyes. There are fragments of carving on the outside walls, probably by some masons of those Norman days or copied from their work; one looks like a wolf biting a man and the other like a wolf between two men's heads. There is also a mass dial.

The gem of this place stands above this Norman doorway under a canopy with three pinnacles; she is a most beautiful Madonna with tiny hands peeping from great hanging sleeves, her veil falling over her shoulders, her face surely one of the saddest we have seen.

Inside, the fine old beams are still holding up the roof, the deeply splayed windows still flooding the nave with light, the low chancel perfectly lovely with the white walls rising unbroken from the rich carved oak panelling to the rounded ceiling.

The church has been refashioned since the Normans set it on this little hill, but it has not been spoiled, and all through its centuries the children of Chesterblade have been brought to its old tub font.

Chew Magna. We come to it over one mediaeval bridge and leave it by another; when we asked an old man how many bridges Chew Magna had he counted six and thought there were seven. The village is surrounded by streams and is charming with old houses and raised pavements. The church stands magnificent with the noble 15th century tower throwing its shadow over the ancient manor and the lovely Church House by the gate, a fine old place with walls in which we noticed a beam four feet round. The manor house was built by a Bristol merchant in 1656 and has a sundial which says:

> *I am a shadow, a shadow too art thou;*
> *I mark the time, say, Gossip, dost thou?*

The noblest house within easy reach of Chew Magna is Sutton Court, which we can visit from Stowey. It stands behind one of the finest walls in England, a captivating piece of countryside which time seems to have passed by. The house has grown round its old tower through many generations, and we wonder if a traveller in Somerset can build up for himself any memory more enduring than to walk up to the old walls of Sutton Court and find himself in such deep solitude.

We swing open a magnificent door into the great 15th century church, a door with splendid iron bands held together by 200 studs. Both porches have windows of upper rooms that have disappeared and the south porch has a big scratch dial. In the middle of the parapet of the other porch sits a man appearing to hold up a pinnacle; he carries a musical instrument. The nave is wider than it is long, a spacious place with carved bench-ends everywhere. There are barrel roofs, and the chancel has fine old beams with painted bosses. A rare screen made up from old carving runs the whole length from wall to wall, enclosing the chancel and the two chapels; it has an elegant traceried parapet, and is painted in red, green, and gold. The modern pulpit rests on a slender stem and is heavily carved with six apostles under canopies divided by lovely columns; we noticed a bird with a worm, and another eating grapes. The ancient reading desk has the initials of an old vicar on it, and an altar table with carved legs like balloons has kept it company for generations. We found on the lectern a chained book written in

1650. A little old glass has been discovered in our time and reset in the windows.

The church has three spectacular gifts from three centuries, a 14th, a 15th, and a 16th century tomb. The earliest one has attracted thousands of pilgrims; the next is the popular sight of the village; the next is in the pompous fashion of its day.

The most remarkable possession of the church is the oak figure of Sir John Hauteville. He is the man who is said to have hurled the Hauteville Quoit from the top of Maes Knoll, and we could almost believe that renowned absurdity, for he looks as strong and fit as the stone giant across the nave. Sir John is one of a very small group of wooden figures in England, and one of the best of all as a museum piece, for he is no conventional piece of oak carved into a man and left lying in a church: he is a vivid figure seen as he probaby was when the end came, sinking back a dying man dressed in his red coat, his boots and spurs, leaning on his left elbow with his right hand on the black and gold handle of his sword.

The giant across the way is the 15th century Sir John St Loe, a colossal figure with his little wife. He is 7 feet 4 inches long, and 2 feet 4 inches across, the very picture of physical energy, with his feet on a lion of which only the tail is left. His wife has with her a little dog, and she wears an elegant headdress with a cap bordered with roses. Both have chains round their necks. The fashionable tomb of the 16th century is to Edward Baber and his wife. He lies in the red gown of an Elizabethan lawyer; she is in black with a Paris cap.

Chew Stoke. We remember riding to it through some of the oddest fields we have seen, with hundreds of molehills like miniature prehistoric barrows; and the ride brings us to what must surely be one of the oddest streets in England. It begins with a stone bridge seven feet wide, it widens out enough to take the post office, the local Harrods, and ten cottages, and then narrows down again to seven feet at the other end. Cars that would come this way must bypass the street through a water splash.

At the crossroads stands the old rectory (now a rectory no more), its front adorned with 20 stone panels of shields and heraldry and lovely angels. The church is fine outside and poor within. Its walls have stood 600 years, and round them rise many lovely trees, a silver birch, a magnificent cedar, a noble beech, and two veteran yews. The tower has four figures mounted in niches in the parapet and gargoyles and pinnacles and corbels all round. The roof of the tower is the best possession of the interior, with three stone heads worked into its vaulting, one of them like a woman with a rabbit's ears. There is a 17th century Bible on a lectern and another lectern has an extraordinary piece of crystal in it, looking like a lump of ice. There are angels everywhere in this small place; we stood in the chancel and without moving counted 100. Some are like toys, some cluster round piers; they run along the cornice and bear up the roof.

In the churchyard wall are two richly carved stones, one with ropework and one with twining foliage.

Chewton Mendip. They spoiled its Norman chancel arch 500 years ago, three arches in one; but gave it something nobler still, a magnificent tower standing out in a wide landscape, compelling us to come. A little bagpiper looks down from the top, joyous and proud to be at the parapet of so great a tower, richly carved with pierced stone windows, slender pinnacles, and figures and sculptured fragments. They are everywhere, corbels, angels, and gargoyles.

The 15th century left a little Norman work for us to see. Outside and in the porch are rows of Norman corbels, one of the smaller chancel arches is still in its place, and what was the central chancel arch is now set in the north wall. It has splendid chevron carving.

A very rare possession which has brought a multitude of travellers to Chewton Mendip is a stone seat under a window by the altar, facing the canopied sedilia. The sedilia have been here 500 years; this stone seat for a criminal has looked across the chancel to them all the time. That is what this frid stool is believed to be, one of three seats of refuge still left in this country for those who claimed sanctuary. The severest punishment was kept for those who violated this sacred place, the only seat of the kind we have come upon outside Hexham and Beverley. It has been doubted whether this is actually a frid stool or not, but it is accepted as one. The fine round font is also from those days.

Two other precious possessions the church has: a lectern made for the first Authorised Bible, with the only Bible it has supported still on it, its date 1611 written inside the cover; and one of the most beautiful engraved chalices in the country, older than the Reformation. It has a paten to keep company with it, and both were made in 1511. On the wall is a fine copy of a Raphael Madonna.

Older than both these are some of the finely carved bench-ends, older still are the figures of Sir Henry FitzRoger and his wife. He died in 1388, but they lie on a 15th century tomb. From the wall facing them looks down the white marble portrait of Frances,

Countess Waldegrave (the wife of Lord Carlingford), whose tomb is below, supported by two angels. Lady Waldegrave was a famous social hostess in the great days of Liberalism, and every year Mr Gladstone would meet his followers at her house in Carlton Gardens.

The fine old door of the church is still swinging on its hinges, and the small door leading up to the bells has kept it company most of the time. The entrance door has a lovely iron ring.

The 600-year-old cross, its little figures still safe under their canopy, is set between two yews in the churchyard, which is rich in trees and has within its view one of the noblest sycamores for miles around.

Chilcompton. The little River Somer comes to it leaping over waterfalls, a lovely sight, and the waterfalls follow us all the way down the lane that brings us to the church.

The church, except for the 15th century tower, dates only from 1839. It has carved oak benches with fine poppyheads, its stone pulpit is very neat, its high windows are filled with clear glass. Three of the windows were given by Darby and Joan of Chilcompton; he died at 95 and she at 88, and the windows were given when he was *permitted to attain his 91st year.*

Chillington. It lies in the wide plain we look down on from Windwhistle Hill, and has a church 500 years old with a delightful chancel arch (almost round, and panelled inside), a curious pillar piscina, a silver cup and dish of 1545, and a font made up from fragments of the original one found built into the walls.

Chilthorne Domer. East and west it has a Roman road; two miles north is the Roman town of Ichalis which we call Ilchester. Yet there is little of great age about this charming place except the church, which has stood 600 years, with an overhanging bell-turret of the 15th century; it has a beautiful Calvary on the top of it. There are two fine crosses on the gables and a curious gargoyle of two figures carrying something. On the wall is a scratch dial.

The ancient studded door opens on to rows of Jacobean seats, their arcaded ends having fan-shaped ornaments, their upper panels carved. The nave is full of them and the old carved doors have been placed along the wall as a dado. They match the Jacobean pulpit with its canopy. Worthy of it all is the splendidly carved modern reredos. A curly-haired man and a woman wearing a wimple have supported the inner chancel arch for centuries, probably since the mediaeval piscina was cut in the sill of a window. The flowers round the font were cut by a 14th century mason.

The oldest possession of the church is probably the 13th century knight, so hidden away in a recess that we hardly notice him. Nobody knows who he is, but most people think him Sir William Domer, who gave his name to his village, as his son, who lies in state at Pendomer, gave it to that village.

Chilton Cantelo. A church at the end of a little lane leading to nowhere is nearly all of Chilton Cantelo. The church has a lovely old tower, pinnacled and with a band of ornament round it, but the rest is Victorian. The massive round font was made a few years after the Normans came and has still its original lead lining. There is a screen of oak and a good stone screen looking delightfully at home under the old panelled tower arch.

Chilton Trinity. Straight lines of pollard willows reach out towards the mouth of the River Parret, across whose muddy waters lie the lowlands of the moor where the last English battle was fought. It is a bare little church we come upon in this bleak land, a tiny 13th century building with the base of its 13th century cross beside it. The preacher climbs up the old rood stairs into the high pulpit, carved 300 years ago. Here also is a font made 400 years ago and four ancient bells.

Chilton-upon-Polden. It has two towers, one down in the valley and one up on the hill. One belongs to the church made new last century, with only a strip of carved oak cornice left from the old; the other can be seen for miles, standing by the road the Romans made from end to end of the Polden Hills. It is part of a curious hotch-potch building raised over 100 years ago by William Stradling, to be a museum for all his discoveries, and it is a museum in itself. Made up from odds and ends of churches and houses all over the county, it has pinnacles from Langport, battlements and grotesque heads from Enmore Castle, a turret from Shepton Mallet, a gable finial from Chedzoy, a bit of Glastonbury, an ironbound door from Stogursey, and an inner one from a monastery. William Stradling filled it with odd treasures, which were scattered when he died. Many went to Taunton Museum, and their old home is now a private house. Through its grounds an ancient British trackway was found running parallel to the Roman road.

Most of Somerset and something of other counties can be seen from the top of this tower, with Wells and Glastonbury to the east (the Wiltshire Hills and Alfred's Tower to the right of them), the Bristol Channel and the Welsh coast to the west, the Mendips to the north, and the tall towers of Sedgemoor to the south. William Stradling used to boast that he could see one cathedral and 35 churches from his own patchwork tower.

However, we need stand on nothing higher than our own feet here for a view so fine that the National Trust has bought for us a patch of grass by Cock Hill. Here the ridge drops almost sheer into the plain, and we see, silhouetted in the distance, the blue hills of the Quantocks and Blackdown. The ridge is never more than 300 feet high, but for its wide landscapes it is as fine as Surrey's far-famed Hog's Back.

Chinnock. The Chinnock triplets, East, Middle, and West, lie in a straight line along the hills near Crewkerne. There is a scratch dial and a font with a Norman base at East Chinnock, a modern church built in Norman style at West Chinnock and a Norman doorway with a carved tympanum at Middle Chinnock.

Middle Chinnock, also with a mass dial, is the prettiest of the three, a place of old stone houses and flower-hung walls. On the gable of the church porch is a quaint sundial, and here (under the seat) we found the head and shoulders of a stone priest, a curious resting-place for one who may have walked through this ancient doorway. The Norman font is twined with leaves, and there are old pews with carved ends. Two sculptured stones are built into the north wall outside, and two stone angels guard the west doorway.

Chipstable. The pleasant country round gives charm to this village of the Brendon Hills, with few possessions save in the church. Here is a 14th century arcade of clustered pillars, with angel capitals very little worn, and bench-ends from whose deep carvings look out faces of 500 years ago. The villagers have set up a fine lychgate to the memory of those who were drawn by a world war from this faraway place, never to return.

About a mile away to the south-east is Waterrow, a white-walled hamlet without a church, crowding round an ancient bridge over the River Tone.

Chiselborough. It has three hills like the three bears, one big, the next middling, and the last one tiny. The big one is Gawlers Hill, the next Brympton, and looking with its fringe of firs rather like a Japanese print is little Balham Hill. From all these hills we see the sea.

The church has a charming old stone spire rising from a central tower with low arches of the 13th century. The remains of Norman arches were found in it a year or two before the Great War, and the chancel arch has been changed back to its old shape with all new work above the base except for one scalloped capital. It is all a little odd as we stand in a nave rather like a barn and see one great round arch with three small pointed ones, the altar just behind. So small is it that the ringers must stand by the very altar steps to sound the bells.

Christon. It has but a small and simple example of the Norman work in which Somerset is so rich, yet the charm of it goes straight to our hearts. No one who has seen this porch, framing in its arch this perfect Norman doorway, can forget it. There are few who will not accept the invitation of the ancient stone seats to stay awhile by this rough horseshoe arch, these lovely mouldings, and look out at the other picture in this frame, where Crook's Peak shoots up like a miniature volcano from the Mendip ridge, an attractive spectacle.

Round the tower runs a line of animals which must have given the Norman sculptor infinite delight as he fashioned them, each with a quaintness of its own. If only the floor could lose its tiles, and the pews and pulpit were worthy of the place, this long sturdy building would be as beautiful inside as out. The interior has neither aisle nor transepts to distract the eye from the two arches of the central tower with scalloped capitals on twisted pillars, while each rib of the vaulted roof between them, ending in a dragon's head, looks like a sea-serpent. Windows to match this Norman splendour have been put into the nave, and the little painted chancel has its windows under trefoiled arches. The Norman font is carved.

Churchill. This quiet place among the elms and oaks remembers in its name and in its Court the ancestors of the Duke of Marlborough, who has another link with Somerset at Sedgemoor, where he helped to win for the king the last big battle on English soil. He has yet another link in this church, where a portrait brass of 1500 shows Ralphe Jenyns and his wife, who sold the Court to the Churchills. Two figures from the 14th century greet us in the porch, a cross-legged knight and his lady.

The 500-year-old church has been made new outside, but has kept much that is old inside, including two fonts (the oldest Norman), a row of stone faces, a splendid oak roof, and fine solid benches with high carved finials. In the 14th century south aisle hang a 17th century breastplate and armour which may have belonged to

Thomas Latch, whose sculptured figure on a painted tomb is the most striking thing in the church. Dressed in scarlet coat, boots, and spurs, he leans forward and gazes with horror at the wife lying beside him, whose shroud he has raised from her face. Seven boys and four girls in red caps kneel on red cushions round them, and one baby in swaddling clothes, some holding skulls to show that they died before that tragic day.

Crowning the hill south-east of the village is Dolebury Camp, a prehistoric hill fort of over 20 acres protected by huge stone ramparts, afterwards used by the Romans.

Churchstanton. Its church is two miles away from most of its people, yet if all its people came they could not fill it. The gallery added early in the 19th century for the lace-workers of Stapley is needed no more. The gallery is fronted with fine 15th century bench-ends.

The oldest possession of the church must be its font, with an unusual shaped bowl looking very like Saxon. The church has the fine window tracery of the 15th century, but the slender arcade with its carved capitals is a century older. The oak pulpit and the prayer desk are old, with lovely carvings. The chancel has two Jacobean chairs with the arms carved as serpents.

The stocks stand by the church gate, and in a field behind the rectory is something of the history not written in books but cut deep into the earth itself—a ditch within a ditch, forming a perfect circle with the ramparts still raised. It guards one of the loveliest stretches of the Blackdown Hills.

Clapton-in-Gordano. It has the best of the once lovely valley of Gordano (the wedge-shaped valley) and in its church are three great rarities, perhaps the oldest of their kind in England—the 13th century screen, the altar candlesticks, and the 700-year-old seats. None of them is very beautiful, but they have grown more precious with age. The masks on the corbels round the squat tower, and the tympanum over the door, follow Norman ideas. There is a consecration cross on the porch, another painted inside, a 13th century font with four ugly faces and four dogs' heads under the bowl, and a piscina curiously placed in a peephole near a stone altar. Round the arcade capitals are oak leaves and the arms of the Arthurs. Their successors at the Court House have written the name of Wynter on many stones, and it is little Edward Wynter who sits in a chair in his red dress, with a skull on his lap, his father and mother praying beside him, and all around cherubs and angels and symbols, a turned-down torch, mown grass, and a closed book, symbols of time gone, for this small life cut short about 300 years ago. More comforting are the lines of a husband and wife beginning, *Greve not for wee tho here wee lye.*

It is more than twice 300 years since the church's three great possessions were made, but the screen, with its double-arched doorway under a wide pointed arch and a rose window, spent most of its long life at Clapton Court, where the boy in red must often have run in and out of it. It was probably the entrance to the buttery, and is valued as one of the earliest domestic screens which have survived 700 years, one of only a few wooden 13th century screens.

When this screen was being made for the Court these pews with their high curving lintels were being made for the church. The 15th century tried to cover up the axe marks on their roughly-hewn sides, but today the church is proud of them. Only a very small group of English churches can boast seats as old as these. So ancient are the candlesticks that the 15th century reredos was made to fit them, its stone shelf having two rounded ledges for their base. The candlesticks look massive yet weigh hardly anything, for they are made of latten, an extremely light form of brass. Veterans all, yet another veteran is here, for still in its place is the sanctus bell which rang before the Reformation.

Clapton Court is fronted with a mighty entrance porch and tower; it must have been one of Somerset's grandest homes when Richard Arthur put his shield over the door 500 years ago.

Clatworthy. It has a few cottages set with their church on the Brendon Hills, all a little old and weary-looking. The great font, plain and round, is Norman and has been standing in the church 800 years; the chancel arch is also Norman. In the tower hang three bells made in Stuart days, one dated 1699 and inscribed, *Drawe neare to God.*

Claverton. Here lies the dreamer of a beautiful city and the maker of it, for he saw his dream come true. Here he rests in the heart of as fair a scene as England has, almost in sight of his city of Bath; yet it is sad that he lies in a grave that is not a part of all this beauty, for he rests with a group of kinsmen and friends under a canopied tomb which has no beauty in it.

We climb up a narrow path between high hedges to find ourselves above a valley stretching to a range of wooded hills. It was

79

the scene Ralph Allen loved; its manor house belonged to him, and here he wished to lie.

The church has lost its ancient character, but has fine possessions. It has kept the curious painted figures of Sir William Bassett and his wife, who have been watching the altar since the happy days of Charles I, she a stately matron with trim ruff and cuffs, and a shrouded baby with a lace collar; he with a sash and a painted belt round his tunic.

They are the oldest possessions of the church, unless we count the mass dial on the sunny wall, and unless it be that the glass in two of its windows is older. One window has four medallions of Continental glass set in a spacious area of glowing crowns and shields and Tudor roses with made-up fragments. The four medallions have in them delicate scenes of the Good Samaritan, the Prodigal Son, the Good Shepherd, and the Sower. The colours are dazzlingly rich. The second window has old and new medallions. The chancel roof is panelled with oak and has 40 carved bosses. Here lies old Richard Graves, the parson who laid his great friend Ralph Allen to rest outside and went on preaching until he had completed 55 years without being absent for one month.

The Manor House, by Wyatville, now houses the American Museum in Britain, containing completely furnished rooms of the 17th, 18th, and 19th centuries, brought from the United States, and other special American exhibits.

Cleeve. Among rocks and ravines and deep woods, it has a mile of one of the loveliest walks in Somerset, Goblin Combe, a long solitary cleft green with ash saplings and beeches, though even they cannot climb to the top of the steep sides where the rock is bare. The cleft winds on and the trees change to pines, with the wind sighing like a sea in their branches; then come great overhanging rocks, till the valley fills with bracken and yew bushes, and comes out into the open heathland. It is a place for legends, and many must have been woven round the highest rocky point called Cleeve Toot. A new church in the style of the Normans has been built for the pretty village.

Clevedon. It is a famous place, gathered about a rocky bay which has come into literature and will not pass out of it. Here Coleridge lived and Arthur Hallam sleeps.

It has grown into a seaside town, but it keeps one of the finest 14th century houses in Somerset; its Norman church still stands high up above the sea; and here we may see the cottage to which Samuel Taylor Coleridge brought his bride. There is still enough impressive solitude about these cliffs (where Turner loved to paint the sunset) to excuse the Clevedon folk for imagining that it was here and not in Lincolnshire that Tennyson wrote "Break, break, break, on thy cold gray stones, O Sea!" As a matter of fact Tennyson knew very little of Clevedon.

She stands here, serene on her own hill and girt by six others which look out to loveliness and grandeur, across to the Mendips and away to the coast of Wales. For Clevedon, like Rome, has her Seven Hills, varying from 100 to 300 feet high, and all a constant delight; Church Hill, Dial Hill, Wains Hill, Hangstone Hill, Castle Hill, Strawberry Hill, and Court Hill (which should be seen when the rhododendrons are out). As if this was not enough for one small town, Clevedon has also the delight of a sea-front, a Poet's Walk round Wains Hill, and a Lovers' Walk along the cliffs to Ladye Bay; and there are many copses, public gardens, and a tree-clad Swiss Valley. We need not wonder that this place is a veritable sanctuary for Nature's children. Over 200 kinds of wild flowers have been found, 45 kinds of butterflies, and 135 birds out of a total of 216 known in Somerset.

The 19th century was well on its way when this small place (then a few cottages round the church, above the bay) stirred with that sorrowful event which was to put into literature the masterpiece of Tennyson. Arthur Hallam, in love with Tennyson's sister, was travelling on the Continent when he died at Vienna, and they brought him home and laid him in this church on the hill where the Severn flows into the Bristol Channel.

> *The Danube to the Severn gave*
> *The darkened heart that beat no more;*
> *They laid him by the pleasant shore,*
> *And in the hearing of the wave.*

> *There twice a day the Severn fills:*
> *The salt sea-water passes by,*
> *And hushes half the babbling Wye,*
> *And makes a silence in the hills.*

Though it is Hallam as remembered by Tennyson who brings the pilgrim here, it is strange that Tennyson himself was not at Clevedon for nearly 20 years after the burial; he called during his honeymoon on the way down to Devon.

Old Clevedon church (into which we come by a mediaeval porch with a fine oak roof) was built by the Normans and has scores of their crude carvings round the tower and the chancel, many of them very quaint faces. There are old faces everywhere, inside and out, with corbel heads 600 years old along the south wall. The 14th and 15th century builders, in transforming the church, kept the old chancel arch with the curious beak carvings, and there are still standing two of the Norman arches of the tower. The nave is 14th and 15th century, the plain font is 14th century with an oak canopy of the 17th, the roof belongs to our own time, and the pulpit is made up with the Jacobean panels of the old one. There are two ancient peepholes in the chancel, and traces of two roodlofts. There are fine old seats with charming poppyheads, and at the back of the nave some pews of Dutch wood with gaunt dogs as finials. The carved panels on the wall between them are from the old lectern.

On one side of the chancel arch is a little girl asleep on a ledge, a dainty figure sculptured in stone. She is Philippa Wake, who used to play in the grounds of Clevedon Court when Charles I was fighting for the mastery of the nation. She lived for seven short years and for eight generations the Wakes lived on at Clevedon, descendants of the family receiving the estate from the Conqueror.

By the chancel wall the portrait of a 15th century knight of Clevedon is engraved on a block of alabaster, its lines fading after much trampling underfoot, for it has been a pavement stone. The knight is believed to be Thomas Lovell, lord of the manor about the time of Agincourt. John Kenn, who added a storey to the Norman tower in the 16th century, sleeps in an altar tomb close by.

There are two notable houses in the town, the home of the Hallams and what has now become the Council House, a finely built 19th century house of Cotswold stone, standing with great dignity in one of the best viewpoints of the town. The house is well worth visiting, for it has a Court Room with a splendid ceiling and stone mantelpieces with carved heraldic shields; a Committee Room with a carved oak mantelpiece; and a Council Chamber with twin doors rich in heraldry, and a wonderful ceiling gay with the colour of 68 coats-of-arms of West Country worthies.

Chief of all the town's possessions is Clevedon Court, the home of Arthur Hallam's mother, the finest house of its period in the county. It has been called one of the most precious relics of early domestic architecture in England, and is now the property of the National Trust.

It stands magnificently with the woods rising high behind it, a structure nobly grouped with its gables and porches and turrets, and the splendour of its windows. The porch has still the old portcullis, which was worked by a windlass in the room over it. The 14th century window with delightful tracery is claimed as one of the finest examples of a square decorated window in existence; it is one of the chief features of its palatial front, and belongs to a beautiful little overhanging chapel, which has another window looking down on the oak-panelled hall with its minstrel gallery. At each corner of the house is a newel stairway, and everywhere we see the harmonious blending of the three ages from which the house comes, 14th century, the Tudor age, and Jacobean days. Here came Thackeray to write part of *Henry Esmond*, and much of *Vanity Fair*; the Mrs Brookfield to whom he wrote many letters was a daughter of the house. Here came Tennyson on his first visit to Arthur Hallam's grave long after he had made it famous without seeing it.

Cloford. It is far away, with a pleasant view from the churchyard, and an avenue of yews to the door. Its tower is battlemented and pinnacled, its east window has two quaint heads outside, and there is an oddly shaped window with five lights. Its oldest possession is one of the very earliest Norman tub fonts, standing on the floor like a tub indeed, with no pedestal.

Once more in Somerset we are reminded of Little Jack Horner who sat in his corner, for here, looking down from the wall, is one of the famous Mells family, Sir George Horner. His long hair hangs over his collar and he is keeping a book open with his fingers. His wife is in black with a white collar and hood, and cherubs smile about them in the style of the 17th century monuments. In a plain altar tomb close by have slept Maurice Horner and his two children for 500 years.

Closworth. Here in a churchyard almost on the Dorset border sleeps Thomas Purdue, Somerset's famous bell-founder. He was 90 when they carried him to his grave in 1911, and carved a bell on his tomb. Five of his own bells, stamped with his initials and the mark of a vine leaf, ring out over him from the fine old tower, and all over Somerset and even up to Scotland his bells resound. His foundry was by the rectory orchard, and we have seen the pit where he melted the metal. He must often have looked in at the rectory as we did, and must have seen the name of a parson of 1606 cut on it. With his bells in the tower are two older ones, one stamped with the alphabet and a jumble of letters. The 15th century tower has a lofty arch and a stone carved with three figures, so worn that it is difficult to say who they are. The rest of the church has been much renewed, but there is a Jacobean pulpit and chest, and a Norman font on which some 15th century craftsman has carved a Tudor rose. Outside are the steps and shaft of an ancient cross.

Clutton. If we come in spring we come to it with aubrietia creeping round and following us to the church. If we come to it at any time we have a noble view. Its church has been made new, but the tower rests on its Norman stone. We come into the nave through a doorway made by our first English builders as Norman influence was dying down, to find a chancel arch by those same builders, who made it lovely with zigzag round it and flowers on the capitals, though vandal hands have put round it a painted text. This and the 13th century font are all that is old.

Combe Down. The best thing we saw here was a sea of buttercups, but it has the magnificent views that give the heights round Bath so great a glory, with the three round towers of Midford Castle, built *c.* 1775.

Combe Florey. It is as lovely as its name and near enough to the Quantocks for the distant blue to change at times to the purple of heather, the green of trees, or an autumn glow of bracken.

It has lost its old manor except for the Elizabethan gatehouse, a tall gaunt block among the cottages, and the present manor house is chiefly 18th century; but a glimpse through the hedge reveals a house 300 years old, with a charming leaded window in the room above the porch.

The lord of the vanished manor has left us his portrait in the church, which is much as he used to see it; he is Nicholas Francis, who died in 1526 and is here in brass. Two centuries before him there came here to rest Sir John de Merriet from Hestercombe, a knight of 600 years ago whose gaunt stone figure lies full-length on the floor with a wife each side of him. He is in armour and his suit is interesting because it shows the shields on each shoulder for lessening the blow from an axe. Above him are a few words in old French telling us that the heart of Maude de Meriett, a nun of Cannington, is buried here; she was an earlier member of the family, who died at Cannington with the sisters there, her heart being sent home for burial.

The oak pulpit was carved in the 15th century, and some of the benches are from that time, but the screen is in memory of a rector's son and seven other men of Combe Florey who gave their lives for

Cheddar: the market cross.

Crewkerne Church.

Claverton Manor.

Crowcombe Court.

Chew Magna Church: the Hauteville monument.

Brent Knoll Church:
a bench-end.

Crowcombe Church:
a bench-end.

Culbone Church.

Downside Abbey: the nave.

us. One of the windows is a memorial to one of the wittiest rectors who ever found himself in a country parish; he was Sydney Smith, rector for 15 years here. In these 15 years the name of the rector of Combe Florey was known all over England.

Combe Hay. It stands in the shadow of many yews in the hollow of the hills round Bath, its 13th century tower peeping up and vanishing as we approach and losing itself when we arrive. It is like an end of the world, for there is no way beyond and we must all come back.

Somewhere here is buried Sir Lewis Dyve, defender of Sherborne Castle, of whom John Evelyn says in his diary that he was indeed a gallant gentleman but not a little given to romance when he spoke of himself.

The church has been made new but has two 18th century wall-monuments by the altar, with cherubs and skulls.

Combe St Nicholas. It has barrows from the Bronze Age, relics of the Romans, a font which may be Saxon, and a bit of a Norman doorway in a church of the Middle Ages.

Like illustrations to its old old story are the odd things making up a tiny museum which we found in the church. There is a shell buried here when the waves of the sea were sweeping over the area, and and fragments from the time when the waves of war were sweeping over Europe. With them are two Roman horseshoes, and bits of carving from the chancel screen, showing an artist's mark and the date 1480. This old screen has been put together again by village craftsmen and is now behind the stalls.

From the Saxon past of the village comes perhaps one of the two fonts here; it is said to be at least 900 years old and to have been saved from the Norman church, of which only one Norman pillar survived the rebuildings of the 13th and 15th centuries. The second font is a neat little copy of 15th century work. One of the bells is 400 years old.

There are memorials to the Bonner family, whose home was the solid Tudor farmhouse called Weston, still with its fine plaster ceilings and a beam in the wall to draw across the old door.

Hereabouts, on the top of a hill near Wadeford, is a curious little temple in which William Pitt may have sat, for it came from the garden of Burton Pynsent, the house near Curry Rivel which was bequeathed to Pitt by a Somerset admirer. It was at Higher Wadeford that seven Roman pavements were unearthed, only to be destroyed by frost and thaw.

D

Compton Bishop. Crook's Peak, the last southern height of the Mendips, rises bare and sombre behind the church, the cave in its side called Denny's Hole now stripped of its amazing stalactites. The church has guarded well its treasure, a precious 15th century stone pulpit. Delicately carved with Tudor flowers and tracery, it is a wonderful bit of work which 500 years seem scarcely to have touched. The Norman font, with a Jacobean cover, looks charming against a last-century screen. The mediaeval tracery of the east window has some of the original glass showing graceful though mostly headless figures of saints. Headless, too, is the 600-year-old cross on high steps in the churchyard. There is a mediaeval mass dial.

Compton Dando. We like the idea of Jupiter holding up the church of Compton Dando, and it is true, for we have seen it. Here he stands to witness if we lie, set in the base of the north-east corner. A noble figure he looked 50 years ago, for we came upon an old man who knew him then, but now his face is worn away with the cold blasts of our east winds and winter rains. Yet we can see that he has been a truly Roman figure, most probably a Roman altar stone, found here last century not far from the place where a Saxon trough was also found.

He is probably the oldest figure in any church in Somerset, perhaps the oldest corner-stone of any church in England, and it is thrilling to come upon it in this small place among the lovely fields round Bath. The image of a Roman god older than Christianity, he would be set up in this country, somewhere in Somerset, before the first church was built in England, and here he stands, chief god of a religion which has passed away, supporting the temple of the faith whose worshippers the Romans hunted down into catacombs and sought to exterminate.

High above him on the 15th century tower a curious winged dolphin points the way of the wind, and on an old stone built into it are three of those scratch dials which were the simple church clocks of mediaeval England. One is the regular circle with lines and two others have figures for the hours.

Compton Dando is rich in its possession of Jupiter, and it has also a glimpse of Wansdyke, the great defensive bank thrown up across the west of England for 60 miles soon after the last worshipper of Jupiter vanished from this country.

Compton Dundon. Compton at the foot of Butleigh Woods has Windmill Hill with its proud column to Sir Samuel Hood, while

Dundon half-circles another of these cone-shaped hills with an ancient camp at its summit; Dundon Beacon it is called, 300 feet up.

Compton has the broken wayside cross, ruin of the centuries, but Dundon has the church, charming with things that have come down to it from many generations. There are the rough old benches for the people and the Jacobean pulpit for the parson, cunningly fitted into the wall on the corbelled ledge which held its predecessor. It is reached through the old roodloft doorway and has back panels, side balustrade, a carved cornice, and a seat inside, altogether one of the most delightful pulpits we have come upon. The nave and the tower are 15th century but the chancel is 14th century, with a piscina and very dignified sedilia. The low stone wall between the chancel and the nave once held a 14th century screen. A few of the windows have fragments of mediaeval glass, here a few crowns and there a few heads.

Compton Martin. Raised at one end of its street is one of the rarest legacies the Normans left to Somerset, shaded in these later centuries by fine yews, a glorious Wellingtonia, and a beech four yards round its trunk.

For 800 years Compton Martin has looked on these walls as we see them, noble inside and out. On one of them is a scratch dial from the days before clocks. Time was when it was proposed to pull the church down, for our superb English builders in the 15th century dreamed of a great transformation. They would take this Norman work and put in its place the lighter pointed arches of their day. They set to work to do so and their mark is sadly plain for all to see, for the chancel arch is all awry, a poor flattened thing that has taken the place of the impressive arch the Normans built, and it seems to be falling down.

The truth is that it has slipped in its foundations. The 15th century men, meaning to cut out all the Norman arches, carried their pointed arch to the top of the Norman clerestory and were proceeding with their transformation when the south pillar of the chancel arch refused to hold the burden put on it and began to come away. It was held up with buttresses outside and with steel rods, and happily the warning was in time to save the church. The builders left it all alone with the chancel arch seeming to be falling down, resting on the leaning pier.

The Norman pillar nearest to the chancel arch is one of the sights of Somerset and one of the architectural curiosities of England. It has ropework carved round it spirally with hundreds of beads running through the rope, and the illusion of twisting is complete. It is the unique possession of the church, and it is odd to think that generations of Compton Martin folk worshipped here without having seen it, for it was long plastered over and not revealed again until 1851.

We look beyond this twisted pillar, beyond the shapeless chancel arch which so luckily saved this fine interior, into a chancel which reminds us somehow of a corner of Durham Cathedral with its double arch and its stone vaulted roof. The chancel is remarkable inside and out, for over it is the dovecot where the lord of the manor used to keep his doves. It was reached from outside; the steps have gone, but the door is still here.

One more rare possession has this remarkable interior, a Norman clerestory looking to the sky on one side and into the aisle on the other. It has been part of the transformation to raise the roof of the aisle on the south so that we see now indoors what generations saw out of doors, windows, Norman corbels, and all. The roofs are charming. Above the eight lovely Norman arches of the nave rises a barrel roof with 42 painted panels of leaves and grapes, resting on six stone heads. The oak roofs of the aisles are in small squares. In the south aisle are the old roof timbers with huge carved bosses, and the beams rest on ten stone corbels of bearded men and sorrowful-looking women; on the north aisle wall the Norman corbel table remains outside. One of the corbels is an extraordinary head of a man with great eyes and gleaming teeth, and most of them are men with neatly trimmed hair.

Under a window of the north wall, in a Tudor recess, lies Thomas de Morton, a tall figure with one hand on his sword and one on his breast, a curly head and a curly beard. He must have been handsome 600 years ago with his collar and cuffs painted blue and his belt to match, his robe in red, his pointed shoes on a lion. The Norman font has a fine band of zigzag round the bowl.

Thankful as we may be that the 15th century masons were thwarted in their work, we must be grateful for the 15th century carvers who gave this noble church its screens. They are in black oak and run round the chapel, most daintily carved, and are dated 1659 when they were moved from Moat Farm at Bickfield. The screen has a double crest and charming tracery, with a band of quatrefoils below the bays. In front of the screen in the choir are the choir-stalls finely carved by Jacobean craftsmen. They were the altar rails in olden days.

Compton Pauncefoot. Grey stone buildings, woods, the little hill of King Arthur called Cadbury Castle, and quite another sort of castle called Compton Castle built about 1825, with lawns stretching down to a shining lake: that and a little more is Compton Pauncefoot. The little more is the church with the 19th century manor beside it. An unusual sight in this county of towers is the low slender spire with a band of carving round it, 500 years old like most of the rest of the church. The font is 700; the charming angels painted on the chancel roof are modern. A stone on the wall proclaims the fine record of James Husey Hunt, who came here as rector in 1838 and served for 58 years. Two stone coffins lie under an old yew in the churchyard and looking into the churchyard is a mass dial.

Congresbury. It is the village of beautiful doorways leading into beautiful places. There is Tudor Cottage with a lovely arch in a timber frame; the vicarage has old stone faces looking out from its windows and a porch round a mediaeval arch guarded by an angel; and best of all is the church, with doorways worthy of a cathedral and one of the most graceful of Somerset's few spires. The 13th century built the church, the 14th altered it, and still the three sundials scratched on the west doorway remain, while rich canopied panels spring from the inner arch.

All this from the outside. Inside is a font with a bucket-shaped Norman bowl on a 13th century pedestal, and with a Jacobean cover. A perfect 15th century screen has its cornice hung with grapes, its doors being in the modern screen at the tower. Yet another screen by the chapel is an interesting patchwork of early carving. There are canopies on each side of the altar and a double piscina 700 years old. The arcade (which is curious for having small black pillars detached from the main columns) leads our eye to the quaintest collection of little people in red and green between the clerestory windows. Many are obviously suffering from toothache, and their swollen faces are thought to be here in memory of Bishop Bytton, whose wonderful cures are remembered in his cathedral at Wells. There is part of a 14th century cross in the churchyard, and a perfect 15th century one rises 40 feet high among the houses, guarded by the Ministry of Public Building and Works.

The old story they tell here is that St Congar stopped beside the River Yeo and built a church of wattle. Wanting shade, he put his yew stick into the ground, where it sprouted like Joseph's staff at Glastonbury. A stump of an ancient yew is even now called

89

Congar's walking-stick. King Ina, hearing of the miracle, gave Congresbury to the saint, and here he founded a monastery, the wattle church becoming a church of stone. He died in Jerusalem, but his body was brought to Somerset. So the story goes, and certain it is that there was a priest here 1000 years ago, for it was one of Alfred's many gifts to Asser, his tutor and friend.

Corfe. It lies at the foot of the Blackdown Hills, with a church rebuilt in Norman style. The font is the one the Normans made, and their designs have been copied by modern craftsmen on many round arches, while two old faces look out from among the newer corbels in the nave.

Corston. Alas; it has lost the quarter-boys who struck the hours on the old church clock; it is sad to miss them, for Southey used to sit in his classroom watching them strike. He was sent to school here after being brought up by an aunt at Bath, and here he spent a year of his life with little profit and much suffering, for the master was almost a second Mr Squeers, and his wife drank.

The church (which has a mass dial on the wall) comes from three periods. The Normans started the tower, now much altered and with a little extinguisher steeple, and they built the two doorways. The chancel is the work of our first English builders in the 13th century, the north aisle is 19th century. The tower has on it the date at which it was restored, 1622. It looks down on a lifesize figure of Christ in the churchyard.

Cossington. A pretty village on the top of the Poldens, its partly 13th century church is set in a lovely garden, with nothing between the rough grass and gravestones and the smooth turf and gay flowerbeds of the manor house. The front windows of the house open almost on to two curiously niched buttresses of the church wall. John Brent, a lord of the manor who died in 1924, lies beneath the chancel floor, his armoured figure cut in brass. His wife has a separate brass portrait, and their arms are also here. The house is not their old home, but a new one raised in its place. There is a quaint 13th century font, and an old sundial.

Cothelstone. The Jacobean manor house which Blake besieged in the Civil War still shelters the church and the cottages behind it. It was held for the king by Sir John Stawell, but he was captured and taken to Newgate, returning here only at the Restoration, to die in this house on the Quantocks, worn out by 14 years of captivity.

His sad life is told on the memorial in the 15th century church, where also is the tomb and the beautiful alabaster figure of his father, who went with Sir Walter Raleigh to Ireland and trained 1000 Somerset men for the fight against the Armada. A curly-headed figure in his ruff and armour, he makes with his wife as perfect a sculptured group as any in Somerset. Near them lie two other Stawells, probably Sir Matthew ad his lady, who were living in the days of Chaucer. She has two angels at her head and two squirrels at her feet.

The chapel in which they lie is separated from the nave by a Norman pier, and the light falls on them through precious windows with six English saints in mediaeval glass. St Dunstan is here with his tongs, paired with St Cuthbert; St Aldhelm of Sherborne is with St Thomas of Hereford, and St Richard of Chichester is with St Thomas Cantelupe. The church is rich in woodwork as well as in glass, for the pulpit and the bench-ends were all beautifully carved in the 15th or 16th century.

The road runs through a mighty avenue of beeches to the foot of Cothelstone Beacon; it is a grand avenue, wide and gracious. Passing this way we come upon the old manor gateway at which Judge Jeffreys hanged two rebels for whom the Royalist Sir John had pleaded in vain.

Creech St Michael. It has a lovely church, though it has seen much change. The tower rises in the centre of a tiny 12th century building which has now become one aisle of the 15th century church. In an altar tomb lies Robert Cuffe, a farmer of Elizabethan England who probably lived on the old farm behind the church. There is much richly carved woodwork in a reading desk dated 1634, the choir-seats and the bench-ends, and a massive oak cornice, all the work of mediaeval craftsmen.

From those far-off days come two sundials scratched on the south porch, and two grinning heads holding up niches at the west door. Two bullet holes in the old doors apparently tell a tale of some battle the village has forgotten.

The village has a bridge at either side of it, both ancient and both across the little River Tone, which rises in the Brendon Hills and flows through Taunton.

Crewkerne. All its streets, with many old stone houses, hurry along to the market square.

Yet it is the church which draws most people to it, one of the grandest 15th century cruciform churches in Somerset, though a little disappointing inside. Its glory is in its windows (so wide on one side that there is room for no more than a buttress between each), in a west front worthy of a cathedral, and in the south porch, where we are greeted by a silent orchestra with harp and lyre, tambourine and bagpipes; delicate figures full of action, though several players have lost their heads and some their instruments. Beautiful stone vaulting with leafy bosses supports a room above this porch, and a new St Bartholomew is in its elegant canopied niche.

Tall gargoyled turrets flank the Tudor gateway of the grand west front, with a bishop on one side, a king on the other, and an empty niche held by a dragon above the bold tracery of the seven-light window. A proud gold cockerel reigns above the lovely pinnacles of the 15th century tower, which encases its 13th century predecessor. Two buttresses to the south transept are roofed over to form a mystery; no one knows whether it was a shrine or something to do with the hermit who used to live in the churchyard.

The lightness of the nave, and its tall arches, are admirable, but we miss the glory of the outside walls. What beauty there is is in the mediaeval roof and the windows. The tower's oak ceiling is fan-vaulted; two lovely panelled roofs are lighted by the splendid windows of the north transept and the chapel; and 13 great stone angels stand full-length to hold up the quaint nave roof.

The font is Norman. Doorways on each side of the altar have splendid stone spandrels, with two boars holding a shield over one, and two angels over the other. Four extraordinary heads support brackets inside the chancel arch, one with leaves like a long moustache growing out of his grinning face. A chest of 1616 has wonderful hinges.

A tiny Tudor brass shows Thomas Golde kneeling in his armour. Two goldsmiths have their brass inscriptions hammered instead of engraved. Hidden behind the organ is another brass inscription with the arms of the Martin family, showing a monkey looking into a glass. On a memorial to two 18th century children a clock points to 9.57, probably the hour when Death, shown with his scythe, came for one of them.

Elizabeth Wyke, who died in 1615, has her name spelt Wike in the verse on her stone to make it easier for the poet to begin each line with a letter of her name. She starts her own epitaph with:

Ending on earth to rebegin in Heaven,
Loving my Maker dearer than my Mate.

Francis Nicholls has his portrait on a bench-end with the Latin inscription, *If you seek my memorial look around.* We look round and see all the bench-ends he carved at the end of last century.

Nelson's Hardy learnt his lessons in a 17th century house north of the church, a grammar school no longer. Another neighbouring house has 15th century windows, and a mile south is 16th century Henley Manor.

Cricket Malherbie. The car swept the foxgloves on each side of the grassy tracks to this small place, so that it was good to have missed the only way to it wide enough to be a road. There is no village, only the Court with pinnacles on its barn, the church, a cottage, a delightful thatched house, and a row of oak trees. The 19th century church has a curiously rich appearance for this tiny place among the wooded hills. It is a handsome building with a little spire, fine gable crosses, and a beautiful pierced parapet of flowing design.

Cricket St Thomas. A great avenue of beeches lines the road the Romans made over Windwhistle Hill, the great road which continues as a drive through parkland to the house and church of Cricket St Thomas, home of Alexander Hood, one of Nelson's band of brothers. He was one of the two great Hoods, sons of the vicar of Butleigh, and he became the first Viscount Bridport, his brother Samuel becoming first Viscount Hood. Alexander was laid in this church the year before Waterloo, and facing his tomb is a memory of Nelson himself, for on a memorial are two little boys, both christened Horatio Nelson, who died one after the other. Nelson's brother William's daughter married into the Hood family, and on her children's memorial the grandfather is shown watching an angel taking them up to heaven. Over the pulpit hangs the flag flown by HMS *Nelson* on her first journey through the Panama Canal.

The church is full of Bridport memories. On the disappearance of the first viscounty with the death of Alexander the title was created a second time and the first viscount of the second creation lies in the churchyard, where he was laid in 1904; the grave is marked by a tall white angel. His wife Mary has a gentle relief of a woman rising into the clouds with bunches of flowers in her hands.

There is no village, and the church seems almost part of this great estate. The men on the estate carved the altar table, the reredos, and the panelling for the 15th century church, now made almost new.

93

Croscombe. A great surprise the Fortescues would have if they came back to Croscombe, for part of their ancient manor house, with its 15th century windows, has become a Baptist chapel. We have found the oldest Nonconformist chapel in England at Horningsham in Wiltshire, but this is the only manor house we have seen turned into a chapel.

We turn up the corner by the 14th century cross, and come to the magnificent church which was here (though not so grand) when the cross was set up. Its aisles have a beautiful arcaded parapet, its nave is battlemented and pinnacled, the tower has canopied niches with figures still in two of them, and above it all rises a stone spire with a band of neat carving round. It was looking out on hills white with blossom when we called, a splendid spectacle, with great gargoyles watching over the village in the hollow. The church belongs to all our building centuries, built in the 13th and remade in the 14th and 15th. It has a mass dial.

It is the church beloved by the Fortescues, which they filled with a mass of Jacobean carving astonishing all who come. We come into it through a porch they knew, with a figure of St George four centuries old and two comical faces at the doorway, one a little like the village simpleton and the other like his wife.

We suppose there is no other interior in Somerset quite like this, for it is crowded with the work of the woodcarvers of the 17th century, all in black oak. It is everywhere, in screens, pulpits, benchends, in the pews, and in the roof. We counted 200 carved panels before we got tired, and found in them eagles, sunflowers, acorns, and shields, among masses of foliage. The great screen reaches almost to the roof, tier on tier with little heads on buttresses and in the border, some sad, some fierce, some laughing, and with the royal arms gaily painted at the top. At each end of the screen is a reading desk to match, and close by it is the colossal pulpit, with panels of shields and medallions all painted red and white and gold, the great canopy crowned with a golden pelican.

It is all early 17th century, and it is remarkable to discover that all this colour on the pulpit and the screen comes from that age. Generations may have missed it but the colour has been there; it was brought to light some years ago by the clever men who use the powers of chemistry to remove the layers of centuries of dust. It has been done in the Chapter House of Westminster, and it has been done at Croscombe.

There are two fine brasses with 34 figures on them; they are to two brothers and their wives, James and William Bisse. William

94

and his wife kneel at desks with their nine sons and nine prim daughters. Mrs James and her daughters all wear highwaymen hats; James has a beard and a ruff and most of his sons have high stiff collars.

The nave has two brass candelabra, a big one and a small one, the small one elegant indeed, and both 18th century. There are two fine Jacobean chairs, charming iron altar rails with a band of red flowers, a chest of 1616, and a little old glass with St John, St Peter, and the Madonna. We come upon the Madonna again in one of the aisles, where she is shown in a most unusual stone corbel of a mother playing with her child.

The church has two odd little rooms, one with a heavy stone roof and the other a two-storey vestry probably used by one of the old guilds. We read that there were seven guilds in Croscombe, for young men, maidens, and wives, for archers, webbers, fullers, and hogglers. The hogglers, we gather, were labourers, and here they would meet to discuss affairs in the days when the church was the only meeting-place they had. With all these guilds of its own the village found it needful to send to Exeter for a mason to carve St George over the doorway, for we found it all set down in the accounts for 1509, where the Exeter craftsman is called the Jorgemaker.

Crowcombe. A bypass has enticed away the cars and left Crowcombe's charming corner at the foot of the Quantocks as peaceful as when its now weathered grey church was built 500 years ago.

Here is the mediaeval church house, now a library with a room above it. The lower rooms were once almshouses, and the children went to their lessons up the covered steps. Early this century the whole place was in a bad way, with two owners, and the tale is told that the top-floor owner called on the ground-floor owner to share the cost of repairing the roof. "I cannot do that," said the ground-floor man, "for I intend shortly to pull my half down." Apparently the trouble was overcome, for the old church house has been restored and is now in the keeping of the Ministry of Public Building and Works.

The split yew in the churchyard may be as old as the 14th century cross which still guards on its shaft a worn preacher in a broken niche above a grinning head. The church is 15th century, with dainty transomed windows, and a row of queer faces and animals under the pinnacled battlements. Fine vaulting crowns the two-storeyed porch, which opens on a mediaeval arcade with carved

95

capitals and as wonderful a collection of Tudor benches as is to be seen in Somerset, their deep carvings perfect still and showing among other designs two men vigorously attacking a double-headed dragon, a grinning face with vines coming out of its mouth and a wild man with a bludgeon out of each ear. One bench seems to have been sheered away to make room for a particularly bulky occupant. A carved Stuart chest matches these old stalwarts, and several fine panels in modern mosaic lend colour to the walls.

The thin Jacobean screen has the top of each arch crossed with delicate tracery. The pulpit was made in 1616, and perhaps the same hands carved the cover which is lowered over the font by a weight like a cannon ball. The font is a gem, older perhaps than the church, with charming little figures carved all round it. We see two hands raised in blessing above a knight and a lady, a bishop adding his blessing, and another holding the model of a church. The Madonna appears with a crown and a sword, and again with her lesson book at the knee of St Anne, and an angel holds a scroll before someone kneeling at prayer.

Raised on high steps above the nave is the manor chapel, added in 1655, with the painted arms of the Carews above the wall-panelling, and on the outside walls are stones to seven faithful servants of the manor, the stately Crowcombe Court we see from the church gate.

In the heart of the village is a second old cross, and farther on a lane leads us to Halsway, once the hunting-box of Cardinal Beaufort, who saw Joan tried at Rouen, and whose figure now faces hers in his own cathedral at Winchester.

Cucklington. Everywhere is a climb in this comely village, and one climb takes us to the top of the boundary ridge with a view into Dorset. The church tower, made new after a storm in 1703, looks across to Stoke Trister's tower on another hill. St Barbara has her chapel within, a good home for this saint of the hills. Her picture is in old glass in the mediaeval window. The arcade and most of the church are 13th century, but the fine font has Norman arcading. The mediaeval oak screen has been moved to an aisle, where we found it beside an old chest with cupboards and drawers.

Cudworth. Lonely among the woods, with the wind whistling over Windwhistle Hill close by, the old church carries its poverty with an air of dignity. The Normans gave it no tower, and the 14th century changed much but added little save windows. For 800 years the villagers have passed through this doorway, with carved capitals and leafy tympanum, to bring their babies to the great font. It is all barnlike inside, with an open timber roof and bare stones. A curious recess lights with a tiny slit a broken altar stone and a charming piscina. The window above them is a simple beauty, and fragments of ancient yellow glass shine from the fine tracery of another. A bracket for a statue juts out from the chancel wall, and by the door a broken head shows its teeth as it sticks out its tongue. Behind the Jacobean pulpit in a panel carved in recent years with two high-backed seats to match. A small collection of fragments of Roman pottery found in the neighbourhood is kept in the church.

Culbone. No noise from the busy world disturbs the quiet of this place, where what is probably the smallest complete parish church in England clings, like a wren's nest, to the wooded cliffs. We must come to it humbly on foot, along a terraced path cut in the hill, with nothing stirring but the sound of the sea and the wind in the pines. The church is complete as planned 800 years ago, not quite 12 yards long and 12 feet wide. The walls, over two feet thick, were raised by the Normans, probably on the site of a hermitage from which the gem of this church was taken—a tiny window cut from a single stone perhaps 1000 years ago. We see how the two lights were chipped from the solid block, and a head roughly traced over the mullion. The font is Norman, the miniature roodscreen was carved in the 14th century, one of the bells is mediaeval and the chalice is Elizabethan. There are ancient benches.

Through the door comes the sound of a stream hurrying over the pebbles to the sea 400 feet below, and all round are dark woods climbing 1000 feet up. Only two cottages keep this small temple company, together with the great house of Ashley Combe through the woods.

Curland. On one hill is a tiny church with a 500-year-old font; on the opposite hill, where dark pines stand stiffly among spreading oaks and beeches, are the ramparts of the mighty natural fort of Castle Neroche. About 900 feet high, on the edge of the Blackdown Hills, it overlooks a wonderful stretch of the central plain of Somerset, and as Norman and mediaeval remains have been found it is probable that this earthwork comes from the troubled days of King Stephen, when forts sprang up like mushrooms.

Curry Mallet. The Mallets came here with the Conqueror, and their arms remain on the grey stones of the manor house, piled on each other without cement and topped with twisted chimneys, the new ones made to match the old. It is to their descendants that the church owes its magnificent oak screen, with figures of Justice, Hope, Faith, and Charity over panels picturing the birth and death of Christ. Between the panels are the Madonna and Child, Peter and Paul, and a woman with what looks like a beehive.

Thomas Pyne had the screen made for his home 300 years ago; his father and mother kneel on the wall opposite the screen, both with rosy cheeks. Rosy-cheeked also is a neighbour of theirs, Ralph Mighill, looking quite lifelike against the chancel wall. At her desk a little nameless Tudor woman prays unceasingly for two children lying beside her. The old bench-ends, fan-shaped at the top, have been faithfully copied, and an ancient almsbox is fixed on a swivel to one of the pews.

Curry Rivel. It keeps a surprise for us up its lane, and pleasant it is to come on the green patch and the chestnut trees, and the church whose stately windows give the scene a touch of wondrous beauty. They (and most of the church) are 15th century, but the lofty tower is new and needs weathering to match the pierced stone windows and St Andrew in his niche. There is a scratch dial from the days before clocks.

Above the vaulted porch, with stone seats and a canopied stoup, a solitary figure plays the bagpipes, and round the corner is another with a fiddle, like a mediaeval Orpheus charming an amazing collection of gargoyles. Oldest of all is the north chapel, with 14th century ballflowers round its east window and six foliated wall recesses for figures of the de l'Orti family, though only four are occupied. On the sill above them is a stone with a priest's head sketched on the top of a cross, the sort of face a child might draw, but extremely interesting, as it marks the period (about 1275) when the cross on a tomb was being combined with a head or a figure, the idea from which the portrait brasses grew. Behind railings under a painted canopy lie two brothers, Marmaduke and Robert Jennings, dressed as troopers with jackboots and jerkins. Their wives and children kneel round them, and tucked up in two tiny stone beds are the twins and the triplets, a sad little nursery, for it seems that they all died as babies.

The chancel has two ancient chairs, one from 1411. A miniature cupboard in the wall where the chalice was kept has still its linenfold door on the old hinges. The font is 15th century. Some 16th century pews are carved all over and some have poppyheads. Across the aisles stretch parts of a 15th century roodscreen rare or unique in its design. There are saints from the 15th century in the windows, Vincent and Isodore, Stephen and Lawrence, with Catherine a little way off, and other fragments of mediaeval glass.

Overlooking Sedgemoor, the last battlefield in England, is a column set up by the first William Pitt in memory of William Pynsent, who so admired Pitt's work (though they never had met) that he left him Burton Pynsent House.

Cutcombe. This is the highest parish in Somerset; it contains the peak of Dunkery Beacon (1707 feet) within its boundaries and the church is 930 feet above sea level, with magnificent views from the churchyard. The church is mainly of the 14th and 15th centuries, with a Norman fragment preserved in the font. The south aisle was built in the 19th century when the iron-mining industry brought prosperity to the neighbouring Brendon Hills.

Dinder. Come to it in lilac time; it is not far from Wells. You will find the church corner wonderful with beauty, a lychgate almost lost in yews as we turn into this beautiful scene, wallflowers ablaze with gold, wistaria, lilac, and laburnum telling us that summer is coming in, and lovely hedges everywhere. It is a charming place with the little River Sheppey falling over tiny weirs in streets and gardens.

We walk up the path to the church with its fine north wall across our view, crowned with a parapet from which friendly gargoyles look down at the top of slender buttresses. Very dainty is the arcading in the battlements, and charming is the tower with its stair turret to the bells.

Yet it is the south wall which holds us captive, for it is Norman, and has three fine consecration crosses. It has a dial scratched on a stone to tell the time to mediaeval England; and it looks down on the cross set on 14th century steps, on an ancient yew which we measured and found 11 yards round, so that it may be 1000 years old, and on the lovely gardens of Dinder House.

Inside, too, we come upon the Normans, for in the chancel wall above a window of St Michael are two dragon heads carved by Norman sculptors .They are from a Norman arch which has disappeared, and have been set in the wall because they are a veritable treasure of antiquity. The rays of the sun shine past the dragons from a window which looked out on the old roodloft and is filled with mediaeval glass still rich in colour. It shows the Archangel

Michael weighing souls, and an ancient representation of the Trinity. Below this window is one of the rarest stone pulpits of Charles I's happy days, carved with fleurs-de-lis and roses, and a band of scrollwork under the cresting. There is a 15th century font with a finely carved bowl and an arcaded stem.

Dinnington. A rugged place on a steep hill, it looks on to the glorious woods and park of Hinton House, where the Pouletts have lived since the days when Sir Amyas Poulett put Wolsey in the stocks. Tessellated pavements, a hypocaust, and other remains of a Roman building have been found here, and there is still something 800 years old in the village. It is the Norman font, decorated with cable moulding, in the small 15th century church now made new.

Ditcheat. St Christopher has come to Ditcheat in our time, with the Child on his shoulder, fishes swimming at his feet (we noticed an eel in the stream), a monk and a nun praying on the shore, and a windmill and a churchyard in the background. The village folk knew him well 500 years ago, but he had been lost for many generations behind the plaster on the wall of the church, and has been brought to light in our own century. There are fragments of 14th century sculpture also found in our own time.

The tower of the church rises on Norman foundations, with a stone seat round each pillar; but the arches were pointed by the English builders following the Normans in the 13th century, and the 15th century builders, who raised the height of the old chancel and crowned it with the clerestory, raised the height of the tower and gave it a fan-vaulted roof, setting figures in its niches. They also sculptured a host of angels to hold up the glorious roof of their nave.

There are two passage-ways from the nave to the altar so that processions can walk through them from the nave, and one has still its original door, probably made at the same time as the original door still leading to the rood stairs. The font and the old chest are both about 500 years old, and there are fragments of 15th century glass in which we recognise St Philip and St James. Sunk in the floor of the sanctuary is a beautiful relief of a rector in his robes with a canopy above his head. A famous name on the rectors' list runs from 1699 to 1891, six Leirs following each other. The grand reading desk is a memorial to this astonishing family, for it is made from their pew, the pulpit being carved in Jacobean style to match it. With the last of the Leirs came to an end an extraordinary rectors' list which we found in the hall of the Old Rectory, a wooden screen carved with the arms and names of all the rectors of Ditcheat from 1433 to 1891. It was made in 1630, and the names after that were added, Leir after Leir.

A charming neighbour of the Old Rectory is the manor house, whose builder, Robert Hopton, set up an imposing escutcheon which catches all eyes in the church.

Dodington. It was on the borders of the royal forest which centred round North Petherton, and here 650 years ago lived Sabina Pecche, master forester, whose business it was to attend in the forest during fawning time, a service commuted into a yearly payment which is still made by the Elizabethan manor house. The house has a hall with a magnificent dark roof of solid oak, formed of richly carved panels, and supported on angel corbels. There is also a minstrel gallery. The date 1581 is over the fireplace, which has an elaborate mantelpiece supported on one side by a man's head and on the other by a woman's. There is a little old glass with the Dodington arms in one of the windows, and in the rooms opening off the hall are two splendid ceilings.

The tiny church was probably a hunting chapel in olden days, for it was once on the borders of the great park. The huntsmen would cross themselves with holy water from the carved stoup now standing on a pedestal by the door, and here is the font at which their children would be baptised. They would look up at the sweet face of the Madonna still looking down from the east window.

The steps and shaft of an ancient cross stand by a tall yew measuring 13 feet round its trunk. Not far away is an old copper mine, and on the hill to the south is Danesborough Camp, first a British and then a Roman fortress.

Donyatt. The yellow stone of Donyatt is cut from its own quarries. Here and there is a thatched roof, and in the midst the tall tower of the 15th century church. On its door are fine hinges like ferns. The Jacobean oak pulpit stands on an ancient stone pedestal carved with small rosettes. The chancel arches have foliage capitals. The Tudor pews are carved with linenfold which were here when Henry VIII was king, and among the ancient bench-ends is one carved with a foal galloping round a tree and one with an odd design looking strangely like a boxing-glove. What is left of the old roodscreen has a new lease of life in the tower.

Doulting. Twelve centuries and more ago there came this way to die a man whose name has lived through all our story. He probably died on the spot where the church now stands, for as he lay breathing his last he told the monks to carry him into the little wooden church, and there he sat on a stone and passed away. The monks of Glastonbury replaced the church of wood with one of stone, the Normans came and built it all again, and to this day we come into it through a Norman arch.

He was St Aldhelm, and the year when he died was 709. He had founded the church at Sherborne and the abbey at Malmesbury (in whose soil he lies), but the great Norman churches there have covered up his work with their splendour, while Doulting still has something intimate to link it with our scholar monk. It has St Aldhelm's well.

The Vicar's garden wall has built into it some of the oldest of Doulting's possessions, fragments of the ancient 15th century church, which has been made new. They are mostly from the old south porch, which must have been a splendid place, for the fragments in the vicar's wall have finely carved faces among them, and very strange the old fan-vaulted roof looks standing upright.

The oldest part of the church remaining is in the north porch; it had fine carving of the time. It has been spoiled by the hands of a Goth of long ago, the ends of the arch cut so as to ruin its round sweep and the whole arch reversed so that the chevron carving is now inside. It was the church's best possession, and it is a pity.

The best possession remaining in the church is the roofing of the transepts, with fine moulded beams, many small bosses, and oak angels looking down. Each transept roof rests on six stone angels and in both roofs we noticed delicately carved bosses in the centre of fine leaves. The best small possession is the 17th century brass of Robert Maiver, an illustrated inscription by a quaint artist who must have enjoyed engraving this skeleton with an arrow, this funny Father Time with his scythe and wings and a flowing curl, this skull with seven teeth and great eyes, and the little spade and pick and crossbones. We may imagine that Robert Maiver would be christened at the 15th century font, a fine piece of carving with a panelled stem and a bowl richly quatrefoiled, borne by eight angels.

The church is rich in parapets, pinnacles, and gargoyles, and its south porch, made new in the 15th century style, has angels bearing up canopied niches on the front, a king and queen at the door, and Peter, John, and Bartholomew looking down. We noticed an old scratch dial, and among the gargoyles something supposed to be the devil devouring an unchristened child, and a fearful-looking dragon climbing up the parapet. The 13th century central tower was made new last century when the spire was taken down and put back stone by stone. It looks down still on the fine cross in the churchyard, 23 feet high on its four steps, carved with the symbols of the Passion, all still clear after 600 years of our English weather. In the village is a noble barn built by the Glastonbury monks in the 15th century.

Dowlish Wake. A shallow mill-stream, one of the sources of the River Isle, flows across the street, dividing the village in two. Horses and cars must ford but there is a stone bridge for those who walk.

It was to this village that they brought John Hanning Speke when he died tragically on the morning he was to tell the British Association of his discovery of the Nile. He lies in the church on the hill, partly rebuilt in the 17th century by his ancestors, with a curious central tower begun in the 15th century. It was a pretty fancy of the builders to carve the corbels above the west doorway, one as a bird clinging to its nest and feeding its little ones, the other showing the second parent bird pecking away at fruit.

There are two fonts, one Victorian, ornate with sculpture of Bible stories and a niche with a figure of Christ bearing the Cross; the other, massive and carved, made soon after the Conquest for a church at West Dowlish burned down c. 1700. It is the only relic of that church. The old font is in the chapel where the Spekes are buried; and here also is the stone figure of an unknown lady wearing a flowing kirtle and a headdress in the fashion of the 14th century, a dog at her feet. Round the recess in which she lies are the faces of two men and two women, turning away from all in the church and gazing down on her. Near by, on a table tomb, lies an armoured knight believed to be John Speke of 1442, with his wife, the last of the Wake family which gave its name to the village. Their figures are almost as new as the day they were fashioned, and round the tomb is a company of little people of their time, an entertaining study for an artist, for they have a fine collection of 15th century costumes. George Speke, who rebuilt this chapel before he died in 1528, is in armour on a small brass.

Downhead. Eight queer men with mouths wide open look down from its tower, which has pinnacles rising above its battlements, and the treasure they guard in this simple place is a font at which children have been christened for 800 years. The porch has the date on it (1751) and from it is a lovely view.

Downside. One of our 20th century surprises, it is like a cathedral that has sprung up unguessed at by most people. Set in the lovely country between Bath and Wells, Downside Abbey is the magnificent home of those English Benedictine monks driven from Douai in 1793 by the French Revolution. They had gone out from Elizabethan England to found a monastery at Douai, and it was persecution which drove them back to freedom. They stayed for 20 years at Acton Burnell in Shropshire and founded Downside Abbey in the year before Waterloo.

It is only in our time that they have crowned their long story with this great white place rising from green terraces, with lawns and banks curving round it in wide sweeps, with noble trees and flowering shrubs. It is a 20th century church, one of the noblest set up in this century. The choir was completed in 1905, the nave nearly 20 years later, and even now it lacks its west end. It is all white and light and spacious, about 110 yards long, the choir about 70 feet high. The aisle and clerestory windows rise magnificent outside with an open parapet above and a great rose window; inside the long line of pointed arches is crowned by a triforium with two double arches in each bay. A dignified angel presides over each pillar of the lofty nave, and the roof is vaulted and has finely carved bosses.

The abbey is filled with small corners of great beauty, chapels complete with altars and glowing with colour.

The Lady Chapel, approached by steps and screened by splendid iron gates crowned with winged angels, has an elaborately carved roof in which the bosses are supposed to represent virtues and the capitals stand for flowers named after the Madonna. The alabaster reredos is panelled with scenes of the Madonna and Jesus, and the frame of the panels is carved into a Jesse Tree. Over the altar of this chapel hangs a canopy of great beauty and tenderness, with angels at the corners and the Madonna in gold. The nine windows are big and fine, and one authority has declared them to be the best modern glass in England. They are effective without keeping back the light, though they have in them about 100 figures, big ones in the lights and small ones in the tracery.

There are more than a dozen other side chapels, all with some features of interest in wood, stone, or glass.

The choir, with impressive arches rising 35 feet, has between these arches stone angels bearing shields recalling men of interest to the abbey—priors, abbots, and benefactors. The richly carved choir-stalls are magnificent with rows of double canopies, one over each side and one over the carved saint in each of the niches above, so that there is probably 15 feet of tabernacle work with delicate wood carving reaching up slender pinnacles towards the height. There are 17 misericords on each side of the choir, all carved as in olden days. The ivory crucifix on the high altar, 19 inches high, is said to be unsurpassed among those of the late 17th century.

There are impressive tombs in the choir aisles. One is a lovely figure of Cardinal Gasquet under a golden canopy. The figure of Bishop Walmesley, who died in 1797, is one of the most beautiful sculptures in Downside. The tomb has been set up by English and American bishops who trace their spiritual descent from him. Also lying in richly embroidered vestments is the figure of Bishop Baines, with a delightful oriel window looking down on him.

Drayton. Its churchyard is like a well-planned garden, with two old yews circled by stone steps, a rockery, and an ancient cross with St Michael fighting the dragon on its shaft. There is a 15th century panelled chancel arch with canopied niches, and an open pulpit with vigorous modern carvings of the winged beasts of the Evangelists.

Dulverton. Set in all the glory of the great amphitheatre Nature made, with the woods and hills of Exmoor closing round it on three sides, it has the River Barle, famous for its trout, flowing under its front doorstep, a sturdy old bridge of five arches. Through the next deep valley the Exe splashes its stony way under the old Hele Bridge to join the Barle at Brushford. The road, following every curve of the Exe through its wooded valley, is one of the most impressive rides in Somerset.

Though the tower of the church is 700 years old, the rest of it was rebuilt in 1852, and much fine work of past ages has been destroyed. Even the Elizabethan cup was stolen and pawned, but chance has returned it to Dulverton. Another inheritance from the old church is a table on carved legs. A bell thought to have come from Barlynch Abbey, now in ruins by the Exe, rings with others of Jacobean days.

There are two memorials to the Sydenhams, who lived from 1540 to 1874 at Combe, a beautiful Tudor house with a bowling green where Drake may have amused himself, for he married a lady of this family who lived across the moor at Monksilver. Was it he, we wonder, who brought here the two Armada medals found under the porch some years ago? The family still has a massive candlestick made of silver and lead from a mine once worked close by the house. A company was floated in the 14th century with a capital of £10 13s 4d, and a messenger was sent to the king on his way to Bannockburn to ask permission to work the mine, a request he granted on being promised half the profits.

Guarding the valley of the Barle are several fortified mounts, of which Mouncey Castle has most to show, though trees now cover the flattened top of this hill. The life of the moor has made great literature, and Dulverton is a name often found in books. Here Jan Ridd met Lorna Doone. Here Richard Jefferies watched the red deer. Here Whyte-Melville found much material for one of his novels. Here also there was born, at Ashway Farm among the hills, a man who left a great mark on the world, Sir George Williams. Every soldier who remembers the Red Triangle in the wars of our time should be grateful to him, for he it was who founded the YMCA.

Dundry. Its noble tower is a welcome sight to Bristol sailors coming home. It was set up by the Merchant Adventurers of Bristol at the end of the 15th century; they set it high on Dundry Hill, 790 feet up, and it is seen right out in the Atlantic.

It rises in plain stone, but at the top becomes a cluster of arcaded turrets and open parapets, with square turrets at the corners like that on one of the towers dominating the streets of Bristol; there must be hundreds of little arches high up. Standing among them we have as wide a view of Somerset as is to be seen from anywhere. There is Bristol with its spires and towers built from the stone of Dundry Hill. There is William Beckford's tower on the hills of Bath. Peeping over the Mendips are the Quantocks. Far away are the hills round Salisbury, north are the hills of Malvern, and across the Severn is the borderland of Wales.

Below us, in this nobly placed churchyard, is an immense square block of stone used by many generations as a dole table for giving out charity, and looking down on the scene are the five ancient steps of the village cross. They are charming. One of the epitaphs time has worn away on these stones once read like this:

> *This earthly spot contains my earthly store,*
> *And after death a king can have no more.*

Except for the ancient figure of a saint locked in the vestry the interest of the church is all outside. The chancel roof has 30 gilded bosses, and above the sanctuary it is picked out with stars of gold.

Dunkerton. Down, down, down, to Dunkerton, under the great railway bridge, over the tiny river bridge, to where a fine old yew has grown up with the ancient church and a magnificent Wellingtonia climbs high above the tower. The altar table is of cedar wood, with two winged angels and panels of wheat and flowers. Even the organ is charming here, made so with delicate gilded carving adorned with angels playing cymbals. Close by it is a fine bench-end by the same craftsman. The font and the piscina are both 14th century. In the tower are remembered two young sons of Admiral Saumarez, one of whom died at sea, and one on an island from yellow fever. There is an old mass dial.

Dunster. It is a surprise for all who have not seen it and the delight of all who have. It seems to belong to centuries past and, lying submissively at the foot of its castle, it brings us back to feudal days. There is no better mediaeval village left in the West than Dunster at the gate of Exmoor; we feel that we are walking through the past, with age-old peeps at every corner; and there is about us everywhere the glory of our English hills, Sedgemoor with its poignant memories and its quiet beauty, and all the wild grandeur of Exmoor, one of the impressive sights all those who would know England must know.

We turn to it off the Minehead road with its fine sweep of the Bristol Channel, and find ourselves running down its wondrous street in the dip of the hills, with the watch-tower in the sky at one end and the castle at the other. At the top of the street the old yarn market keeps company with the ancient inn, and all the way down are houses quaint and old and curious, with lattice windows, low-beamed entrances, and queer chimneys, some with doors still on mediaeval hinges some with wide hearths inside and fine carved stairways, some with timbers said to have come from the wrecks of ships.

One house there is that captivates us as we pass; it is round the corner up the steep hill leading to the church, a long gabled house with a tiled roof and pantiles in front, arranged in a pattern. The storeys overhang each other and each storey has six windows in a row. It is a 15th century block and is now three cottages, but was the guest house of the priory which nestled by the church with the goodwill of the castle. Its walls still stand. We saw the old fireplace at which the monks would warm their hands; we saw lavender growing in their old garden with Madonna lilies, over the wall their old barn (a little spoiled with its new tiled roof), and at the end of the garden the dovecot still as they would see it with its fine round walls, its conical roof rising to a lantern, and about 500 nests inside, any one of them accessible from the revolving ladder.

It is all by the church, part of the same 15th century group which brings mediaeval England back to us. Even now the church is two in one, for there is still the monks' church and the people's. It has been so since 1498, when the transepts, the central tower, and the choir were given to the monks, and the nave was made the people's church. It was then that there was thrown across the church this screen with 14 bays filled with rich tracery, 11 feet high and 20 yards long. It has five rows of carving along the top and 56 slender panels along the bottom. Each of its 14 arches is fan-vaulted, and the whole screen is one of the most impressive pieces of craftsmanship the Flemish artists ever made for an English church.

There is another 14th century oak screen in the south chancel aisle, and a modern screen runs across the tower arch at the entrance of the chancel. Over this screen and over the long one are the doorways of two roodlofts, for Dunster had the western roodloft of the monks' church and the eastern roodloft of the people's. Tucked away in the rich carving of the great nave screen we found two charming heads no bigger than half-crowns, one the head of St James, whose scallop hat we also see among the few specks of old glass which are all that Dunster has left of the original windows.

For 500 years the noble wagon roof has looked down on this old place. It is impressive in its dignified simplicity, with more than a thousand yards of beams spanning the wide space, and 50 finely carved bosses of roses, quatrefoils, and heads. The roof of the south aisle is flat and heavily panelled, with about a hundred small bosses in a lighter oak. It is one of the magnificent legacies of the mediaeval craftsmen who came to Dunster.

They left behind them three chests of three centuries, one of elm from the 12th century, another from the 13th heavily clamped with iron straps, and one of the 14th roughly hollowed out of the trunk of a great oak. They left behind one old bench-end which has been a model for the carving of the others; and some 13th century tiles with the Luttrell arms and fleurs-de-lis on them, companion tiles to those in the floor of the ruins of Cleeve Abbey, where we have seen 1000 as the monks left them. The tiles at Dunster are in the chantry of St Lawrence, a thrilling little place off the chancel, for it has still the old stone altar of the monks, standing where it stood in their own day. The great stone has all the five crosses with which such altars were carved to represent the five wounds of Our Lord, and it has an unusual sixth cross carved on the front.

We found by this old altar a processional cross carried here five centuries ago. In the centre on one side is an engraved portrait of Christ with the emblems of the Passion, and at the four corners are angels and a pelican; the other side has a cross in the centre and gems of colour in enamel representing the Four Evengelists. It is all 14th century and perhaps the rarest small possession of Dunster. There is also a Tudor chalice dated 1573. The font is 15th century, its eight sides carved with emblems of the Passion. The stone pulpit on its fan-like pedestal is modern.

There is a noble group of sculptures of the 14th, 15th, and 16th centuries, mostly of the Luttrells from the castle, or of those who were at the castle before them, a family descended from William de Mohun and his wife Adeliza, who founded the church as the 11th century was closing. The oldest figure here is that of a de Mohun lady who may have married one of the 13th century benefactors of the church. She lies under a canopy with four stately heads hanging from the cusps, two of crusaders and two of their wives.

Sir Hugh Luttrell has lain 500 years on the left of the altar with his wife beside him; he was the gallant knight who built the castle gatehouse, and the first Luttrell to live at Dunster; and still he wears the proud SS collar, though his face is battered away. On the floor of the south chapel is a great stone with the portrait of Lady Elizabeth Luttrell. She has been sleeping here since 1493 with two small angels attending. In the same chapel, on a tomb which must once have been of great splendour, lies her descendant Thomas Luttrell and his wife, their son kneeling at prayer beside them with his own wife sleeping, a very beautiful figure. One portrait brass alone survives from the 15th century; it has the portraits of John and Agnes Wythers.

Though the church is mainly mediaeval we come into it through a splendid Norman doorway, and the west arch of the tower has two slender round columns older than the ruined cross in the churchyard; they come from the days when William de Mohun, a knight high in the favour of the Conqueror, came here from the Battle of Hastings and founded this priory on land the Conqueror gave him. The best features of the fine west doorway, which has been well restored, are the pillars on each side, with bold capitals and the dainty beaded moulding of the outer arch, ending in two fierce heads. The door itself has elaborate iron hinges.

In those days the Normans raised the round towers of Dunster

Castle on the hill. One of them remains with half its wall intact; this and the round columns in the church are almost all that is left of Norman Dunster. Its Norman castle had the tragic boast of being the only one of a dozen Norman castles in Somerset which were dismantled or destroyed by war. It was held for the Empress Matilda against King Stephen by William de Mohun, who coined his own money here even while Stephen's forces surrounded him. The castle has belonged to only two families in all its history, the ancient house of Luttrell having bought it from the widow of the last de Mohun. The fine 15th century house which leads us into it was built in 1421 by Sir Hugh Luttrell; it is 45 feet high and has three storeys with battlements. The mounting steps are still outside it.

The gateway is as it was in the Civil War, when the castle was defended first for the Parliament and then for the king. The Luttrells were for the Parliament, but the castle passed into the hands of the king, and for the last year of the Civil War was the only place in Somerset flying the royal standard. It has a room they call the Leather Gallery, which still has leather hangings of those days painted to look like tapestry, and showing the story of Antony and Cleopatra. The castle passed out of royal hands after furious fighting for 160 days, during which it is said that Blake, annoyed by the long resistance of Colonel Wyndham, threatened to put the colonel's mother in front of the fighting line, but was too proud to carry out his threat when the old lady gallantly told her son to do his duty.

The castle has changed much throughout the centuries, and except for the Norman tower the oldest walls are now in the Tudor half of the front. The oldest part of the structure still in use is the gateway leading up to the terrace; in it, bound with iron bands, hangs a door which has been opening and shutting for 650 years. In this gateway is an ancient prison with an iron keyplate which has spaces for eight keys. In the woodwork of the door is a bullet fired in the Civil War.

We leave this noble place with its famous walls and are down in the street again, looking up to the great watch-tower built for its view and as a landmark for ships in 1775. At the top of the street is the yarn market which has stood here since 1600; it is like no other we have seen, for it has wide overhanging eaves and eight gabled windows, crowned by a lantern. In the centre is a stone pillar from which oak beams spread all round, one with a hole in it said to have been made by a cannon ball. This famous cross was the market for yarn; there is, a little way off, the ruin of another cross where butter was sold, a pillar on broken steps. By the yarn cross is the mediaeval house in which lived the Abbot of Cleeve, now the Luttrell Arms. It is a fine piece of old England and its 15th century gabled porch has openings for crossbows. There is a huge fireplace in the kitchen, and one of the rooms has a plaster fireplace illustrating a classical fable. On a small hill behind the inn are the remains of an embankment made by the Parliamentary troops for bombarding the castle. This and the bullet of the gatehouse door are the witnesses of the last historic events which left their mark on this historic place.

Durleigh. Its most curious possession is a round dovecot with 900 nesting niches made of mud. It is thatched and the walls are protected with plaster and brick, but inside this quaint place is as it was when pigeons were used for training falcons or as the staple winter food of parsons and squires. The dovecot belongs to Bower Farm, a curious building with two round towers circled with grotesque gargoyles. A spiral staircase leads to one tower, its steps worn by the tread of feet, and a stone in the porch has a deep groove where swords were probably sharpened long ago. There is a little old glass.

The church has lost its dedication. Its tower has a gabled roof. The chancel arch is 13th century, the new-looking font is 16th, and three of the oak doors and two of the bells are mediaeval. One of them, inscribed *Ora Pro Nobis*, is believed to be the oldest bell in Somerset.

Durston. Its oldest possessions are the yew still flourishing in the churchyard, and the materials worked into Buckland Farm from the old house of the nuns attached to the priory of the Knights of St John of Jerusalem, the only example in England of a community of women of this Order. The old church was made new in the middle of last century, but the fine tower is the old one with its beautiful traceried windows and its ancient bell, and the carved bench-ends and the altar table had been here about 300 years.

East Brent. Its stone spire, seen for miles, rises from a tower sculptured with three groups one above the other, of God the Father, Our Lord, and the Madonna. Indoors it is the ceiling and the mediaeval glass which draw all eyes. In one window are pictures of the Betrayal, the Judgment, and the Scourging, all 14th century, while the Crucifixion and the Ascension (with just the feet of Jesus appearing under his robe as He rises out of the picture) are copies of the old. Three golden figures in the north windows are thought to be mediaeval German. The ceiling is a rare one of embossed plaster with huge pendants, its crown-of-thorns design picked out in brown in 1637. Glass, plaster, ironwork, and carving—here are fine examples of them all. For ironwork there is an ancient ring and handle to the door; for woodcarving there are lines of 15th century bench-ends, a fine Jacobean pulpit, a bold old eagle with gilded wings; and the Jacobean gallery on newer pillars satisfies us that even galleries are not necessarily bad.

The arms of Glastonbury and the winged beasts of the Evangelists are on the bench-ends, with the initials of Abbot Selwood who built himself a house here. In a Glastonbury manuscript of 1503, called the Terrier of Abbot Beere, is an exact description of this house, with its cloisters and stables, apple and pear orchards, and the elms and oaks where the herons nested; but now the house and the orchards and the herons have gone.

Two stone priests of the 14th century lie in the church, while a layman, probably one of their congregation, lies outside in the grass.

There are paintings on the wall done by Prebendary Denison when curate to his uncle, Archdeacon Denison, who was rector for 61 years last century. He is remembered in the churchyard where he lies, for the old cross has a little sculptured figure in his honour. He died in 1896. He it was who started the village celebrating its harvest home with great festivities which are still carried on.

East Coker. It was an East Coker boy who piloted the ship which brought Robinson Crusoe home. He was William Dampier, born at Hymerford House, the charming thatched place by the mill stream, still with the stately porch he knew so well and the Gothic windows through which he took his first peep of the world he sailed round. His memorial is in the church, which makes a gracious stone group with the Court and the 17th century almshouses reaching up the hill towards them.

The Court is mainly Tudor, with a Georgian wing; the church is Norman and mediaeval, with a tower curiously placed at the east end in the 18th century. A grand carved door with a massive wooden lock and part of an old iron handle opens on a round-columned arcade, the work of Norman masons. Often Dampier must have opened this door; at this Norman font he was baptised. He saw this old chest when it was new; and he may have wondered at the stone figures of two women who lived in his village 600 years ago. One lies by the font, worn and broken, for she was dug up from the churchyard a few years ago; the other, thought to be

Elizabeth Courtenay, has aged too, but a dainty beading still edges her wimple.

On the wall is a brass to the famous son of the village, embossed with his portrait and the sort of ship which brought Alexander Selkirk back from his island. On it is this inscription:

Buccaneer, Explorer, Hydrographer.
Thrice he circumnavigated the Globe, and first of all Englishmen,
explored and described the coast of Australia.
An exact observer of all things in Earth, Sea, and Air, he re-
corded the knowledge won by years of danger and hardship in Books
of Voyages and a Discourse on Winds, Tides, and Currents which
Nelson bade his midshipmen to study and Humboldt praised for scienti-
fic work.

Born at East Coker 1651
He died in London 1751
and lies buried in an unknown grave
The world is apt to judge of everything by the success, and whosoever
has ill fortune will hardly be allowed a good name.

There is treasure to see up a rough lane a mile away, an exquisite gem in the wall of Naish Priory. It is a pointed arch ten feet wide, with moulding spreading into fan-tracery to support an oriel window crowned like a queen on her throne, and with an oak door rich with tracery, through which a small portal is cut. There are octagonal chimneys with bricks arranged like bands of embroidery, and a 15th century window with two heads believed to be Henry IV and Joan of Navarre. All this is to be seen from the lane, and much more if we are fortunate enough for the great oak door to open to us.

We have seen something else from East Coker in Taunton Museum, a tessellated pavement showing two men carrying a stag, dug from a Roman villa on the road to Yeovil.

One of the first Englishmen to see Australia, William Dampier was educated at Yeovil Grammar School, which made him master of a delightful English style of writing and sharpened his faculties as a naturalist. An orphan at 16, he sailed west to Newfoundland, east to the Dutch Indies, came home at 21 to fight against the Dutch, and then began a career of adventure which took him round the world. He joined a gang of privateers who ravaged the isthmus of Darien, capturing towns and ships. With intervals of terrible privation he touched the coasts of China and Australia, returning in 1691 to write his immortal *Voyage Round the World* and a masterly treatise on winds and currents. In 1699 the Government gave him a ship to explore the South Seas, and he sailed along the south-west and north coasts of Australia, finding them horrible, with apparently barren shores, savage men, and terrifying kangaroos. Not until Captain Cook had seen the east coast did Englishmen covet a foothold in this strange land.

In recent years, East Coker has been known particularly as the place which gives its name to the second of T. S. Eliot's *Four Quartets*. Its significance for Eliot lay in the fact that his New England family originated in this Somerset village. The cordwainer Andrew Eliot left East Coker in the middle of the 17th century and settled in Boston, where he became town clerk and assisted at the Salem witch trials. There is a further link. East Coker is the reputed birthplace of Sir Thomas Elyot, whose treatise on education and politics, *The Boke named the Governour* (published in 1531), is echoed in the poem. The American poet who adopted English citizenship chose this village as his last resting place, and the church of East Coker holds his ashes:

In my beginning is my end.

East Cranmore. We look out across Somerset for miles from the tower on the hill above it, 900 feet up. The tower was built last century by one of the Pagets of Cranmore Hall; the hall itself, about a mile from the tower, is now a school.

To this quiet corner, where noble cedars grow higher than the roof of the hall, we come by a lane arched with beeches, passing a church standing in a blaze of rhododendrons in due season. The church is 19th century, but we come to it through small gates which have been opened by generation after generation of Cranmore folk. There has been a church on this spot since Saxon days, and it is thrilling to find a Saxon cross that has been here probably 1000 years; it is from the church built by the Saxons, and is now over the vestry door. This, with the Norman font and four quaint stone heads in the vestry, is all that remains from those ancient days.

East Harptree. Its chief spectacular possession meets us in the porch of its church, a porch as big as some chancels. It has a Norman doorway with a design that is unfamiliar, but its great possession is the huge canopied tomb of Sir John Newton, who lies on it in armour as he was in the days of Henry VIII, Mary I, and Elizabeth I. Under a canopy richly carved all round, resting on six fluted columns with sculptured capitals, its ceiling panelled with

Tudor roses, this proud man lies a bold and stately figure, his hands clasped at prayer. He has lost his wife, but in front of the tomb are groups of his sons and daughters, 20 in all, a captivating procession. Above them is a little man in black and gold, a kneeling Moor delivering up his sword but carrying a crown to show that he is a king. It is the crest won by one of Sir John's crusader ancestors.

There is much old panelling still left—in the tower, on the choir-stalls, on the doors of the aumbry; and some of the benches have fine ends. The splay of one of the chancel windows has the painted head of a saint. Side by side are a peephole and a passage through the chapel to the altar; in the chapel are two old candlesticks painted white and gold, and a dainty silver lamp. There are many old beams in the roofs, and the chancel roof is painted red and green and gold. The font, in spite of its appearance, was made by the Normans.

East Harptree has a great surprise for us, a fine glimpse into a past far older than any church in England. In a stand made from ancient timbers of the church is displayed a pewter vessel nine inches high in which some Roman hoarded his savings. He hoarded them and buried them in a field at Harptree, and in time went away with the Roman legions, his secret hoard remaining unknown. It happened that the summer of 1887 was very dry, and East Harptree was short of water. It was necessary to find a new spring and a search was made in the Mendips. William Currell's spade struck something hard not more than a spade's depth underground; it was the Roman's buried treasure, safe in its pewter hiding-place. In it were 1496 coins of nine emperors, most of them of the fourth century. A few of them are in the British Museum, where we see them as the Harptree Collection, hundreds are scattered elsewhere, but 68 are in this stand above the pewter pot which held them all these centuries, the thrilling possession of this little church, which has arranged them splendidly for us to see. These 68 are of five emperors, Constantius, Gratianus, Julianus II, Valens, and Valentinianus.

In one of the fields hereabouts are still fragments of the old mediaeval fortress of the Harptrees, and in a lovely park is the 18th century Harptree Court with ponds and waterfalls and magnificent gardens. Yet the great house and the fortress are young indeed compared with this handful of coins which come to us from Caesar's world.

East Lambrook. In its ancient church is a window through which the morning sun has been shining for 600 years, and a traceried font to which fathers and mothers were bringing their little ones when the first Tudor king sat on the throne. How long the two men's heads have been looking at each other across the nave we do not know. Two bells hang there in a modern turret, and those who want to hear the parson from the gallery must climb up steps outside.

East Lambrook Manor, a 15th century house with 16th century additions, can be visited by the public once a week during the summer.

East Lydford. The church, rebuilt in 1866 by a rector in memory of his wife, has the carved wooden pulpit from the old church and a font used in Norman England standing by a new one. Another old thing is a charming little alabaster carving of St George on his horse charging a dragon, while a king and queen pray for him from their castle top, and a beautiful damsel, near enough to be in danger if he does not win, adds her prayers to theirs.

Easton-in-Gordano. Its 15th century tower, with pinnacles and parapet, stands among pines and firs, yews and cedars, and it has the unusual type of windows with tracery in the lower half. There are still ancient figures in the four canopied niches. Inside the tower is a lovely arch with four great depths of moulding, and let into the wall above are two old tombs with columns resting on heads of beasts. This and the Norman font are all the church has that is old, for the rest is 19th century.

East Pennard. Cottages eye us from among the trees and an old farm stares through mullioned windows, till we think the road has brought us into private grounds, so neat is the open space with the shrubs in the middle. It is, however, just one of East Pennard's pleasant ways. Here is the church with its lovely windows, and a rose carved on the thickset tower. We look up at the mediaeval roof with embattled tiebeams, carved bosses, and stone angels. We admire the exquisite panels fronting the gallery. We note how time has faded the radiance of the painted angels above the new screen. We wonder whether the oak pulpit was carved by Grinling Gibbons, for it has his open-peapod signature among its fruits and flowers; and we pass on to the Jacobean stalls with their slender balustrade, and the fragments of mediaeval glass above the rich silver candlesticks on the altar.

It is by the font that we pause, a splendid Norman font with four weird heads grinning below the arcaded bowl, one like a monkey,

Dunster Castle: the Leather Gallery.

Dunster: the yarn market and main street.

Exmoor: Badgworthy Water.

Farleigh Hungerford Castle.

Glastonbury Tor.

Glastonbury: the George and Pilgrims Inn.

Glastonbury Abbey from the east.

Glastonbury Abbey: the abbot's kitchen.

one a bearded demon, and two sphinxes, all with bird claws, and with four horned heads at the base. The ancient cross holds up a new carving of the Crucifixion in memory of men who died in the Great War.

Wrax Hill here is well worth the climb for the lovely view.

East Quantoxhead. It is said to be the only piece of Somerset that has not been sold since the Conqueror came. Here was a Luttrell in the days of Magna Carta, and here was a Luttrell when we called. They built this village group with the church, the house, and the farm over 500 years ago on the rising ground above the pond.

We came to the church by a path of soft turf through a bower of roses, sweet briar, and honeysuckle, and indoors we found the beauty of dark oak carved against grey stone. These bench-ends were carved 500 years ago, and the pulpit of Cromwell's day matches them in bold design, as do the altar rails and the screen. There is a fine piece of carved stone in the canopy of Hugh Luttrell's tomb, the work of a 16th century craftsman. The east window is in memory of another Luttrell with an astonishing record, Alexander Fownes Luttrell; he was rector here for 70 years last century, but was actually ministering here two years longer. It is one of the oldest records of service we have come upon in all our visits to 10,000 places.

In another window is ancient glass with a curious and intricate pattern symbolical of the Trinity.

Edington. This and Wiltshire's Edington both claim to be the Aethandune where Alfred defeated the Danes and saved Christianity in England. If it is to lose this claim (as we fear it must), Somerset's Edington has little left to it save its view of the Polden Hills, and for intimate beauty its Norman font, deeply carved with festoons and cable moulding, and bits of oak carving left in the chancel from the 15th century church, out of which look quaint faces with long moustaches. Herons may sometimes be seen flying to their home in the trees, and here came the Romans, leaving a kiln and heaps of pottery behind.

Elworthy. On Willett Hill is the tower a rich man built to look at from his window, and on the other side of the road is the long ridge of Elworthy Barrows, 1300 feet up. The tiny church has a delicately carved screen painted with roses and thistles, its early 14th century tracery let into a framework made in 1632. The old pulpit is approached by the roodloft stairs.

E   117

Emborough. For 700 years this church has stood in a lonely place, now with a farm beside it, its tower rising above the low farm buildings with a view of the great world below. There is a noble group of fields at the corner and a fine old yew at the gate.

It has one of the oddest little interiors in Somerset, a poor nave with a white ceiling simply adorned with six bunches of roses and lilies, and a tiny chancel seen through the tower. Set at the foot of the parapeted and pinnacled tower, the chancel out of doors looks like a miniature, and so it is, little more than a wide passage as we look into it through the two tower arches.

In this tiny sanctuary floor is a stone with two small portraits cut in it. Often must some mother's heart have almost broken as she looked at these small faces, drawn as a child might draw them on a slate. Poor little John and Elizabeth! They left this world in 1700, and much would we give to know their story. Below their portraits we are told:

> These pretty babes for long did play
> Before the Lord called them away.

There is one more village portrait on the wall of the nave, a white medallion of Robert Bath, who would see these pretty babes at play. In this same floor is another pathetic tale of little ones, three who died under three, one in 1726, the second in 1729, and the third in 1730. The father followed them in 1732 and the afflicted mother lived on another generation. There is a fine Norman font. Near it at the west end a gallery rises on oak pillars.

Englishcombe. It has been the home of Saxons and of Normans, and both have made their mark on it. The Saxons carried Wansdyke through it; it marches past the church. The Normans gave it the tower with three stone seats for priests in its arches, the font at which its children are still baptised, the doorway through which we come to it, and those lines of carved stone underneath the cornice, half-worn away but some of them still with the faces the Norman craftsmen gave them—a toothless man with glaring eyes, a man asleep, a muzzled dog, a melancholy looking fellow, and a savage fellow holding his mouth open to show his teeth. On the wall is a mass dial.

The tower arches inside have been pointed since the Normans left them. One of them has a projecting round column with a capital sculptured into a face with goggle eyes and a dozen great teeth showing. Above the eastern arch, looking down on the altar, is a remarkable bambino, a tiny figure of Christ in swaddling clothes. A roughly carved stone on a bracket in the nave is supposed to be an ancient head of Our Lord.

Above the chapel off the nave is a clerestory window of the 15th century, with glass which has been in it all the time, still rich with gold. Other great windows have panelled splays carved with the arms of the monks of Bath Abbey who refashioned the church, and with the emblems of the Passion. The Norman font has a 15th century cover. The chancel has tall early 14th century windows.

The tithe barn near the church belonged to the monks, and in the days when it would be filled with corn the green mound we see from the churchyard was crowned with a castle. It was the home of the Gournays, one of whom was summoned in 1297 for keeping in it a pillory, gallows, and tumbril.

Enmore. Two yews guard its ancient cross, one 19 feet round and hollow, the other 15 feet round and solid. Waving its branches to them from the garden of Enmore Hall is a venerable cedar as lovely as a tree can be. The 15th century tower of the church has long pinnacles rising from the buttresses and small ones crowning the turret. We come in through a deeply carved Norman doorway to find a Norman font which has been refashioned, a magnificent oak pulpit of Jacobean days, and an old chest. Hanging on the walls are two ancient helmets, one of the kind worn at the time of the Armada, the other with a crest of a wyvern, a fearful-looking beast.

Evercreech. It has a fine square at the heart of the village with the cross on five worn steps, an old wall and old cottages, a vicarage, lovely almshouses bordering on the churchyard, and a church dominated by a tower noble with rich carvings, its great windows filled with open tracery, its buttresses pinnacled all the way.

One above the other rise the parapets of the aisles and clerestory, and round the walls runs a wonderful gallery of gargoyles, among the best in Somerset. They climb up and run down and creep along the cornice. At one corner two cats seem to be playing a game, one catching the other; a wrinkled creature with sharp claws has a face like Mr Punch; and there is a laughing monkey on a stick, climbing up a pinnacle. The quatrefoiled parapets have roses and shields and one a lovely head, and St Peter stands in a niche of the tower, greeting all who come. There is an old mass dial.

Indoors the eye is drawn to the fine painted roof of the nave, its ribs red, black, and white, with 16 painted angels and gilded bosses.

The roof has been here here 500 years but the colour has been renewed. The stone pulpit and the font match one another though there is 500 years between them. The modern pulpit is borne on a group of the merriest angels we have seen; the 15th century font has fine niches with a band of foliage under the bowl and a row of little windows and shields above. There are two brass candelabra, both 18th century and charming, and both crowned with doves, and hanging in the tower are ten old leather fire-buckets from the days before the fire brigade.

Exford. This Exmoor village has within recent years come into a great inheritance. In its church stands a 15th century screen where before was only the low stone railing now by the font. Though newly patched, it is hard to believe that the screen has not always been here, and still harder to believe that such work could lie forgotten for over forty years. In 1857 the screen was in the church of St Audries, on the sea side of the Quantocks. The next year the church was pulled down and rebuilt, and the fan-vaulted screen was not wanted. It was packed in pieces, stored in a barn, and forgotten. For over a generation it lay there, till found by someone who knew its worth. It was offered to the neighbouring village of Williton, but would not fit the new church there; so it was packed up again and sent to South Kensington. Although it had once been quoted by an authority as a model for church builders, it still lay in pieces, for it would have cost too much to set it up in the museum; but it was no longer forgotten. Church after church in West Somerset was measured till they came to Exford, and here was a church which had room for it, was worthy of it, and was prepared to pay for it. Everyone in Exford gave something till £700 was collected, and the screen set up with the missing parts replaced.

The church has another interesting possession in the arcade of clustered pillars with wreathed capitals, built about 1532. The oldest part is the 15th century tower with a quaint little demon with two angels outside the west window, while the font is 100 years older.

Beyond the broken shaft of the ancient churchyard cross a path leads to a labourer's home, with a high wide porch and fine arches which proclaim it no ordinary cottage. We may guess from its name that it was once used by priests, for it is called Prescott. The rest of the village gathers round a delightful old inn at the bottom of the hill by the shallow Exe, which flows on through a valley once covered with mighty oaks. Only a few feet below the soil we come upon the blackened trunks of this primeval forest.

Exton. The bare bones of Exmoor show in humped grey rocks through the surface of the steep road to Exton, and as rugged as the road is the roughly built church. The tower is 700 years old at the base, and a patch in the nave walls looks like the herringbone masonry of the early Norman builders. One of the bells has the initials of Roger Semson, who was making bells in Somerset 400 years ago. The chalice was made by an Elizabethan silversmith. Below is the hamlet of Bridgetown, with two old bridges over the Exe.

Farleigh Hungerford. It is a thrilling corner of Somerset. For centuries its fine little bridge across the Frome has brought great people this way, some to the church on the hill, all to the castle below it, the church carrying on with all its memories of 500 years, the castle a shadow of its former self (though now in the care of the Ministry of Public Building and Works), with noble chestnuts and beeches standing sentinel among the ruins. The grass is green in the moat, the watch-towers are broken and silent, but it is a famous place to which we pass through Farleigh's great gate.

Here the Hungerfords lived from 1369 to 1681, one of the richest English families, whose pride it was that they could ride from here to Salisbury on their own land. Their wheatsheaf and two sickles are on the gatehouse, their marble tombs are down these steps, their crests are carved in oak on the roof, their shining armour is hanging on the walls. Here lies the man who built this place, first Speaker of the House of Commons, the proud Sir Thomas Hungerford. He laid out this court 180 feet long, he raised four towers 60 feet high, and set up these walls six feet thick. The castle, started by Sir Thomas and finished by his son, was a stronghold of the stately Tudor Age, stood through the Civil War, and was brought low by a favourite of Charles II, who himself was banqueted here; today all that is left complete is a 14th century chapel, one of the most stirring museums in our countryside.

We reach it down seven steps and are astonished at the treasures in this small place. The walls are hung with armour, and the chantry is enriched with about 100 painted shields. By the altar is a wall-painting of St George battling with the dragon, a kneeling knight beside him. On the walls hang a crusader's sword, some coffin handles, a set of Saracen mail, and a scimitar.

On a Jacobean pulpit is a fine carving of a man smiling on his unseen congregation, and the oak reredos has a Madonna among cherubs. Everywhere about us is something beautiful in wood and iron and glass and stone, and everywhere is something moving to those whose minds run down the past. Here is a font which is all that is left of a church, with two fragments of stone which is all that is left of a village; the church was St Michael's in the lost village of Rowley. Here are tombs rich with carvings and colour, a gallery of painted heraldry, iron grilles, and scores of old glass panels, sculptured figures among the best in Somerset, armour and spoils from Agincourt and Crecy.

In five table tombs and in the lead coffins below sleep lords and ladies of this famous house, the first and the last of the Hungerfords. They brought Sir Thomas Hungerford here in the 14th century, and his wife Lady Joan in due course. They had seen great days, for he had been at Agincourt with Henry V and had presided over the House of Commons as its first Speaker in the days when it met in the Chapter House of Westminster Abbey. We can see where he sat today. His tomb, lying just inside the 14th century iron grille, is finely painted with coats-of-arms and has five charming small figures between them. By the tomb hangs a copy of the last will of Lady Joan, wishing to be laid here and desiring that on her funeral day twelve torches should be borne by twelve poor women, clothed in russet with linen hoods and wearing suitable shoes and stockings. She willed 200 marks for prayers to be said for the health of her soul and the souls of all her ancestors for ever, and to her son's daughter Katherine her black mantle furred with miniver, to her grandson a green bed embroidered with one greyhound.

Next to them, in a black and white tomb of great magnificence, sleep Sir Edward Hungerford and his Lady Margaret. Their white figures rest on a bed of black marble eight feet long, set up by the widow in her lifetime. She founded the Hungerford almshouses at Corsham in Wiltshire, and here at Farleigh in 1648 she laid her lord. Their two figures are among the best sculptures of Stuart times, and time has suffered them no wrong.

In another tomb sleeps Sir Walter Hungerford who died in 1583; in another Sir Edward and his Lady Jane; and in another that Mary Hungerford of whom we read that she was the wonder of her sex.

At the west end of the chapel is the gravestone of a 15th century priest who still sleeps here. His figure is engraved on the stone, and he was seen when the stone was raised in the 19th century, his teeth still perfect; he lived in the house still standing by the chapel.

The old glass is of great interest, most of it being Continental work of the 15th century. That in the east window shows Moses and the Brazen Serpent, Job and his wife, with various saints, among them being St Collette praying with two devils, one flying out of the window. In the chantry the light falls on the tombs through a window in which we see the story of St Collette in Flemish glass. She is shown as a dwarf in her little bed, with her mother praying that she might grow up tall and graceful and become an abbess. The prayer was answered, and the cripple girl grew up miraculously to be the beautiful St Collette, who is shown doing penance with scourge and scorpions.

The pitiful memories of two women cling about these walls, both in the desperate times of Henry VIII. One was the wife of the first Lord Hungerford, who was imprisoned by her husband in one of the towers; the other was that bravest woman of the brave, Margaret Pole, Countess of Salisbury, last of the Plantagenets. She was born within these walls while the Hungerfords were away; these towers would be the first impressive sights she saw in the long and crowded life which ended in her butchery by Henry VIII.

A little way up the hill stands the church which looked down on the Hungerfords in all their glory. It has a wagon roof with carved bosses and a cornice with winged angels and grotesques. The chancel has fine iron gates, the panelled oak pulpit is carved with strange birds, the altar rails are curious 19th century work looking older, and one of the pews has some Tudor linenfold. The altar is made from a chest of the Commonwealth period, and an old altar stone is set in the floor of the sanctuary.

There is much old glass. The east window has fragments showing St Leonard, St Christopher, and the Madonna. There is also in Flemish glass a picture of the Day of Judgment, and the picture of a hunted hind appealing to St Leonard for protection. Another panel has the head of a man in armour, probably Sir Thomas Hungerford.

A peaceful little place, it has over the doorway an ancient stone with a Latin prayer 700 years old, praying that it may be a temple of peace for all who come this way.

Farmborough. It has a little stream running through it coming down from Barrow Hill, and four fine gargoyles keeping guard on the pinnacled tower which has looked down on it all for 500 years. A rose window in the north aisle has a little old glass and there are a few more fragments in a small round window at the end of a curious passage into the chancel. Built into the south wall are fragments of old stone carving.

The font is curious because it is made of plaster. There are thousands of stone fonts in England and about 30 lead ones, but this is the only plaster one we have seen; it has roses in its panels.

Farrington Gurney. All the church has to show us is outside, a little old man in his niche above the west door. The village folk call him Old Farrington and think he may have been Thomas Gournay, lord of the manor 700 years ago. A quaint little fellow he looks, holding something worn away, very much like a crucifix.

Fiddington. On the flats near the sea, its only treasures are in the 14th century church. The new seats have old carved bench-ends, and there is a Jacobean oak pulpit, a font looking new yet nearly as old as the church, a mediaeval bell, and the base and shaft of an ancient cross.

Fitzhead. A high buttressed wall runs along one side of its street guarding Fitzhead Court, the home of the great family here in Stuart days; but far older than this house is the elegant church-yard cross looking as it has looked for 700 years, but with the tiny canopied figures made new. The church has a glorious 15th century fan-vaulted screen and there are many bench-ends probably carved by the same craftsmen. The tithe barn still belongs to the church, but is used for people instead of corn.

Fivehead. The treetops are dark in Swell Wood, where the herons have one of their chief colonies in Somerset. It is on other trees, the stately elms, that the 15th century tower looks out through a window with traceried transoms, the best in this church; but most we liked the little Norman font with the band of cable moulding and a delicate design along the top, and the curious palimpsest brass, which is really three in one. A smiling lady has on the other side of her the praying hands and part of the cope of a 15th century priest, linked to two little figures like saints and the words in Latin *Who died Friday*.

The smiling lady is Jane Seymour, wife of Protector Somerset's eldest son. The name of her father, John Walsh, is on the house he built here, Cathanger Farm, a lovely home with a Court Room and a paved way across the turf to an ancient gatehouse. It is said that one day this lawn was crowded and the windows were flung open, for young John Wesley was preaching one of his first sermons.

Langford Manor is another old neighbour, so old that in 1518 it was given by Sir John Speke, ancestor of Africa's great explorer, to pay for masses to be said for his mother and children in the Speke

Chapel of Exeter Cathedral. It was altered in Stuart times, and today, in a walled-in garden, its old dovecot stands without a roof.

Flax Bourton. We need not be surprised if we are told that the preacher here stands on a pinnacle of the tower, for it blew down and became the foundation for the pulpit. The church comes from the 12th and 15th centuries, with a Norman font, a Norman doorway, and a Norman chancel arch. The doorway is curiously tall and narrow, with banded pillars and various mouldings, and above is a crude carving of the Archangel Michael spearing the dragon with a bishop's crozier. The chancel arch, still marked with the axe which hewed it, is lovely, and has dragons coiling below its capitals, on one of which an animal is peering out among the ferns. Two little animals like rabbits are at a window in the charming chancel, with its new panelled oak roof. On the outer wall is an old mass dial, opposite the church is the old Angel Inn, and not far away is the fine wooded gorge of Bourton Combe.

Foxcote. It is the last place we should expect to find in Pepys, for it is almost nowhere; but it comes into Pepys because there were born here the twin maids whose stone figure he went to see in the church at Norton St Philip. They had one body between them. The little church was rebuilt in 1721 and is a simple attractive fabric. There is a large monument to Robert Smith (1714) of reredos type and another to the Rev Robert Smith (1769) of obelisk form, with weeping cherubs between a skull and urn.

Freshford. Its street runs up to a height and down again, and at the top is the 15th century church, with a friendly man looking down from the cornice of its western tower, where two angels above the door have two wings between them. Its Norman font is its chief possession. Its walls are rich with tablets of thankfulness for lives well lived.

Frome. It runs up and down and in and out with steep and narrow streets full of quaint old houses, and with a river from which it takes its name. The roads out of it lead into some of Somerset's loveliest villages and bring us in a few minutes to Wiltshire.

At the top of one of its hills, in the shadow of the wall of its oldest church, Bishop Ken lies in an unromantic grave. Millions have sung his hymns, for he wrote such famous lines as, "Glory to Thee, my God, this night," and millions remember his name as one of the seven bishops who sounded the death knell of the Stuarts. For him his

125

death knell sounded at Longleat, the famous and beautiful Wiltshire house a few miles away at Horningsham, where he was staying in retirement. They buried him here outside the walls, six poor men in the parish carrying him to his grave at sunrise; it was his wish that it should be so, but it can hardly have been his wish that his grave should be so poorly housed.

The church stands where St Aldhelm built his church more than 1250 years ago, and there is still in one of the walls, close by the chapel with Bishop Ken's window, a stone from St Aldhelm's church. It still has on it knotwork carving of the Saxon mason and a lion with his tail between his legs. The next oldest thing is the 14th century Lady Chapel; the rest has been made new. From the 18th century comes the bell with the inscription:

> *God made Cockey and Cockey made me,*
> *In the year of our Lord 1743.*

It has much that is fine and good to see, but Somerset has hundreds of churches with more charm and more of ancient beauty. We feel that Frome has done too much with this old place. It has too much of everything. Somebody has not been able to leave it alone. Inside and out it is ornate. We climb to it up steps from the street, lined with a gallery of sculptured groups of about 50 figures, scenes on the Road to Calvary. We reach the door and find stone figures everywhere. They fill every corner, on the guttering, round about the walls, a remarkable collection. Out in the rain are bats and griffins and crocodiles, heads of all kinds, a wild man tearing his mouth open to show huge teeth. On a capital on one of the doors we noticed carvings of birds among flowers, one looking at its eggs in the nest.

The most beautiful possession of the church is its oldest, the Lady Chapel, with a series of fine modern Kempe windows of 12 little scenes from the life of Christ. It has a lovely iron screen dividing it from the nave, and a tomb with open stonework through which we see the stone image of a skeleton. It has been here about 400 years, and is believed to be the tomb of a knight of the Leversedge family. It was Robert Leversedge who built the iron screen of this chapel in the 17th century.

On the wall of the chapel is a relief by Westmacott of two sisters embracing each other, daughters of Lord Cork. On another wall is a monument to two infants lying with a skull, two of six children of one family all dying as infants. A curious old painting on iron has on it the fading figures of a man and his wife with their 11 children.

In the floor of the chapel of St Nicholas is a pavement of 14 square tiles daintily engraved black on white with the Seven Virtues and the Seven Vices. They are very neat. Neat also is the roodloft, which has been set up in place of the ancient one; it is painted in red and blue and gold and green, with a cross made by the peasants of Oberammergau. The ancient piscina is still where it was set in the wall for use from the old roodloft.

Perhaps the most effective of all the decorations of this much-decorated church are the windows, mostly by Kempe. In some of the great windows of the nave the figures are striking and the colours fine.

Glastonbury. It has been in the dreams of men from the days of King Arthur till now, and there are those who will always believe that the Glastonbury Thorn is the child of one planted by the man who buried Jesus, Joseph of Arimathea. The story is that he was sent to bring the good news from Galilee to the Britons, that he thrust his stave in the ground of Wirral Hill where it burst into blossom, that he buried the Holy Grail at Glastonbury Tor, and built a chapel of wattle and daub which grew through the centuries into the noble Norman abbey which stands magnificent in ruin to this day. It is known throughout Europe as Avalon, the Sleepy Island of the Blest.

If we believe all its legends Glastonbury should be our sacred place, for the legends tell us that St Patrick's bones lay here, that here King Arthur was buried, and that here was the tomb of Joseph of Arimathea. It is not necessary to believe them, for Glastonbury is enough. If the modern town had been worthy of its ancient fame it would still have been one of the loveliest towns in England, with a glow about its streets that would bring the pilgrim here from the world's end. The pity is that this shrine of so much that is woven into our island story has been in the keeping of those who have betrayed their trust, and Glastonbury, Isle of Avalon, has become a town of mean streets and commonplace houses, its jewels mixed with vulgar things. Its Tor draws the traveller for many miles round and we all come here on pilgrimage, but having seen what we came to see we hasten away.

What Glastonbury has for us to see is the famous Tor standing out for miles as we ride about Somerset, a magnificent 15th century church standing proudly halfway up the street with the Glastonbury Thorn growing between trimmed yews, the tithe barn with its great roof, the noble front of the old guest house by the ancient Tribunal of the abbots, the remains of a lake village older than the Roman Empire; and the abbey ruins nearly 600 feet long, with the walls of a nave that rose 100 feet from floor to roof.

The Charter of the abbey, signed by King Ina, is still in existence, one of the oldest charters in England, for it has seen 12 centuries go by. The real greatness of the abbey began with Dunstan about 1000 years ago; he was born in 924 at Baltonsborough near by, and rose to be the most powerful man of his age.

This wonderful Somerset man, who lived through more than 60 years of the tenth century, rose to be Primate of England in the days when the Church ruled the State. He was one of the most famous men of our first 1000 years, and his influence was in all ways beneficent and humane. As a boy he lived at the court of King Athelstan, but was too scholarly and mystical for the boisterous sons of the Saxon nobles. He was happiest in solitude, poring over books, and he carried a harp about with him, for he loved music; it has been said that he was the greatest English musician before the Conquest. He was painter, calligraphist, worker in silver and gold, and took a great delight in the company of craftsmen and skilled metal-workers, loving to be with them at the forge. When Edmund became king he recalled Dunstan to his court, although he had become a monk; but jealousies arose and the king did him wrong, for which he afterwards grieved and, calling Dunstan to follow him on horseback, he led him to Glastonbury, took his hand, kissed him, and made him abbot. Dunstan was but 21, but he began the building-up of Glastonbury, working out plans for education, and he was in the midst of his reforming zeal when Edmund was murdered by a robber in Gloucester; he lies there in a magnificent tomb. His successors chose Dunstan as their adviser, but the abbot, opposing King Edwy in an unlawful marriage, found himself out of favour and fled to Flanders, being afterwards recalled by King Edgar and made Archbishop of Canterbury, joining with the Archbishop of York in crowning Edgar at Bath as a formal declaration of the unity of all England under one king.

Dunstan lived on into the last quarter of the century, burying King Edgar, and also his son Edward the next king, who was murdered at Corfe Castle; it was Dunstan who gave him a dignified burial at Shaftesbury, where we may see his grave and something of his remains. He helped to crown King Ethelred, and for the last ten years of his life lived apart from kings, teaching, studying, and encouraging charity among the people, and closing his life in great serenity, having left a deep impression on a rude age.

The Conqueror found Dunstan's monastery one of the richest in these islands, so that it was said that could the Abbot of Glaston marry with the Abbess of Shaston their heir would have more land than the king. Then it was that the belief grew up that King Arthur was buried here, and we read in the books that a massive oak trunk was found, 16 feet deep, with the words: *Here lies interred in the Isle of Avalon the renowned King Arthur.*

In the 12th century the wattle church of Joseph of Arimathea was burned and a new church was opened in 1186. These are its ruins. In fashioning the choir they set up a stately mausoleum at the east end in which were placed what were said to be the relics of Arthur and Guinevere. It is a legend, but tradition has made the spot a sacred place.

It is 600 years since the cloisters and the domestic quarters were built, and in the 16th century Leland described his rejoicing at the sight of this great place and all its literary treasures. Then came the fall of the monasteries; the first monastic foundation in England, it was one of the last to go.

Standing in this thrilling place, roofless but beautiful, it is pitiful to remember the last day of the last abbot of Glastonbury. The martyrdom of Richard Whiting has been called the blackest page in the history of the dark work of Thomas Cromwell. The old abbot was lodged in the Tower of London and the treasures of the abbey were sent up to Whitehall. There is a letter from Richard Pollard informing Cromwell that the old abbot had been drawn through the town on a hurdle to the hill called the Tor and put to execution there. His old head, white with 80 years, was stuck on the abbey gate and his body was quartered and sent to four Somerset towns. The king took the treasure and the abbey buildings were left to be a common quarry, anyone taking what he liked; so that down to the 18th century the stones of Glastonbury were used in making roads to Wells.

We can stand on the spot where the wattle church stood before Alfred was born; it is called St Mary's Chapel. It has been roofless 300 years but there is colour still on the walls. Its north door is the most wondrous fragment of the abbey still left to us, a marvellous piece of Norman sculpture, black with age. It has four bands of moulding rich with foliage, decorated ornament, and scenes from the New Testament. It has carvings of the Annunciation, the Salutation, and the Adoration of the Wise Men in one band; another shows the Wise Men returning to their own country, and others the Flight into Egypt, the Massacre of the Innocents, Joseph hearing of the death of Herod, and the Return from Egypt. It is an astonishing survival of a piece of art exposed to the winds and rains of centuries. In the opposite wall of the chapel is the original dedication stone marked Jesus Maria, with bullet holes above the inscription.

We are able to see here a remarkable piece of building work, for we can go down into a crypt built under the floor of this chapel after the chapel was complete. The floor has vanished, so that the crypt is roofless except for one small fragment, but it is known that there was carried out here a feat of our 15th century builders which can only be compared with the relaying of the foundations of Winchester Cathedral by a man who plunged into the morass below it and set the cathedral on a mass of concrete. The chapel was here when the crypt was formed, and the chapel floor was raised to allow the crypt sufficient height, massive walls six feet thick being carried twelve feet below the foundations. When clearing this crypt in 1925 about twenty oak coffins were found, and in one coffin was a skeleton with a pilgrim's staff.

No less remarkable as a piece of early craftsmanship is the abbot's kitchen, with four fireplaces; it was built 600 years ago and remains complete. It is 70 feet high and 40 feet square, and is built of stone. Eight arched ribs carry scores of tons of masonry in the roof, the ribs meeting at a centre ring out of which rises a lantern, meant for ventilation. The lantern is stone, 12 feet across, and weighs many tons, yet it seems to hang lightly in space, and a builder who has examined it failed to find a single crack that could be thought a sign of weakness.

As an impressive spectacle the great nave of Glastonbury, open to the sky, ranks with our noblest ruins. We have here the whole range of the abbey church spread about us for 600 feet, 200 feet longer than Wells Cathedral, with transept walls reaching 175 feet and columns 100 feet high.

There still stands just below the church the old guest house of the monks, now an inn. Built in 1475, it has one of the finest fronts of any inn in England. Set in the battlements is the stone figure of a craftsman, and in the panels are painted heraldic shields. We can take coffee in a parlour which is much as it was when the monks were here, and sleep in bedrooms with oak beams which have not been changed since the 15th century. Almost next door is the old house where the abbot dispensed justice with the powers of a judge; below the court house is a dungeon.

To not a few pilgrims who come this way the most captivating of all the possessions of Glastonbury will be its great stone tomb. If the story woven about it were true it would be perhaps the most sacred thing in England, for the story is that in it they laid Joseph of Arimathea.

It is a wonderful sarcophagus, sculptured in quatrefoils with little ornaments, and it has been known as a remarkable tomb for hundreds of years. Some time in the fifth century it was written that Joseph lay in Glastonbury, and in 1367 a chronicle said that the bodies of Joseph and his companions were found there. In the 15th and 16th centuries there was talk of a celebrated shrine in Glastonbury churchyard, and men went on pilgrimage to Joseph's tomb. The story may be a myth but the tomb is here for all to see, set in the middle of St Catherine's Chapel in Glastonbury church. Looking down on it from one wall is the cope of the old abbot and his apron with three roses on it, pathetic witnesses of the glory that has passed away. Looking down on it from the opposite wall is a picture said to be almost certainly a Correggio. It shows two women and a boy with a snake, and is one of many fine pictures of Italian masters hanging in the church.

On each side of the chancel arch is an altar tomb. In them sleep Richard Atte Welle and his wife; they have been here since the end of the 15th century, her tomb with six weepers, his with seven. There is a great chest which Richard and his wife must have seen, for it was bought for the church in 1421; it has the arms of St George.

By the altar in the chancel are two windows rich with 15th century glass. One shows a small green cross made of thorn, and there are Tudor roses, doves, a bishop, and flaming suns. The other window has twelve charming figures, with the Madonna in white wearing a crown of gold. The old hourglass-stand is still in the new pulpit, the panels of which have the Twelve Apostles in stone.

Facing St Catherine's Chapel with its famous tomb is St George's Chapel with another tomb, in which lies John Cammell, a 15th century treasurer of the abbey. He is a fine alabaster figure and has four weepers and five camels round him. The chapel has become the War Memorial, and the simple wooden screen through which we enter is in memory of the men who died for us. Along the top of its open panels are pieces of ancient oak carving found built into Glastonbury's cottages; one is a vigorous St George slaying the dragon, another is the old carver's expression of extreme sacrifice, a pelican feeding its young with its blood.

A painting of the Crucifixion brought from Liège during the Great War has been set up in a reredos made from 15th century linenfold.

Inside and out the tower has something for us to see. Outside, looking down from the top, is the Glastonbury Imp, a queer grinning fellow, and below him is a bishop on a bat's back; inside is the old clock of the tower, resting on the floor. It beat out the time from 1719 to 1929 and then stopped suddenly, and after an inquest it was put on the floor as a museum piece, with the old carillon beside it. Two of the oldest church clocks in England were made by Glastonbury monks; they tell the time at Exeter and Wimborne.

Round the marketplace with its modern cross are many old houses, including almshouses built by two ancient abbots, one of whom built St Benedict's Church, close by, about 1520. The almshouses have battered stones which were once greyhounds and dragons, roses and crowns, and they have a small chapel with a very beautiful stone window. In St Benedict's Church, which has a fine little tower and a mediaeval stone pulpit, lies Sir Henry Gold, the judge who was grandfather of Henry Fielding, father of the English novel; Fielding was born at Sharpham two miles away. A little way above the ruins stands the fine old abbey barn, shaped like a cross and nearly 100 feet long. It has a splendid timber roof and stone carving of religious emblems in the gables, where we see the symbols of the Four Evangelists; it is about 500 years old. The roof is an ingenious piece of timber work, forming a double series of arches resting on the tiebeams.

Glastonbury's small museum has a remarkable collection of things concerning the old town and its lake village. We saw an abbey key found in the ruins, a small medallion of old glass painted with a Tudor rose, a pilgrim's staff from a stone coffin, and a pilgrim's leather bottle. There was a little stone man from the old market cross, a fragment of wattle from a house, and two draughtsmen from Saxon and Norman England; our fathers played draughts 1000 years ago.

Up above it all, above the hill where Joseph of Arimathea is said to have thrust his staff into the ground, and above the high place where he is said to have buried the Holy Grail (the site today known as the Chalice Well) rises the Tor, the Island Mount of St Michael, 500 feet above the sea and crowned by all that is left of St Michael's Chapel, shattered by an earthquake or a landslip in 1271 and rebuilt in the 15th century. It has a ruined tower, built probably in the 14th century and restored in the 19th, and over its west doorway are two queer sculptures, a woman milking a cow and St Michael weighing souls.

Goathurst. Longer than man can remember the herons have made their home with the red deer of Halswell Park; there were about forty pairs when we called, the biggest heronry but one in Somerset. They are protected by the Tyntes of Halswell House, who built their home in this great park in Tudor days, and decorated it with the art of Grinling Gibbons. Their memorials are in the church. One of their proud sons sat in seven Parliaments, and one of their 17th century knights is here with his wife and nine children kneeling round him; a small child of the family is here asleep, sculptured in 1835. The family pew has a peephole cut through a wall to the altar, and in it rests armour carried at the funerals long ago.

By the church (which has an old mass dial) is the old manor house in which the rector was living when we called, dining every night with a magnificent plaster barrel roof over his head.

Godney. The monks called it the Island of God; one of their seals has been found among the ruins of Glastonbury Abbey. Yet it is older than any monk, older than Christianity itself, for the chief possession of Godney is the field to which we come through a white gate on which is written British Village.

Hardly a car would stop to look at it, but those who are wise are not indifferent to this field with the little mounds which were once islands in themselves standing high in the marsh, each one with a hut of wattle and daub set on piles, a hearthstone in the middle and a thatched roof overhead. There have been counted 80 or 90 of these little mounds, so that here must have lived a few hundreds of people who walked to their huts over paths of beaten earth and clay and brushwood. Their village was surrounded by a palisade, the first human attempt at security. They had a good knowledge of agriculture, spinning, and weaving, and they loved beautiful things, for Glastonbury Museum has a bronze bowl found here decorated with bosses, ornaments of amber, glass, and jet, and many other treasures found under their clay floors, layer after layer of which was renewed from time to time, as the brushwood and cinder sank lower into the marsh. It was all in the centuries just before Christ, from 300 BC to AD 100.

Here little else seems to have happened for thousands of years, but the 19th century gave Godney a handsome church built to look like Norman. It has a window with some ancient glass in which we noticed two prehistoric ruffians who may well have lived in Godney's lake village, and one with a head like a cat's.

Great Elm. The church has in its walls herringbone masonry put there by Norman craftsmen, and in the tower are stones which may have been laid by Saxons.

The doorway to the tower is Norman, with the old door still swinging in it, carved and studded with amazing hinges. Above it is a curious little lancet window which must be one of the earliest of its kind, and has over it a tiny window of five leaded lights looking like an early attempt at tracery. On the south wall of the nave is one of the first rough sundials from which the villagers learned the time in mediaeval days. The interior is charming and of great simplicity, white with attractive plastered ceilings, filled with low box-pews by Jacobean craftsmen and their imitators, and with an Elizabethan gallery reached by steps from outside, supported on oak pillars inside and fronted with panelling in Jacobean style. The litany desk is true Jacobean, a quaint cupboard with a woman's figure on its door hanging between two queer childish figures carved on the buttresses.

Greenham. It is a hamlet set among hills and trees, with a manor house built in Chaucer's time and added to in Tudor days. On one side of the battlemented porch is a beautiful double row of mullioned windows belonging to the great hall, which, with its huge fireplace, its tapestried walls, and the great table on a raised dais, gives us for a moment a longing for those rich mediaeval days.

Greinton. It lies at the foot of the Polden Ridge near the field of Sedgemoor, and its 15th century church is rich in oak doors with deep tracery done by Tudor craftsmen, many old bench-ends, a fine chancel roof with bosses, and a panelled roof in the nave with a carved oak cornice.

Halse. It has a mill centuries old and still working, a nunnery which has turned farmhouse, several delightful old cottages, a charming street, a view of the Quantocks, and a church filled with good things. Here is a mass dial, a font made by the Normans, and a wonderful screen with four cornices, fine cresting, lovely fan-vaulting, and rich carving of 500 years ago. Keeping it company are bench-ends carved by the villagers in our own time, some with scenes from the Creation and some with the arts and crafts of the countryside—the shepherd with his lamb, the blacksmith and the builder, and a woman at her spinning-wheel. It is all very good, carrying on the fine tradition Somerset has had for at least five centuries. The east window has old Flemish glass which was made for a church in Florence but has become the picture gallery for the children of Halse. It has pictures of many of the old stories, two by 14th century artists who show St Catherine at her wheel and the young Madonna having her first lessons.

The tithe barn not far from the church has been thatched as a pavilion for the playing-field, and a mile away, at Stoford, is a little old barn and other remains of mediaeval work.

Hardington. It is one of the pathetic corners of our land, like Old England vanishing. A tiny stone bridge, a walk across a field, and we are at the manor house with the little church across the yard.

If walls have ears and windows eyes, these walls ringed in by trees must have heard and seen strange things. This was the home of the Bampfyldes from the 15th to the 18th century, when the end came with the gay Sir Charles, who fell so heavily into debt that they sold his deer park. A deer's antler was decaying on his door when we called. His strange son followed him, a desperate man who somehow became rector and would gallop across country and take service with his top-boots showing under his surplice; he would sit receiving tithes with a brace of pistols on the table. His father was shot dead in London and brought here to be buried; he was the kind of man who was the gay villain of the novels of that time.

His great stables are still here; we found the farm horses in the old stalls with the name of Sir Charles's coach horses still up—Marmion and King Arthur in gold letters.

The little church has seen it all, for something of it was here before the Bampfyldes came. Its tiny tower, with pinnacles too big for it, is inside no more than a small recess. Charming the little nave looks as we stand in it, with its crude Norman arch running almost from wall to wall. It is full of oak box-pews, and has a two-decker pulpit with a seat in which the old parish clerk must have sat half trembling with the desperate rector above him in his top-boots. The plain painted font appears to have been cut out of solid stone. The little holy water stoup by one of the pews has a carved canopy. The roof is charming, oak panelled with two Catherine wheels and 16 bosses.

The Stuart coat-of-arms is still bright with paint on the walls and the Bampfylde arms are in the windows. By the altar is a wall-monument with the story of four Bampfyldes: the colonel who died an old man in 1694, the gay Charles who died in 1823, one who perished at sea in 1853, and the wild rector whom they laid to rest in 1855. Below this are carved in stone the emblems of their rank—shields and gauntlets, axes and swords, drums and banners.

Hardington Mandeville. Far out of the way, on the hills which cross the border into Dorset, it has a church rebuilt last century by John Hancock, vicar of the neighbouring village of Haselbury Plucknett. It was he who carved the splendid arch in Norman style opening to the transept, and also the fine corbels and bosses in the chancel. The church still has its mediaeval tower, and there is also a Norman font with carving round the bowl, and a Jacobean pulpit with more carving.

Haselbury Plucknett. It is Wulfric's village. Here he lived in a cell; here he sat and talked with our Norman King Stephen; here they buried him. He was born near by at Compton Martin. Once a country squire who loved sport more than all, he gave up sport to be a priest, shut himself up in a cell clothed in a suit of mail, and lived a hermit's life. People came from all parts to talk with him, and it is said that one day as Stephen rode by Wulfric hailed him as King of England. On Stephen answering that he was no king, for his uncle was on the throne, Wulfric cried out that it was no error, for the Lord had delivered the realm into his hands.

He lived to be 90, and they buried him under his cell, where the north chapel of the church now stands. A priory was founded in his name, and his tomb was long a place of pilgrimage.

The church outside is mainly 15th century, but the inside is modern except for the 13th century arches where Wulfric lies. There is a round Norman font, a carved chest of the 17th century, and a lectern with an old wood carving of the angel staying the hand of Abraham as he is raising his arm to slay his son.

A little way off, where the road to Merriot crosses the Crewkerne road, is a mediaeval bridge almost untouched for 500 years.

Hatch Beauchamp. Almost lost in the deer park, we come suddenly upon its 400-year-old church with its parapet and pinnacles and the fine belfry windows looking over the high wall of the great house.

One of the church doors is opened with an iron handle centuries old, solid enough to last as long again. All these years five painted faces have looked down from the windows of the north aisle, and St George on his horse, vigorously attacking a dragon, has been keeping company with all the delightful figures on the bench-ends. The font is 16th century.

Hawkridge. It is one of the loneliest of all the lonely Exmoor villages, perched on a ridge about 1000 feet high, with one steep side leading down to Danes Brook, the other to where the River Barle is crossed by one of the oldest bridges in England, made of giant stones in a forgotten past.

The church is the oldest inhabitant. Here it has stood 800 years, the base of its ancient cross beside it. Its rough doorway seems to have been made by a local mason who had vaguely heard of Norman ideas in architecture. He has rounded it with a simple band of carving, and has even tried to ornament the capitals, a pathetic attempt resulting in not much more than scratches on the stone. More rough lines are cut as ornament round the fine wide font hewn out of the stone of these hills soon after the Conqueror landed; and here is a stone to another Norman William, a coffin lid inscribed in old French to one who was Warden of the Moor. It is a plain low narrow church, but brightened at one end by the astonishing green grotto beneath the tower.

Along a narrow lane, down an almost precipitous field track, in and out of the trees following the curves of the Barle, we reach the famous Tarr Steps. Cars must ford the wide stream, for this bridge was made long before the days of pack-horses by men we should not recognise as kin. It links up two ridgeways where Bronze Age men buried their dead, and we who cross it today are part of a procession whose beginning is lost in the past and whose end may stretch as far into an unknown future. No one knows where these stones came from, for there is no rock like them here; but it is suggested that they may have been brought to Exmoor by glaciers in the great Ice Age.

The whole bridge with paved approaches is 180 feet long with 17 openings or arches, each formed by a great flat stone balanced on low piles of other stones built against the flow. Nothing but the weight of the flat stones holds them in place. Some in the middle are 7 feet long and 5 wide, but when the bed of the stream yielded up no more giants smaller ones were used in couples for each end.

Heathfield. Two figures kneel in the church of this small place. From the lady's Elizabethan headdress we guess her to be Margaret Hadley of the manor house with either her brother or her husband. We have seen her again at Dunster, this time with another husband, Thomas Luttrell, in the family group set up by her son. On the wall is a stone to Thomas Cornish, rector of this farming parish for 54 years till "like unto a shock of corn, heavy and ripe for harvest, he was gathered into the heavenly garner". The pulpit, a splendid piece of work, has been made up from fragments of carving, possibly part of the old screen.

Hemington. It has something lovely from two ancient centuries, a small chancel arch built by the Normans, and a great tower from that 15th century when our English building was at its height. The tower is one of twins hereabouts, being like the tower of Buckland Denham. It is magnificent, pinnacled and battlemented, with colossal arches set with blind traceried windows. On each side are two gorgeous gargoyles, short and sturdy and rather like pigs. Along the parapet of the nave are two animals ready to spring, and between them is a sundial painted on a battlement.

A very old door brings us inside, the huge wood block of its lock being over two feet long, with the mark of the carpenter's tools unworn by centuries. The tiny door of the rood stairs is still by the pulpit and the open doorway above. Older still is the rather queer font, for the Normans fashioned it when they built the chancel arch, which has been lost and was discovered again when Sir Gilbert Scott was restoring the church last century. The 14 little stone heads in the aisle are modern. The church is peculiar for having but one aisle and a clerestory, the roof held above it by ten great winged angels with stately headdresses and shields. There is just a fragment of ancient glass to give a touch of colour to this church that lies so quietly down in the hollow.

Henstridge. For a village pond it has part of a moat, but of the house the moat guarded nothing is left save the stables, with two archways for the carriages to pass under, and the gateway, with a mysterious niche on each side. A new house has grown up beside them, with two majestic weeping ashes in its garden. An old neighbour is Toomer Farm with curious battlemented gables, heraldic decorations on its walls, and two stone dogs to guard the door.

Roses lead us to the door and climb up the walls of the church, made new except for its 15th century north arcade and tower arch, and part of the north aisle. William Carent of Toomer Farm, High Sheriff of Somerset, lies with his wife on a grand tomb of 1463. Their arms are on a canopy above, and 17 small figures are round them, but they are all very worn and there is only a trace of their ancient colour. A niche cut in the tomb has probably something to do with the pilgrims who were granted 40 days indulgence for saying a prayer at it. An elaborate stone canopy and a dainty carved doorway with a face on the shield over it add to the interest of this much refashioned church.

High Ham. Here is one of Somerset's fine 15th century churches, built of the stone of the hill it stands on, with a tower 100 years older and an amusing row of gargoyles. One plays on a trumpet, another strains to listen with a hand behind the ear; there is a fiddler and a piper, and a man throwing a stone as if maddened by the rival musicians. Among them a chained monkey nurses her baby. There is also an old mass dial. The screen, the oak roofs, the bench-ends, were all made for the church when it was new 500 years ago. The roofs have many carved bosses and stone angels; the panelled bench-ends and the choir-stalls have poppyheads; the oak screen is as lovely as any in this county of exquisite screens, still with its roodloft and rood stairs and a roodbeam carved with leaves. It is said that Glastonbury monks started work on it just before the dawn of the century which saw them homeless. There are two old lecterns, the Jacobean one with two old chained books on one side and a chained Book of Remembrance of our own day on the other. There is a Norman font with cable moulding, an Elizabethan chalice, an altar table of 1633, and two figures in ancient glass, one carrying a small cow.

At the rectory is a description of the village written in Latin by Adrian Schael, an Elizabethan rector.

High Littleton. It stands 500 feet up with a wide view of the Mendips; its hills have memories of the Romans, its tower has stones of the Normans, and the church as we see it is mostly 15th century. It has a lovely carved and richly pinnacled pulpit with panels of roses and 15 tiny heads on the pinnacles. There is an old font and a new one. Who can fail to be interested in the great square stone by the altar with its story of all the Thomases of the Hodges family? They range from one who was born before the Spanish Armada and come down to the last of the male line of the family, all neatly and clearly set out so there can be no misunderstanding. There are two big gargoyles looking down from the tower, one like a huge bat.

Hillfarrance. A few cottages by the River Tone cluster round a small green and a church with an early 16th century tower made beautiful by a delicate parapet. Here hang four bells which rang in the first Stuart king. The pulpit was made in 1611, and there are some carved bench-ends in splendid condition in spite of their four or five hundred years. Stone angels help to support the archway into the little chapel built by a lord of the manor in memory of his mother before he died in 1333.

Hinton Blewett. It is hidden away on a hill looking out to the Mendips, but was not too hidden for the Romans to find, for here they built a forum, and men have picked up coins of the Emperor Claudius.

The 15th century church has one of the most charming interiors in the county, with stone floors and a low chancel arch. The nave is filled with splendid 15th century benches with arcaded and traceried ends, and the chancel, seeming to grow naturally out of the nave, is a charming little shrine, carpeted to the altar, with no altar rails and no screen, with two old chairs and a desk such as we should expect to find in a house. The dainty piscina has a shelf and the bottom of the bowl is beautifully carved. The altar has a touch of black and gold, and the east window has the three dragon-slaying saints in subdued colours: St Margaret, St Michael, and St George. The east window of the aisle has a dainty Madonna in blue and gold. There is a little old glass in the window tracery.

The font is Norman, but surprisingly delicate for Norman work, and it has the marks of the staples with which it was locked. The pulpit, which was a three-decker in the 17th century with a seat for the clerk, a reading desk above, and the preacher's place above it all, has still its very neat canopy. The way to the old roodloft is preserved through a very tiny door. There is an elegant doorway into the chancel over which Symon Seward carved his initials. The door through which he came to his altar faces a charming back wall of a row of cottages rising from the green turf of the churchyard.

Hinton Charterhouse. We come to it by a glorious run along the hills from Bath, and the great possession we come to see is the ruin of the priory founded more than 700 years ago (in 1232) by the Countess of Salisbury, wife of William Longsword, son of Fair Rosamund. Here she must have come to realise one of her dreams, and few houses have a more beautiful story enshrined within their walls.

Ela was only seven when her father died and left her all his wealth; she was the rich Countess of Salisbury. Richard Lionheart was King of England, and he chose as a husband for Ela his own stepbrother, William Longsword, the marriage being most happy. Longsword served three kings faithfully, and was one of the men who saw King John in his rage seal Magna Carta at Runnymede. He went to the wars in France and no news came of him, but the faithful Ela refused all advances from those who begged her to marry again, declaring that she would yet see the earl's ship come into the harbour of Poole and her husband waiting on the deck to welcome her. It happened so. It happened also that Longsword died a tragic death soon after, and was the first man to be buried in Salisbury Cathedral. Ela waited till their son came of age and then went into a convent and gave herself to a life of religious activity. She founded the Abbey of Lacock in Wiltshire, becoming its abbess and dying there, but before she died she founded also this priory at Hinton; it is one of the monuments of her most gracious life.

Today the priory is scheduled as a national monument and has been admirably restored. The 13th century chapter house with a vaulted roof above it is set in a quaint three-storeyed building with many gables, and there are two dovecots from olden days, with hundreds of nesting-places. In the 16th century the lovely manor house was built out of the ruins of the priory gatehouse and porter's lodge, and it remains a picture of Tudor grace. The house has two interesting spiral stairways, one of stone and one of oak, both in the hall.

Hinton Charterhouse has also a mediaeval church much restored.

Hinton St George. It is one of the perfect villages, with a wide and lovely street, old houses, a beautiful church, and the ancient home of the lords of the manor set in 1000 acres. The Pouletts were there in the 15th century, and they are there today.

The mediaeval village cross is still standing, with John the Baptist carved on its shaft; the stones of Priory Farm and the thatched Priory Cottage are weathering with the centuries; the scratch dials are still on the buttresses of the 15th century church, which has a fine tall tower with pinnacles and pierced battlements, and a window on every side to let out the sound of the bells. The porch has a ribbed stone roof and an old traceried door, and ancient timbers make the panelled roofs of the nave and the south aisle.

Somebody 500 years ago chiselled the three daggers of the Pouletts and the cross of St George on the font which had been made by the Normans 300 years before. The pew of the Pouletts is raised apart, and a place has been found at the foot of it for the alabaster figure of the man to whom they owe their great possessions here, Sir John Denebaud, whose daughter married William Poulett. Here lies their son Amyas, knighted for valour on the field in 1487, and remembered as the sheriff who put Cardinal Wolsey in the stocks when he was a young nobody at Limington.

Beneath the stone canopy of his great-grandson's tomb we may look into the chapel where the beautiful sculptured figure of Sir Amyas lies with three generations about him, their wives and their children, their heraldry, and little weepers on their tombs. A wonderful picture these white figures make, lining the whole chapel, while their shields held by satyrs, their records, and the monuments to their successors, reach almost to the ceiling.

By Sir Amyas is his son Hugh and his grandson Amyas, who lies on a roll of carved matting perfect in alabaster. One of the poems to him is perhaps the last inscription in French on an English tomb, and the initials E. R. signing another inscription are thought to be Elizabeth I's whose loyal servant Amyas was, though she thought him "a dainty and precise fellow" for not liking the suggestion to murder Mary Queen of Scots, when she was in his care. His reply to her has echoed down the corridors of history. It was his great grief and bitterness, he said, that he had lived to see the day when he was required by his sovereign to do an act which God and the law forbade. His life and his goods were at Her Majesty's service, but God forbid that he should make so foul a shipwreck of his conscience, or leave so great a blot to his poor posterity, as to shed blood without law or warrant.

Next comes the son of this Amyas, Sir Anthony, with his wife on his right to show her higher rank. He is in armour like the rest, but has a distinguishing feature in a six-inch beard. She wears a charming gown and has jewels in her Paris headdress. Round their tomb are 48 shields, and they have all their children about them, five kneeling sons and five girls. The eldest son John has a classical monument, and all round the walls of the church the Poulett name appears again and again. A brother and sister have portraits in medallions, and on a stone is remembered a man who served the family as bailiff for 62 years and died in 1792, leaving five acres of his land to buy shoes and stockings for the poor each St Thomas's day for the next 3000 years. Near the bailiff is a small brass which shows dimly the figures of John Thuddile, his wife, and their 11 children.

It was the first Sir Amyas who built the great house, and it has been much added to and altered since. In 1636 it gained a beautiful plaster ceiling, and in 1664 it had 47 hearths to be taxed. It was to the White Lodge in this park that the Duke of Monmouth came on his progress through the West, and here it was that Elizabeth

Parcet broke through the crowd and touched the duke for King's
Evil.

Holcombe. The long street climbs up the hill to the new
church, but it is the old church down by the farm that we love. Yet
the new church suits its people well and is fine. It christens its
children at the Norman font from the old church, looking like two
or three round bowls one above the other.

Along a lane, through a farmer's gate and down a field, the little
old church stands alone, beloved by the farmer who took us over it
but forgotten by the world, except that now and then in summer it is
full of people who love a service in these venerable walls. How long
they have stood we do not know. Although the church was refashioned 500 years ago it has three Norman arches, a Norman
window, and one tiny window as wide as the palm of a hand which
looked to us like Saxon. It is in the little tower with the ancient
bells; we rang one and sent its melodious note across the fields.

It is the magnificent doorway that enchants us as we come, for it is
pure and noble Norman with carved shafts and capitals, a little rope
round the cushion of each capital, and deep zigzags round the arch,
with a lovely stone angel above it all. She has been watching in this
place for centuries. One of the old stones in the arch below her has
a curious inscription upside down which nobody can understand.

We stand inside between two Norman arches, a wide one across
the chancel and a smaller one behind the squire's pew, reached from
the tower. The nave is full of white box-pews, with a small pulpit
painted to match and a lovely little box for the clerk below. There
are hat pegs on the walls. Marble tablets tell us of generations of
people who have sat in the pews.

Holford. "There is everything here," wrote Dorothy Wordsworth; "sea and woods wild as fancy ever painted." She and her
brother William had rented the manor of Alfoxden to be near
Coleridge at Nether Stowey; it is odd to think of these two in this
great country mansion with only a servant and a young boy, but their
rent was only £23 a year, and most of their days they spent out
of doors, walking with Coleridge.

For hours they would wander over these beautiful hills, up to the
line of far-famed beeches and down in the glens, exploring Tannery
Combe and Hodder's Combe, or the old camp on Danesborough
Hill. At all hours, in all weathers, they would set out (they walked
35 miles to Lynton from here), and so strange did their behaviour

seem to the villagers, so wild was their talk of the Revolution in France, that the owner of Alfoxden became alarmed and refused to renew the lease.

By the gates of Alfoxden House are the pretty cottages of Holford, with a small church hiding its curious gabled tower in the trees. Little is left save part of an ancient cross and a list of rectors to show that a church was standing here in 1319.

Holton. In its churchyard the old cross has been made new in memory of four men who gave their lives for us in the Great War. It is a pretty place they had to leave for ever; we found one of its cottages wrapped completely round in jasmine. The tiny church is 700 years old and has an ancient sundial over the porch. The font is older than the church itself, and the stone pulpit has been here 500 years, delightful with its carving of flowers and tracery. It was long lost and was found again in the last years of last century.

Hornblotton. If we think the name strange it is interesting to know that it was once still stranger, though why or when it was first called Hornblawerton we do not know. Its cottages are gathered round a green, but the church hides its spire, covered with oak shingles, behind a big house looking out to the Roman Fosse Way. An avenue of firs and acacias leads to the house, but the only way to the church is along paths hidden in the meadow grass. It is 19th century, but beside it stands the small tower and bellcot of the earlier church, whose fine Norman font is within the newer building. Tub-shaped, it bears the marks of the hinges which locked it. Much has been done to enrich the new church, so small that it holds only 85 people. On the walls pictures, stars, and texts show in brown plaster beneath the white, and the oak chancel seats, pulpit, and lectern are inlaid with many woods.

Horner. It is the gateway to one of the loveliest of all the valleys leading to the high land of Exmoor. Woods follow the little stream and creep halfway up steep hills to where heather and whortleberries grow. It is good to know that this beauty will not fade, for it is safe for 500 years, having been leased to the National Trust by that great lover of Somerset Sir Thomas Acland. Near its group of cottages is a slender-arched pack-horse bridge, almost hidden among trees which dip their branches in the valley stream.

Horsington. It is fortunate beyond most villages in having managed to keep the old preaching cross, with a canopied figure on the pillar with skulls and bones, a crown above his head, and an animal's head beneath his feet. The church has been made new since then, refashioned last century, but it has kept the old tower with two bells that were ringing before the Reformation. It has also the old font with crudely carved angels on it. One ancient possession has come to it, a west window made 600 years ago for a manor house, then used for the rectory dovecot, and now bringing light to the sanctuary here. The rectory was built by the first of a long line of Wickhams in 1686, and the family provided the rectors here for more than 200 years.

Huish Champflower. A delightful place, it lives up to its name, the white walls of its cottages set in green hills and deep valleys with a background of larch and pine. Its church is 15th century with a 14th century tower. The nave has a fine arcade of plaster pillars, and in an east window is some ancient glass with quaint figures in animated conversation; they are apparently part of a Tree of Jesse, and probably from the ruined abbey of Barlynch, which we see from the Exe Valley Road. The mediaeval wooden eagle has been given new wings, the chalice is Elizabethan, the font is Norman, and one of the five bells is mediaeval.

Huish Episcopi. Here is beauty in abundance, for a gardener has planted a peony valley near the church, and we walk among the perfumed bushes. And here is one of the stateliest and loveliest structures in Somerset, the exquisite 15th century tower, stately and crowned with pinnacles, garlanded with quatrefoils, decked with ornaments. The 15th century refashioned the church after fire had destroyed the Norman structure, except for a doorway which is crowded with carvings still red from the flames of 600 years ago. A queer creature's head looks out from among them, and on one side a sundial is scratched in the stone. Here is the door, strengthened with long hinges and a great lock, which a mediaeval carpenter put in the place of the burned one.

The perfect little Tudor screen under the tower arch was thrown out of Enmore's church, but Huish cared enough for beauty to save it. It has a 15th century font to keep it company, a carved oak pulpit of 1625, and an arcade of curiously pointed arches. It has lovely windows, one by Burne-Jones showing kings and shepherds and red-winged angels worshipping round the stable.

Huntspill. Its new houses crowd the highway, but the old ones go with the trees by the rectory and the church, a long church superbly proportioned with a 15th century tower heavily buttressed against sea winds. Only reddened pillars and an unknown knight and his lady are left to tell of the fire which destroyed most of the interior last century. The knight's shield was cracked in the heat, after lying here unhurt since the 14th century, and the lady's robe was tinged red by the flames, but they lie here still, hewn from the same quarry as the church itself. Also saved from the fire was a Jacobean chest and a magnificent pulpit 300 years old, its black oak finely carved with lilies and roses in sunken arcades, and its ten sides cut with texts from King James's Bible. Strange that less than 100 years ago such work should have been so little valued that the man who put in Stogursey's stone pulpit should have been offered this old one for a few pounds. Luckily Huntspill was ready with ten pounds to buy it from him, and it remains for us in this worthy place.

Everything new here since the fire has been admirable; the font, designed by Sir Edward Beckett, has an old carved cover; Balliol College (Huntspill's patron) sent the altar candlesticks from its own chapel; the nave and chancel seats are models of carving; and the new roofs are held up by a choir of oak angels, many with instruments, among which we noticed bagpipes. There is a Bible of 1640; and one curious small thing we noticed was a doormat with the name William Rodney worked into it in the 17th century.

In our own time a book from the Jacobean chest has been identified as a very early copy of the English Prayer Book issued by Edward VI, with comments by the reformer Martin Bucer.

Hutton. Long ago they found a great cave here, filled with bones of wild beasts which we can see for ourselves in Taunton Museum. The church (which has a mass dial) has seen its own great past, for here lies a man whose portrait is before us in the armour he wore at Bosworth Field. His portrait is in brass, and his name is Thomas Payne, a squire with his wife and 11 children. On another brass is John Payne, also with his wife and 11 children in costumes of the 15th century; he is a generation older than Thomas.

The church has another family group engraved on a stone; they lived at Hutton Court, the old house by the church which has still its 15th century open timber roof and the fine hall in which Nathaniel Still and his wife would sit with their five children in the days of the Civil War. There is a 15th century font, and a charming little 15th century stone pulpit. Every inch of it is carved, probably by the mason who made the group of twenty or so pulpits like it found in the Mendips.

This is one of the smallest in the group yet it is raised so high that the preacher must climb the old rood stairs to get into it.

Ilchester. Here was born the wonder man of the Middle Ages, the friar Roger Bacon, whose learning the 13th century tried to crush behind a prison wall. It is one of its memories, and memories are nearly all it has today. Five Roman roads which met within its city walls, the mint of Saxon times, the nunnery and friary and workshops which fashioned beautiful stone figures for Somerset churches, are all gone. It was once the chief town of Somerset; today it is a place of a few hundred people.

In its barnlike town hall is the chief relic of its lost glory, the brass headpiece of a 13th century mace, with niches in which are set three kings and an angel, and with an inscription which has been translated: *I am a mark of amity: do not forget me.* The old pillar of its 17th century market cross has a sundial on the top. The bridge which links the Roman Fosse Way across the River Yeo was made new last century, though an ancient pack-horse way still carries people lower down, at Pill Bridge.

Of the seven mediaeval churches only one is left, and it has a tower so odd that Roger Bacon, who would see it growing up, may have wondered at its being farther round it than it is to the top. It has Roman bricks in its eight sides. The chancel dates chiefly from the 13th century, but the north and south windows were inserted in the 15th century. To the 15th century belongs also a chapel with canopied niches and odd bits of vaulting in its walls, and a few carved stones under the tower, where we found the holes for the beam which barred the door. The Jacobean pulpit has arcades cleverly cut as if receding.

Another memory Ilchester has of a poet whose verse the 18th century applauded, though the 20th century has forgotten her name. She was Elizabeth Rowe, whose father was a prisoner here when her mother fell in love with him on one of her visits of mercy. Their daughter married Thomas Rowe, and wrote such fervent poems that her fame spread to France and Germany. Bishop Ken and Matthew Prior were among her admirers, Pope printed her elegy to her husband in one of his own books, and Dr Johnson, linking her with Isaac Watts in fame, declared that for such as them human eulogies were vain; "they were applauded by angels and numbered with the just."

It was in the dark Middle Ages that Roger Bacon was born here, in 1214; in 1914 his birthplace set his portrait in brass on these walls. He was her greatest son, the most astonishing figure of the mediaeval world. He studied first at Oxford and afterwards in Paris, where his fame grew so that he was named the Marvellous Doctor. Returning to Oxford he began the studies which were to lay the foundation of modern science. Brilliant experiments enabled him to make a magnifying glass, and possibly a primitive form of telescope, whose principle he understood. By mixing charcoal sulphur, and saltpetre, he anticipated the discovery of gunpowder, and he foresaw the use of steam vessels.

With the light of learning blazing on his brow he towered above the misty superstitions of his age. His jealous rivals charged him with black magic, and, as he had become a Franciscan friar, his superiors were able to confine him in Paris for eight years and to deny him intercourse with the world, the use of books, instruments, and pen and ink. It happened that the one friend he had became Pope Clement IV, and asked for an explanation of his teachings. In reply Bacon wrote an encyclopedia of the world's knowledge, with a magnificent plea for freedom in learning. Clement died too soon to help him, and he was imprisoned again, this time as a sorcerer and a heretic, and he regained his liberty only two years before his death in 1294.

Ile Abbots. A joyful surprise is its 15th century tower, rising from the marshland of the River Isle. It has pinnacled buttresses and niches still with their statues, one a symbol of the Resurrection, another St George on his horse. The south porch is lovely with pierced battlements, a fan-tracery roof with a central pendant, and an ancient studded door with bands of ornamental ironwork. An odd window is cut through the roodloft stairway to give a peep into the early 14th century chancel, where is an enormous stone coffin, a piscina richly bordered with panelling and canopied niches, and a spacious triple sedilia with tracery which is copied on all the ends of the old oak pews. The balustered tower screen is Jacobean; there is also part of a mediaeval painted screen. The Norman font on five legs has been roughly carved with such scrawls as a child might scrawl on a scrap of paper; we noticed a dragon-like creature upside down. The north aisle, added by that great church builder Margaret Beaufort, mother of Henry VII, looks curiously modern for its 400 years, and it has wreathed piers and an oak panelled roof.

Ile Brewers. No brewer, but a Norman de Briwere, gave his name to this place on the banks of the River Isle. The red-capped

Lullington Church: the north door.

Huish Episcopi Church.

Kingsdon: Lyte's Cary.

Langport: the hanging chapel.

Montacute House.

Meare: the Manor Farm.

Martock Church: the roof.

tower and the red roof of its 19th century church are pleasant against the green marshland, and inside is a Norman font with cable moulding round its bowl.

Ilminster. It has most of the things that a little town needs, and a tower which any great town might envy. Only at Wells is there another like it, for it was inspired 500 years ago by the central tower of Wells Cathedral. It is glorious, with 24 pierced stone windows to let out the sound of the bells, 22 pinnacles at the top, and, rising above all, the cap of a stair turret with 16 gargoyles and 32 canopies. The great tower crowns a church with an exterior worthy of a cathedral, and the transepts have magnificent windows, niched buttresses, and gargoyles running round a panelled parapet so delicately carved as to hold us spellbound. The south porch is also of remarkable beauty.

After all this it is disappointing to enter and find that the 19th century has spoiled so much, for it rebuilt the nave and broke the harmony of the whole. The fan-vaulted roof of the tower is as enchanting as anything outside. The chancel arch is panelled, and in the chancel is a striking modern reredos with many saints under canopies, seen also from the transepts through ribbed slits in the walls. On each side of the altar is a little doorway with charming spandrels leading into the vestry. There are quaint corbels, an 18th century candelabra and a 17th century pulpit, and the 500-year-old font is curious for being flat on one side where it was once fixed to a pillar.

Here are the monuments of the Wadhams, whose name is held in high honour at Oxford, and in the south transept is the tomb of Humphrey Walrond, an Elizabethan who gave Ilminster its grammar school. Over his tomb hang two crested helmets, one of wood, and both made to be carried in funeral processions.

Two real helmets of the 16th century, crested with a rose, hang in the north transept over the grave of Sir William Wadham, who gave the money for both transepts, for the south porch, and probably for the tower. His brass is on his tomb, looking up to the carved oak roof on which he saw the craftsmen working 500 years ago. Sir William lies in armour with a lion at his feet, and at his side lies his mother in widow's mourning; her little dog has a collar hung with bells. The niches round their tomb are empty, but at one end a knight and a lady kneel in prayer. Nicholas Wadham and his wife Dorothy lie near Sir William's tomb, both with their portraits in brass. His is a vigorous likeness, and a speaking one, for out of his

F

mouth come the words: *Death unto me is advantage*, and his wife replies, *I will not die, but live, and declare the work of the Lord*. He died and she lived, and she carried out his dream of building Wadham College. Nicholas died in 1609 and the work of the college was hardly begun, so that, as he said in his will, he left the "whole menagery" of the college to his 75-year-old Dorothy. He had been 40 years her husband and she knew his will. Roman Catholic though she was, she faithfully observed the Protestant precepts of her husband, and Wadham College rose as a home of the reformed religion, with statues so liberal and free from bigotry as to seem centuries ahead of their time. Dorothy saw the work finished and lived nearly five years more to see the College flourish. She was a fine old lady, and before she died the words she put in Latin on the tomb came true:

He still shines. Do you not see? Look at the towers set on the other side of Isis. What habitations he built for the Muses, what temples for gods!

They lived at Merrifield, near Ilton, on the other side of the River Isle, but their home, which Thomas Fuller described as being "at all times an inn and at Christmas a court", is now but a heap of stones inside a gloomy moat. On that spot the great Wadham College was born.

Ilminster School, which Nicholas and Dorothy must have known so well, is still flourishing, though it now houses the girls' grammar school, the boys having moved to new buildings. The grammar school (founded in 1549 by Humphrey Walrond and Henry Greynfylde) stands proudly facing the churchyard, a fine Tudor building with massive walls, stone mullions, a grand old doorway, ancient glass in the windows, and a sundial which has marked the sunny hours since Elizabeth I's day. Among the other interesting buildings of the town are the colonnaded market house, with the stone pump close by; the Chantry, an old house by the churchyard in which the priest once lived, still with its fine old doorway; two other houses with similar origins, Abbot's Court and Cross House; a Unitarian Chapel 200 years old; and Dillington House at the fringe of the town, approached by a fine avenue in a park of 136 acres.

Ilton. A stalwart chestnut tree stands sentinel at the fine old rectory and a church of the 14th and 15th centuries. We found there bells which rang in the first of the Stuarts at the foot of a tower no longer strong enough to carry them; but doing duty still are an old oak pulpit on a stone base dotted with flowerheads, two veteran chairs in the chancel, and a font 500 years old. A miniature brass of 1508 shows Nicholas Wadham in swaddling clothes. Near him is a dainty little figure of alabaster. Generations of ninnies have scrawled their initials all over her in the fashion of our modern litter-louts. Above her are old tiles bearing the arms of the Wadhams and pictures of the Oxford college founded by another Nicholas a century later, whom we meet with his wife at Ilminster. It was this later Nicholas who gave the pretty row of almshouses on the way to his home of Merrifield.

Another group of 17th century almshouses has an inscription to John Whetstone, Gentleman, and we were told that this gentleman was a poor little waif who got his name because he was found in a manger with a bundle of whetstones. The villagers here cared for him, and when he grew rich he gave them this row of cottages. A charming old farm called Scotts has a wing which looks as if it might fall across the road at any moment.

Keinton Mandeville. It has spread itself about but has left its church away in the fields, a barnlike church of 1800 with a 13th century chancel and a simple Norman font. On the walls hangs one of the many crude pictures of David with his harp that we find in Somerset. There was born in this village a man with the little known name of John Henry Brodribb. Few who read this will have heard it, yet this boy from Keinton Mandeville was famous through-out England as Sir Henry Irving. The grey stone house in which he was born (now standing as one of a row) has been christened Irving House, and a brass explains why to the passer-by. He was the great-est actor of his time.

His father was a small shopkeeper, and the boy was brought up in the home of a Cornish miner who was a Methodist. He learnt elocution and rejoined his parents on their coming up to London, and, finding his way on to the stage at 18, he had a versatile career for ten years, during which he played nearly 600 parts. He woke to find himself famous at 33, when he appeared in *The Bells* at the Lyceum, and from that time he never looked back. He engaged Ellen Terry as his leading lady for an autumn tour in 1878, and the association lasted till the end. Their appearance in Shakespeare drew all London to the Lyceum, and they enjoyed triumph after triumph together. He was superb in *Hamlet*, but good in most Shakespearian characters, and was far the most popular actor of his time, known the world over. He received high honours, and was the first actor ever knighted for his services on the stage and the first actor to speak at the Royal Academy banquet. His ashes were laid

151

in Westminster Abbey, and his statue is outside the National Portrait Gallery, looking towards many of London's theatres.

Kelston. We come down the hill and round the hill to Kelston, to find a little church which has in its keeping something beautiful 1000 years old. Old houses cluster round about, some built from the stones of the great house which has disappeared, in which Elizabeth I stayed with her godson Sir John Harington. The house was built for him in 1587 by an Italian architect. There were Haringtons here for centuries, and one of them has an almost unique brass on the wall of the nave, for it has an anthem with music engraved on it, the musical epitaph of Henry Harington, founder of the Harmonic Society, who was buried here in 1816.

Proud names we found in this small place, for the ancient church was made new by Colonel Inigo Jones (whose family has long owned the living), and a tablet on the wall tells us of Sir Caesar Hawkins, for whom the famous architects, the Woods of Bath, built the house still standing on the hillside near the church. Sir Caesar wore himself out in the cause of humanity and died in 1786.

The great possession of the church, its Saxon stone carving, is built into the wall by the altar. It has been part of the churchyard cross and has delicate carving of interlaced foliage carved in panels divided by rope moulding. It is thought to have been done about the 9th or 10th century.

The church has been made new but keeps its ancient tower and has an old door still swinging on its hinges. Four 18th century bells ring under the saddleback belfry roof. There is old glass in the chancel and the nave, two chancel windows having two saints, one with a cross and a bell, the other carrying what appears to be a tower. In the nave are fragments of weird figures with roses, foliage, and crowns. One of the figures is an extraordinary angel with colossal wings. There is a charming font set on an old round stone base, its bowl springing from something like a cup of leaves.

Kenn. The last of the Kens to live here, in the house changed out of all recognition, make a quaint family group in the church. The father, who died in 1593, kneels on a cushion with two daughters behind him, his wife reclining below with a baby in one hand and a book in the other. All three women wear wide skirts over farthingales. Through the marriage of one of these girls the Ken home passed to another family, and so the villagers cannot claim Bishop Ken as one of them. The great man of the village was Sir Nicholas

Staling, Gentleman Usher to Elizabeth I and James I, as a stone in
the church tells us.

Except for its tiny 700-year-old tower, capped with a wooden
pyramid, the church has been made new; but there is a 13th century
font, an Elizabethan chalice, a fine old door with tracery, a 14th
century cross with a new head, and as pretty a row of cottages as
ever led to a church door.

Kewstoke. A lovely way from Weston-super-Mare brings us
through the woods of Worle Hill, with peeps of the sea through a
canopy of windswept trees. From the church door starts the climb
up about 200 steps to the top of the hill; they are called St Kew's
steps, and perhaps it is true that the saint had a hermitage at the
top, where all to be seen now is the broken outline of a prehistoric
fort and a thrilling view of Somerset. From the churchyard we see
the Welsh mountains.

From Norman days to the 15th century men have been building
this church. There is a wonderful Norman doorway with twisted
pillars, a 14th century font bowl on a Norman stem, and a comical
face on the arch of the mediaeval rood stairs. The 15th century pulpit, richly and delicately carved, is one of about twenty old stone pulpits left in Somerset. Among some bits of mediaeval glass are the
arms of the Priory of Woodspring, of which much is left still in the
fields near the cliffs.

Far off it looks like a church, its high tower beautiful with an open
parapet and pierced stone windows, but people have been living
in it since 1550. There are charming stair turrets and a parapet still
marks the shape of the old place. The buttressed tithe barn is in the
farmyard, its 14th century porch blocked up. The walls are strong
and firm, though ferns and flowers grow in a hundred crevices, as
pretty a picture as one could wish to see, with the fish pond of the
monks and the spring which gave the Priory its name.

Most remarkable of all the treasures of Kewstoke is the Becket
Cup now kept in Taunton Museum. Here it was found behind a
sculptured figure built into the wall. Not for rich metals or fine
workmanship is it precious, for it is only a broken wooden cup; but
it is stained with a man's blood, and it is almost certain that it came
from Woodspring Priory, and had been sold by the monks of Canterbury as a relic of the murdered Becket—the cup which caught his
life blood.

It may well be so, for Woodspring was founded in 1210 by William
Courtenay, grandson of one of the four murderers, three of whom

were Somerset knights. Reginald Fitzurse, their leader, had already set up a chantry chapel here that prayers might be offered for his victim's soul, and the granddaughter of the third of these knights offered an endowment for the priory. The prior's own seal was a cup, and here this wooden cup from Canterbury must have been treasured till the priory was dissolved. Then someone hid it in the wall of the church where it was found hundreds of years later, its hiding guarded by a tiny sculptured figure.

Keynsham. It has given its chief treasure away; it was a Roman pavement in which Caesar's craftsman gave us long ago a mosaic picture of what Shakespeare gives us in words:

> *Orpheus with his lute made trees,*
> *And the mountain-tops that freeze*
> *Bow themselves when he did sing.*

The pavement was found when they brought the railway here, and we have seen it in Bristol Museum. Its other great treasure Keynsham nearly lost when the massive tower of its church fell in in the 17th century; it crashed into the nave, broke down the lovely chancel screen, but just missed the chancel, which stands as it has stood about 700 years. What was saved from the old screen is now at the end of one of the aisles. It is the finest piece of workmanship in the church, with eight glowing suns in the vaulting and a traceried parapet. There is a finely carved Jacobean pulpit with ten panels and a quatrefoiled border, and in the chancel is a heavy screen of Charles I's day, with a central opening and two arches on each side, the Stuart arms gaily painted above it all.

The nave has lost its ancient roof, but the magnificent roofs of the aisles remain, divided into hundreds of small panels with delicate quatrefoils carved in them and with many gilded bosses. There are queer stone corbels.

The chancel walls have many skulls and cherubs and on each side of the altar are two great tombs from the days when skulls and cherubs were much beloved by sculptors. On one lies Sir Henry Bridges, a doughty warrior of Elizabeth I's day. Facing this warrior on his tomb kneels Sir Thomas Bridges (1661) who founded the almshouses here for six poor widows and must have been a kindly man.

The fine 17th century tower dominates the long street of Keynsham, which leads us one way to Bristol and the other way to Bath. It has two sundials, buttresses rising to the top and open parapet work. Round one of the aisles runs a band of 14th century ball-flower ornament and on the wall of the other aisle is a line of queer men and strange animals. There is an ancient scratch dial on one stone, and we noticed a curious thing we have not seen before, for all the buttresses round the church are numbered in Roman numerals. The south porch has a vaulted roof with carved bosses.

Kilmersdon. It has not lost the wondrous charm of Somerset. It lies comfortably among its wooded hills and clusters round a noble tower almost 100 feet high, full of windows, stone tracery, canopied niches held up by angels, buttresses climbing to the top, with battlements and rich pinnacles over all. All round the battlements are fierce beasts on guard. There are about 50 sculptured figures on the outside walls, the oldest of all on the south, where a Norman corbel table still remains.

The door is dated in studded nails—1766; but there is a finer old door into the vestry, panelled with charming floral tracery and still with its ancient lock and key, the lock encased in a block of wood about four feet long with the old key fixed in front. In this vestry is the oldest memorial stone inside the church, to Robert James (1528). The inscription is cut in four small arches. The oldest stones inside are a few Norman fragments in the chancel, but the interior of this fine structure is 15th century.

The nave has six magnificent benches that have been here all the time, with timbers four inches thick; ten stone angels look down on them from the roof. The long and narrow aisle has a fine oak roof with carved bosses in each of its 144 panels and a little black-and-white work. The chancel has still a little of its old roof left.

There is a splendid 15th century screen in front of the north chapel, as clean as if it had been finished yesterday, yet it is one of the best pieces of craftsmanship from the 15th century with four angels on its cornice.

In this chapel are two richly carved niches with charming angel brackets. They are by the rich east window set here by Lord Hylton to his daughter.

There is a little mediaeval glass in the tracery of one window. The font is decorated from top to bottom and is an unusual shape, rather like a bell upside down, with three bands of arches and quatrefoils round its three tiers.

Close to the school is a quaint stone lockup. Across the valley rises a stone column 50 yards high with a lantern at the top, shining among the trees for miles around in normal times, which must please the proud Joliffes if they still remember this world, for the tower was raised in memory of them, as we read on its walls in three languages.

Kilton. It lies with Lilstock in a lovely and secluded spot, the sea in front and the Quantocks behind, and a little hill close by to give it a view across the Quantocks into Wales. The 14th century church has been made new, but Lilstock, nearer to the beach, keeps the chancel of a church older still. Yet in both these parishes there are only 20 houses.

The church has a charming high font of the 14th century, richly carved and with angels under the bowl. There is a brass of 1592 with a long hymn of praise to Charles Stenninges. Both churches have silver chalices older than the Armada, but Lilstock has the chief possession, for in the tiny chapel is one of the earliest Norman fonts, a deep bowl ribbed with lines and chevrons round the rim.

Kilve. Wordsworth and Southey both sang of Kilve shore, a rocky place with low broken cliffs. Near it is a ruined chantry, the stones of its arches and windows held up by ivy when we called. It fell on evil days after the death of its founder, for whom prayers were offered in it in 1329, and it has been the home of smugglers. So too, no doubt, has the tower of the church, in which is still kept an arch of the ancient screen, all that is left to show how beautiful this church must have been 500 years ago. An old yew tree, with a trunk over 20 feet round, has seen all this beauty come and go.

Kingsbury Episcopi. The River Parret flowing slowly past sometimes turns it into a lake and sends the villagers about their business in boats brought from the osier beds.

Up a pretty lane, which an old house appears to threaten with a wide leaning chimney, we come upon one of Somerset's proud towers, which has defied wind and water 500 years. It is 120 feet high, with beautiful pierced stone windows, bands of carving, pinnacles, a rich doorway, and many niches with headless figures. In one of the niches is the War Memorial, on which is represented the martyrdom of St Martin. A tiny figure of Christ is over the south porch. There is an old mass dial. Owing to the soft foundations, the tower buttresses have been carried inside for greater strength, there to form a kind of second arch, panelled like the inner one and with four canopied niches. Stone fan-tracery completes a tower all beautiful without and within. The 14th century nave, with a curious collection of high box-pews, has a spacious 15th century chancel of the same height, lit on each side by splendid windows with traceried transoms. In a lovely transept window are fragments of mediaeval glass, some showing pinnacled buildings like a new Jerusalem, a panel of the Madonna, and another panel of St Matthew with his Gospel, the book being open and a quaint little angel speaking to him from its pages.

The 600-year-old font has an unusual design of lines and ledges.

Kingsdon. The little River Cary runs here between two mediaeval buildings, the church on one side and the lovely manor house of Lyte's Cary on the other. The church is among the cottages, a 15th century place with some 14th century windows, a thistle-shaped Norman font, a Jacobean pulpit, and the stone figure of a 13th century knight who reigned in Kingsdon when Edward III reigned over England. He lies with gauntlets, sword, and shield, a coat draped over his armour, a lion at his crossed feet.

Lyte's Cary (now National Trust property) is a typical Somerset stone-built manor house of the 15th century. It has a chapel 100 years older which was for years used as a barn but is a chapel again, its east window filled with quaint figures in blue and gold from the life of Christ. It is a 19th century copy of 13th century glass, and came from the Lyte Chapel in Charlton Mackrell church. The Lyte arms are round a painted frieze. An old prayer desk has drawers and a cupboard, probably from a bedroom of the manor.

There is a minstrel gallery in the stately hall, which has an open timber roof with angel corbels. Swans and horses are moulded on a plaster ceiling, and more swans and horses are outside a lovely bay window; they are the heraldic emblems of John Lyte and Edith Horsey who built this portion more than 400 years ago. Their son Henry made a wonderful garden here and wrote about it in a book called *Lyte's Herbal*.

Kingstone. It has an old church with a farm to match; the church tower rises in the middle of the building, and the bell-ringers stand among the people. A few of the windows have fragments of 15th century glass. A blocked doorway is carved with rosettes, and the font is probably early 13th century.

Kingston St Mary. Here for 500 years was a French king's sword, brought by John de la Warre from Poitiers. He hung it up in the church, above a magnificent tomb ten feet long, with coats-of-arms all round. There the sword remained for centuries, later

157

to hang in the hall of Hestercombe, the home of the Warres, till the last Warre died and the possessions of the house were scattered. That is the last we know of the sword of the French King John.

There is another fine old house in the village called the Grange, with a turret look-out and a mass of the tall chimneys which were the delight of Tudor builders.

The church tower is one of the finest of a noble 15th century group in Somerset. It has pinnacles, parapets, and niches borne on angels. The 15th century porch is in fine contrast to the plain narrow arches of the 13th century nave. The font is 16th century, and the pulpit 18th. One of the bells is mediaeval. There are old bench-ends with homely carvings of oxen and their yokes, and a weaving shuttle which speaks of the days of Somerset's great prosperity, when the wool trade flourished and the merchants gave the church its tower.

Kingston Seymour. The sea has several times tried to swallow this rich marshland village, which owes its name of Seymour to a lord of the manor, one of the barons who stood with King John at Runnymede as he sealed Magna Carta in his rage. Painted on wood in the church is an old account of the time when the waves broke down the village defences and filled the Norman font with sea water. For ten days the flood was five feet deep, the water above the pews. However, the work of our three great building centuries was here to defy the sea. The open parapet of the tower, from which springs a short spire, was finished about 1400. Cut through a wall and the splay of a window is a peephole to the altar. On the font are four crosses. A new cross tops the fine shaft of the old one in the churchyard.

Kingweston. Half of it is in the park, gathered round the great house and the church, the simple spire of which is an uncommon sight in this county of sturdy towers. Kingweston's church was destroyed last century, but three good things survived. One is the magnificent Norman doorway with its waving lines of chevrons and its sides criss-crossed to the ground; it is one of the finest of these arches left in Somerset. Another survival is the simple Norman font, and the third is a chair from Glastonbury, a thrilling possession, for it has on it the initials of Richard Whiting, the last of the abbots of that famous abbey. In this chair would sit that good old man in the days before the imperious king and his servile Thomas Cromwell broke up the monasteries, pulled down churches, and sent out a command that Richard Whiting should be dragged to the top of Glastonbury Tor to take one look at his abbey, and then should be butchered.

The shaft and base of the old churchyard cross have been used for a new one.

Kittisford. Its high church tower is buttressed to the top, the finest thing in this lonely place above the Valley of the Tone. Inside the church is something we have rarely come upon in our tour of England, a 16th century south arcade made of oak. The seats are four or five centuries old, and the oak pulpit has the date 1610 cut twice, the carver miscalculating the space the first time and deciding to try again. Only half a dozen times in our visits to 10,000 churches have we come upon such oddities. In a chest is some armour put aside after the Stuart wars. On a wall are the brass portraits of Richard Bluett and his wife, who lived on the other side of the river at Cothay Barton 400 years ago. It is one of the loveliest homes in England. First we come to a small lake, then to a gatehouse opening on a green where peacocks tread serenely, then to a perfect 15th century house. The crooked porch was probably part of an earlier building, and there is an Elizabethan wing, but the fireplaces and the panelling of the Bluetts are older still, and the lead guttering on the roofs is as fine today as when the people looked up to it and wondered at this clever new idea. The hall has a magnificent roof on arched trusses with angel corbels, an oak screen, and a gallery leading to the bedrooms. On the walls are two Madonna pictures, simple and with a rare charm, and other paintings of life in England 400 years ago.

Knowle St Giles. Past a manor house with fine old windows and up a grassy lane we must climb to as hidden a place as Somerset has if we want to see how well this old church has been made new, even to the font and the stone pulpit with its many little heads.

Lamyatt. The 15th century church is in the farmyard with the barns and with two yews, one a fine old tree, the other shading the porch. The tower has outside steps to the belfry. It has two turrets with stone vaulting, one with two Tudor doorways and four stone corbels. The chancel arch is panelled, the roof of the nave has 15th century tiebeams with open-work impressive for so small a church, and there is a fine Norman font with cable moulding round it.

Two heads of saints have been wearing away in the west wall for centuries and two bells in the tower are mediaeval. There is an old mass dial.

Langford Budville. The village has a bushy heath of its own, and a mediaeval church with a handsome carved parapet and rows of tiny wooden angels with gold wings under the roof of the south aisle. The beautiful font is 16th century. No one here seems to know more than we do about the little mystery of a slender stone needle about a foot long, with a stone thread running through the eye. The needle is under one of the rings of foliage which take the place of capitals on the columns of the nave.

Langport. It has the charm of an old-world market town, with the narrowest of main streets over the River Parret, a noble church on the top of its hill, and a curious chapel on an arch over the road, to surprise the traveller and set him wondering if he has come unexpectedly on a bit of some walled city.

This hanging chapel was built for a tradesmen's guild in mediaeval days. It became a school, and the Freemasons have made it their own.

Norman and 15th century, simplicity and adornment, meet at the church door, where is a tympanum carved with angels worshipping the Lamb of God, a bishop and priest among them. The door itself is traceried and transomed like one of the windows which make the 15th century chancel so rich a setting for its wonderful collection of mediaeval glass. Among the host of saints in the soft blues and greens and reds of the east window is a little pig with a bell round its neck. It is Anthony's pig. Clement is here with his anchor, Rhoda with her palm, Dorothy with fruit and flowers, and an endearing Joseph of Arimathea with the Holy Grail. They crowd with their fellow saints round Mary as the angel announces to her the glad tidings; and above them all are the arms of John Heron, who gave Langport this glorious window 500 years ago, mullions, tracery, glass, and all. On the wall hangs a fine oil-painting of the Madonna mourning her Son. The font is 500 years old.

Langridge. There is no more delightful experience for an Englishman than to be lost in some of the lanes round Bath, and if it is in the valley by the Gloucester Road it is all the better. When we come to Langridge there is nothing about us but the lovely group made by the barn, the farmhouse, and the church.

160

We are lost to the world in the presence of the past; we stand where Romans, Saxons, and Normans must have been, for hereabouts have been found the foundations of a Roman house.

Yet it is Norman England we begin with. We come through the yew arch at the gateway and up the steps to the roses climbing about the porch (with mediaeval tiles in its walls), to find ourselves at a magnificent Norman doorway. It has a triple arch, carved with flowers and zigzag, set on rounded columns, and inside these an inner arch like a rope of stone curiously twisted round. It leads us into a perfect little Norman building 50 feet long and 18 feet wide, with a tiny modern apse seen through the chancel arch. The arch was made by the men who made the doorway, and has also three orders of moulding, with zigzags and balls all round. It is set on huge square columns with a rounded shaft running up the centre, both columns with cushioned capitals, and above the arch, set in a tiny Norman recess, the Madonna and the Child have looked down on this small place for 800 years. They have been in this quiet hollow of the hills since the days when Norman barons were fighting for our liberty.

On the wall of the nave is the brass portrait of Elizabeth Wallshe, who may have lived in the house next door. They laid her here in 1441, and on her brass her little dog is sitting at her feet. On a tomb in the tower is the stone figure of another lady probably from next door; she lies with long wavy hair and a scarf about her neck. In the chancel lies Ann Gunning who lived across the valley at Swainswick; she lies with her father and mother, and in spirit at least she must have been worthy of the beautiful Gunning sisters of whom all the world has heard, for we read of her that she was a woman of admirable art and beauty, uniting in a high degree a strong understanding and a good heart. The 700-year-old font is mounted on a great base.

The delightful farmhouse, set back from the lane across a little lawn, is the old home of the Wallshes, mediaeval lords of the manor; it was built in the 13th century and refashioned in the 16th and it has the old trefoiled windows.

A little way from this deep solitude, up on the broadbacked hill of Lansdown, stands the monument set up by Cornish men to keep alive the name of Bevil Grenville, who fell here in the hour of victory in one of the fiercest of the early battles of the Civil War.

Laverton. This little place has something left from Norman England in its 13th century church. It has all been restored so neatly that we see its Norman doorway with the old shafts and capitals; its saddleback tower has still two Norman windows with no glass in them, and the arch of a vanished Norman window is visible in the western wall. Here, too, is something of the old rood stairway.

At this font 15 generations of Laverton children have been baptised. There are 16th century tombs in the churchyard and an 18th century monument with cherubs in the nave. The altar has two neatly carved oak panels and a dainty embroidered frontal between them. The plastered roof of the nave has charming floral bosses, and shields along the cornice. The windows have angels and apostles.

Leigh-on-Mendip. The 15th century church of this bleak village on a ridge of hills is a splendid place.

Notable among its many treasures is an uncommonly complete set of mediaeval seating. Magnificently carved, some with small arcading and spandrels, some with double arches and quatrefoils, some like 14th century windows, the old benches are all extraordinarily impressive, heavily marked by the hand of time.

Here is the rough Norman font, the marble altar slab which has been buried in the earth and found again, and here are 30 stone angels holding up magnificent roofs. The splendid chancel roof has 96 oak panels with fine carved bosses, and oak angels along the cornice. The nave roof has deeply carved beams, the tower arch rising up to them and revealing the splendid west window. In it is a captivating blaze of colour in squares and diamonds with wheels and little panels of every shape and size, into which are worked the emblems of the Passion, pretty little portraits of angels, one of Our Lord, and two with crowns. It is one of the loveliest pieces of colour for miles around, and is 15th century. The east window tracery has other mediaeval fragments.

Among all that is old in this fine place what will probably appeal most strongly to many are two stone angels which seem to be on guard in the sanctuary. They are looking down from the wall on each side of the altar rails, and are remarkable because they are among the very few survivals in all England of angels whose purpose was to hold up the Lenten veil before the Reformation.

One of the precious possessions of the village is the parish register of 1566; we found its pages fine and clear after all these centuries. Guarded with great reverence is another ancient possession of

Leigh, a fragment of a mediaeval carving of a figure of St Catherine. She lies on a windowsill, having lost her head, but still with part of her wheel.

Perhaps we have left the best to the last, for this fine church has a noble exterior. Its 17th century porch has a crude mediaeval pillar stoup, much battered by time, but for the rest the outward splendour of the church remains.

Was ever a tower so pinnacled, were ever walls so rich with parapets, in any village church? Round the walls of the aisles and round the clerestory above run the open parapets with great bands of quatrefoils carved with roses and shields, and up the tower, which is built with oyster shells between its stones, run more pinnacles than we have seen on any tower we remember, on the buttresses and on canopied niches borne by winged angels.

Limington. It was in our great Tudor days that Limington was buzzing with the news that its young rector had been put in the stocks for being (it was said) scandalously drunk at a performance of the Lopen Play. An unfortunate day it was for Sir Amyas Poulett, the High Sheriff who had to mete out this justice, for the rector became the most powerful man in the land next to the king, none other than Cardinal Wolsey, and he never forgave Sir Amyas.

Only a print of Holbein's portrait reminds us here of the cardinal, but we know that he held the village babies before this fine font when it was new, his hands rested in the carved piscina of this 15th century chancel, and surely he smiled, as we do, at the two grotesque heads supporting the 14th century tower arch, the arms of one clutching a pair of tiny legs and those of the other a tiny head to match. We see the north chapel as it was in his day, with its fine vaulted stone roof, of which the ribs run in parallel arches. Here lies, cross-legged in his chain mail, Richard Gyverney, builder of the chapel in 1329, with Gunnora his wife resting her wimpled head on a tomb below, and close by a nameless couple who may be his father and mother. Father and mother, son and daughters, are worn and black with age. The initials of a later lord of the manor, the Lord Harington killed at the battle of Wakefield in 1460, are entwined with his wife's in a lovers' knot on the choir-stalls. There are some excellent linenfold panels, Jacobean and mediaeval, a few of them from an old screen of which only the base remains.

Litton. We burst suddenly upon a great and quiet scene with the village in a hollow, sheep lying across the road as we run down to it.

Its streets are steep and winding and its long stone walls run everywhere, one of them six feet deep in white arabis when we called. It is an old, old place, and in its churchyard is a great stone bowl which it is thought may have been the font of a Saxon church.

Looking down on it all is a green cockerel perched above the rich pinnacles of the tower. On the walls are four fearful gargoyles and two angels with a row of about 30 stone heads in which we noticed men with beards, women with wimples, and a man laughing. There is a mass dial. Indoors are ancient benches with the marks of the axe on them still clearly seen after 500 years, and there is a Jacobean pulpit and a 15th century font.

Locking. It has the remains of an old windmill from its near past, and from the distant past come the mystery of a small chamber, nine feet square, found in a mound like a tumulus, and the huge stones forming a miniature Stonehenge on the manor lawn. Several are over eight feet high, and we could scarcely believe the story of the rector who brought them here in bullock wagons from a stone circle on the Mendips.

The 19th century built a new church, but kept the pleasant 15th century tower and two ancient treasures, the pulpit and the font, both of old stones. The stone pulpit is a rare one, 500 years old, its carving unhappily covered with paint. The font, like a trough on one old leg and four new ones, is Norman, with figures at the corners which might have come out of a Bayeux tapestry. They stretch out their hands to each other across a snake-like pattern, wearing little skirts such as a child might draw. Outside the west window are two quaint heads, one with long ears and a lolling tongue.

Long Ashton. Though so near Bristol, here are beautiful woods and dales which set us dreaming of Exmoor; and behind a wall five miles long is what is thought to be the oldest deer park in England, with Ashton Court set in the midst. There have been deer here since the park was planted in 1391, and here is a tree called Domesday Oak supplied with crutches to rest its weary limbs. The house is 15th and 19th century, two houses as one, the ancient front designed by Inigo Jones. The windows have 15th century heraldic glass.

The church has much treasure from mediaeval days: an old altar stone, a bell older than the Reformation, two stone figures worn and broken from the 13th century, ancient glass in the chancel, and fine tombs. On the oldest tomb lies Sir Richard Choke, a red and white figure in his judge's robes with a dagger and a rosary hanging from his belt. So he was in 1454 when he bought the great house in the deer park. His wife lies with him in a red cloak, with a heavy gold necklace and a pointed black cap, and we may wonder if there is a painted tomb more perfect anywhere. Time has not spoiled even the little bird-like angels about their pillows, or the angels on the painted canopy, or those golden winged ones carved at the back holding prayers for God's mercy.

In an old carved tomb under an arch lies the tenant of Ashton Court before Sir Richard came to it, and there are wonderfully carved alabaster memorials to the Smyths who lived at the Court in Elizabeth's day. Thomas Smyth was a Stuart MP, and lived in grand style with nine maid-servants and 20 serving men; he was one of the last people to keep a jester.

Matching with its vivid colours the judge's tomb is a rich and heavily gilded screen which has stretched the whole width of the church since mediaeval days. The rail of the roodloft has been brought down and made into a second cornice for it. Its doorways are beautifully carved, and it is an impressive sight.

Long Load. Long it is, for it straggles nearly a mile down the road, with only one thing to make us pause all the way—a massive 17th century pulpit in the 19th century church. The bridge over the Yeo has four triple arches of the 15th century.

Long Sutton. We remember it for its village green and its delightful windows, many of them set in the old Court House, where each has a different level from its neighbour. The 15th century church has fine old windows, three in a row in the belfry of its high tower. The tower has a vaulted roof and a tall panelled arch. We come through an old studded door to find the church gay with colour. The fan-vaulted screen of 1520 stretches across the nave and aisles, bright blue, red, and white, like a barber's pole. The blue ceiling is dotted with gold stars, the only original colouring left. Even the Jacobean cover of the 15th century font has been painted. The pulpit is a gorgeous spectacle in wood, 400 years old with a 17th century canopy. It rests on a base carved in tiers, rising from a slender and neatly panelled pillar. Round eight sides are modern figures in pinnacled niches under richly carved canopies. Round the top is a crest of delicate foliage and elegant candelabra.

Lopen. It is remembered chiefly because a young rector of Limington sat fuming with rage in its stocks; he had come over from his neighbouring rectory for the Lopen feast, a merry affair at which he is said to have drunk not wisely but too well, so that the High Sheriff, Sir Amyas Poulett, put him in the stocks for disorderly conduct.

The rector grew up to be a famous man although he was only a butcher's son, for he became Chancellor of England as Cardinal Wolsey. It is said that he never forgot or forgave the insult of the stocks at Lopen, and in his days of power he had his chance to avenge himself by ordering Sir Amyas not to leave London without his permission. Sir Amyas was Treasurer of the Inner Temple, and was virtually a prisoner there until he flattered Wolsey by putting his badge on the new Temple gateway, so that the Cardinal relented and allowed him to return to Somerset.

Wolsey must often have been in this 15th century church, but it is not as he saw it, though the font has been here 700 years and there are old altar rails and two old chancel chairs. There is also an architectural puzzle, an odd little splayed arch in the porch.

Lovington. Under a tall yew in the churchyard is a post and a bit of wood almost eaten away, leaving enough for the village to boast that it still has its stocks. It has lost its mediaeval church, which, except for the heavily buttressed tower, has been made new. Its old font has needed patching, too; but there are some bench-ends with poppyheads 500 years old, and the mediaeval stone carving round the aumbry makes it unique in Somerset. The piscina with a shelf in it has also survived, and outside the west window is tracery with Tudor roses above it. There is a dial from the days before clocks.

Low Ham. For more than 300 years its church has stood in a field at the foot of High Ham Hill, but still no path is worn to it, and we must walk among the sheep to reach the door of one of Somerset's most interesting churches, a rare example of imitation Gothic from the 17th century. Its builder was Sir Edward Hext, who was brought here to lie by his wife. Their beautiful stone figures rest on a railed tomb, both with ruffs and he in armour with his head on a plumed helmet and a lifelike dog at his feet. Their only daughter married Sir John Stawell of Cothelstone, but their grandsons came back to finish the church, George completing the building and Ralph giving the altar silver still in use, with the red velvet altar cloth looking as if it would last for ever. Their arms are on the chancel door, and there is a railed monument to Ralph, his two wives, and his son John, the boy who left the puzzling maze of embankments beside the church, foundations of a dream which never came true.

Young John meant to build here a mansion which should be the most beautiful of its kind, but it was a broken dream. He made plans for a veritable palace, 400 feet by 100. He sold 26 manors to pay for it, but died almost before it was begun. Only the gateway seems to have been complete and even that is gone, carried away in 20 wagons with 40 horses to where it stands as an entrance to Hazelgrove House near Sparkford.

Within the church the stone screen with its carved oak doors confronts us as a delightful surprise as we enter; and the chancel has another screen, a tiny oak one carved on both sides, with a vine trailing along the east cornice and back again along the west. The stone screen came from another chapel, but this one was put here by Edward Hext, his grandson adding the 14 gold cherubs. The carving of the old pulpit is gilded to match.

In a patchwork of 17th century and modern glass Mary and John stand sorrowfully by the Cross. Unusually fanciful is the tracery of the clerestory windows. One of the bells is 14th century, and there is a door older still, with hinges made seven or eight centuries ago.

Loxton. Above its old houses looms Crook's Peak, the last of the Mendips; and in the dark narrow church is one of the mediaeval stone pulpits which are the pride of Mendip villages. Made about 1460, it is very fine with pinnacled canopies, though not quite so rich and delicate as its fellow at Compton Bishop. A stone man helps to support it The 13th century tower forms the porch too, and here is a curious peephole to the altar, cut six feet or more through the wall, probably so that the ringer could see when to sound the bell at the raising of the Host. The font and a rather poor screen with linenfold panels are both about 500 years old. A patchwork of 14th century glass lights the vestry. The venerable shaft of the 15th century cross in the churchyard holds up a new head with little figures like those which time had broken.

Luccombe. It is the way of the world that the accommodating Vicar of Bray should be famous and the Vicar of Luccombe unknown. Here he lies, the staunch Royalist Henry Byam, born at the foot of Dunkery Beacon. He became its parson, and he it was who roused the Exmoor men to fight for the king, placing four of his sons as captains at their head. However, the invincible Blake was out against them and all was lost; even the vicar's wife and daughter were drowned in trying to escape to Wales.

Yet Henry Byam lived. He followed Charles abroad, and we can still read the sermons he preached to the exile. He lived to see the Stuarts back and then returned to Luccombe, happy again in this church so delicately and so beautifully made.

Luccombe is a village of charming cottages, with the base of an ancient cross much older than them all.

Lullington. It is a gem of England as it is and has a gem of England as it was in Norman days, for the church is a place of pilgrimage to those who love the things the Normans left behind.

The lychgate gives us a lovely view of a thatched corner of the countryside, with a pine against the sky, trimmed yews lining the path, and a farmhouse which comes into the picture as if it were part of the church. The noble 15th century tower has the lovely windows we are so familiar with in Somerset, and round the walls are fierce animals ready to leap down.

We come into the nave by a Norman doorway, with twisted pillars, carved gables, and beak-heads. Over it is a tympanum probably carved by master masons brought from Normandy, for the whole of this doorway appears to be inspired by work we have seen at Caen. The Conqueror gave Lullington to a bishop friend who may have brought the masons over. The tympanum is much worn by eight centuries of wind and rain, but the figures are still recognisable as wild beasts devouring the Tree of Life, with God over all on the throne, a hand raised in blessing. Above this are five grotesque sculptures with rows of five on either side, many of them crumbled away.

The lovely Norman chancel arch has clustered columns and bead ornament. On one of the capitals are two animals sharing one head, and two grotesque birds which seem to be putting their heads together in earnest conversation. The font is worthy of these Norman masons, who probably made it. It is shaped like a tub and has three bands of stonework round it, a frieze of animal heads and human faces, a band of flowers, and a ring of arcading, while round the bowl runs a Latin verse which means that in this holy bowl sins perish.

There are two narrow Norman windows, and set in the wall of the vestry is a coffin stone going back almost to Norman days, showing the Hand of God reaching down from the clouds to a cross.

Luxborough. We who climb to this solitary place can only wonder at the indomitable spirit of the men who built it; it stands a lonely outpost on one of the peaks of the Brendon Hills. The old church has lost most of its old possessions save for the 16th century font. The shaft of the ancient cross is broken, and even the bells are new.

Lydeard St Lawrence. It was the home of Old Man Rich; he may have been christened at the curious font in its 14th century church, and he must have loved this view of the Quantocks, which seem here to change their green to blue and back again like a chameleon. The Norman font is curious, like a Norman font placed upside down with a bowl placed on top of it, the whole capped by a pointed cover.

The capitals of the nave are 15th century, and one has a fox creeping round it with a goose in its mouth, another has four angels. There is a much-battered screen of the same age with Jacobean paintings, a beautifully carved Jacobean pulpit, and some fine Tudor bench-ends. Above the south porch with its decorative battlements is a sundial of 1653. Perhaps we may like the outside of the church better than the inside; certainly it is finely planned, and has a very handsome tower.

Lympsham. The manor house is richly decked with pierced parapet, pinnacles, and great windows. It is imitation Tudor, but the church is real, with a beautiful 15th century tower, double belfry windows, and massive pinnacles. The light flows into the chancel through the fine tracery of two low windows of an earlier church which for centuries lay blocked in the walls. In a window of the north aisle are two roundels of mediaeval glass showing in vivid colours St Christopher and a church built on a rock. From two raised seats generations of churchwardens have kept an eye on their congregations. The tub-shaped font cut with zigzags is the work of a Norman craftsman, but unfortunately it has been spoilt.

Lynch. Something of the past has come back to Lynch, for its 16th century chapel was a barn and is a church again, with seats for 36 people, a choir gallery built from oaks grown in the neighbourhood, and panelling from 18th century pews at Selworthy. Nearby is the manor house, a treasury of ancient oak. Up a narrow lane by the old mill is a picture to remember: a group of white thatched cottages with rounded chimneys, and a rock garden watered by a stream which curves round the roots of two walnut trees as the sea curls round the foot of the wooded hills.

Lyng. It belongs to Athelney, or rather Athelney now belongs to it. Its small church was a chapel of the monastery Alfred built as thanks for the shelter Athelney gave him in his struggle with the Danes. Its site is marked today by his portrait in relief on a block of stone set up last century close to where his old fort (Burrow Mump) heaves its steep sides above the plain.

The church has a 15th century tower with pierced stone windows to let out the sound of the bells, a charming crown to the turret stairs. The bare stone walls inside make a pleasant background for a remarkable collection of 16th century bench-ends. There is a font made soon after the Normans came to England, an old pulpit, a chest hollowed from a tree trunk and now crumbling to dust, a patchwork of soft-hued ancient glass in the chancel, and a canopied stone seat.

On 16th century bench-ends here are many pictures, from Tudor England and the land of fantasy. A woman carries a pitcher on her head, a rider has a sack on his; there is a dog after a rabbit, and a heron catching an eel (we may see a real one fishing in the dykes close by if we are lucky). Two wrestlers struggle together, and then one stands triumphantly on the other. We see a woodcutter, a child riding something half-bird, half-bull, and holding on to the tail of its queer mount, and many birds and beasts of all kinds and shapes; and through this queer assortment a young couple wander hand in hand. High on the chancel wall are fragments of a painting centuries old.

Maperton. Its ups and downs and woods are lovely in all seasons; its road is best when the rhododendrons are out; while a glance round the church (hiding behind the big house) reveals that here are those who love beauty and the dignity of age. Not that the church is old. All but its 15th century tower has been made new, but the porch has been turned into a museum of things from the old one—a piece of interlaced carving like Saxon stonework, a piscina thought to be Norman, and several curious stone heads. The Norman font has been brought in from the churchyard and given place of honour instead of the new one; and lying in its old place under the tower is a stone of 1677 bearing an epitaph which appears in various forms in many places, but in none more gracious than this earliest of all:

> *Short were her dayes, yet dyed she never.*
> *Death had his will, yet lives she ever.*

Mark. It straggles through the now drained marshland to the north of the Polden Ridge, and has a big and splendid church 500 years old. The parapet of the nave is a lovely thing to see, but surely no church has quainter corbels than those which catch the eye indoors, king and queens, abbot and bishops, all carved in wood and painted in bright colours, all old save three newcomers, King Edward and Queen Alexandra and Bishop Kennion of Wells.

Stone angel corbels are under the carved roof of the north aisle, where oak angels spread their wings along the frieze, some bearing the ladder, pincers, nails, and other symbols of the Crucifixion. It is a noble array of carving, and there is more to see; a glorious old traceried door, a 15th century screen and another which is partly mediaeval and partly Jacobean, a Jacobean pulpit, and four splendid statues of the writers of the Gospels, rising from the backs of the choir-stalls, each with his winged symbol. They are a precious set of wood figures brought by a vicar from the Continent, where they are believed to have been made for the Cathedral of Bruges. It is said that the vicar paid £70 for them, and that they may be worth £2000. The artist's conception of the Four Evangelists is entirely original, Matthew being curiously gaunt and tall.

The font has a row of angels under its bowl, one with a naked figure in its arms; it is 16th century with a cover of the 17th. By it are some rough old benches of the usual mediaeval uprightness, so that none could loll in them. In one of the windows is a little mediaeval glass with eight old figures of saints.

The inn by the church gate has the royal arms on the ceiling at the entrance. A mile or so away the road crosses the River Brue by an ancient bridge.

Marksbury. It is a long time since John Chinnock, the Abbot of Glastonbury, lived here, and only a few stones are left of his moated house.

The small tower of the church was crowned 200 years ago with pinnacles rather like upturned trumpets, rising 20 feet above the roof and bearing four weathervanes. The stone of the old rector William Quintyn has been used outside as a windowsill, and other tombstones have been built into the walls. One has a quaint assurance that those who sleep beneath it outside are quite as comfortable as those within; being poor, we read, they rest out of doors.

The sanctuary has a beautiful Jacobean oak table with massive legs carved with the heads of dogs. On the wall by it is a tablet with cherubs, skulls, and crossbones. Another tablet tells us that

Francis Popham lies here, heir to the fortunes as well as the virtues of his family.

It was from this old manor house, built in the 18th century near the site of the Abbot of Glastonbury's home, that there set out in 1797 the funeral procession of Francis Popham's wife, who was buried at midnight, the road from Hunstrete to Marksbury church being lit by torches. Many tales are told of this eccentric old lady. Once she arrived at Chew Stoke when the famous Bilbie was recasting the tenor bell now in the tower, and she threw in a lapful of silver to sweeten the tone. Certainly this bell is very soft and sweet, though it has had to be recast.

Marston Bigott. We dip down into the quiet hollow of a park, up a little path by a thatched cottage, through a tiny lychgate with a verse from Lewis Morris to greet us, up a flight of steps, along an avenue of trimmed yews, to a new tower built in Norman style. The tower has memories of the Corks—a mother-of-pearl tablet to a Countess of Cork by her four daughters, and a white sculpture of Louisa Boyle who was *peculiarly dear to the inhabitants of this parish where she spent her few years.* We see her lying with her sorrowing parents and her brother at her head. From the tower we reach a heavy stone gallery used by the people of Marston House, an 18th and 19th century mansion set in 400 acres.

The church is built as the Normans built, but is all made new. The chancel roof is vaulted and the modern arch has a fine line of zigzag round it. There is a chest of 1666. Its finest possession, however, is the glowing east window with five panels of Continental glass, charming with the quaintness of the Flemish and German artists. In one the Archangel Gabriel with wings like a bat's, and in a gold and scarlet robe, is coming up behind the Madonna, who has a white dove on her golden halo. Another window has three nobles at a feast with fine views of the rooms in the house, where we see people walking. Another has a procession of people gaily dressed in red and green and gold, followed by sheep, oxen, and queer men on camels. The fourth shows two old men in rich colours carrying an enormous bunch of grapes on a stick between them; and the fifth is a Crucifixion, rather cruel and terrible, with the Cross set as in an eastern palace and blood flowing in streams, filling a huge bowl of blue and gold.

Marston Magna. The brook running through the village turned the mill on its way until shortly before the last war; it once served the moat of a manor long since vanished. West of it is a delightful Jacobean house with a sundial of Shakespeare's day. The church is of late 11th century origin, as is shown by the herringbone work in the north wall of the chancel.

The chancel arch is late 14th century, but the beautiful font is Norman, with a fluted basin and its original lead lining. On the east side of the door is the hole for the beam which barred it in mediaeval days, and on a buttress is a scratch dial which marked the sunny hours long before the old clock came in 1710. Opening from the north porch through a 16th century screen is a 15th century chapel with splendid windows and a lovely canopied niche. Recently several paintings were discovered, including one depicting the martyrdom of St Thomas of Canterbury. There is a plain 18th century pulpit with a sounding board, and in the windows is some old glass showing two golden-winged angels, a king's head and shoulders in ermine, and a chalice.

Martock. What many people here call the grandest roof in Somerset is in the beautiful church of this charming little town. A long avenue of tall trimmed yews approaches the church, framing the plain 15th century tower and transforming it to a thing of beauty. Human gargoyles sit precariously round the top, and a winged dragon creeps round.

Rich men rebuilt the nave in the 15th century, putting their arms on the lace-like parapet and on a shield inside; but the humble chancel is as the 13th century left it, with its steep gable resting on two corbel heads, one with hands raised to help to bear the weight. Huge clerestory windows light up every detail of the stately nave with its panelled shafts and crested cornice, its shields and spandrels and angels, and its vaulted niches with 17th century paintings of the Twelve Apostles, curious sombre pictures set in dazzling white. A curious thing the builders did was to carry buttresses of the tower through the wall to form a panelled arch.

High above it all is the famous roof, its timbers fretted and pierced and ornamented till there seems no inch uncarved. There are no fewer than 750 panels, with designs seldom repeated. Angels spread great wings on each side of kingposts ending in massive pendants, and pierced tracery joins the crested tiebeams to the beams above. No tribute of wonder is too high for the courage and skill which conceived such a roof and finished it more than 400 years ago.

Under an arch of flowers lies a worn and nameless figure. Behind the new altar table a big stone cupboard is hollowed in the wall, an unusual double aumbry. A crude wood painting shows David playing his harp. The font is 500 years old. The organ was built by Father Schmidt, to whom Charles II gave a workshop in Whitehall Palace, and one of the bells is twice as old.

The vaulted porch is a beauty, with stone seats put here 500 years ago, and with two dials scratched on the wall. There are five more dials on or about the south buttresses, a remarkable number we do not remember ever to have seen exceeded. Lads playing fives against the tower notched a buttress by the other porch and used it as a ladder for retrieving balls stuck in the roof; we can see the holes they made for scoring.

Facing the church is the old manor house, with a broken archway for carriages and a smaller one for those who walk. It has 13th century arches, a 14th century hall, and a Tudor kitchen. The buttery windows with a 14th century sun-room above them make an exquisite corner of mediaeval England.

That is the old manor house; the new one is 17th century, and the ruin of one of the 15th is in a field guarded by a water-filled moat. By the church corner is the old court house, now the church house but turned into a grammar school by William Strode in 1661. By the 18th century market house is an old column with a new sundial on the top and seats round the base. Near by flows the River Parrett, crossed by an ancient bridge, and not far off is Hamdon Hill, whose golden stone built Old Martock.

Meare. Its ancient past has been among the waters. We may stand in the fields and see the mounds on which the mud and wattle huts stood on piles in the marshes before the beginning of the Christian era, and even in days long after that the great Meare Pool was flooded for 500 acres in winter, so that there is a record in the church accounts that in 1765 the sexton was paid eighteenpence for rowing the church clock from Glastonbury.

Today Meare has a green meadow set in the midst of one of our lovely English groups, the church, the manor, and the house of the ancient fisherman of the Abbot of Glastonbury. All three are from the 14th century. The fish-house is the property of the nation, the manor has become a farm, the church remains, the one unchanging thing throughout the centuries.

The abbot's fish-house would be a cottage in those days, 600 years ago, the fisherman living on the upper floor and keeping his fish and his tackle below. He had no communication between the floors inside, and the outside steps have gone. Through the windows of this stone house we see the central room, the massive timbers, and the open fireplace. Round about it in olden days were three small pools stocked with fish.

Across the meadow is the lovely manor house with a room over the porch and a quaint stone bishop on its gable. It has Gothic windows with beautiful tracery, a hall 60 feet long, a roof covered with lichen, and a long low barn close by.

We come to the church down a charming pathway under the limes, bringing us to one of the rarest doors we have seen, reminding us of the marvellous door to the Treasury at Wells. This one swings on two remarkable hinges 600 years old, fashioned into something wonderful, appearing to represent vases with foliage coming from them. One of them spreads out so far that it is ten feet round. There are few if any better examples of mediaeval ironwork in England.

We open it into an attractive nave with a panelled roof in which the great moulded beams are well lighted from the clerestoried windows. Stone angels hold up the roofs, and in the chancel the roof is of open woodwork like the hall of a manor house. Two sturdy little angels watch at the chancel arch. The chancel itself is 14th century, and by the sanctuary, leading to the vestry, is a Tudor archway with an elaborate traceried window over it. From the roof hangs a brass chandelier of 1777, and in one of the windows are bits of ancient glass no bigger than a man's hand. Set in the chancel wall at an odd angle is a curious piscina, and there is a fine alms-box on a stem, carved with dainty arches by a 15th century craftsman. The stone pulpit is 15th century; it is a fine example, panelled and pinnacled and carved with roses. The nave in which it stands was rebuilt 500 years ago by Abbot Selwood, and his monogram is on the parapet above the south aisle.

Four miles west of the old lake village of Glastonbury the Meare lake village lies on one side of the drained Meare Pool, five miles round in Elizabethan days.

The village was in two parts, divided by a water channel, the two parts having about 150 dwelling-places, now seen as round mounds seldom rising more than two feet above the flat peat moor.

An excavation of one of these mounds disclosed three clay floors of a circular hut, not laid on a timber foundation as in many lake dwellings, but on the bare surface of the firm peat. On the second floor was a clay hearth. The upper floor was roughly paved with stone in patches. Other mounds were sites of houses generally round but sometimes rectangular and built on a timber foundation in swamp or shallow water.

Most of the huts seem to have been raised on a mass of timber resting on the bed of the swamp. On to this, clay brought from higher ground was beaten into a hard mass and a wattle and daub hut was raised over it, with a hearth in the middle. If the foundations sank another layer of clay would be raised and a new stone hearth built on top of the old. One of the huts had had seven floors laid down.

The age of these remains can be discovered from the objects discovered in and about the dwellings. Among them is pottery probably made centuries before the Romans came. With these were flint and stone implements of the old Stone Age, which the villagers had probably found or inherited.

Glass beads and bronze brooches have been found, a jet ring, a finely worked knife handle, and a great butcher's knife; there were many bones of birds and young animals, including the remains of a pony, a pig, and a dog.

The discoveries most clearly dating the village are Roman coins of Constantius and Valentinian of the 4th century, which show that some of the sites were inhabited for a time towards the end of the Roman occupation. They must certainly have been occupied some centuries before, and their discovery and exploration afford a most interesting insight into the life of this populous place 2000 years ago. We may see many of the objects found in the Lake Village in the county museum at Taunton.

Mells. Every child will love it and every grown up too, for it is Little Jack Horner's plum. Lovely it was to find that the ages have not spoiled it.

At the wayside is a stone-flagged resting-place with seats about. Across the road is the children's corner, beyond are charming thatched cottages, herbaceous borders along the street, a long stone wall that runs round the rectory garden and never seems to end, and, opposite the rectory, a narrow way between the cottages leading us to a pillared gateway.

The magnificent church rises in front of us with one of the richest exteriors we have seen, and over the stone wall is the lovely Tudor manor house built in the shape of an H. It was largely built by Little Jack Horner who sat in a corner in the office of Thomas Cromwell when he was breaking up the monasteries for his royal master. We do not wonder that, seeing his opportunity to make Mells his own, Horner put in his thumb and took out this plum.

The great church was here then, for it is 15th century everywhere. It rises in battlements and pinnacles, like a mass of beautiful stone that climbs and climbs until it reaches the top of the wonderful tower, handsome with its blind tracery and its pierced stone windows, adorned with slender pinnacled buttresses all the way to the parapet. The loveliness of it all grows on us as we walk round it looking up to its gargoyles, enchanted by the old priest's door, and tempted by the pathway through an avenue of yews with the wreck of a venerable elm in a field beyond the stile.

Inside this majestic place we come to find that Mells indoors is worthy of its out-of-doors. We step into the tower to find fan-vaulted roofs, old pews in front of us, the heavy timbered roof of the nave resting on 12 stone angels crowning the rugged walls, the light falling through clerestory windows, and on each side of us something moving and something of a delicate beauty.

On the right is Raymond Asquith's sword, the sword he had with him when he fell in France on September 15, 1916. Who that was living then forgets the day when the Prime Minister who led us with high dignity into the valley of the shadow lost his firstborn son? Here he lived, out there he lies, and his sword is the proud possession of the village he loved. The white cross from his grave in France is also here, in the Horner Chapel. We read of him that in the flower of his youth he took up arms for his country and died fighting bravely, that his body lies in a distant and friendly land and is followed by the grief of those who loved him.

Facing this sword, carved on a great stone on the wall, is a handsome peacock designed by Burne-Jones as the ancient symbol of the resurrection, in memory of Laura Lyttelton, wife of Alfred Lyttelton, who many times crossed political swords with Raymond Asquith's father.

We pass from this tower down the nave to the east end, rich in screens across the chancel arch and round the chapels, four of them finely carved with rich and elegant cresting. The fine stone pulpit has delicate arcading and deep little niches under its carved panels, and beside it is the door of the rood stairs leading to the open doorway at the top.

The lectern has fragments of the ancient chancel screen worked into it, and everywhere is new and old panelling and new and old carved pews. One mediaeval bench-end has been set up at the west end to form a small table for the visitors' book; it is perfectly charming, and has a delightful panel of David playing his harp to Saul, an old man enchanted as he listens, holding his sceptre yet forgetful of all but the little harpist he loved. A carved figure sits on the arm-rest under the richly carved poppyhead. Close by is the oldest thing in the church, a tub-shaped font the Normans made, with a band of cable round the bottom. The church has received in our own time an embroidered silk picture after the design by Burne-Jones of Love Gathering the Children into her arms; it is a magnificent piece of work.

It is the small Horner Chapel that draws us here—not only for the lovely roof with 96 oak panels and floral bosses resting on stone angels, but also for something which is the great surprise of this fine church, a bronze rider on his horse.

It is a remarkable thing to come upon, and it is as good as it can be. It stands in the centre of this small chapel raised on a high pedestal, and, sitting on the horse which carried him to France, is Edward Horner from the house over the wall. Very handsome he is, with his sword and helmet hanging from the saddle, a noble group designed by Alfred Munnings on a pedestal designed by Sir Edwin Lutyens.

Mells has little good glass, but in the tracery of its north windows are a few fine 15th century fragments showing a saintly lady with two keys and three loaves, Catherine with her wheel, Margaret and Helena, and other saints.

What many will think one of the most charming corners of the church is its south porch, its fan-vaulted roof borne on slender shafts and adorned with rich bosses; there are two saints over the door.

Merriott. Like its neighbour Crewkerne, it is busy making sail-cloth, and a little stream running through to join the Parret is here to turn the mill. The 13th century church was made new in the 15th century except for the massive tower with its pinnacled turret. Scratched on a stone of the porch buttress is a sundial used in the days before clocks, and a stone perhaps as old as the 12th century, set in the wall over the vestry, has a carving of two birds with one or two other mysterious things about them. Here also is a stone cross with a crude carving of Our Lord made centuries ago.

Middlezoy. Its church is five or six centuries old, and has a fine tower looking out across these flats which were once marshes and are even now sometimes turned into an immense lake in winter. The tower has a turret and a pierced parapet, and is adorned with canopied niches; its lofty panelled arch has two pairs of angels looking down. More old panelling is seen on the font, both on the bowl with its flowers and on the beautiful stem. There is much excellent woodwork. Across the 14th century chancel is a graceful black oak screen of the 15th century, with tracery in the solid panels below and with a light and beautiful network of it above. The barrel roof has carved bosses, the Jacobean pulpit is enriched with arches and foliage, and among the fine old bench-ends there are some with poppyheads, and one showing a man in a kilt. Richly carved, too, is an old chest in the chancel, with elaborate geometrical designs on the front and writhing dragons round the top. A lancet window in one of the aisles is oddly placed low down, and a window behind the organ has a yellow St John in old glass.

On a small brass in the nave we read of a Frenchman who served 18 years in the English Army before he died fighting gallantly at what the inscription calls the Battle of Weston. The reference is to the Battle of Sedgemoor, when some of the Royalist soldiers were bivouacked within these walls.

Midsomer Norton. The little River Somer comes splashing through it. The vicar has a Norman gateway in his garden and a Norman font in his church, but they are all that is ancient except for the poor knight of the tower. Outside in a niche of the 17th century tower is a bold figure of Charles II, who gave the tower some of its bells.

Inside the tower lies a battered wooden knight of 700 years ago. There are only about a hundred of these wooden figures still surviving from mediaeval England, and only two or three like him in Somerset, and he lies here as if he were one of the dark secrets of the church. No wonder, for we found him in a sorry plight, lying on a box among much lumber on the first floor of the tower. He still carries a decayed shield, but the mail protecting his face is gone and a sort of knobble is all that is left of his sword. Lost under his shield we found the last touch of colour on this old wooden knight whose dignity has passed away.

The church has a curious double arch in the tower, a 17th century one and a 20th century one, and the stone barrel roof of the chancel, though made new with all the rest of the church except the tower, is charming with tracery.

Milborne Port. On this peninsula which Somerset thrusts into Dorset the Normans built a church so grand that we could wish the 15th century had left well alone; but the church grew with the busy little town. The niches and the stoup from its west front were given to the tiny chapel in the churchyard, and one of its Norman doorways is now at the old guildhall, its zigzag arch framing a door

179

there with an ancient iron handle. The church still has much of the heritage of its first builders, for Norman are the panels and arches in the chancel walls, Norman the lower part of the tower with its stair turret and stone arranged in diamonds, Norman the lancet windows of the vestry, and Norman the inner south doorway with carved capitals and a tympanum of two lions. (We found another creature sticking out its tongue at us, a horned demon, one of many old heads supporting the buttress pinnacles.) Most impressive of all are the four Norman arches propping up the tower between the chancel and the nave, two with their round heads changed to points, all with carved capitals. They are high and massive and awe-inspiring. The font, too, is Norman, with its arcading spoilt in the 15th century. The cover is nearly 300 years old.

Beneath the charming 15th century barrel roof of the south transept an unknown lady lies in a recess, and we can only guess her age from the fact that her dress was the fashion 650 years ago.

The screen is perfect still, with the carving for its roodloft on a canopy, its doors on their hinges. There are two chained books and the Vinegar Bible, in which a printer's error changed the parable of the vineyard into the parable of the vinegar. In a case are some odd things found here (British pottery and ancient pipes).

The road to Salisbury passes a Queen Anne house called Ven, with two glorious cedars and trimmed yews like well-drilled sentinels on its lawn.

Milton Clevedon. The Madonna greets us in the porch on the bracket of a canopied niche in which is a figure very much like St Christopher. We have come to this place, so small and simple, past a charming house and through a farmyard, the farmyard in which they found the old font with all the marks of out-of-doors on it. One of the most interesting small possessions of the church is a mass dial, and another is something we find it difficult to interpret, a startled-looking face with red hair and in a high collar; it is a frag-ment of ancient glass in a window. There are stone angels bearing up the roof, and three panelled arches by the transepts and the chancel. In a niche by the altar lies a stone figure of a priest with a chalice, bareheaded with his robes, as he must have been about 700 years ago.

Milverton. It is a small place with as many trees as roofs, and with one of the most delightful streets we know running past a row of old houses opening on a raised cobbled pavement. Up this road

Mells: the church and Manor House.

Muchelney: the Abbot's House.

Norton St Philip: the George Inn.

Nether Stowey: the castle mound.

Nunney Castle.

Oare village.

Porlock Bay.

Preston Plucknett: barn and farmhouse.

we climb to the church, where is a splendid collection of 16th century carving. Nearly every bench-end is as perfect as when the carvers left it 400 years ago. The Apostles are carved on the choir-stalls, St John being shown with the chalice and the serpent, and many benches in the nave have portrait busts. Others show the two spies returning with an enormous bunch of grapes, a man drinking out of a goblet, and a bird pecking away at grapes. Praying figures kneel along the front of the pews. More old bench-ends are worked as panels in the new screen, and the pulpit is made up from old carving. The font, with two bands of ornament, was hewn when the Conqueror was making his Domesday Book, and marks show where the lid was locked. Above it two bearded heads support a curiously curved tower arch.

By the church, built of the same red stone, is the vicarage, an example of a small house of the calmer days which followed the Wars of the Roses.

Minehead. It is the sea-gate of Exmoor, and is three places in one: the group of cottages with the old church on the hill, the fishing village tucked away by the quay, and the growing seaside town beloved by thousands. It has the old thatched cottages of Alcombe at one end and North Hill at the other. North Hill, which dominates the bay, is one end of a crescent of hills curving round Minehead, putting their broad heather and pine-clad heights between it and the winds of Exmoor. It is a haven of flowers, its walls hung with purple aubrietia, geraniums climbing up the houses, and fuchsias everywhere. The hill rises 850 feet above the sea, and we climb by zigzag ways through woods with superb views at every turn—valley and moor in front of us, far-off the Quantocks and the Brendons, and Wales across the Channel. Below lies the old town and its harbour, which has kept itself untouched from the plague of red brick villas. Minehead has many touches of old time domestic architecture, and in the old village quaint handmade door-knockers tell of the days before factories, when Minehead was a busy port. One low room with long beams in its roof, opening on to the quay, is now the Chapel of St Peter, where prayers are offered for fishermen and all at sea.

St Michael's Church stands on the hill, and for 500 years men have sailed into the harbour guided by the light at the roodloft window. We can ride up to the church by a winding road, but if we are wise we shall climb up the steps which make this corner of Minehead like a glimpse of Clovelly.

G

The steps are the delight of artists, and a lovely picture they make, climbing up the narrow street between the yellow thatched cottages, with the church tower above us silhouetted against the sky. On the south wall of the tower is a mediaeval carving of the Trinity (God with the Crucifix and the Dove), and on the east wall is a quaint sculpture of St Michael weighing a soul, with the devil clinging like an ape to the weights to weigh it down, and the Madonna helping the soul to turn the balance. Carved above the east window on the outside wall is a prayer for Minehead's fishermen of long ago:

We pray to Jesu and Mary
Send our neighbours safety.

The window below the prayer is beautiful with 16th century tracery, and has a pompous little figure on each side, one of them bearing a shield with the date 1529. We may stand in the church-yard and look out over sea and land for many miles.

Most of the church was completed in the 14th century, but the tower is 15th. The font is delightful 14th century work, with little figures in niches at the stem, and others sitting round the bowl, all their feet dangling except for one rising from a tomb. There is a magnificent screen with fan-vaulting, and a platform for the roodloft about eight feet wide; the screen was made locally about 1500, and was apparently carved by the same craftsman as the Dunster screen. Perched on the top of it is Jack, a little man in green hood and jerkin who used to strike the time with his hammer. The 17th century reredos was found in our own time among a heap of lumber. Sil-houetted against a window with subdued colour is the Jacobean pulpit. Six ancient books, two still with their chains, rest on a chest with cupboards and drawers instead of the usual lid; it has on it the arms of a vicar of 1484. The worn stone figure of a priest of about 1410 is believed to represent Richard of Bruton, a friend of Mine-head in those far-off days. He has a canopy above him, angels about his head, and at his feet a dog sleeps with his paws on a bone; while the priest's hands are clasping the stem of a broken chalice.

A mediaeval chapel with a carved wagon oak roof is now used as the vestry, being approached through a wide timber arch. The mag-nificent altar table in the chancel rests on two winged angels, a massive and splendid piece of Elizabethan carving, and before it lies in brass the portrait of a lady with a high horned headdress. She is Mary Quirke. It was Robert Quirke the mariner whose money built the old-fashioned row of almshouses at the bottom of the hill. There is a picture of his ship and an inscription over a door, telling us that he built the row in 1630 for the poor for ever, and *cursed be that man that shalt convert it to any other use.* By these cottages is the shaft of the old market cross. An old house known as the Priory was once the Court House, and a fine old coaching inn, opposite St Andrew's Church, has an alabaster figure of Queen Anne looking into its ever-open door; she is very like the plump figure looking down Ludgate Hill from St Paul's. The statue was given to the town by Sir Jacob Bancks, a Swede who sat in nine Parliaments for Mine-head, helped on his way by marrying the rich widow of Colonel Luttrell of Dunster Castle. A walk over the hills brings us to the ruins of a very ancient place called Burgundy Chapel, and not far away is Bratton Court, a beautiful home now a farmhouse; it has great doors under a massive timber archway into the courtyard, giving us a glimpse of the gem of the house, a lattice window set in a carved oak frame.

Misterton. Those who come here today may never have read the book woven round it, but our grandmothers wept over it, and we all know its title, *Coming Through the Rye.* Helen Mathers wrote it in the house next to the church; she was born here, and here began her life as the writer of 20 novels and some poems. In the year of her great success she married a well-known surgeon, Dr Henry Reeves.

The old home of Helen Mathers is long and low and beautiful, its mullioned windows peeping out through the wistaria at a trimly shaped yew and a sundial. Time has only lightly touched the Norman font in the church, but the church itself is 19th century.

Monksilver. Here came Francis Drake to woo a lovely lady, Elizabeth Sydenham, daughter of the grand old house called Combe Sydenham. It was Sir George Sydenham, Elizabeth's father, who built the great house, putting the date 1580 above the porch and having these words carved in Latin above the door:

This door of George's is always open except to ungrateful souls.

That the door has at times been shut for necessity is plain, for there are bullets in its timbers, probably from the Civil War.

The village is snugly set in another combe, and it has a 15th century church with a Norman tower. All round it are impish gargoyles, and within is more of that wonderful carving which beautifies so many of Somerset's churches: in the panels of the screen, in the 16th century pulpit, and in the 15th century pews, on which we noticed a fish and a lamb looking like Noah's Ark animals. The oak lectern is a mediaeval eagle, and the font has a mediaeval cover. A Jacobean almsbox is inscribed with a prayer for charity. It is said that the village blacksmith built the aisle with the money he found in the 15th century buried in a field, and some of the original glass he put in is still in the windows. Another village blacksmith, following his good example, planted the yew in the churchyard in the year 1770. There is a beautiful cross near it in memory of a rector. One of the bells is mediaeval.

Monkton Combe. It is down a hill to paradise, down into one of those beautiful hollows which make the country round Bath like a little Switzerland. Here is one of our fine schools and we may envy the boys their youth in such a superb piece of Somerset.

The little 19th century church set in this earthly paradise has a black-and-white floor and a charming oak pulpit in memory of 18 village men who died for us in the Great War. It is neatly carved with tiny linenfold panels below and open tracery above, and of the 18 heroes of this little vale it says:

> *Christ died to make men holy,*
> *They died to make men free.*

Montacute. Within a few miles of each other are Somerset's grandest houses—Brympton, Barrington, and Montacute. The village of Montacute itself is a village which might be chosen with half-a-dozen others to represent Somerset, with its charming wide square flanked with weathered homes of golden stone, its Norman and 15th century church, its priory gatehouse, and the sharp wooded peak which marks out its great house for miles.

The legend of Montacute, told in a 12th century manuscript, is that a shining black cross was dug from the hillside, and Tofig, Canute's standard-bearer, built for it the abbey at Waltham in Essex. The peak on which it was found is called St Michael's Hill. An 18th century tower on the top, 60 feet high but only just peeping above the trees, marks where Robert, Earl of Mortaigne, half-brother to the Conqueror, built a castle. It was the earl's son who founded the priory at the foot of the hill. Its perfect 15th century gatehouse stands here still, home of a farmer, and alone in a field is the pigeon house of the monks. The glory of the gatehouse, with its embattled tower rising above the rooms on each side, is the exquisite oriel window corbelled above the great door. Another oriel looks from above the gate on the other side, between two stair turrets, and over one and under the other oriel are the initials of Thomas Chard, prior from 1514 to 1532. Inside is a mantelpiece and some beautiful vaulting, with bosses of the arms of France and England, a cardinal's hat, and some faces.

Close by is the village church, built in Norman days and added to during the next three centuries by the English builders. The noble tower with its panelled arch and bands of quatrefoils, the buttressed porch with a canopied niche and a vaulted roof, the nave with its gargoyles and stone angels, are all 15th century. So is the font. Norman is the plain chancel arch, and Norman the uncouth stone figure supporting the organ.

The altar has a beautiful niche on each side, and in the chancel wall is a stone cut with a text in the lettering of Tudor England. There are big and bold stone heads round the transepts, looking down on many memorials of the Phelips family of Montacute House. First to come here were David and Anne, two gaunt figures who have peacefully smiled away nearly 500 years; David measures 6 feet 9 in his armour. On a canopied tomb are Thomas Phelips and his wife, the Elizabethan couple who started the building of the great house and left it for their son Edward to finish. Thomas is in armour and trunk hose, his ruff closely fitting under his beard; his wife wears a divided gown with a ruff and a Paris headdress. Another lady similarly attired, but with the added beauty of an embroidered petticoat, is probably Edward's first wife, Margaret Newdigate, who died in 1590.

In the churchyard is a massive stone coffin, and the shaft of a mediaeval cross with the figure of a bishop or a prior under its canopy.

However, it is the great house which enchants us here, and it belongs to us, for it is in the hands of the National Trust. It was begun in 1580 by Thomas Phelips, the date 1599 in the drawing-room probably marking when it was finished by his son Sir Edward, the Speaker of the House of Commons who was sitting in state when Guy Fawkes was creeping below in the vaults. His was the first speech in the Guy Fawkes trial, and the original minutes of the Gunpowder Plot inquiry were kept at his old home till a few years ago. He also took part in the trial of Sir Walter Raleigh. We remember him again because his father was godfather to Thomas Coryate of Odcombe, and it was probably through Sir Edward that Coryate gained his introduction to Court; certainly Edward encouraged him to start his tramp round Europe in the shoes which he hung up in Odcombe church on his return. In some respects the splendid

Tudor west front is the most interesting part; it was brought here from Clifton Maybank just over the Dorset border in 1786 and is about 50 years older than the house.

Montacute remained in the Phelips family for over three centuries, and Lord Curzon rented it for some years before three unknown friends of England gave it to the nation, so giving a new significance to the old words over the front door, *And yours, my Friends*.

We walk to this great house, between its living walls of yew, to find ourselves before an architectural splendour unmatched even among Somerset's great houses. The richness of its walls, the handsome windows, the ornamental buttresses crowned with beasts, the curved gables, the open parapet, the projecting wings, the rounded oriels, and the statues of warriors, are an amazing array of craftsmanship blending in a perfect whole. The warriors looking out from the garden front are the Nine Worthies: Hector of Troy, Alexander, Julius Caesar, Joshua, David, Judas Maccabeus, King Arthur, Charlemagne, and Godfrey of Bouillon. The architect has sculptured as many dogs on the roof as ever frolicked around the door. They are all over the house, sitting on the gables, creeping round the parapet, or on guard at the corners.

Inside are huge fireplaces and wide stone staircases, panelled rooms, plastered overmantels, old heraldic glass, and a magnificent gallery 170 feet long, running the length of the building with an oriel at each end.

The traveller's chief delight at Montacute is outside. In the spacious garden we feel like Prospero among these gorgeous towers and balustrades and terraces, for it has a magic and delicate beauty everywhere. The great house is set in the serenity of wide lawns with terraces of golden stone, and deep yew hedges. Great stone balustrades reach out from the house, golden with lichen and broken by small classical temples with six round columns, crowned by a circular stone roof with a cornice from which three ribs spring to form a cupola topped by an open ball. At the end of the balustrades are two garden houses which are delightful to see, having round bays, pillared corners, enriched cresting, and quaint roofs rising to a central pinnacle. Between these two houses are noble iron gates leading into the meadows. In the middle of this enclosure is a fountain, and the verge on each side is planted with yews. Along the terrace leading to the lawn from the house stand six dignified columns crowned with lanterns, and they are matched by lines of tall stone obelisks running on each side along the balustrades.

Moorlynch. It has one of the finest views in Somerset from the churchyard on the southern edge of the Polden Hills, 300 feet up. Here the villagers stood 250 years ago and watched day dawn on the tragic plain of Sedgemoor, the last English battlefield. The moor is stretched below, the stately towers of Othery, Middlezoy, and Weston Zoyland marking where the King's men were seen by Monmouth from the tower of Bridgwater church. To the left is High Ham Hill with another church on the top; to the right Chedzoy Tower can just be seen.

The broken shaft and pedestal of an ancient cross are in the churchyard; a sundial is scratched on a stone in the porch. It is a 13th century church altered in the 15th century. The chancel has kept ten of the stone consecration crosses marking where the bishop touched the outside walls with holy oil. Also carved in stone above the east window are a lamb and an eagle with the cross of St Andrew between them. A chancel door has 13th century ironwork, and door, pulpit, reading desk, and bench-ends are all of old carved oak.

The oldest possession of the church is the Norman font with its cable moulding, and there is also a curious ancient piscina and some old glass in the chancel. We found, propped up in the vestry and looking very uncomfortable, a lady of the 14th century with an elaborate headdress of stiff goffered linen like a wig.

Through Loxley Woods runs a Roman road to remember, first through wide green verges and trees, and then opening out on a magnificent view which the National Trust has preserved for us for all time. On each side is the vast central plain of Somerset.

Muchelney. It has guarded its corner of mediaeval England 500 years, and a noble corner it is to guard, so fine that the National Trust and Ministry of Public Building and Works have protected it. Very precious is this group of church and abbey, priest's house and village cross.

The priest's house is a low thatched place with beautiful windows of the 15th century, perfect from outside though cut in half inside by the floor of an upper room. Iron serpents entwine on the ancient handle of the door, and pointed arches lead from room to room. We found the creepers hiding a stone carved with a priest giving alms, which the new house on the almonry site has built into its wall.

Nearly every cottage in Muchelney has mullioned windows, many quarried from the ruins of the abbey, but some of its carved stones and wooden angels have taken sanctuary in the stately 15th century church, where is a coffin lid cut with a crozier, and some old tiles, one showing a fine fellow on a white horse, another a saddled elephant. A row of dainty niches found in a cottage wall is now a reredos. Little figures are at prayer on the Tudor font. A boss on the vaulted ceiling of the tower carries the Daubeney arms. Painted angels in 17th century dress wave texts all over the nave roof. An 18th century barrel organ fills one porch, and the 19th century has a noble representative in the fine stone pulpit.

Only the foundations of the great abbey church remain, but there are extensive portions of the domestic buildings virtually intact; these include the abbot's lodging, the kitchen and guest house together with the south walk of the cloisters, which has lost its lovely fan-vault. The north wall of the refectory survives, covered with stone panelling, and a little distance off is the rere dorter or latrines building. Very striking is the wide stair to the abbot's room, worn with the feet of many generations. In all Somerset we can only remember the famous steps of Wells Chapter House as comparing with these in beauty. At their foot an arch frames the tracery of a window flecked with mediaeval glass; at their head a panelled arch stands before a stone doorway with carved spandrels.

Stone lions on pillars 12 feet high crouch at each side of the abbot's fireplace, and an oak settle 25 feet long with Tudor linenfold runs the length of one wall under great windows with glowing fragments of towers and turrets in their glass.

The community lives on in the fly-leaves of a book in the British Museum. It is the 14th century *Muchelney Breviary*, whose illuminated vellum pages make the most complete monastic breviary we have; the 56 fly-leaves at the end particularly fascinate us, for here the monks wrote down their news of battles, recipes for dishes, ways of curing the plague, and all the hundred and one things which interested them.

Mudford. Its ancient bridge spans the pleasant River Yeo, by which stands the church among the willows. The church tower is a beauty, carved with a band of quatrefoils and a broken figure of Our Lord on the Cross, angels hovering about Him. The long 15th century nave is filled with 17th century pews. There are box-pews in the chancel, and a carved partition leads from the Jacobean pulpit to the minister's prayer desk. The 15th century font is carved with Tudor flowers and there are two old scratch dials built into one of the 15th century buttresses; they come from the days before clocks, and may possibly be as old as the 10th century, remnants of a Saxon church.

Nailsea. Many people remember it for its early glass, still preserved in some museums.

Nailsea's church is mainly 15th century, with a font a century older, and a stone pulpit of about 1500 cut with the arms of the Medes of Failand Hill. It stands so high that the parson climbs up to it by the steps to the vanished roodloft.

The chancel arch has gone but its capitals are left, a curious couple. On one crouches a man with his face distorted as he bears the weight of the stone above him, though a winged bull is doing its best to help at another corner. Edward IV's badge of a white rose and a sun are among fragments of mediaeval glass; on an old stone is outlined a shrouded figure in a coffin, a skull at its feet.

Panelled in oak and with a peephole to the altar is a pew for the owners of Nailsea Court. Their old home, reached by an avenue of pink chestnuts, is at heart 13th century, with a Tudor shell. It has passed through very bad times, but is once more a stately house, almost a museum, for stones and furnishings have been brought from all over Somerset to bring back its ancient glory. Here is a Crusoe room which has one of the most interesting of all the old possessions of this place, a mantelpiece from the Bristol home of Mrs Daniel, where Daniel Defoe met Alexander Selkirk after his rescue and Robinson Crusoe came to life as they sat and talked together.

Their hostess was the daughter of Major Nathaniel Wade, who bought Nailsea Court in 1695. A constant trouble to our Stuart kings, he was mixed up in the Rye House Plot and captured after fighting for Monmouth at Sedgemoor, the only officer, it is said, to bring his men from that ghastly battlefield in anything like order. He was taken to the Tower, but King James II pardoned him, and he came down here to live.

Nempnett Thrubwell. Seventeen miles of parish roads lead to its church, and a great treasure it has to show us, though we found it tucked away as if it were an ordinary thing. It is a wonderful font the Normans made, with an oak pyramid cover it has had for half of its 800 years. All through the centuries it has been guarded by 18 little men carved all round it, comical faces such as a child would draw, each one set in an arch and appearing to spring out of a vase. The stem of this remarkable bowl is arcaded with shields.

The font is the chief possession of this 13th century church, which has a list of rectors going back to 1242 and a stone still in the churchyard which covers the grave of the first rector of all, Robert—just Robert. By his grave are the old steps of the churchyard cross, and on the wall is still a consecration cross on which Robert may have put his hand on consecration day. The chancel has a modern roodscreen designed by the elder Pugin; it has four oak angels in it.

Nether Stowey. Beloved Stowey Coleridge calls it, and even to those who pass through it all too quickly it has a charming air, with many little houses crowding a narrow street and more houses standing back behind small pavement bridges, to make room for the stream running down from Castle Mount, where digging has revealed the foundations of an ancient fortress. That, however, is not what we come for; it is for an Ancient Mariner.

It was in one of these houses behind the stream that Tom Poole lived, he who found a cottage for Coleridge in which the poet spent the happiest years of his life. It is not a beauty, as Coleridge himself said, but it brought him to his friend Tom Poole and it links us with a piece of immortality. It is good that it should belong to us all, in the care of our National Trust.

For here he wrote *The Ancient Mariner*, and it was at Nether Stowey's church door that this grim tale was told in imagination to one of the wedding guests. Except for the shadowy vision of an ancient mariner that we seem to see about its doorway the church has little to show us. It has lost the loud bassoon which blared out hymn tunes from the gallery, and the little vesper bell, but it has the memorial of Thomas Poole, the tanner whose love of learning and great power of affection attracted all who met him. We read a little of him on the stone here, enough to realise that when De Quincey described him as being appointed guardian to his children by every third man who died in Nether Stowey, he was not far wrong.

The lovely old manor is next to the church, hidden from the road by a wall with an overhanging hedge of yew. At the end of the wall is a quaint gazebo (as lookouts used to be called). The house was begun in the time of Henry VII and left unfinished until Elizabeth I's time, for its builder had in the meantime had his head cut off on Tower Hill for joining the Cornish men who marched to London protesting against new taxation.

Nettlecombe. Its church and its Court stand together, a charming group in a park of giant trees.

A treasure house indeed is the 15th century church, with glorious 15th century glass of saints and heraldry, a chalice of 1479 which is almost the oldest silver known to bear a date, the original altar stone with old tiles about it, bench-ends of the 16th century, a fine old pulpit of the 17th, and a font like no other in Somerset. There are only about 30 fonts in all England like it, and only two outside East Anglia, this and one at Farningham in Kent. On the font are seven delightful little sculptured scenes of the Seven Sacraments: Baptism, Confirmation, Communion, Penance, Ordination, Matrimony, and Extreme Unction. The font was carved about 1470, and the ladies on it wear the horned headdresses of that time.

Two stone knights have lain here sheltered in recesses for six or seven hundred years. One is John Raleigh, a giant of seven feet in armour with his sword strapped to his side, and with him his wife and his hound; the other is his ancestor Simon Raleigh. They would live at the Court, though the house we see is mostly Tudor, built long after them. It has ceilings and fireplaces richly decorated in plaster work in Stuart times.

Newton St Loe. It is one of the quiet corners of the world, a delightful little place, a small church on a hilltop, a great park round about, and fine views everywhere. Down in a dip, from a gate in the churchyard is a peep of one of our lovely English groups through the trees.

In the garden of the mansion are the ruins of a castle in which King John is said to have been held a captive, but scratched on a stone of the church is something possibly older still, a 24-hour dial which was telling this village the time before King John sealed Magna Carta. In the churchyard, which has a fine yew at the gate, the steps of the old cross are crowned by a new cross with a dainty head.

The church has also been made new, but the old tower still has the hideous gargoyles the mediaeval masons loved. The 14th century doorway has ballflower ornament and the south arcade still keeps its ballflower capitals, the oldest part of the church. The door opens upon a great surprise, for it is all a little unchurchlike as we enter. We come into a transept and find ourselves looking through a group of columns 600 years old. On our left is a huge marble monument within magnificent iron railings, all spikes and balls; it is an 18th century structure with marble columns crowned by rich capitals and borne by angels. The modern pulpit, enriched with oak panelling and tracery, is raised on a slender stone pillar and on a bracket in the wall; it is charming. The floor of the chancel is paved with black and white tiles.

One of the windows has St Michael with his sword and scales and the Madonna with a purple cloak, with two small medallions of St Margaret with her dragon and the brave Carlo Borromeo of Milan visiting the sick in the plague which befell the city. Facing this is a companion window with two saints and small medallions of St George and St Martin giving half his cloak to the beggar. The altar has one of the oldest chalices in Somerset, with a paten to match. It was made in 1511.

We noticed on a lovely stone house by the church, over the door, one of the finest ammonites we have seen, looking like a splendid piece of carving, with a sundial over it. The great house is now a college of education for women teachers.

North Barrow. We do not wonder that the shaded path to the church has grown mossy, for there are not 100 people in this Caryland village. Last century saw the old church come down and the new one go up, but the old misshapen font remains. It has a new pedestal, but we have seen nothing else like the bowl in Somerset, and we doubt if there is another in England. It widens in the middle and then turns sharply in again, so that top and bottom are the same width.

North Cadbury. The little River Cam separates North Cadbury from South with its fortified hill, the Cadbury Castle of the Romans and the legendary Camelot of Arthur and his knights. North may leave to South its famous hill, for it has its own abundance of good things.

It is a charming village of old stone cottages, a place of orchards and grassy walks through nut groves, with a dark beech avenue leading to its two beauties, the wonderful church and the gabled Elizabethan house standing side by side in grey stone. The church (which still has its old mass dial) was set here by Lady Elizabeth Botreaux in the 15th century to be a college for a rector and seven priests. It has a fine and spacious chancel with a canopied niche painted and gilded on each side of the altar, canopied sedilia, and the ancient altar stone with its five crosses. There is a room above each porch, complete with fireplace, heavy oak doors opening into them. The church has some of its old oak seats and a wonderful collection of carved bench-ends, with the date 1538 hidden at the back of one. Many have portraits of men and women of the time, and here, too, is a gay troubadour playing his pipe, two dragons hatching from eggs, a windmill, a pack-horse and its driver, and surely the only bench-end in the world which has a carving of a Tudor mousetrap, *with a mouse in the claws of an old tabby cat beside it.*

An old prayer desk matches these bench-ends, and there is more woodcarving in the bosses and above the tiebeams of the splendid roofs. The font was made for Lady Elizabeth's new church. Eight blue-robed saints in ancient glass stand in the west window, restored to the church from the big house beside it. Below them is Lady Elizabeth herself, to whom we owe all this beauty. She lies on an altar tomb beside her husband, under a vaulted canopy; she wears a lovely horned headdress and has two small dogs at her feet, Sir William being in armour with a lion.

There was another pair once keeping them company, but they have gone, and only a brass inscription marks their tomb. In a long rhyming epitaph it tells how Lady Magdalen was forced to marry a man older than she, but when he died she obeyed her heart alone and married Sir Francis Hastings, whose statue was here with hers. Next to the vacant tomb is a nameless tomb of 1611, a heraldic stone above it, probably belonging to the family of Matthew Hales, whose funeral helmet is still on its original bracket in the vestry. Below it is a series of photographs of the misericords carved for the college priests, but taken out of the chancel and now in a private collection.

Cadbury House has fallen on good days after some bad ones. The hall, with a delightful oriel and many old coats-of-arms in its windows, has been panelled with oak from the beams of the original roof. A portrait of the builder of the house hangs in the hall; he was Henry Hastings, 3rd Earl of Huntingdon and nearly King of England, for most of the Protestant noblemen supported his claim to the throne in succession to Elizabeth. He it was who settled the rectory of North Cadbury on Emmanuel College, Cambridge.

North Cheriton. Only the shaft and the steps are left of the ancient cross built in the days when the church was new. The font, shaped like a bucket, was made by Norman masons long before Adam, the first known rector, came to North Cheriton. The lovely chancel screen has tracery as delicately poised as a bed of lilies; it is made up from fragments of a 15th century screen from Pilton. There is a new screen in the tower, behind which hang the original clappers from four old bells still ringing.

North Curry. Its headland thrust into the moors was chosen for safety in warlike days, and has given it safety today from the noise and terror of the public highway. Giant elms lead past an ancient cross with a new pillar to a church sometimes called the Cathedral of the Moors. Its beauty is rather patchwork, the 15th century nave being too big for the older tower, but its size and its noble windows (it has a double clerestory) give it dignity.

It has inherited from Norman England a doorway carved with zigzag; from the late 13th century come the massive tower piers, the south transept, and the queer windows of the lower clerestory; and from the 15th came both the strangest and the best—the gargoyles and the stately south porch with statues of Jesus, Peter, and Paul, and a pierced parapet running the whole length of nave and chancel. A beautiful Madonna and Child are borne up by an angel in the porch, while more angels hang from the stone fan-vault. A village blacksmith of last century added another touch of beauty with hand-turned iron hinges for the door, and the villagers of today panelled the chancel, which has an oak reredos by Bligh Bond of Christ appearing to the disciples, with charming statues between the panels.

It was the 15th century which made the font and roofed the nave with oak beams on resting stone angels. The mediaeval craftsmen must have marvelled as we do at the enormous wood coffer over six feet long, studded and bound with iron. The lid, cut from a block of wood four inches thick, can scarcely be lifted by a man. As it is lowered two iron pins fit cunningly into staples. In front is a rare lockplate. From the fact that the lid fits into and not on to the coffer it is reckoned to be over 700 years old. Some of the windows contain beautiful painted glass by Burlison and Gryll.

We recoil with horror from the emaciated stone body lying near the coffer, with shroud thrown back, ribs protruding, and head tonsured. Another stone figure is thought to be John of Slough, who lived at Slough Farm before it was refashioned in Tudor times. His manor figured in a curious custom called the Reeve's Feast, when an enormous mince-pie with an effigy of King John on the top was eaten, and John was toasted and sung up to 1868 as if he had been a gentleman, all because he gave the village permission to hold this feast. We noticed an account of it on a stone in the vestry, where is also an old picture of David playing his harp to the accompaniment of two angel trumpeters.

North Newton. We owe North Newton an incalculable debt, for it has preserved for us, though all unknown to it, one of our most precious gifts from antiquity, Alfred's jewel. Here was found in 1693, by Sir Thomas Wrothe, lord of the manor, the lovely thing that now reposes in the Ashmolean Museum. The field where it was found, behind the rectory, is three miles from Athelney, where Alfred withdrew to plan his attack on the Danes and received a scolding, as every schoolboy knows, from a peasant's wife for burning her cakes.

The plain tower of the church has not even a parapet, and its curiously unfinished look is stressed by the ugly wooden structure on the top containing a peal of tubular bells. Slits and windows like cottage casements light the tower, which is possibly 700 years old.,

Sir Thomas Wrothe found the rest of the church in ruins in Stuart days, the minor canons of Wells having built an alehouse and stable out of its stones for use when they came to collect their rents and hold their courts. Sir Thomas made it a church again, and though its walls have been renewed it keeps some magnificent woodwork from his day—a beautiful pulpit, a carved door, and an unusual kind of screen. The screen is carved with four figures in relief, Faith with her shield, Hope with her anchor, Charity with her dove, and the Madonna with the Babe in her arms and the Holy Spirit hovering over her. The carved arch of the reading desk matches the screen's, but the greatest treasure is the vestry door with the parable of the Wise and Foolish Virgins carved in two panels.

It is the chief distinction of this village that here for 800 years lay buried the earliest surviving Crown Jewel of England. Farms have been cultivated for centuries in what was once known as Petherton Park, and it was in this soil that the jewel King Alfred wore in his crown lay hid. The pulling down of the old house led to its discovery in 1693. The jewel, two and a half inches long, bearing on its stem the head and snout of a boar, has a Saxon inscription in Roman letters, *Alfred Mec Haht Gewyrcan*, which in our English means, Alfred had me made.

It was presented to Oxford University in 1718.

When the Ashmolean Museum was founded the Alfred Jewel was handed over to its keeping, and there it is today for all to see, with exact duplicates in gold and enamel that any one of us may buy.

Northover. Where a paved Roman ford once crossed the Ivel between Ilchester and this place was found a coin of Augustus Caesar, now in the British Museum. The 16th century built a bridge, but it was made new last century. Northover's church is mainly 15th century. It has a 15th century font and a carved Jacobean pulpit.

North Perrott. The church is mainly 15th century and of cruciform plan with central tower. It has been much renovated but retains its original form. Four panelled arches support the tower and are believed to cover Norman work; certainly the thickness of the walls suggests Norman work hidden within. The modern reredos incorporates two painted panels of Spanish provenance. The pleasant village set among trees has many attractive old stone houses.

North Petherton. The 15th-century tower of its church is a miracle of beauty. It is 120 feet of perfection, banded with quatrefoils like openwork embroidery and right royally crowned with pinnacles.

Old statues of saints fill the niches in its six-foot walls, and pierced stone panelling lets out the sounds of the bells. Its quatrefoils are repeated along the parapet and on the base of the 15th century cross; and inside the tower is just as beautiful, with a high panelled arch, a fan-vaulted roof, and an ancient clock with the bold look of two faces.

Most of the church is 15th century, but two angels hold up a 17th century gallery, ornate with carving even round the window-frame, filled with box-pews, and with something from early days as a kind of figurehead. He is old Father Time standing on the world, a skull above his head and an hourglass in his hand, and he is fixed to the front of the gallery.

A thistle, a lily, and an acorn branch are among the flowers on the Jacobean bench-ends. Flowers and leaves run round the 15th century font, and the tracery of the pulpit, made only a few years later, reappears again and again in the chancel panelling, the altar rails, and the fine screen, all the work of a modern craftsman, who found another source of inspiration in the black oak door by the altar, with its canopied tracery and its Tudor roses. It leads into the old sacristy, where iron bars still guard the window.

Kneeling at her prayers on a brass is Katherine Morley, whose *godly life and death wrote her own epitaph.* She died in 1652.

North Stoke. It is perched on a throne that Nature gave it, high up above the world about, looking from Bath to Bristol and across to Wales, with the Avon running below. We climb to it up steep and narrow lanes, past small stone cottages, by barns and farms and fine stone walls, up group after group of steps with gurgling water running by until we reach the Norman tower with tiny windows and a turret stairway. We come through a doorway 700 years old, with two heads fading away and a scratch dial older than any clock in the world, and we swing open a door that men have been swinging open for many generations. It brings us into a simple corner of mediaeval England with slender roof beams seeming hardly able to bear the weight of the great stone roof above them; with one of the roughest Norman fonts we have seen, the corners of its massive bowl adorned with tiny heads; and with a plain Norman arch from the tower into the nave. Much of the interior has been refaced, but its quaintness remains.

North Wootton. Over its tiny stone bridge thirty men went away to the Great War; they fought in nine countries and all but two came home again. It is a little place worth sacrificing something for, with a small church in orchards white with blossom when we called, and noble hills beyond. There is a sundial over the door, with an odd little stoup below it, and we found two 18th century tombstones lying in the porch. The oldest possession of the village is its leaning font, leaning quite as much as the tower of Pisa or the spire of Chesterfield; it was made by the Normans, and has a band of cable moulding round it. The vicar stands in his old panelled pulpit by the rood stairs; one preached here last century for 47 years, and there are two windows in his memory. In memory of a vicar's wife is an oak screen carved with six panels by village craftsmen.

Norton Fitzwarren. The men of this proud village boast that

> *When Taunton was a fuzzy down*
> *Norton was a wallèd town.*

Today Norton is a winding street of great charm, and no walled town. Certainly its folk may boast of the magnificent chancel screen in their 14th century church. It is the best of three old screens the church has kept, and attracts the eye by its richly carved cornice and its astonishing dragons. To the children of Norton it must be as good as a picture book, for here is a ploughman with his team of oxen, a sower following behind, and behind them all a dragon creeping up, its jaws already closing on one poor unfortunate. Other men crouch behind great bracken leaves, and a second dragon is stalking a small company of men and dogs.

Grotesque creatures in stone crouch round the church as gargoyles, peering out from many odd places.

Norton Malreward. Standing by the fine yew in its churchyard, we look down on the white walls and red roofs nestling among elms and fruit trees and copper beeches, a lovely sight in May. It is all under the great hill called Maes Knoll, in which lie unknown warriors of Ancient Britain.

There is little that is old outside, except the tower from the 13th century; but in the refashioning of the church the Norman chancel arch was saved and it remains the great possession of the village. It is carved with zigzag, balls, and chevrons, and has shafts with twisted rope-work round them. The font, much spoiled, has kept the arch company through 800 years. For most of those years there has been in this place a rough coffin lid now in the tower, carved with the heads of a man and his wife. It lay for centuries in the churchyard and the years have worn the couple down, but they are pressing close to one another, as if time could not divide them.

Norton St Philip. It has a fine inn, a fine church, and a fine Elizabethan dovecot on a farm. The ancient hostelry has stood on the street 500 years with oriels and bay windows, outdoor steps to an upper room, a small figure wearing away on the doorway, a gallery at the back and timbers at the front—altogether a lovely glimpse of Old England. Here would stay mediaeval merchants coming to the great cloth fair, and here, it is said, stayed the Duke of Monmouth ten days before the Battle of Sedgemoor, narrowly escaping from a bullet fired through the window.

We imagine that the church was built by the same builders as the hostelry, for both are 15th century. The porch is tucked in between the buttresses of the tower with two lions on guard under the roof. It is thought the tower may have been built with re-used material; certainly it is an extraordinary tower, after no known design, with oddly arched windows and elaborate niches, with four rich canopies at the two sides; we see fine heads and niches on each side of the outer porch, and a continuous line of enrichment from the bottom to the top. The roof of the porch is richly and deeply carved.

There is a stone effigy of *c.* 1460, an unknown man of the law lying on an elaborate canopied tomb, his hands clasped, his tunic fastened with buttons, a high cap on his head with a band of fur, the pointed toes of his shoes curling over the back of a dog.

In the window tracery of the north wall is a little of the oldest glass in England; it has rich blues, and among the fragments we noticed a comical face.

The chancel has an old barrel timber roof elaborately panelled with tracery and oak screens on each side. The east window has fine glass by Christopher Webb.

The roof of the nave is heavily timbered, borne by eight big angels with long hair. The old rood stairway is still here. There is a Jacobean oak bench. The south porch has nine old bosses and fine timbers in the roof; in it are two doors, one low and one high in the wall.

Norton-sub-Hamdon. In the high ridge to the east of it is quarried the famous Ham Hill stone of which this charming village and many others are built. A very pleasing building-stone it is, warm and golden with its weathered shades of grey, and here is a tower to show it at its best, a dignified church with pinnacled buttresses, great windows, and an impressive loftiness in its nave and chancel.

The church is mainly early 16th century, though fire has destroyed nearly all that was put into it at that time. In the heads of some of the windows a few little angels survive and a few saints in old painted glass, and the 13th century font has survived to outlive its usefulness, for it has been displaced by something more elaborate. The south porch, with its vaulted roof, belongs to the last church but one on this site.

One odd possession we found in the churchyard, unique in our experience for such a place, a buttressed dovecot with about 500 niches for birds, a mediaeval relic of the manor house which stood next door.

Nunney. It is a surprising picture of mediaeval England, for in less than a minute we can cross the moat of a 14th century castle, cross the bridge of a little stream, and be in a 15th century church. The village clusters round these ancient monuments.

There can hardly be a city which would not be proud of this castle, with its four round towers standing as they have stood 600 years, in one of the best moats we have seen, neatly walled and filled with sparkling water. Standing in the castle we counted 30 doorways and windows, some of the windows with a splay of 10 feet, some of them still dainty architectural fragments. We can trace the marks of five floors on the walls, and in one tower is the line where the staircase has been. There are the doorways leading from the staircase to the rooms, the lookouts from which the defenders watched for enemies or shot their arrows, patches of carving, brackets, fireplaces, and through one of the windows is a fine peep of the church tower which the people of the castle must have seen rising 500 years ago. Its fine weathercock shines like pure gold above the roofs.

The tower has an open parapet with battlements above it, a tiny turret and four pinnacles, gargoyles all round, and windows and arcading all the way. It has a fine sundial with a painted sun.

The proud possession of the church is a stone man lying on a windowsill, one of a group of five mediaeval figures of knights and their ladies tucked away behind the organ. They are the proud Delameres, and the man on the windowsill above the rest is the builder of the castle, Sir John. He has his hands clasped but his face is lost inside his helmet though his belt is still finely carved, and the lion is still at his feet.

On the two tombs below him, their panels elaborately carved with heraldry, are two Delamere husbands and wives. One has a military sword and belt with lions on the breast and skirt of his coat, and on his head something we have not seen before, something like a prim wig or an elaborate skull-cap. There is a delicate chain collar round his neck, and his wife has a long veil from the head to the waist, with a beautiful head-cover like a crown. Her cloak is held in place by two buckles, and she wears a girdle. The other knight lies in heavy armour wearing a ruff, with his wife in a tight-fitting bodice and a flowing skirt; she has a charming headdress and a ruff.

There is much here that all these old people would see. They would see the rough old Norman font like a basin, the mullioned peepholes on each side of the 13th century chancel arch, and the mediaeval painting which is fading away under glass; it is apparently a crusader. Some of them would see the fine oak screen across the chancel arch, one of the best bits of ancient timber screen in Somerset. It has central gates with two bays on each side, spandrels finely carved with foliage crowned by a neat row of Tudor roses, and above it all a double band of rich cresting from which project longhaired angels. Above all this is a small fretwork parapet.

Nynehead. Here John Locke stayed with his friend Edward Clarke. A magnificent avenue of limes brings us to Chipley, with the secluded bowling green, where he began his famous *Essay on Human Understanding*, and at the house when we called was a box full of his letters, many of them written to little Betty Clarke whom he loved dearly. It was of the children here that Locke was thinking when he wrote his *Essay on Education*. One of the greatest of English philosophers, he was born in Somerset at Wrington, but he lies at High Laver in Essex.

Another fine house spreads its beautiful garden and park round the 13th century church, where now lie many of the Sandfords who lived in it. Theirs is the chapel through whose rose window the light falls on the white figure of an angel. Other pale statues stand round the walls, and here are two blue and white reliefs by Della Robbia, gentle pictures of the Madonna and Child. Hanging in a curious frame is an old painting from a chapel in Italy thought to be the work of Mino da Fiesole.

In a corner kneel Locke's friends, Edward Clarke and his wife, sculptured figures with their family arms painted above them as a canopy.

A small 15th century carved oak screen is across the chancel, and there is a deep narrow slit through one of the piers to allow a glimpse of the altar from the side, for the church is unusually wide. The south aisle was built about 1410, and in a window is a bit of glass put there at that time, showing Saint Catherine. In the churchyard is the base of what must have been a magnificent old cross.

Oake. It would seem as we pass through it that a charming old farmhouse and a tithe barn are all it has to show us, but the church is secluded behind the farm, and is worth finding. It still keeps the old dial by which the villagers told the time of mass in the days before clocks, and it has a remarkable font, a misshapen 13th century bowl which, all askew on rough sandstone, has lasted 700 years. There is a beautiful Tudor pulpit, a Jacobean chair in the 13th century chancel, and fragments of old glass from Taunton Priory.

Oare. In a deep Exmoor valley, hidden from the sea which is so close, it has wild hills round its green patch of fields, and a silence broken only by the splashing of Oare Water and the twitterings of the swallows which scoop up its mud for their nests under the chancel eaves. Before it has gone another mile the little stream joins Badgworthy Water, and together they run into Devon under an ancient stone bridge with lofty arches.

It is the country of Lorna Doone. From Oare her lover walked to meet her; in this 15th century church they were married; through this window was fired the shot that spilled her blood on the altar steps. Almost it seems that we can hear the shot; almost we can see the white figure lying there; and almost we forget that she lived only in the pages of a book. Her creator, Richard Blackmore, whose grandfather was rector here more than a century ago, is pictured on his memorial stone in the church.

The narrow little church, entered by an ancient oak doorway, is filled with high box-pews. Very curious is the centuries-old piscina in the new chancel; we have seen no other piscina quite like this stone head held up by two hands. The chalice is Elizabethan. The bowl of the font is Norman. There is an odd painting of Moses signed Peter Spurrye, Warden, 1718, and a stone carved with a knight kneeling in a wood and two hounds sighting a stag with a cross between its antlers—the old legend of St Hubert, here in memory of another huntsman, Nicholas Snow, whose life ended in our own time at the long low manor house by the church.

Odcombe. It is more than 350 years ago since Thomas Coryate, the rector's son, hung up his shoes in his father's church after having walked in them across Europe. The shoes are no longer here, for, worn as they were, they probably fell an easy prey to church mice; but we like to think of the odd man of Odcombe returning to this village of ups and downs and narrow ways to write the book of his travels, *Crudities hastily gobbled up in five months' travel, newly digested in the hungry air of Odcombe*. He brought with him something else, too, a strange implement called a fork, the first in England.

At this font with its Norman bowl, its 14th century pedestal, and its 15th century cover, Thomas was baptised. He would sit in this charming panelled porch. Perhaps he and Old Yew were young together. Perhaps he would read the time of mass by the dial which has come down from the days before clocks. He would look out on the view and long to be off on his travels, yet we doubt if they took him to any homes more lovely than two he left behind him, for Brympton d'Evercy and Montacute are near. Montacute he knew very well, for there lived the patron who encouraged him in his travels, and as for Brympton the Beautiful, who for miles round does not think it like a dream?

Thomas could not win a degree at Oxford, yet he came away with a perfect mastery of Greek and an astonishing knowledge of out-of-the-way facts. Above all, he came away with the fixed determination to see the world.

He found his way to Court, where he was the butt of every courtier's wit. Prince Henry allowed him a pension. In 1608 he set forth to travel Europe. He visited France and Italy, returned through Switzerland and Germany, and was back in five months. He wrote a volume of his travels, the finest thing of the sort up to that time, but he could not find a publisher. His good nature, his importunity, his wit, induced 66 of the famous men of England, poets, preachers, princes, and statesmen, to write him verses with which to introduce his book, and with these the volume at length appeared, establishing itself as a classic.

It still makes good reading, for he was a born observer and writer. Whether it is the first umbrellas in Italy or the new cathedral rising in Cologne, he misses nothing. He meets armed footpads near Baden, and instantly knows what to do. He has only one shirt to his back, one pair of shoes to his feet, and there is money in his girdle which he is in danger of losing to the brigands. Instead of waiting to be robbed he snatches off his hat, steps forward, begs, and is rewarded by the astounded robbers.

The ink was hardly dry in his book before Coryate came down to Odcombe, hung up his old shoes as an offering in his father's church, addressed the villagers at the market cross, told them he would be absent ten years, and was away again. He searched for the tomb of Homer, explored the plain of Troy, delved into the mysteries of Constantinople, visited Jerusalem. He reached India and, being brought into the presence of the Great Mogul, made a speech in Persian. He was destined, however, never to leave India, for his health broke down and he died at Surat in 1617.

Old Cleeve. It has a noble outlook, through the trees across the wide bay to where North Hill rises like a mountain from the sea. Raised above the cottage roofs, the church has the best of the view, for which it took its seat 500 years ago. Even then the monks of Cleeve Abbey, close by at Washford, were an ancient institution.

All these years there has lain here the stone figure of an unknown man in a loose-sleeved gown, a cat crouching at his feet with its paw on a struggling rat. Carved panels from the old roodscreen decorate the chancel wall, and the lovely strip of carving in the aisle may be also from the screen. The poor box has a prayer for charity written on it in 1634. An old chest in the porch has been hollowed from an oak, and the cobbled floor of the porch has alabaster stones from the beach below set in the shape of a heart 300 years ago.

On a tomb in the churchyard is the familiar blacksmith's epitaph in memory of George Jones of 1808:

> *My fire's extinct, my forge decayed,*
> *And in the dust my body's laid.*

A cobbled path leads by a churchyard cross made new, to a chapel which stood too near the sea, so that the cliffs fell away and the chapel disappeared. Near its site is the fine house of Chapel Cleeve, a modern house with just a fragment of what may have been a mediaeval monastic grange.

Orchardleigh. It is like a jewel in the crown of Somerset, an enchanting gem of the delicate beauty of this countryside. We turn down to it at the signpost leading us to Lullington and Orchardleigh:

> *What a peace steals over me*
> *Born of happy memory;*
> *Lullington and Orchardleigh.*

Here is the only island church we have seen in our grand tour of England, a rare little place set in a lake two miles from the highroad. We found the lake overhung with trees on a glorious summer day when the silver birches and copper beeches were at their best, the rushes were coming up from the water like green sword blades, and here and there the surface was solid with lilies. Round the great house are noble oaks and beeches—we measured a beech and found it 18 feet round the trunk; and at the church door rises a Wellingtonia of remarkable beauty, twice as high as the ancient stone roof.

Such is the setting of this 14th century shrine looking almost like a moated church as we come across the bridge. It has a little world of its own where no sound breaks the solitude save the singing of birds and the bleating of goats. The inside of St Mary's has a nave and chancel with much to see and a little chapel with nothing. It is one of the surprises of the countryside to walk through this great park and to find ourselves confronted with many things of beauty and rare craftsmanship, fine windows and lovely sculptures.

The sanctuary has great possessions. At the entrance to it, high above the altar rails, are two monks carved in stone, one with a hook he has been holding for centuries. They are older than the Reformation, for they belonged to those mediaeval days of roodlofts and Lenten veils, and on the hooks was hung the sacred veil which screened the altar in Lent. On one side of the sanctuary well is a piscina and on the other an aumbry, both unusual and most elegantly carved, the piscina having four heads and a six-leafed drain, the aumbry having its original door, angels in the spandrels, and in an oval niche what seemed to us like a figure of Our Lord with a head between His feet.

On the east wall at each side of the altar is a stone pillar rising from the ground and becoming a beautiful sculptured bracket, both with quaint conceptions of a mediaeval artist on them, the central figures being a king and a queen, the queen between two queer men and the king between a man and a dog, all seeming to be pulling at the hair of the royal couple.

The light falls on the altar through three windows with mediaeval glass, the central figure of the east window being a saint in a white robe with pale gold borders, surrounded by seven panels of musical angels; very charming the saint looks with his face dimly discernible as in a mist, against a ruby background. From the north and south windows eight saints look down on the altar. We do not think we have seen these disciples more quaintly shown, all of them strange figures with beards, and some with curly hair. Simon is carrying a fish, and John has the snake coming out of the chalice.

There is 15th century glass also over the charming 14th century priest's doorway, and in the windows of the nave, where we noticed the lion of St Mark and the holy lamb, and a bishop and a king and a fragment with St Michael slaying his dragon.

There is a Jacobean pulpit and an arch crowned with three stone pinnacles leading into the small chapel where the Champneys lie.

The font is of remarkable interest, for it was chiselled by a Norman mason who left the sides of this massive bowl quite plain. In course of time a later sculptor came and started decorating the bowl, chiselling round the top and bottom of it bands of floral ornament and conceiving the idea of decorating the space between with figures in oval niches linked up with foliage. He carved three ovals, in one of which is Our Lord, in another the Madonna, and in another St Anne teaching the Madonna to read; and then the 13th century sculptor stopped in the midst of his work. He began to carve his fourth oval niche and laid down his tools and did not come back.

It seemed to us a beautiful thing to find in this enchanting place the grave of a poet who loved England almost more than all, Sir Henry Newbolt. Orchardleigh is described in his historical romance *The Old Country*, where he gave it the name of Gardenleigh. His poems have rung round England and the Empire, and, whether he wrote poems or prose romances, from the day he was a Clifton schoolboy (with Thomas Edward Brown as a master), he wrote nothing unless he wrote it well. He was a Staffordshire vicar's son, born at Bilston in 1862, and was knighted during the Great War.

Orchard Portman. The church in the fields is all it has—that and a few scattered cottages and farms. It is 15th century with something left from the Normans—a carved arch and a rough-hewn font, and a 20th century chapel built by Viscount Portman. It is like an old-fashioned family pew, with chairs round the panelled walls, and on two helmets sit quaint painted models of the Portmans' heraldic dog. The chancel has two fine old chairs and is panelled with linenfold. The chancel has some ancient stalls and a carved oak pulpit, and in one of the windows are four saints in ancient glass.

Othery. It stands high on a ridge in the middle of Sedgemoor, the island once called Zoyland. Its cottages crowd together to be beyond the reach of floods, which many times have made Zoyland an island again after winter storms.

The church has grown from our three great building centuries, with a cross which may be Norman on its eastern gable. It has quaint and precious possessions, its chief treasure being part of a 15th century cope which has been cut up for a frontal. It is a lovely piece of mediaeval embroidery, showing the Madonna rising to Heaven, the whole shimmering with silver threads and rays of glory. On the magnificent mediaeval bench-ends are birds, flowers, and butterflies, and many remarkably good figures: David playing his harp, a soldier with the head of John Baptist, and a knight and his lady. In the window of a chapel are medallions of mediaeval glass with the heads of three saints (Gregory, Augustine and Jerome), each wearing a little black cap with a tuft on the top. The font is 14th century, the tower 15th, and the old carved door, with an ancient ring and a key over a foot long, has Tudor roses in its tracery. The churchyard has a curiosity on a buttress of the central tower, which has been pierced so that a window in the chancel can be seen. It is possible that the hole was made so that a light burning in the window could be seen outside.

Otterford. From two hollows of these lovely Blackdown Hills spring the Otter and the Yarty rivers, on whose banks walked the early Stone Age men, whose sharpened flints are found in the valleys.

On a hill between the rivers is a 13th century church, with three bells of the 15th century. Here lie many Combes from Fyfet Court, one 17th century Combe defying Death's power in lines of brass:

> *Injurious Death, thou now hast shewn thy spite*
> *And yet my dust shall see Eternal Light.*

Otterhampton. A tiny place near the mud flats of the River Parret, it has a 600-year-old church shaded by a spreading yew reaching almost up to the bells in the old tower, with a font made soon after the Norman Conquest, a bell which was ringing before the Reformation, and a Tudor screen with curious oak carvings as perfect as in the days of Elizabeth I.

Over Stowey. It is a happy village at the foot of the lovely Quantock Hills, safe from motor roads and railways and the ugliness they bring. Its 500-year-old church was made new by the great Victorian Radical who became the first and last Lord Taunton. He was Henry Labouchere, and he lies in this quiet place after an exciting life in politics. There is a Burne-Jones window to him, and one to his daughter; it was his nephew Henry who became a notorious politician and edited the well-known weekly, *Truth*. The font, the splendid bench-ends, the 18th century candelabra, and two of the bells, are all original possessions of the ancient church. On the wall is a memorial to two brothers, both of whom died at 78. They were rich farmers who lived much in the village, and below their names is a group of farm implements, some rakes and a plough; an interesting little collection for an antiquary in another 500 years.

Paulton. We found ourselves sorry for two old people here, both in this church built rather like a chapel, and neither of them quite at home, for they were tucked away on the first floor of the tower. One of them stands in a corner and is thrilling enough to be by far the greatest possession Paulton has. He is a 13th century knight, and handsome he must have looked in his chain mail when they shaped him from the limestone hewn from Paulton's own quarry. A little unlike the English work of those days, it is thought he was fashioned by a French sculptor, perhaps the artist who fashioned Thomas de Morton, whom we have seen at Compton Martin.

Keeping company with the old knight in his corner is a stone lady battered and worn, a memorial to one who may have been baptised at the 14th century font that lies unused in this new place. It was dug up in the foundations.

Pawlett. Stretching out to sea are the Pawlett Hams, 2000 acres of the richest pasture in Somerset, once belonging to John of Gaunt. His own lands lie below sea level with beds of peat sometimes 30 feet deep, securely banked from the tides and drained by dykes. The village is safe on high ground.

Pushing open the massive church door we are in a delightful

207

interior quite unspoilt, having come through a Norman doorway with three moulded arches, all much worn but with their curious beak heads still here. The font was probably made by the Norman craftsman who carved these heads, and its cap is probably Jacobean.

The line of ancient seats, with doors into them and carved ends, wave up and down where the floor has sunk a little. A Jacobean pulpit matches them. The chancel is filled with box-pews, and old rails guard the altar on three sides, a rare survival. The 15th century chancel screen is painted and gilded and still has its heavy door; there is a fine bold carving along the cornice.

Pendomer. It is on the way to nowhere. Its little lane (the only road we found) ends in a path across the hills to Dorset. It is one of the loveliest lanes in Somerset, with a glorious view of hills and woods as we stand in an avenue of oaks.

We climb up the cart track to the old farm, and in the 14th century church close by will stay awhile to keep Sir John Domer company. His stone figure, in chain mail and a flowing surcoat, has been above his grave 600 years. Two peasants of those days stand on pinnacled brackets and hold over the gallant knight an embattled cornice with iron spikes for candles, to be lit on the anniversary of his death, and an angel, broken with years, bears in its hands a tiny mannikin, Sir John's soul on its way to heaven. The whole tomb is a wonderful piece of sculpture, probably from the workshops of Ilchester.

By the tomb is a round Norman font, and two ancient beams help to support the new roof above his tomb. There is old glass in three windows of the chancel, and the head of Our Lord looks down from one, while in another angels carry the arms of John Stourton of Preston Plucknett, who bought the manor in due course. He bought Brympton, too, so that there was a manor apiece for his three daughters when the old man was drawn in his best wagon to his grave in Stavordale Priory. It is his manor house, made new in the 16th century, which stands by the church, sharing the delightful view, and adding its own beauty and a great apple orchard to the lovely scene at the end of the lane.

Penselwood. We come into this little shrine through one of the loveliest doorways for miles around, but indeed Penselwood is a shrine itself, set high on Nature's throne with a view across miles of country to the ruined tower of Glastonbury Tor, with winding ways and a scattered group of people who love their church.

The pride of the village today is something it has produced itself, something not unworthy of the lovely doorway the Normans left behind. It is a group of bench-ends filling the nave, made from locally-grown wood, cut and moulded by a village carpenter, and carved by a skilful lady of the district.

We felt it was good to be sitting in these pews looking through the open Norman doorway at the splendid profiles of a king and queen who look down on all who come. Here they have reigned these 800 years, holding up the lintel, yet seeming anything but weary with the burden of their crowns. They are charming, gazing across to each other so that we catch their faces against the light of the sky. On the lintel is a holy lamb between two other creatures, and there is double chevron and zigzag moulding above. Over the outer doorway of the porch, protecting this fine Norman work, is set the head of the mediaeval cross, with the Crucifixion, two kneeling figures, and the Madonna. There is more mediaeval sculpture on the tower, where we noticed among the gargoyles one of a man looking wonderfully cheerful in spite of his toothache.

There is a very low Norman font, a cupboard made from the ancient timbers of the roof, a Jacobean table, an ancient coffin lid, and a few specks of early glass; and in the tower still rings a bell which has summoned people to worship for about 700 years.

The country round is rich in stones that are older than history. It is part of old Selwood Forest, where stood ancient strongholds and moated mounts. There was a battle of Penselwood in Saxon days, but older far are these great hollows stretching over perhaps 200 acres called Pen Pits, which may have been villages or hiding-places in prehistoric times.

Pensford. It has a character, and a good one; could any tiny place be more crowded with quaint loveliness? Perhaps we found it at its best, for it was a glorious spring day and the aubrietia was creeping down the stone walls through which the river runs, ten feet down from the cottage gardens to the water, and it is all bridges—three little stone ones and a colossal viaduct dwarfing the village, the tower, the roofs, and everything with its 16 great arches carrying the trains 100 feet up in the air. A perfect miniature is the little domed lock-up looking down the street. Wansdyke which runs close by is hardly noticed.

The 14th century church is nearly moated with the little river; in its long history the nave has been flooded four feet deep. It has a 15th century font with quatrefoils and roses; a Jacobean pulpit of which every inch is carved with squares and circles and leaves, and in the tower we found an odd little man most certainly winking.

Pilton. It is part of the pride of Old England, a lovely place full of beauty.

On the hill above is the tithe barn, 100 feet long. It looks out across the valley to the grey wall of the church with its fine row of windows, the manor house below and the vicarage above, the grey stone village lying about it all, framed in grand chestnuts.

The church has a lovely parapet all round, with hundreds of little arcades and great stone heads. It has a Norman doorway and a nave built when Norman work was merging into English, 700 years ago. It has a magnificent timbered roof of 15th century beams, carved and parapeted, angels with outspread wings centred on each beam, some with painted faces; there are about 30 wooden angels in the roof and 30 stone ones supporting it. The oak roof of the chancel is cut out into nearly a hundred panels with bosses shaped like leaves; it is lit by clerestory windows. The chancel arch is deeply panelled and of stately beauty, arcaded in the soffits with three stone angels in a row along each capital. In the chancel is a 15th century window portait of Thomas Overay. The glass shows him kneeling with suns and crowns and birds and queer creatures about, and the sill of his window is made into a seat for priests, guarded by two dogs and two angels. The 13th century piscina is a beauty, with lovely spandrels and a tiny stone vaulted roof complete with boss; the drain hole is covered with a flower.

In a delightful little chapel is a most unusual Easter Sepulchre, Christ's face carved on it below the arms of the cross. The reredos of the altar here is covered with Tudor embroidery, blue with golden seraphim. In the window above is a little old glass with a bishop's mitre and a Tudor rose.

Round this small chapel is a remarkable 15th century oak screen with heavily carved gates and a cornice on which the grapes have not lost their colouring. The screen is a mass of curious engraving, with queer dragons and monsters snarling at one another.

Perhaps the chief of Pilton's treasures is the mediaeval embroidery hanging on the wall, given to the church from Wells in 1492. The silk face of one of the pieces, showing the Madonna, was eaten away by spiders and a company of ladies of Wantage have renewed it. The embroidery was found in a curious Jacobean chest still here, with a long domed lid and rings once used for tethering calves or sheep or fowl or whatever living tithes the farmer brought. There is a mediaeval chalice, a brass chandelier of 1749, a 400-year-old font once used as a cattle trough, and an old flute and a clarinet which Mr Beecham used to blow in the 18th century.

Rich almost like a cathedral is this great church in the hollow of Pilton. High above it stands the barn shaped like a cross with its projecting porches, its four gables carved with the emblems of the Evangelists. It is now a roofless ruin since fire destroyed its thatched roof. It presides over this village so greatly endowed by nature, and looks across to Glastonbury Tor raising its head above the fields around.

Pitcombe. Delightfully surrounded by meadows, it has an old farm and an old tower to link it with the past. Godminster Farm is mainly 15th century and has a carved stone chimneypiece of that time; its chief entrance is in a west front made new when William and Mary were on the throne. The tower with its hideous gargoyles and its gracefully panelled arch watches over a church that has been refashioned, but here still are a Norman font bowl, an old high-backed chair, and a panelled chest. In the churchyard a new cross is rooted firmly on the high base of the old one.

Pitminster. In this land of great towers it is pleasant to see a small lead spire peeping above the treetops. The great house, Barton Grange, is now but a shadow of its ancient self, part of Taunton Priory. Poundisford Lodge and Poundisford Park have been more fortunate for they have kept their plaster ceilings, and the latter has a great hall and gallery, with an old fireplace and very curious window fastenings.

It was to Humphrey Colles that they gave Barton Grange when the monks were turned out, and he lies in the church alone, carved in stone, his cloak flung open to show his girdle and jewelled pouch; while his son and grandson, both in armour, lie with their wives and children on each side of the chancel. Carved in alabaster, they make two beautiful groups. Anne Colles died just three months before the Armada, and one tiny baby lies at her head with another at her feet, little motherless twins, for they hold no skull, as does the eldest daughter, and so we know that they were living when the mother died.

On the font is a vigorous picture of St George and the dragon with other carvings of 500 years ago. The bench-ends were richly carved a century later, and in the windows is heraldic glass of the great families of that time.

Pitney. Only the mediaeval tower of its old church has been left untouched by the ages, but though the walls have been re-fashioned it has much for us to see indoors. The key of the door itself is shaped to form the sacred letters IHS, and by the door is an unusual holy water stoup which has escaped the battering hand of time. We found a delightful little lamb on one of the corners of the 14th century base of the font. The bowl is 15th century and has the marks of the hinges. The cover of the font is made in Jacobean style by village craftsmen of our time, who also made the reredos and some of the panelling. The lectern and the pulpit are actually Jacobean, the pulpit carved with a rose for England, lilies for France, and realistic thistles for Scotland. Fixed on a window close by is a preacher's hourglass stand, and in one or two windows fragments of old glass have survived. Two of the bells are mediaeval.

Podimore. From inside its old tower we may see with what cunning arches the builder has fitted eight sides to a square base. Only tiny lancets light his tower, and it is a plain little church, but with a mass dial, fine old pews, fragments of mediaeval glass in the east window, and a font made over 800 years ago, when the Conqueror was reshaping England and giving slices of this flat bit of Somerset to his favourites.

Porlock. Every motorist knows it for the famous hill that climbs up steeply towards Lynton, and every lover of poetry knows it because it was a gentleman from Porlock who broke the dream of Coleridge by calling on him as he was writing out *Kubla Khan* which had come to him in a dream; he drove the vision from the poet's mind and it remains for ever an unfinished gem of English literature.

Yet Porlock has inspired poetry too, for Southey, caught in a shower, sheltered in the old Ship Inn, and wrote a sonnet there.

So this village, with its friendly cottages crowding on the narrow twisting street, the green hills closing it in on three sides and the sea on the other, comes into literature. Its tiny harbour is now a mile away at Porlock Weir, for the sea has crept back across the fields. There is one more old house left, once the little manor of Doverhay Court, now a village room, and on the moor by the ancient earthwork of Berry Castle Camp is the oldest thing of all hereabouts, a sort of little Stonehenge, with ten stones standing and eleven fallen.

It is good to see that Porlock's quaint wooden spire has been

Taunton: the south porch of St Mary Magdalene's Church.

Shepton Mallet Church.

Pitminster Church: the monument to John Colles.

Taunton: the font in St James's Church.

Trull Church: the pulpit.

Tintinhull House.

Timberscombe Church.

Washford: the gatehouse of Cleeve Abbey.

Washford: the refectory of Cleeve Abbey.

retopped and reshingled after losing its head in a thunderstorm 300 years ago. The church is 13th century, and it has the distinction of being dedicated to the saint who is said to have crowned King Arthur, the Celtic Dubricius. The font is 15th century, and there is a delicately carved Easter sepulchre of the 16th; it was made to replace the old one now in the porch. Here lies in his armour, with his feet crossed, the good knight Sir Simon FitzRoger who helped to build the church, and under a rich canopy, wonderfully chiselled in alabaster, is one of the knights of Agincourt, John Harington and his wife. She has a mitred headdress with fine lace; he is as Henry V would see him, and his hands are clasped in prayer over his badge. They lie on a table tomb of great splendour, but it is pitiful to see the silly names of many ignorant louts scratched over it, even on the forehead of this fair lady.

Portbury. It was apple-blossom time in Portbury when we passed by the ruined tower of its vanished priory and stood amazed before its massive church. Two yews have been standing here so long that one is hollow and the other nearly bald, with only a little tuft on top, but what a church it is, with its panelled parapet, its sanctuary bell and bellcot both 500 years old, its old mass dial, an enormous porch with a room above, and a lovely Norman doorway!

The interior is impressive with the height of the aisles, the nave being Norman at the core with the Norman chancel arch pointed on its original round pillars. The Norman font, a square-cut bowl inside a scalloped capital, has a niche by it for the holy oil once used for baptisms. Stone seats over 700 years old are round the walls and pillars, put here for the ancient and infirm when there were no pews, and the weakest went to the wall. Whenever we raise our eyes there seems to be an old head watching us. Two strange ones are on the chancel wall. Another Norman capital served as support for the Lenten veil. The head from some abbot's statue is in a recess. Sharing arches with the piscina is a beautiful 13th century triple sedilia. Across the tower arch is a handsome oak screen 500 years old. The chest and the silver chalice were made before the Armada, the chest with three locks and a slot for alms and fines.

William Goodwin, a 95-year-old yeoman, has the old altar stone with five consecration crosses for his epitaph. Framed on the wall, a small brass of 1621 shows Sara Kemish of Naish House kneeling with two daughters and two baby sons, all neatly labelled with their names.

The Romans made Portbury a big place when Bristol was hardly

H

213

thought of. Many of their foundations have been found, but their old port is a tiny inland village now.

Portishead. No place in the Old World, and only the Bay of Fundy in the New, has higher tides than Portishead. In March the sea here rises as much as 45 feet.

The Romans fortified its headland, and the Saxon Wansdyke ends in one of its fields, after climbing the hills and sweeping the plains of three counties, like some young Wall of China overgrown with turf. It is one of the most astounding British monuments that has survived from the days after the Romans.

Now this prehistoric place has become historic, for the old port is transformed and new houses are everywhere. It has managed to keep the woods of its headland in spite of new docks and the naval college which has taken the place of the old *Formidable*. At Nore Point is an odd little lighthouse on legs like a step-ladder.

The church marks with its stately tower what is left of the old village, and gives sanctuary in its churchyard to the village cross, 20 feet high and with a new head. Beside them glows the mellowed red of the manor house, with an Elizabethan turret. The church has rare possessions; one of the rarest of all is the ring in a stone head on the chancel wall, which used to hold the veil drawn across the sanctuary in Lent before the Reformation. There are very few left. Here, too, is a mass dial, and the sanctus bell of those mediaeval days, which for 500 years has sounded from its niche, and here is something else rarely seen today, the musician's gallery opening into the church from the porch. There are two fonts, the Norman one like a Corinthian capital, square cut inside, having been found buried and brought back. The two chairs are made from the old chancel screen.

Preston Plucknett. A wonderful mediaeval group calls us with its beauty as we pass down the village street. House and mediaeval tithe barn stand side by side, stone from top to bottom. The buttressed barn has finials on its gables, a fine timber roof, and a great pointed archway for the carts. The house is cut through with another archway, its spandrels carved, its ancient door barred with a beam. The high porch has a vaulted roof with a rose in the centre and a room above. In a fireplace stretching the whole width of the house is a cupboard and a hiding-place, and the octagonal chimney has been pierced to let out the smoke.

This was the home of John Stourton, a local character and MP for

Somerset from 1420 to 1435. He had three wives, three daughters, and three manors, and so was able to give to each daughter a manor when he was drawn in his best wagon by his best team of oxen to his grave in Stavordale Priory, which he had rebuilt and endowed. Fortunate were the two daughters who won this and the more humble Pendomer.

Three generations of another old family, the Freakes, have their memorial under an arch in the church. Mainly 14th century, with a tower of the 15th, the church gives sanctuary to the fragments of a 15th century cross found buried outside. They show Christ on the Cross, with his mother and his friend turning their heads in grief. A hare creeps round one side of a chapel arch, while a greyhound pursues it everlastingly from the other side, and the heads of a man and a woman in a wimple hold up the arch of the chapel opposite.

Priddy. We are on the top of the world above the Cheddar Gorge, a wild and desolate place where dead men lie on the skyline in their barrows, where the grass creeps up the side of a Devil's Punch Bowl, where Romans dug out hollows and cut out steps and made their camps. The British Museum has a cup found here.

It is a bright little world to which we run down the hill, gathered round a splendid green on which we found the hurdles packed up like a haystack and thatched over, all ready for the great sheep fair. Down by the green we found an old man at a water trough into which water was running hard in a time of great drought. It seemed a curious sight when hundreds of our villages were crying out for water, and we learned that this water runs hard without ceasing day after day, year after year; the old man remembered it being captured here in a pipe, and he had never seen it dry.

Just before we called, the District Council had been pumping up the spring, for the water had slowed down to a trickle and it was thought to be the drought. It was not the drought, for after the pumping the spring flowed faster than ever; the level of the water rose where the spring came out at the top of the hill; and down here by the green it renewed its strength like a little river, as if it would never stop. The stream comes from the desolate world of waste and rocks up on the hill, where we are told there are marvellous caves of stalactites and stalagmites, reached by a sheer drop of many feet, and where the rocks are so hard that men must blast to dig a grave.

All Priddy must climb to church, as all its children must climb to school. They stand side by side on another green. The church, with stone seats by the walls, has a huge Norman font not now used, a small oak font taking its place. The chancel has an oak screen by a Tudor craftsman, with an old one on the left and a new one on the right to match. There is an old chest and fine barrel roofs resting on stone heads, a beautiful collection of kings and queens and women with wimples.

Priddy keeps in a great glass case its ancient altar frontal, on which 500 years ago some patient English needlewomen embroidered a flower like an iris many times over on fine damask. It has lost its colour, but the flowers in gold thread are perfect still.

Priston. Nature has made it lovely and man has made it irresistible. He must come to it who would know the wonders Somerset has. It is one of the far-off corners, easily lost yet much too good to lose, with a church standing where the Normans left it, set between the rectory and the farm, with a yew which must have been a sturdy youth when the Spanish Armada came, and a chestnut six yards round, its branches sweeping the ground.

Over this fair scene, to which the rector comes through a glorious avenue of elms and beeches, preside Dignity and Impudence. Dignity sits on the gable, Impudence struts aloft above the tower.

Impudence is the cockerel which dominates this scene, a weathercock afraid of no wind that may come, looking to us six feet long. It would seem that the makers were told that it was for one of the highest towers in England, but the tower of Priston is no great height, and this weathervane, fashioned as for the spire of a cathedral, reminds us somewhat of the frog in Aesop which blew itself up. Yet the people of Priston were undaunted. It is said that they filled the cockerel with beer and drank it before hoisting the great creature up; it must have held enough for all the population.

Dignity is a proud Norman lion crouching on the western gable. We have seen such a lion on the gable of a manor farm not far away, and it is said that there are only a very few in England. This king of beasts was shaped by the Norman sculptors who gave this church the odd gallery of queer things running along the north wall under the eaves. There are creatures with goggle eyes, cats with sharp ears, and a dog with a snub nose.

Neither these nor the great lion are the supreme legacy of the Normans here, for there is something nobler yet, something facing us as we come to this small porch. It is an inner doorway built by the Normans, a fine arch on two shafts with slightly carved capitals in which swings one of our most interesting doors, hung here by a

Norman carpenter when the masons had finished their work. It is about nine feet high, swinging on two hinges ending in dainty spidery webs, held together by ornamental iron bands and about 100 studs. Inside it has criss-cross timbers about two inches thick held by 100 nails, and a huge block of oak for the lock roughly cut with an axe 800 years ago; the marks of the workman's tools are still on it, and in the middle is a chiselled-out piece into which a man's hand would fit while he was working it.

This marvellous door brings us into a tiny place in which the builders of our time have been moved by the spirit of the Normans. It has all a noble dignity, the nave and chancel one width all the way along with two tower arches between the chancel and the nave, both built as the Normans built, with three depths of moulding decorated with beaded zigzags and three patterns. Under the tower stands the round stone pulpit, and there is an elegant 15th century font on an arcaded stem with heraldic panels. There is one of the rare pillar piscinas.

Publow. It has one of the five mediaeval bridges that cross the River Chew within ten miles, and is so deep in the quietness of the countryside that birds were nesting all the way up its 15th century tower when we called, and the pinnacles were alive with jackdaws. The tower has a charming turret with arcading and tracery, and there are fine gargoyles. Three possessions has this small place: a silver chalice of Elizabeth I's day, a pulpit made out of two old pews when Charles I was a boy, and a font made by the Normans. In the tower is a small table carved with lions at the corners.

Puckington. It had three old friends not long ago, and now the ancient yew is alone in its churchyard, for the great oak on Oak Tree Hill, and the Puckington Elm 16 feet round its waist, have toppled over in a storm. Old Yew was planted as recently as 1724, but it is a magnificent tree and almost as high as the tower.

The village has an old-world look, especially about its 15th century church, with a chancel 200 years older in which is still the original piscina and the triple sedilia added when the church was 100 years old. In the sanctuary are two old carved chairs. The font has the Norman mason's cable moulding round it, and in the tower is still a bell which rang out before the Reformation. On the wall is a mass dial. Near the bridge over the River Isle is a long low line of thatched farm and barn with oak timbers, and plaster ceilings on which is a heraldic pig above an eagle with two heads.

Puriton. It has lost the manor house which once belonged to Admiral Blake, but has found a sham castle set up to please Pelagie, the daughter of a French count who married Benjamin Greenhill and came to live here at Knowle Hall. Benjamin hoped this home-sick daughter of France would be comforted to look out on a tower, and set up the castle on Knowle Hill with two towers which were still here when we called, but seemed crumbling and unsafe. The lady did not pine away, for she died in the last year of the 19th century, 73 years old, and here she lies. The grey stone church has a charming oak screen, and the sanctuary has old panelling. The most curious possession of the church is the winding stone stairway in the south porch, leading to a room which has disappeared.

Puxton. The pretty lane bordered with willows almost ties itself in knots in winding its way to this tiny home of about 100 people. We found here, from the notice to the Dyke Reeves on the church door, the delightful names of some of these rhynes, as the dykes here-abouts are called. Many are Yeo, an old word for water, and so come Blind Yeo, Old Yeo, Lythy Yeo. But who can tell us the origin of Grumblepill?

The small church is 700 years old, with windows of our three great building centuries, and it has a low tower leaning away from the nave. Three feet out they say it is, and it looks as if it may topple over any day. Here hang two old bells, one inscribed in the beautiful lettering of mediaeval days. Probably the north porch has not been repaired since 1557, the date cut on its stone. The old wooden beam still bars the south door. We found the inside as tumbledown as outside, the old benches, roughly hewn out of oak 500 years ago, looking as if they could not last much longer. An iron bracket for the hourglass still hangs by the old oak pulpit, matched by a curious reading desk with high sides like a miniature pulpit and both decorated by a Jacobean carver. Between the nave and chancel is a massive low wall, all that is left of the mediaeval stone screen. The oldest possession of Puxton is the plain 12th century tub-shaped font, and it has also an old mass dial and an Elizabethan chalice.

Pylle. There is something of Elizabethan England in the manor house, which still has the arms of the Berkeleys on its gateway. Though little is left of their home as they knew it, they would recognise the pleasant 15th century tower across the road and the Norman font with its unusual design of short and long lines. The rest of the church was made new last century, and most of the villagers now live at Street.

Queen Camel. Two streets it has to please the eye, one wide and straight, one a cobbled way between old cottages; and among the bridges over the Cam is a midget for pack-horses, three feet wide. In the church a 14th century arcade reaches up to a 15th century roof on angel corbels, and everywhere we look is craftsmanship in wood and stone. The panelled chancel arch has vine leaves like those on the cornice of the screen. Both are 15th century, and the screen is one of the loveliest in Somerset, perfect in every part, with delicate fan-vaulting and original doors still on their hinges. There is a mass dial from the days before clocks.

Matching the screen in grandeur is the Tudor pulpit with nine canopied niches, and the 15th century font on a hollow panelled stem, with statues on its buttresses and a Jacobean cover. Fragments of mediaeval bench-ends have been framed in the new seats, and a bold eagle on a rocky perch carries on the tradition of fine carving. There is an elaborate canopy over the sedilia and piscina, and framed as a picture is some rich embroidery on velvet. A cupboard and a vestry screen have been made from the Jacobean pew where sat Sir Humphrey Mildmay, whose memorial in the wall tells us that he lay with seven wounds among the slain at Newbury, but lived to see the Stuarts regain the throne.

His Elizabethan home in Hazelgrove Park was turned into a copy of a Genoese palace by another Mildmay in 1720. An elm avenue leads through the park, where we found a giant oak 37 feet round. The imposing entrance archway was dragged in 20 wagons by 40 horses from Low Ham, where John Stawell started 300 years ago to build a mansion that was to be the most beautiful of its kind in the world, but built this gateway and then stopped. He had a gateway but no house.

Queen Charlton. We must say of this small place that it is charming without and within, for its church corner is like a garden, its church is like a well-kept house.

The village clusters round a tiny green on which the shaft of a cross rises on five great steps. The gabled manor house with the little rock garden at the gate, between a lovely chestnut and a noble yew, has a Norman neighbour on each side—the fine central tower of the church and a magnificent gateway, one of the greatest surprises

219

we have come upon on a country road. The front door of the manor house looks across the road to this fine arch made 800 years ago for the vanished Abbey of Keynsham. It has chevron mouldings, slender fluted shafts with carved capitals, and two small heads worn away with the winds and rains of centuries, and very impressive it looks, leading into the garden of the manor with another arch beyond.

This fine manor house which has grown through the centuries, and must several times have transformed itself, has two greyhounds on its gables, an eagle on the parapet, and the heads of a king and queen. It is Catherine Parr, the third Catherine of Henry VIII and his lucky widow, who is said to have slept here and to have given the village its royal name.

The lovely church is white from floor to ceiling, the tiny chancel like a drawing-room through the pointed arches of the tower. The sanctuary has a blue carpet, blue curtains, and a brocaded altar frontal, all standing out daintily against the clean walls of rough white stone, the four tower arches and the two arches on the right of the altar which led 700 years ago into a vanished chapel. The fine face of a man which once looked into the chapel has for centuries looked at nothing but a wall, but the queer creatures of these capitals mostly look into the charming chancel; one of them is something like a stoat biting a man, and another extraordinary creature is peeping out from fleurs-de-lis.

The sanctuary is paved with ancient gravestones, and on the wall is a bracket with a mediaeval carving of a woman's head. The font is Norman. Near it stands an old bell that will ring no more; it is seven feet round the rim. The nave roof is barrel-shaped and daintily panelled in oak with little carved bosses; it is all very light. The Norman tower has the open parapet familiar in this part of Somerset, with gargoyles and pinnacles. It has dominated this small corner of a fair countryside through eight centuries that have brought little change.

Raddington. Walking up a lonely lane which seems to lead us nowhere we catch sight of its quaint church in a ring of firs balanced on the top of a small round hill, looking for all the world like a picture in a fairy tale. A climb up a stony pathway brings us to the porch, where we found a white owl warming his five wits. For 500 years and more the church has stood here, leaning a little wearily, for it has hardly been touched. The chancel screen, which must have been dazzling when the craftsman left it about 1380, has suffered through the centuries, but the carved oak bosses are still fine on the painted roof. The font made 800 years ago was decorated by a 15th century mason, and the bell he may have heard ringing still rings across the fields and farms of Raddington.

Radstock. It is in the heart of a great surprise, the coalfield of Somerset. Strange it is to find black pits in this fair countryside, but pleasant to see the fir trees creeping up the slag-heaps, making new little hills for Somerset.

Here, 50 generations since, passed Roman chariots; on the Fosse Way a piece of the old road was once laid bare, and paving stones were found marked with the chariot wheels. Today it is the church that draws us here, an unbeautiful place made beautiful by those who love it. It stands in a garden which runs uphill, and everywhere when we called the flowers were bright, and a fringe of forget-me-nots was creeping round the walls.

Poor battered kings and queens greet us at the porch, inside and out. The porch itself, with an old mass dial scratched on its front, has a stone barrel roof carved with quatrefoils and bosses of animals and faces. With the wall to which it belongs, and the tower, it is all that is left that has not been made new, and it has within it the broken lid of an old stone coffin with fragments of a Latin inscription, dug up in the churchyard.

Keeping company with this stone is the old cross finely set on great stones in the nave, its sculptures of the Crucifixion and the Madonna all weathered and battered, but safe at last from the storms of time. Part of it had been built into the porch and part buried in the churchyard, but the cross is now complete. Older still, yet looking new, is the font the Normans made, with a band of cable moulding.

Redlynch. It is in the lovely countryside round the pleasant town of Bruton, and on the edge of a park which has twice lost its great house in our time. The original house was built in 1672 by Sir Stephen Fox, who lived in the reigns of six kings and whose name should be remembered by the old soldiers we see walking about London in scarlet coats, for it was he who planned their Chelsea Hospital and largely paid for it. His house was enlarged in the 18th century by the Earl of Ilchester, who left it practically two houses linked by a covered way, an east wing and a west wing; but the 20th century has destroyed them both, the east wing being demolished in 1913, and the west burned down in 1914 by a band of angry suffragettes who chose this way of asserting their right to the vote and displaying their unfitness for it. The west wing was rebuilt and is all that now stands.

Redlynch has a little 18th century church by the wayside, charming, beautiful in its simplicity, with white walls panelled in oak, the east wall pedimented and adorned with cherubs. A small recess at the side of the altar leads to a pulpit with a sounding-board.

Rimpton. Its cottages look out from mullioned windows almost on the borderline of Dorset, with the famous Ham Hill quarries not far away. The church has a pelican on one battlement and a sundial on another, amusing gargoyles which have looked down for 500 or 600 years, and the quaintest face cut in a stone over the chancel door. There are fine seats with carved ends from the 15th or 16th century, an oak pulpit carved in the days of Elizabeth I, and a beautiful oak eagle in memory of ten men who did not come back. The font is 15th century, with an old carved cover, and outside is all that is left of the cross which stood in the churchyard when the builders brought the font.

Rodden. It is out of the world, an odd corner with a church in a farmyard where we found a bar across the gate to keep the cows away. They come to drink at the pond in front, with a row of three noble yews between them and the 17th century walls. From the names carved on its door by 17th century louts we gather that the door is original. So are the bench-ends with simple Jacobean carving. The font is very unusual, and the bowl is borne on three detached shafts round a central column.

Rode. It is far from the rushing tide of life and little known, but has any village in our 10,000 a more dramatic memory? It is three generations since its name was heard in Parliament, printed in every paper, and on all men's lips. Quiet enough now it seems, though it has two churches and a small green with a monument which pays the village's tribute to those who fell in the Great War.

The 14th century church (which has kept its old mass dial) has a strong tower from which colossal gargoyles with flapping ears look down. Some of the stone heads at the windows are remarkably lifelike. The door swings on its original hinges and by it is a tiny stoup. Above the door inside hangs a bishop's mitre painted on wood, presented by one of the rectors who became a bishop.

By the pulpit is the upper doorway of the old roodloft, divided by a piece of stone carving set across it; and there are two peepholes by the chancel arch, both interesting, for one is very long with a miniature peephole beside it, and the other has a coffin lid set in it. Many fragments of neat sculpture are let into the walls, and there is dainty carving on the capitals in the nave. One of the walls has a lovely niche with a canopy. The elegant font has a stem with tiny trefoiled arches and a bowl carved with roses. Behind the twisted altar rails are two old chairs, one neatly carved in the days of Charles II. There are good old rafters with carved bosses, well seen with the light from charming clerestory windows. The west window in the tower has four medallions of old glass.

It has been a church of faithful servants. We found here a tablet to an organist of 50 years, a parish clerk who attended 664 funerals here in 53 years; and two parish clerks who lived in *friendship during their long service for Rode and Woolverton*, and died so that they were buried on the same summer's day in 1799. We found a wonderful family of Browns, four parents and four children with 630 years of life between them, three over 80 and five over 70, and an old rector of Queen Anne's day who used to say that bishops and parsons must die preaching and praying—and did so.

Not a year passes by in this little place but somebody comes to ask about Constance Kent and the house in which she lived. The house is by the 19th century church, across the road from the village green, set in a lovely garden and seen well from the road, hardly changed since that day in 1860 when all England was startled by a mystery within its walls. A little boy of three was killed in the night by someone in the house, and the mystery could not be solved. Within living memory there has been no case like it; in the annals of crime there have been few so baffling.

"Be sure your sin will find you out" the preacher chose as his text the next Sunday, and Constance Kent sat there, but they did not find her out. Nobody found anything out, and the Kents left Rode. Years passed by and then the mystery was solved by an almost incredible confession.

Rodney Stoke. It has a delightful church. A famous family gave the village its name, the ancestors of Nelson's Admiral Rodney. On a farm across the road from the church the gatehouse of their old home stands. We went up the stone steps outside it and looked at the fine beams in the roof.

In the tiny chapel off the chancel lie Edward Rodney, who gave the church its lovely screen, its pulpit, and the cover for the font;

George his son, who died at 21; and Anna his daughter. The best of them all is Anna, perfectly charming under a window, serene in a richly embroidered bonnet with lace collar and cuffs, her sash and sleeves looped with bows, and double rows of pearls on her neck and shoulders. Looking down on her is the grim figure of George, grim because he is getting out of his coffin with his shroud still on, his hands raised, his long hair falling on his shoulders, and above him an angel blowing a trumpet to announce his resurrection. Looking across the chapel towards them are Edward Rodney and his wife, in oval recesses under a curtained canopy, their eyes wide open.

Between the chapel and the chancel sleeps the oldest Rodney of them all, Sir Thomas of 1478. Cherubs and angels hang from the canopy of his richly sculptured tomb, a dragon peeps out from a spandrel, and on the tomb he lies, a neat and captivating figure, his head on a helmet with his eagle crest, his feet on a dog, his dagger at his side. Five queer little women look from the front of his tomb into the chancel, one kneeling at prayer for his soul, two counting their beads; and looking into the chapel on the other side, daintily carved on shields, are St Anne with the Madonna and Child, St Leonard with the shackles he struck off the wrists of prisoners, and a bishop. A fascinating group the Rodneys are.

Fascinating also is the little screen Sir Edward gave in 1625, with the Jacobean pulpit to keep it company. We have seen no other like it, for it broadens out with its great cresting so that it fills the nave from wall to wall, and has nine little bays above it. It is heavily carved with acorns, grapes, flowers, leaves, and the sharp-beaked eagles of the Rodney crest. Three bands of carving have simple moulding running between. The pulpit has ten little arches to match.

It would please Sir Edward Rodney, if he could come back, to see that Rodney folk are keeping up the high tradition of the Somerset carving men. The heavily panelled oak roof of the nave, and the barrel roof of the chancel with its dainty carvings, are as he would see them, but the bench-ends are simpler and of our own time. They are simple but they are the fine work of the amateur craftsmen of the village, a little group of carvers working under Miss Evelyn Coleridge Smith, whose father was rector here.

Sir Edward Rodney's oak canopy covers a Norman font with a twisted bowl, unlike any other we remember, and it is curious also for having four crosses on the rim. Another interesting possession of the church is a pair of pewter bowls, one of which bears the name of a "churchwarding" in 1739. There is a carved stoup with a canopy in the tower, and a lovely little canopy over the priest's doorway outside. There is also the old mass dial on the wall. The nave and chapels have dainty pierced parapets with pinnacles.

Rowberrow. It is like Goldsmith's deserted village, for its mines have closed; but something far more precious than lead and calamine has been dug up from the churchyard: a delightful bit of Saxon carving, believed to be part of a cross, through whose pattern winds something like a serpent. Here it is in the church. A cherub supports the royal arms of 1637, and little worn heads look out from under the bowl of a 15th century font with a wooden cover. The church and the manor house share the same courtyard on their high perch under Dolbury Camp, and the lane which leads to Shipham opens on a glorious view of the Bristol Channel.

Ruishton. They began to build a beautiful tower for Ruishton 500 years ago, with pinnacled buttresses, canopied niches, and bands of ornament round it, but time moved on with hastened step, as the sundial over the porch reminds us, and the tower was never finished. It ends abruptly 66 feet high, with neither parapet nor battlements. A pillar from a Norman doorway is the oldest thing the church can boast, but it has still a few panels from its wonderful roodscreen, and a delightful speck of a window in the stairway which led to the top of the screen. There is a curious 14th century font elaborately carved on a central pedestal, with four smaller pedestals at the corners ending in short pinnacles. The old oil-painting above the font shows a crowd of worshippers round the Child Jesus. The base of what must have been a fine cross is in the churchyard.

St Audries. It is West Quantoxhead if we go by the map, but it is St Audries to everybody. The church stands proudly near the home of the man who built it, in a park sloping down towards the sea. A stream falls over the cliff to the beach, where the tusks of a mammoth were found. They are now in Taunton Museum, a relic of a monster which roamed in the shadow of the great forest here when the stumps we see at low tide were trees waving their branches in the wind. Here is little else that is old (a broken cross, a yew, and hidden in the crypt a stone coffin and a Norman font), for the church is 19th century; but it has in it the spirit of those old builders who loved to carve in wood and stone. The clustered columns were cut from single blocks of Devon marble; the roof with its angels is from the oaks of the hills around; and on the walls are figures as grotesque as any that delighted the eyes of our ancestors.

St Catherine. It is incomparable. We have seen nothing in our 10,000 villages more like the spirit of Old England, tender, enduring, and altogether lovely. We come to it through miles of narrow lanes where often the only inhabitants must be a stoat or a weasel crossing the road or the nightingale singing in the treetops. We pass trees in these lanes that would ennoble any park; one elm seemed to us about 200 feet round and over 80 feet high.

We are in one of the valleys that rise to make the great ridge of the road from Bath to Gloucester, on a slope of those marvellous hillsides looking down into depths we cannot see, with beauty round us like a fairyland, and treetops climbing like a mass of great green balls until they reach the skyline.

The fine old house is set in lovely gardens of stately trimmed yews and firs and beds with old-fashioned forget-me-nots. Among the treasures of the house is a portrait of Catherine of Aragon from Holbein's studio, and there are noble views from the windows; but one odd thing we remember here is a tree trunk which runs from the basement to the roof, with steps running round it in a spiral. The house has been built round it.

Time had changed this scene little in 500 years, since Prior Cantlow came from Bath and found this lovely place. He, too, could find no fairer scene, and here he built this spectacle, this gracious group of gables, walls, and windows, of climbing steps and terraces, church, manor house, and a tithe barn like a cross. He took down the Norman church and set up his fabric in its place, and he laid out a garden and set up his great house, St Catherine's Court, which has been greatly altered and enlarged since then. They stand together, nestling in the hills, one of the greatest surprises a country lane ever had, a rare and perhaps a matchless group.

The oldest stones of the church tower are as the Normans left them, with the mark of the axe still visible. The old door is studded and panelled and its lock is in a block of wood about three feet long. The best possession of the church that has remained unchanged 800 years is the fine Norman font, chiselled all over with a charming band of interlaced circles at the top.

We found ourselves in a tiny nave, with a peep through the low chancel arch through which we see the glory of the church at its best: it is its glass. Most of it is original as Prior Cantlow saw it. It is lovely everywhere, and especially in the east window, which has a Crucifixion with Mary and John at the foot of the cross, and Peter carrying the key. In the tracery are ten small medallions of roses and flaming suns, and below are shields. On the right of the altar is a medallion of Continental glass with a tiny and very odd St Catherine in the fields. On the north and south walls of the chancel are dainty windows bright with shining heraldry and tracery of roses and suns, and there is a lovely St Catherine in the nave. She stands on a broken wheel with tiny gold wheels all over her robe, and on each side of her the mitre and crozier of Prior Cantlow. St Catherine is his monument, but his brass portrait is at Widcombe, where he lies.

The chancel has a charming barrel roof of blue; its oak ribs are painted where they meet, and has tiny painted bosses of roses set in sun. It rests, like the roof of the nave, on stone angels. On the left of the altar is the quaint tomb of William Blanchard (1631) and his wife. Both kneel on red and green cushions as do their four children below, one son with a red sash and three daughters in black with white collars. A most excellent man was Blanchard:

> *Blanchard, thou are not here comprised*
> *Nor is thy worth characterised:*
> *Thy justice, charity, virtue, grace,*
> *Do now possess another place.*

In this quaint church the preacher climbs into the little oak pulpit by the roodloft steps, passing through the clerk's desk, in which is a fine old chair. The pulpit is 15th century and is a perfect gem, set on a slender bracket in the wall, panelled with window-like tracery and painted all over in red, green, white, and gold.

St Michael Church. Behind the farm buildings, past hayricks twice as big as itself, stands the tiny, much renewed church with a gabled tower. Its interesting possession is its 700-year-old font, at which was baptised a child who grew up to be an officer in the British Navy and an Admiral in the Turkish, Sir Adolphus Slade. In the middle of last century he was lent to Turkey and was for 17 years the head of the Turkish Navy under the name of Mushaver Pasha.

Saltford. We found here a lion from Norman England looking down from the gable of the manor farm. It is one of a very small group now known, perhaps less than a dozen; there is one on the church at Priston close by.

The font in the church is probably as old as the lion; it has eight heads below the bowl, long prim faces all well groomed. The church has been made new, rather like a charming chapel with high box-pews, a pulpit with carved panels, and a simple chancel with an

227

arch springing from the wall. In one of the windows St Michael and St George are killing their dragons.

The quaint possession of the church is a curiosity in memorial stones, the work of a mason of Charles I's day. He managed it all very well, crowding his square stone with fine deeply cut lettering, until he found that he must carry on round the sides and somehow started wrongly. Beginning halfway up on the left and going round, he found himself at the right-hand corner at the bottom with still some words to come, and not knowing what to do. If he carried straight on the sense would not read; if he turned the stone upside down it would be absurd; what was he to do? He spelt the words backwards until he reached the corner, when he went straight on again, thinking himself a very clever fellow.

The stone is in memory of Lamorock Flower and of him we read:

> *Flowers they were, nipt in the spring,*
> *But flourish now with God their King.*

Sampford Arundel. Built into a wall of the church are two stone hands raised in prayer for centuries, holding between them a symbol of a heart once buried here. The church has a 13th century tower with later top. The rest was much renewed in the 19th century.

Sampford Brett. Two tragic tales await the traveller here, in the curious old church shaped like a cross. The ends of the seats are beautifully carved and the work of 15th century craftsmen is on the benches and stools in front of them, and in the lectern and the pulpit.

One of the tragic tales is of the stone figure of a knight who lay for centuries in the graveyard and is now indoors. Rain has worn away his face and time his name, yet it is thought it may have been his sword which smote Thomas Becket on the steps at Canterbury. The terrible assassin, Richard de Brett, was Lord of Sampford Brett, with Sir Reginald Fitzurse, leader of the bloodstained knights, as his near neighbour.

The other tragic tale is of a mother and her two children whose portraits are said to be those carved on one of the bench-ends. The story is that she is Florence Wyndham, of whom the tale is told that she woke in her coffin when a thief broke into it to steal her rings.

Seavington St Mary. A magnificent yew with a solid trunk 22 feet round spreads its branches to protect the little church; it was probably a sapling when the oldest part of the church was young. There is still the 13th century doorway, an old mass dial, the original font, and the triple chancel arch with peepholes through which the village folk were looking at the altar long before the days of Joan of Arc. The tower is 15th century. One of the old seats is a long carved bench on which many old folk have rested on their way to the grave, for it was made in 1623 as the parish bier.

Seavington St Michael. The Fosse Way of the Romans runs near by like a ruler eight miles long on the way to Ilchester; the pavements and foundations of one of their houses have been found hereabouts.

A stone figure from some tomb is propped up against the chancel wall exposed to the wind and the rain.

The church itself is a tiny 13th century place without a tower. The font is 13th century.

Selworthy. Holly and oak and ash spread their branches over the lane that leads us to this refuge in the hills; then the round white chimneys above the treetops give away its hiding-place.

First we come upon seven thatched cottages with bulging bread ovens, grouped as though in a garden round the great walnut trees on the green, almshouses no longer, but guarding their air of serene old age. Farther up the lane a stalwart 14th century tithe barn stands in the rectory grounds, with the worn tithe symbols of animals on its walls, and between the barn and a farm 300 years old is the surprise of this hidden place, a church perfect in beauty.

England has no gem more richly set than this. Here is one of the most thrilling views from any church door in the land, looking far over the vale to the heights of Exmoor where Dunkery Hill in olden days would blaze its message from beacon to beacon. Behind us as we stand and stare is a great oak door, studded and carved with linenfold. It leads into a south aisle perfect in every detail, with windows worthy of a cathedral, and roof timbers carved and painted with all the skill of the 16th century. The tower is 14th century, and the chancel probably as old, but the rest of the church is 16th, the plain north aisle added first, and as a grand climax this wonderful south aisle. The arcades are full of grace; there is no tracery in Somerset finer than these windows overlooking Exmoor, and the superb wagon roof is one of the richest in England, its dainty bosses with the face of Christ looking down from among the symbols of the Passion. The bosses in the nave roof are even more remarkable, some showing figures in high relief, saints with the Trinity in the midst of them, all repainted last century.

There is a handsome 18th century west gallery, and the room over the porch, turned last century into a pew for the people of the manor, looks with its balcony curiously like a box at the opera.

The great Chantrey has sculptured the memorials of three of the Dyke Aclands, who followed the Steynings at the manor, and who have done so much to preserve the splendour of this corner of Somerset.

There is a restored early 16th century pulpit with a 17th century tester and hourglass. Some mediaeval glass is left in the east window of the north aisle, including the angel of St Matthew and the eagle of St John.

The oldest possession of the church is the Norman font, shaped rather like a thistle and with a wooden case made for it out of linen-fold panels. On the altar are 16th century candlesticks, and the two chairs within the old altar rails are 17th century. Some of the pews are old, and others have been carved in our own day by the villagers. The timbers of a great coffer are crumbling under iron bands. There is a chained copy of Bishop Jewel's *Apology*. In the churchyard is a cross 400 years old, perfect still except for its head.

Older far than church or cross are the remains of a British earth-work on the hills above Bury Castle, looking to the sea.

Shapwick. Among the fields to the north of the Poldens is a little wood over which herons flap and cry, and in whose depths is a cavern with a domed roof and a hole dug deep. It is an ice-house, a kind of refrigerator, where ice gathered in winter was stored during summer for the great house. The duck-like quacks of the herons add to the mysterious gloom of the place. Near by is Shapwick House, its fine gable front (spoilt by a brick addition) built by Judge Rolles when Cromwell deprived him of office. We caught a glimpse of another old gabled house (Down House) from the village street, with a round dovecot on the lawn.

A cedar stands at each corner of the church, the tallest over 14 feet round the trunk. The central tower is on 13th century arches, but most of the church has been made new under a fine timber roof curving like the inverted hull of a ship. There is a mass dial. A red bull's head marks stones to the Bull family, who with the Strangways have lived at Down House from 1657.

Shepton Beauchamp. It has two old neighbours, the church and the house opposite, which have come down from the 15th century. The church tower is splendid inside and out, with a band of carving, a transomed window, an ancient bishop in one niche and a new St Michael in another, a tall panelled arch, and a stone vaulted roof. Over the porch is an old statue of the Madonna. A massive pier in the arcade appears to have supported a central tower. The font is Norman, triple sedilia and a piscina all under the same arches are 13th century, the east window with tracery something like a swastika is 14th. No church was complete in mediaeval days without its cross in the churchyard and its Calvary on the rood beam, and here are both, but they are new. A Crucifixion has been set up on a carved beam in the chancel, and in a niche on the cross outside is the Good Shepherd.

Shepton Mallet. The traveller motoring through Somerset comes to it again and again, and never once too often. It is one of the old towns of the Mendips, lying in lovely country just off the chief Roman road in Somerset. The Shepton in its name is short for Sheeptown, and goes back to Saxon days; the Mallet is Norman, the name of the 12th century lords of the manor.

The town has four great treasures of antiquity, two indoors and two out: the market cross and the church tower, and the roof and the pulpit of the church, and there is also by the market cross a curious survival unique in England, the Shambles. The market cross is famous among our mediaeval monuments. A brass tells us that it was set up in 1500 by Walter Buckland and his wife Agnes, who beg our prayers for ever. It has a stone-paved floor and six arches, and is altogether a remarkable piece of decorated sculpture, with its beautiful pierced parapet, its leafy pinnacles, and a central spire rising over 50 feet.

Keeping company with this fine cross in this small marketplace is a curious fragment of the past that was here before the cross was built —a little row of market stalls under a narrow roof. It is hard to believe it, but they have been here five centuries, and are the oldest wooden shambles in the land. They have been the centre of the market life of Shepton Mallet for a dozen generations. Two worthy institutions from the 17th century still carry on: the Strode alms-houses founded in 1699, and the school founded in 1627 but now housed in a new home. Overlooking the marketplace is a small museum which carries us back to the world beyond history, for it has relics of the hyena's den at Wookey Hole and of other animals in other Mendip caves, and Roman remains, including pottery and coins. It has also a fine collection of geological and insect specimens built up by Mr John Phillis, and many interesting old pictures of the town.

Rising high above all this is the first of the famous Somerset towers, the forerunner of a long and beautiful line that gives this county a splendour unique in the land. It is a bold structure with pinnacled buttresses and immense gargoyles, capped by the stump of a little spire which on second thoughts the builders left off, so setting a new fashion in towers of dignity and strength. Its roof is fan-vaulted. Set above the doorway of this noble church is the mediaeval conception of the Trinity (the Almighty with the Crucifix and the dove) and statues of St Peter and St Paul. We found many old carvings being replaced by new ones, and recognised the face of George V above one doorway, the work being done by a father and two sons in their own quarry. We open the splendid door to find ourselves in an interior which we must think disappointing at first sight, for it has made itself poor with windows and galleries, and with painted figures above the chancel arch, but all England may be thankful that the spoilers allowed to remain the two wonderful possessions of Shepton Mallet: the 15th century roof of the nave and the 15th century pulpit. They are among the nation's treasures. The roof has 350 panels all carved in oak, each panel with its own carved boss. Every one of these carvings is different, and the oak is curiously light and dark so that the rich craftsmanship stands out plain for us to see. There are few more impressive roofs in any of our churches, and it rests on 36 figures of angels bearing shields.

While the craftsmen were carving the oak for the roof the masons were carving the stone for the pulpit, a marvellous piece of work cut from a single stone and ingeniously set on a post so that it must be reached by steps climbing through a stone pier.

Looking across to each other from the east and west windows of an aisle are two stone knights who have lain here for 700 years; they lie cross-legged on the windowsills, and are probably Mallets. There is also a quaint brass showing William Strode of 1649 with his wife and their nine children, a skeleton of Death in their midst aiming a dart at the wife. Near it is the bust of Edward Barnard of 1641, a pompous-looking fellow with a moustache and beard like Charles I's, and this queer epitaph:

Such dust as I am now, so shalt thou be.
Live here with God, then shalt thou live with mee.

The plain round font bowl, rescued from a garden where it was long used as a flower-pot, is believed to be the oldest of all the possessions of the church; it may have belonged to the church which was here before the Conquest, of which part of the walls are believed to be in the nave and chancel, and it is the one Saxon possession of this mediaeval church. The chancel has a charming timber and plaster roof with carved bosses and stone angels, and high up in the north wall is a double window left from ancient days. It looks down on a dainty piscina resting on two pillars which has been here since the 13th century.

Shepton Mallet has among its other churches a Unitarian chapel built in the 17th and 18th centuries, with a richly carved oak pulpit, and another of the town's proud possessions is a fine park with a lake, 13 acres of natural delight given to it by a native.

Shepton Montague. It lies tucked away in a green hollow. The mainly 15th century church was recently gutted by fire but it has now been partly restored and attractively refitted. There is a Norman Font and remains of a churchyard cross. The Royal Arms panel was presented by the present Queen.

Simonsbath. It is called the capital of Exmoor in the guidebooks but never were words so abused. It is a featureless little village, yet most welcome to the traveller in the middle of this unruly kingdom of rock and heath and marsh and tumbling streams. There is not another village for five miles round, and it lies on the one good road we found here.

Somerton. Our New World is here with nine giant aerials seen from afar and raising spidery webbing to the skies, while the Old World forms a pleasant grey group round a 17th century market cross with a battlemented shelter. Here is the church, the town hall, the grammer school, and two inns, one with thick walls used first as a castle and then as a gaol. A little way down the street the old folks are at home in the almshouses Sir Edward Hext built for them in 1604.

Older far than these things is the memory of Somerton, for it played a great part in the life of England twelve and a half centuries ago. It gave England a king, one of the most remarkable men of his age, King Ina. As David came into history tending his father's sheep, Ina comes into history driving his father's oxen, and they chose him one day in 689, "by divine command" it was said, to be king. He was an admirable ruler and gained supremacy over all England south of London, the first king with this distinction. He passed a series of laws (drawn up with the aid of his bishops, the Witan, and a great assembly of God-serving people) which show humanity and mark the change coming over the treatment of the conquered under Christian influence. He was the first king to give rights to Welshmen, but he seems to have been too sensitive for this rough world, and was filled with shame when war broke out and went with his wife on pilgrimage to Rome, where he lived simply as a peasant, and saw his own kingdom no more.

The glory of Somerton is in its church, which all our great building centuries helped to build. To the 15th we owe the best of all, a roof so magnificent that we gaze on it as Wordsworth gazed at the daffodils. In all Somerset only Shepton Mallet and Martock have anything like this. Each oak panel is pierced with a pattern delicate as lace, and along the carved beams creep monsters like dragons. We do not wonder that the master carver was so satisfied with his work that he put his initials on one of the pendants. Other carvers came to look and to leave their best in these high bench-ends and on the splendid reredos, where Charity stands with her dove in a group of four statues.

Then came the Jacobeans to add their gifts, the painted pulpit and the panelled chancel. James died and Charles reigned, and another master craftsman set to work on an altar table for Somerton, carving and colouring a quaint picture on each leg, Adam and Eve on one, Noah hammering away at the ark on another, a ploughman on a third, and the last a curious symbol of Time and Eternity, two hands pressing a Bible on an upturned hourglass. Three chairs in the chancel were made about this time, the back of one ending in a bishop's mitre. Panels railing off the 500-year-old font may be from the screen which completed this magnificent collection of carving.

There are two brass candelabra of 1782, and we were delighted to find a panel on the wall gay with heraldry giving Somerton's history as tracked down in 500 documents. Even the vicars' list is illuminated with the arms of the patrons, a charming touch in an ark of beauty.

South Barrow. Among the flat fields of Caryland is its 15th century church, altered last century but keeping a bit of Norman carving on a curved stone above the south door, an oak pulpit which looks Jacobean, a fine balustrade before the altar probably as old as the Tudor bench-ends, and a 16th century font.

South Brewham. Two old yews have guarded this shrine since the days of Joan of Arc; they would see the old church when it was new. We imagine that the beams in the barrel roofs have been looking down on the nave and chancel since then; the roofs are crowded with them.

It was sad to see the old font in the churchyard filled with rubbish, but it was good to see two charming brasses on the walls indoors. One is to Francis Lynewraye, who was steward of the manor here for 44 years and left *this wretched world* in 1596. His skeleton is lying down and under it we are told that as he is so we shall be. The other brass is an illustrated verse in memory of Edward Bennet, the rector who died *of a suddain surprise* in 1673. There are engravings of a flying hourglass and a skull and crossbones.

Dominating the landscape for miles around is the great tower rising as if from a wood on the skyline. It is 50 yards high and is the famous Stourton Tower, set up in the 18th century in memory of King Alfred's valour against the Danes. It looks down on the wide plain in which he wandered as a fugitive, followed by his people and guarded from his foes.

South Cadbury. Indoors it has little for us to see, for the church has been made new; it has a sculptured group as reredos, a curious little window cut in a buttress to light the pulpit, and in the splay of another window an old painting which may be meant for St Thomas.

Out-of-doors, however, it has much. Climb the lane opposite the house with 1587 below its thatch, and more than half Somerset is to be seen, for here is Cadbury Castle, one of the finest natural hill forts in Somerset, used by Briton and Roman. To the south its grassy slope is gentle, but to the north are ditches and ramparts strengthened with stone walls, now half-buried and overgrown with trees and bushes. In a field to the west the bones of many men and boys have been found heaped in a trench, probably Britons who had bravely resisted Saxon invaders. In 1922 a hoard of over 300 Roman coins was found here, probably the contents of a pay chest for the Romans.

Yet it is more than a great natural fort; it is one of the legendary Camelots of King Arthur and his knights. The crest is Arthur's Palace; there is also Arthur's Well and St Anne's Wishing Well, both now muddy drinking-places for cattle; and at the foot of the hill, making its way towards Glastonbury, is a track mostly hidden by the plough, but still marked on the map King Arthur's Hunting Causeway.

South Petherton. Oriel-windowed houses and little Tudor cottages rub walls with shops and villas; and in the church, set in their midst, modern and mediaeval meet again. The church, which goes back so far that it has the names of all its vicars since 1080, may seem disappointing, yet an hour had passed before we had seen all that it had to show us: the Norman stones by the south door, with Sagittarius on one and a lion on the other; the carved stones on a sill in the chancel; the 13th century vaulting of the tower, springing from winged symbols of the Evangelists; the odd staircase cut through two pillars to reach the belfry; the fascinating 14th century tracery of the north transept window.

In the 15th century lady chapel the light falls from another splendid window on a curly-headed knight dressed in chain mail, with his hands on a sword. He was dug out of the roadside a few years ago while a pit was being dug for a petrol tank on the road from Yeovil to Ilminster: odd, surely, to come upon a mediaeval knight in digging for a petrol pump! He is Sir Philip de Albini, who died in 1292. It is pathetic to think of the lord of this countryside dug up in a road. One of Sir Philip's descendants, Sir Giles Daubeney (as the name became), who died in 1445, has a beautiful brass portrait in full armour with holly berries at his helmet. His first wife is by him with a yapping dog; the second wife has her brass portrait on the floor.

Two men of the Tudor house called Wigborough, still in its park of 400 acres, have their monuments on the wall, one Henry Compton (1603) an absurdly long thin figure in breeches and high-boots kneeling opposite his wife. There is also a monument to William Ashe (1677) with three kneeling figures.

On the wall hangs an extract from the diary of Richard Symonds, the Royalist soldier who loved old things better than wars. He was quartered here in 1644, and had much to say of South Petherton in a diary now treasured in the British Museum.

The attractive choir-stalls have been set up in our time, and thereby hangs a tale. In 1771 there was a dramatic scene in South Petherton, for, amid the scoffs and jeers and the clanging of church bells, the curate was drummed out of the town by an angry vicar and his people. Little did they think the day would come when the curate would have great honour paid him in this church from which he was being driven; yet in 1935 there was a Methodist pilgrimage to the church, and the bishop dedicated these stalls in the name of Methodist laymen of England to the memory of Dr Thomas Coke. Coke was the curate whose preaching had shocked his vicar; he joined the Methodists and became for many years John Wesley's Chief of Staff and right-hand man.

A bridge carrying the Roman Fosse Way over the River Parret has two old stones, one so worn that it is impossible to guess who were the two figures on it, the other telling us that *The right hand roade leade to Yeo.*

King Ina's Palace, as the oldest house in the neighbourhood calls itself, was begun centuries after King Ina and was probably completed by the Giles Daubeney who lies near his royal master in Westminster Abbey.

South Stoke. It lies in as fair a scene as Nature has given us from her chalice of beauty, and in the heart of it when we called the banks were aglow with aubrietia and arabis and a flood of sunlight over the little church and the great tithe barn. One of the gables of the barn is filled with pigeon holes. The 15th century tower of the church has four of the biggest gargoyles we have seen, their mouths open wide enough to drop a loaf in.

It is a beautiful doorway that leads us into this old church made new. One of the loveliest approaches the Normans left behind, its arch rests on two richly carved pillars each with a different pattern, one with diamonds with fleurs-de-lis in them, the other with a sort of rope round it, also making diamond shapes. The tympanum has three forms of carving with two neat medallions at the end, and over it are three depths of zigzag with an outside band of scrollwork. The font is 13th century.

Sparkford. It is here, there, and everywhere, with the Roman fortification of Cadbury Castle as its highest neighbour. We pass two stone cottages sharing a charming old porch, and are glad to find the church just as simple and charming, though all but its 15th century chancel and the tower arches was made new last century. It has kept its 14th century font, the Jacobean pulpit, and has added old carved bench-ends to the new choir-seats. One of the bells, inscribed with a prayer to St Catherine, is mediaeval. The River Cam flows by the churchyard.

237

Spaxton. It has ever before it a representative of Somerset's most prosperous days, for one of the bench-ends in the 15th century church is carved with a fuller working on a piece of cloth with all his tools around him. He is one of the men who were making Somerset rich with the woollen industry, enabling her merchants to spend their money on beautifying her churches. On some of these bench-ends are the dates 1536 and 1561, the time when the carved fronts of the pews were made to match them and the mediaeval pulpit. The carving of the wooden posts before the altar has been laid bare by the removal of coat upon coat of paint and varnish and whitewash, and the village blacksmith has now made for them a set of fine branching candlesticks. The curiously shaped almsbox is 17th century; a 15th century brass almsdish is in memory of a verger who was here for 50 years, following his father also here for 50 years.

Time has dealt gently with two 14th century figures under a stone canopy by the altar; the man is thought to have been a Hill who lived in the manor house at Merridge.

Outside is an array of gargoyles and a splendid cross, its figures worn by five centuries of sun and wind and rain.

Stanton Drew. Everything man has made here seems young: the Norman font in the 15th century church, the 13th century doorway into it and the 13th century tower, the old tithe barn, the mediaeval vicarage built by Bishop Beckington with two monsters at the corners of a window, the farmhouse with its traceried mullions and its carved finials, the mediaeval bridge on the road to Chew Magna, and the odd little round house which has been made new and charming, as it used to be when it collected the tolls.

Yet new seem all these ancient things at Stanton Drew, for here stand the crude temples of our Ancient Britons, reminding us of the great stones at Avebury and the monuments strewn about the Wiltshire plain ending at Stonehenge. These colossal stones in a field at Stanton Drew were here, we may believe, when the Egyptians were building the Great Pyramid. Some are standing, some have fallen, but it is easy to see that they formed a stone circle comparing with Stonehenge, and it is believed that they would have some relation to the worship of the sun, being designed for the observation of the time of sunrise on Midsummer Day. Smaller circles, Sir Norman Lockyer believed, were set up to watch the rising of a star which once began the new year, and it is thought the three great stones over the churchyard wall, known as the Cove, is the place where the observer sat to watch.

One odd thing we came upon here, a glazed recess, enclosing the entrance to the old roodloft steps, in which are now preserved fragments of mediaeval tiles found in the churchyard. Built into the churchyard wall are fragments of 13th century windows.

Stanton Prior. The church is of 13th century origin with a deep contemporary porch; the tower is a 15th century addition. A drastic renovation of 1869 destroyed much of its character, but it retains an old wagon roof with carved bosses and the font is Norman. A mural monument shows Thomas Cox (1650) kneeling at a desk with his wife holding a baby and below four sons and two daughters.

Staple Fitzpaine. Who will see a Somerset village looking at its best, let him come to this church gate with its row of 17th century cottages. It is a charming place with an old-world setting for one of the loveliest towers in the county of great towers. The pierced battlements, the balcony windows, and the comical gargoyles are all 15th century, but the south doorway is Norman, the arch rich with an unusual plan of decoration. The small wooden screen came from the neighbouring church at Bickenhall; all that is left of Staple's own screen is in the chancel and in the beautiful chair at the clergy desk.

Stavordale. Here in a remote spot below Alfred's Tower is a pleasant country house which incorporates the 15th century church of a priory of Austin Canons, founded in 1263 and largely rebuilt two centuries later. After the dissolution in 1539 much of the building was pulled down and eventually the chancel of the church became a farm house and the nave a barn. About 60 years ago it was restored as a private residence. The north chapel has a lovely fan-vault and the nave and chancel retain their splendid timber roofs.

Stawell. Like a great farm set in the flat dyke-land near Sedgemoor, the surprising tower of Chilton Prior is spying down on it from the top of the Polden hills. The churchyard has grown higher and higher till it reaches above the six-foot wall of the street. Yet there is little left of the old building save a blocked 13th century arcade and a 13th century font. The tower was never finished but stops halfway, with a gable to cover it.

Stawley. Its tiny church has stood by a great oak for many generations, with the village of Ashbrittle peeping down from the hill; but it is we who feel dwarfed as we open the fine old door and walk between the high pews, past the high pulpit with its domed canopy, up to the long box-pew shutting in the choir. The font is probably early 14th century, and a frieze of twelve panels over the doorway of the tower asks us to pray for Henry Hine and his wife, 1522.

Stockland Bristol. The church was rebuilt in 1865 but it retains its 15th century font and a restored mediaeval screen.

Stocklinch. A small place looking as if it must have struggled hard to keep the grass from overgrowing it, Stocklinch has two old churches, one among its thatched roofs and one in a field at the top of the hill. The one among the cottages has been here 700 years. Three bells and their wheels show through its gabled turret, and it has a stone sundial which was fixed in Shakespeare's day. Its windows call the antiquarian to them, for the outside of each window is cut from a single piece of stone and has no joins, and no two are alike. It has a Norman font, a charming piscina of the 13th century, and an old and rather shabby oak pulpit with a canopy; the pulpit is joined to a reading desk.

Higher than anything else in the village stands the other church, a mediaeval structure near the manor house. Charmingly set among trees in a field, with no path leading to its door, it has a perfect Norman font with a delicately carved band round it and spurs at the base, a piscina resting on an old carved head, and two other sculptured heads under an arch. On a windowsill we found a stone lady 600 years old, with a kerchief on her head.

Stogumber. Cardinal Beaufort, the wealthiest subject in the land, would come here for the hunting, when the church was new. It was in the heyday of his fame, about the time when he conducted the young King Henry to Paris to be crowned as King of France and England. He found the church new and could well afford to add a little loveliness to this small place. He gave it this aisle, with the turret stairs leading to the roodloft, crowned the walls with pinnacles and battlements, and set the gargoyles round them. Outside the wall of the cardinal's aisle runs a stone seat where old folk would sit and listen to the preacher on the steps of the churchyard cross. The door leading out of the aisle and up to the roodloft, and the door at the top of the stairs, are both interesting, the lower one having a lovely 15th century handle, the upper one decorated with panels from the mediaeval screen. We believe that there are only as many churches as we can count on one hand where two piers have been cut through for a peephole to the altar, and this is one of them; it was done when Cardinal Beaufort's north aisle was built.

Stogursey. Between the Quantocks and the sea, ten miles from a station, this little village lies two miles or so off the Bridgwater road to Minehead. It is well worth finding, even if we come on pilgrimage 100 miles, for it has much to see. Two round towers, a moat, and a broken wall have survived the 13th century castle destroyed in the Wars of the Roses. There was a castle even before that built by the Norman De Courci, to whom this village owes its name and its church. He gave the church to an abbey in Normandy, and we may see the original deed of gift at Eton College, for Stogursey came to be given to Eton for an endowment and the college still retains the tithes, the patronage, and the Priory Farm, with its round barn once the dovecot of the monks but now rebuilt without its 1000 niches.

The church is of Norman origin with later refashioning and additions. The wide tower rises from the centre on two noble arches of 18-feet span, with two smaller ones added when the chapels were built 700 years ago. These and the grand west doorway all bear the marks of the Norman carvers, who also made the deep tub font, where four old faces look out between bands of ornament. The nave was rebuilt in the 15th century, and in the church accounts is the name of the artist who carved the splendid bench-ends 100 years later. In them is a man climbing a tree, a great fish, and many birds playing hide-and-seek among the foliage. The old oak roof has gone, but oak angels still spread their wings above us as we stand in the nave looking up the steps to the altar. The pulpit is made from an Elizabethan reading desk.

The stone figures of two Verneys from Fairfield House lie in the south chapel, the 14th century William holding his heart between his folded hands. Each figure is in armour, each alone; though in niches round John's 15th century tomb 12 little figures a foot high, men and women of his time, stand as weepers, sculptured with a delicate grace, with St Christopher and St John among them.

Stoke Pero. An old rhyme runs something like this: Culbone, Oare, and Stoke Pero, parishes three where no parson'll go. Though there is no road, only a rough track over the moor or a stony lane plunging sheer into the valley and up a climb steeper than far-famed Porlock Hill, a parson does go to Stoke Pero every Sunday over the hills from Porlock. Only a farm keeps the forlorn church company among the heather and bracken, but there is another farm and a small house across the valley and Cloutsham farm a mile away, quite a big enough population, according to Somerset reckoning, to have a church. Though the church has had to be restored, the pointed doorway of two solid posts of oak is still here after centuries in wild Exmoor winds and mists.

Stoke St Gregory. Sleepy and on the road to nowhere we may think it is, at the end of a headland thrust into the moors of central Somerset. We found a farm (Slough Farm) still on guard against the phantoms of the past with half a moat round it and arrow-slits in its walls, and in the churchyard the stocks still wait under a tall yew tree for any ne'er-do-well.

It has a noble church, with a handsome pierced parapet, glorious windows, and a central octagonal tower built in the 13th century fashion before such towers were ousted by the stately towers of 200 years later, for which Somerset is renowned throughout the land. The tower has eight sides cunningly fitted on four arches, with smaller arches joining the corners. Niches and statues are everywhere—19th century apostles round the tower, a mediaeval St Gregory in the south porch with a dove in his hands, and the statues round the Jacobean pulpit. We have seen pulpits like this at Thurloxton and North Newton, but nowhere else in Somerset.

The deep tracery on the bench-ends is scarcely touched after more than 400 years; a door is still barred by a beam in the wall and another old door is heavy with great strappings of iron. Near the 600-year-old font is a cupboard made from a 16th century reading desk, its panels crudely portraying the Wise Virgins with their lamps burning. A massive altar table has a proud two-headed eagle in front, probably a gift hundreds of years ago from the Speke family, whose crest it was. The pewter candlesticks are 17th century. There are fragments of ancient glass, and an oil-painting on wood of David playing his harp.

Stoke St Mary. This little village at the foot of a wooded hill, with a long white house of Charles I's days giving a touch of charm to its street, has kept a joke in its belfry for 400 years. It was a curious whim of Roger Semson, who made one of the bells, winding round it half the alphabet *backwards and upside down*. The font is 500 years old, but most of what we see has been made new.

Stoke-sub-Hamdon. All over Somerset and all over Dorset we see the golden stone from its hill; it is in church and house, tower and cross. For 1000 years and more builders have come with their horses and dragged from Hamdon Hill great blocks to make a wall or an arch, an angel or a mullioned window. How much has this place contributed to Somerset's glorious towers! The hill-sides are scarred with quarries.

The Romans fortified the hill to make a camp three miles round, and from this golden stone hewed a column for a statue of Flavius Valerius Severus, one of the Caesars who rose to share for a short time the emperor's title of Augustus. Since the days of the Romans generations of Norman and English builders have been quarrying here. We may climb the hill if we will, or a car may run up its rough trackway to the marvellous view-point all round as we wind our way to the top, where stands a great stone column with 44 names of the fallen and a bronze wreath.

The Normans came to Stoke and used its golden stone to build a church; the 13th century added a tower which the 15th topped and hung with gargoyles; the 14th raised the porch and the room above it, with amusing corbels to the vaulting and coloured plaster work; and at some later time a mysterious canopy with a consecration cross above it was let into the wall of the nave. Our own century put the ancient figures from the churchyard cross back on their broken shaft.

There is still much left of the fine Norman church. The carved doorway has a tympanum of Sagittarius, the human-headed horse of the Zodiac, aiming an arrow at Leo the lion while a lamb holds a cross above them and three birds perch in a tree. Over one of the three Norman windows is the Archangel Michael with his dragon. Round the Norman chancel walls are odd-shaped corbels and a stone scratched with a primitive sundial. Inside is a Norman font with cable moulding, a double piscina under a trefoiled arch, and a magnificent chancel arch rich with the Norman mason's work. The 13th century added a piscina in a pier for the roodloft altar; the 14th added a transept lit by four lancets with heads between them, and laid here the stone figure of a rector; the 15th roofed the nave and the south transept, carved the bench-ends, filled the east window with glass, and painted the walls, though only scraps of the colour with which they decked the church are left, a few patches on the walls and fragments in the window. The Jacobeans carved the altar table and the grand pulpit, which has still its old hourglass. The 15th century stone screen, one of the small groups still surviving, came here, like the stone altar in the north transept, from some other chapel.

Then in Stuart times came John Strode in ruff and armour, to lie here in stone under a fashionable canopy. His home, now called the Priory, is still one of the architectural glories of the village and something like the fine place he knew, with its Tudor gateway, the bellcot over a tiny gabled oratory, and the panelled hall. The round house where he kept his pigeons is still among the barns. The whole property now belongs to the National Trust.

An interesting old place is the Fleur-de-Lys Inn, with carved spandrels in the doorway and a fives court set up in the days when the lads of the village were no longer allowed to bang balls against the tower of the church.

Stoke Trister. Only two miles from Wincanton, it seems 100 miles from anywhere by the time we have climbed the hill, as the new church did last century when the old one at the bottom was burned down. Up the hill with it came the Norman font with its carved cover, the old pulpit, and a mediaeval bell. What we miss most is an east window, the wall being filled with the commandments on tablets of stone. The church tower looks out to the great tower on the skyline marking the spot on the Wiltshire border where Alfred is said to have raised his standard against the Danes.

Ston Easton. Stone Easton it should be, and in stone is its best possession, an impressive Norman arch leading into the chancel of the little church. Seven centuries after the Normans set it up Ston Easton took it down again, taking its stones one by one and numbering them and putting them back as they were. It has three orders of carving and rests on round shafts. The peepholes on each side are new and the chancel as we see it is 18th century. It has a neat oak barrel roof and an ornate font rather oddly used as a reading desk, a newer font being used for christening. There is a neat oak pulpit and screen, and an elaborate nave roof with four dormer windows.

Here lies John Hippisley, who lived to hear of the Great Fire of London, and has this warning on his monument:

> *Reader, prepare, and be not vext*
> *To think your turn may be the next.*

Stowell. We come down a lane which stops before a big house, a farm, and a church. There is an amusing winged gargoyle on the mediaeval tower. The parson still climbs the old rood stairs, though

Wells Cathedral: the west front.

Wells Cathedral: the nave.

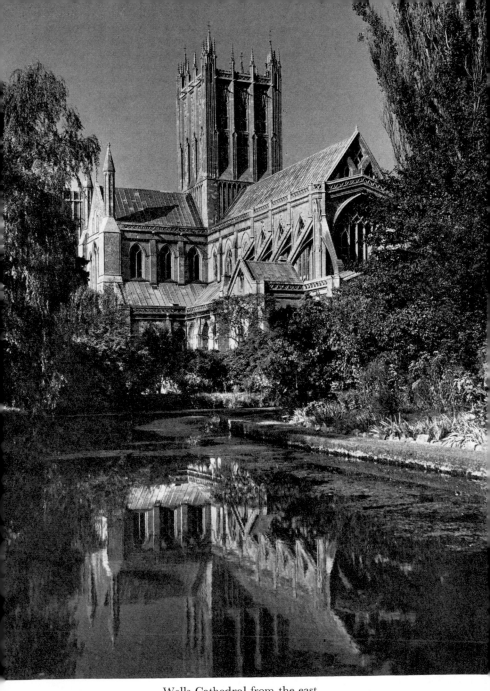

Wells Cathedral from the east.

Wells Cathedral: looking from the south transept to the north transept.

Wells Cathedral: the undercroft.

now on the way to the pulpit. The font is 500 years old. The chalice is Elizabethan. The doorway is imitation Norman. In 1760 CTT, amateur artist, cut a peacock and his initials on the end of a chancel seat; and in 1913 along came RAC to cut his initials and a cock on the seat opposite, 243 years between two odd little pictures. The manor house has gone, but its great 15th century window survives after a varied life, for it has been in a rectory dovecot and is now the west window of Horsington church.

Stowey. It has a lovely climbing street with great banks and little steps to the houses; it has a lovely work of art open to the wind and the rain; and its great house is tucked away in a world of its own where none can come except to feel that life is good indeed.

Its artistic treasure is the little sculpture on the outside wall of its church, a 13th century church in a cluster of noble beeches and two fine yews; we measured one of the beeches and found it five yards round. On the chancel wall is a lovely Madonna perhaps 18 inches high, a gem in spite of the wear of centuries, which have left her still with her crown and a veil. On a stone not far from her is a pair of shears set here by the wool merchants who remade this church in the days of their prosperity. The shears are on a buttress.

The windows are odd, with no two alike, and one has been a door. In one are fragments of old glass from Rouen with mitres, crowns, and roses in them. The chancel walls are covered with modern paintings of Bible scenes by Henry Strachey, a scene of gloom and terror looking down from above the chancel arch on the nave, where the Angel of Death with huge black wings appears to be receiving the dead from their graves. There are two tablets in the nave from the days when these pictures and tablets were fashionable, one to two people favoured richly with fortune who *sought not the distinctions of the world*, another to a girl of 19 who was *suddenly taken away before evil could alter her understanding or deceit beguile her heart*.

Best of all at Stowey is Sutton Court. Here, behind one of the rarest walls in England, about 15 feet high and battlemented, with beauty creeping about it everywhere, stands this fine Tudor house built round an ancient tower. We are looking at the growth of centuries, perhaps at something older than the Norman Conquest, for life has been going on here through all these generations. It is as quiet a place as we have found.

Stratton-on-the-Fosse. An old place overshadowed by a magnificent new neighbour, the school and abbey of Downside, its

I

village street is part of that long paved road the Romans made to the south coast from Lincolnshire. They made, too, the wide flat bricks in these church walls, rebuilt in Norman days.

We come by a 15th century traceried door into one of the two churches in England dedicated to St Vigor, a Norman saint of the 6th century. It has a Norman font and an elegant stone pulpit made about 1400, with long sunken panels. A gay patchwork of old glass has a charming golden-haired Madonna and the symbols of the Passion—the Cross, the whipping pillar, and the nails.

This small church has something never made for a church at all; it is its organ, which was made for Brighton Pavilion and was listened to there by thousands in Brighton's royal days. Later it became the property of Downside Abbey.

Street. It looks across the fields to Glastonbury, and the most interesting things it has to show us of itself are older than Canterbury, older than England, and older than civilisation. They are ten prehistoric lords of the land, a plesiosaurus and nine ichthyosauri which roamed about these fields and died in this place perhaps 1,000,000 years ago. They were found in the quarries of blue lias from which the village was made, and they are now preserved for us to see in the walls of the small museum.

The church is old but poor, yet it has a fine treasure in its sculptured sedilia, the stone seats for the priests enriched with decorated arches and pinnacles, with tiny heads the size of a penny; we noticed 21 of them among the leaves. There is a pinnacled piscina with a canopy.

Street has a fine viewpoint held by the National Trust, Ivythorne Hill, looking across to the Mendips; and here also is Marshall's Elm, the place where the first 25 of Charles I's soldiers were killed soon after the king set up his standard on Castle Hill at Nottingham.

We have seen in Glastonbury Museum a Norman draughtsman picked up in Street churchyard; it lies with a Saxon draughtsman.

Stringston. The ancient church has been restored in our time by the Prior family, whose tomb, carved with names for about 300 years, is near the wonderful cross in the churchyard which still bears high its figures after about 600 years. There is Christ on the Cross, Mary with her little Son, a knight to guard both, and a bishop to bless those of us who pass this way. The 400-year-old font is still used, and three very old bells still ring. One is from the ruined chapel at Lilstock near by, where a new church has kept the roughly carved

246

font the Normans made. On the walls at Stringston hang memorials to the St Albyns who let their house to Wordsworth and his sister and then, fearing that they were revolutionaries, turned them out.

Sutton Bingham. Up a tiny lane almost on the border of Dorset is a church, a waterlily pond, and a simple manor house. That is all we found of Sutton Bingham, and the only sign of life we saw was a crowd of goldfish in the pond.

Yet here is not only a 14th century cross with a pillar cut from a single stone, but one of Somerset's most perfect Norman churches and a wonderful collection of 13th century wall-paintings. The church has no tower; its two old bells hang in slits in the gable. It has not 50 seats for its people; but everything it has is of the best.

A modern porch shelters a Norman doorway. There is a Norman font with cable moulding, and a perfect Norman chancel arch, rich with chevrons. It is only six feet wide, but is big enough for the miniature 13th century chancel, with paintings on its wall, in the splay of the east window, and in the trefoiled arches of the lancets. They have been unfortunately touched up by a modern artist. During the Great War another 14th century painting was found under the plaster of the nave wall, depicting the death of the Blessed Virgin.

Sutton Mallet. It lies at the foot of the Polden Hills, with dykes and willows about it, the Roman road on the ridge above giving a view comparable with that from the Hog's Back in Surrey. By no means a beauty, the church has the charm of quaintness. It is a tiny place with an apse at one end and a rather queer tower at the other. It is full of box-pews, some so high that we can barely see into them. In the middle, in the little space left free by these pews, is a Norman font and a harmonium.

Sutton Montis. Under the pine-grown ramparts of Cadbury Hill, the biggest Roman camp in Somerset, a church was built in Norman days, with a very low tower and a massive stairway to the belfry, where 200 years later was hung a bell inscribed with a prayer to St Cuthbert. Here it rings still. By the Norman chancel arch (splendid with chevron carving) stands a canopied pulpit from which ten generations of parsons have preached. The font is 15th century, and in the rectory garden is a sundial of the early 17th century.

Swainswick. It lies in one of the great valleys of the hills round Bath, off the beautiful Gloucester road. Its church, with a huge

247

barn close by, stands where the Saxons built their church. The splendid Norman doorway has zigzag carving, four-leaved flowers, and faces fading away; and stone faces have been looking down from the arch of the tower for centuries. In a chapel off the chancel, approached through a panelled arch with neatly carved capitals, is a canopied recess above which is a tablet to an accomplished daughter of 17 who died in 1764. There are many finely carved pews as memorials to those who sleep in this place, a fragment of a canopy in the nave wall, and over the pulpit a charming little window with St George and St Margaret.

The rectors of Swainswick have established one of the longest records we have seen, for one of them preached here 67 years from 1744 to 1811, and two others followed him for 46 years each, three men out of the first part of the 18th century into the 20th.

It was here that William Prynne the Puritan was born in 1600; his parents have a memorial in the church. He would be baptised at the 14th century font, and must often have looked at the old brass which shows Edmund Forde with his hunting knife in the everyday dress of a man of 500 years ago, his wife with him.

Swell. Poor little Swell, we may think, for it hides itself behind the manor house, with no village left to its name and nowhere to hang the two bells on the floor when we called. Yet the old place goes straight to our heart. Except for the chancel, it is just as its builders measured it out 800 years ago, 16 feet this way, 32 feet that. Its little Norman doorway has the same simple criss-cross carving, but the Norman font has been cut to a new shape. Crowns and flowers and Tudor roses gleam from fragments of old glass. The chancel, with a panelled arch and pillar piscina under another carved arch, was built in 1450. The niches by the altar, each with a tiny vaulted roof complete with a carved stone boss, have still the painted backgrounds for the statues they have lost. The dainty inlaid double chair in the sanctuary is fit for a lady's boudoir, in strange contrast with the pulpit and reading desk of 1634, and the 15th century pews which fill three-quarters of the nave with their worn white oak, made to look even smaller than they are by some tall box-pews. The Tudor manor house, though altered internally, retains much evidence of its original beauty.

Tatworth. It has a new church and an old inn where once a year a bit of No Man's Land, a meadow with a watercress stream, is sold by auction to certain farmers who claim rights in it. It is one of the quaintest sales in England, for an inch of candle is set burning and the last bidder before it flickers out owns the meadow for the year. There are many things to be careful about, for you may be fined if you sneeze or cough or run the risk of putting out the candle in any other way; but when it is honestly out the solemn auction ends in a less solemn way with a meal, and every guest has watercress from No Man's Land.

Close by is the hamlet of South Chard, where an old cottage and an ancient chapel share the same thatched roof, and hereabouts is the Roman Fosse Way.

Taunton. It wears the cloak of a busy town, and busy it is, with clothing trades, engineering shops, and railway works; and yet as we ride up to it it has the distant enchantment of a cathedral city, with high towers drawing us from afar, and when we reach it we are in the midst of history. Twelve centuries ago King Ina founded Taunton. We see the great earthworks he set up for his castle; as it guarded the little settlement in ages past, so Taunton guards it now. The earthwork of Ina's castle, 80 feet wide and half as long again, held up by powerful stonework, remains within the precincts of the rambling castle by the River Tone. To those who understand it is a thrilling spectacle, for King Ina was building up the kingdom for Alfred and Athelstan to consolidate. He had driven back the Welsh and built his castle at Taunton to defend his kingdom, and from here he dominated all England south of London, the first Saxon ruler with such power and unity.

He was the founder of the town that has grown so great today, and he was one of the best of our early rulers, for he called his Witan together, with the bishops and a great gathering of God-fearing men, and drew up laws which marked a great advance in the moral life of the people. The influence of Christianity was clearly on them, and they provided for more humane treatment of the conquered than any other laws passed in these islands till then. It must have been a tragedy for Ina when the tranquil life of his kingdom was disturbed by war, for he went on pilgrimage to Rome, and there, though he himself would go to kingly feasts, his wife led him back to simple ways and he lived like a peasant until he died in the Eternal City.

The castle has grown through the ages, but we enter by a modern gatehouse raised on arches 600 years old, in which we may still see

249

the groove which held the chains of the portcullis in mediaeval days. The gateway opens on to Castle Green, where, with modern buildings about it, stands all that is left of the castle of the Norman bishops of Winchester. Here Geoffrey Chaucer's son Thomas was Constable; he took a Somerset girl as his wife. In the Civil War it was held for the king and for the Parliament in turn, but the redoubtable Robert Blake held it for a year against the king's forces, which he punished so rigorously that at the Restoration Taunton was deprived of its charter, until Charles II relented and sent the new charter now hanging in the council chamber.

The Royalists set 10,000 men to take the town, but Blake held on till Fairfax came. What we see of the old building from the seven acres of Castle Green is the Drum Tower of the curtain wall and another gatehouse of the 13th or 14th century. The tower has two Norman windows, and the gatehouse leads us to the inner ward with the Great Hall rising from it, built by Bishop Langton in the 15th century, 40 yards long. It is here that we see King Ina's earthwork, and to the left is the Norman keep with walls 13 feet thick, huge buttresses, some 14th century windows above, and a vaulted chamber below. The keep is the old part of the castle, built by the bishops of Winchester when they were lords of the manor here. The Great Hall has been the scene of most of the historic events of Taunton for more than 400 years.

It is the name of Judge Jeffreys that leaps to mind here, for here he held the Assize after the fall of Monmouth. Taunton had hailed the duke as he rode into the town on a June day in 1685, proclaiming him King Monmouth, cheering him through the streets, and decorating the castle with flags. They presented him with a Bible in the marketplace, and the duke, flushed with the sense of triumph and impending glory, kissed Miss Blake who gave him the Bible and paid the same compliment to her 26 scholars.

Three weeks passed, and another memorable day had come, for the battle had been fought and lost and the prisoners were arriving from Sedgemoor, wounded, terrified, starving, with the ferocious Colonel Kirke pursuing them. He hung 30 of them within sight as he sat over his wine at the White Hart Inn, and for days the town was at his mercy, with men hanging in the marketplace.

Thirteen weeks passed, and on September 18 Judge Jeffreys arrived at the castle to try the rebels.

The River Tone glides slowly through the town, and the old marketplace, with its stone market-house, draws all roads into it. Before the market moved away it was the centre of life, as Taunton is the centre for all the rich meadows, orchards, and cornfields of the vale around, the vale of which Michael Drayton wrote:

What ear so empty is that hath not heard the sound
Of Taunton's fruitful Deane, not matched by any ground?

and over which Macaulay became enthusiastic, writing that "every stranger climbing the graceful tower of St Mary Magdalene sees before him the most fertile of English valleys". This tower is one of the two beautiful towers of Taunton, the other being St James's. Both churches are magnificent, 15th century refashioned in the 19th, when both these towers were taken down for safety and rebuilt stone by stone. We see them as they have looked for 500 years.

For miles we see the stately tower of St Mary Magdalene, rising 163 feet high, its four stages lit by windows, its buttressed pinnacles at each corner, its summit crowned with pinnacles and turrets on the high panelled parapet. There are statues in niches by the noble west window, and in the spandrels of the doorway are mediaeval carvings of Judgment and Doom. The delicate fan-vaulted ceiling of the tower completes its splendour.

We come in by the south porch, which has on it the date 1508. Two curious animals peer out from the buttresses, and in three elaborate canopied niches over the outer doorway are Crucifixion scenes, with the thieves on their crosses, and Mary and John at the feet of Jesus. The hands and feet and the heart of Our Lord are carved on the inner doorway. The vaulted ceiling of the porch is rich with flowery bosses, and the porch has a room above it.

The nave is remarkable for having four aisles, and a forest of slender pillars rises with clustered columns to the clerestory, some of the pillars carved with angels, some from the old 13th century church, the rest from the 15th, and one of them with a delicate niche from which the gentle face of Mary Magdalene looks out, a modern sculpture. More angels look down from the massive roof beams of this mediaeval nave, and figures of the Twelve Apostles fill the niches between the great clerestory windows, where 15th century glass glitters with little scenes and saints. There is more ancient glass in St Andrew's Chapel, picturing the marriage feast at Cana.

There is on the wall a monument with a gaily painted figure of Robert Gray, his head bare, his beard pointed, his ruff starched, and a red cloak over his black gown. He built the almshouses in East Street, and when he died in 1685 he was so beloved that they gave him this epitaph:

Taunton bore him, London bred him,
Piety trained him, Virtue led him.

St James's Church, 15th century, but refashioned like St Mary's, has a tower 116 feet high, with a spired turret at one corner of its pierced parapet, with pinnacles and statues, and a vaulted roof. Its lofty arch looks into the long nave which, with the north aisle in which the mediaeval roof remains as it was, and the slender columns of the north arcade, are all 15th century. In that same century the grand font was made, with saints and apostles, with 21 figures in groups of three, and with the Madonna and St John praying at the foot of the Cross. This splendid font was found half-buried in the wall last century. The Jacobean pulpit is remarkable, for it has a carved scene of seven mermaids swimming with proudly curving tails; we do not remember such a company of sea-maidens in any other church. A chest of 1697 has a bird perched on foliage and two dogs with outstretched tongues. The altar chalice is Elizabethan. The church has lost its mediaeval screen, a fragment of which we see in the castle museum, but it has two fine chapel screens which have been seen by a million people who have never been to Taunton, for they were shown at Wembley Exhibition.

Taunton has done well with its municipal buildings, keeping as a touchstone for their architecture the lovely lines and tall windows in the 16th century grammar school. The corporation meet in the old school dormitory, with a fine open-timbered roof over their heads. An imposing new home for the county council has risen in the centre of the town.

Taunton School has a splendid home with 50 acres of playing-fields at one end of the town. Its creeper-covered buildings with a central tower, rising above two fine ilex trees, are seen from the road. The school has grown from its foundation in 1847 to an important school with 600 boys. The oldest school in the town is King's College, founded in mediaeval days and rebuilt in the 16th century by Bishop Fox of Winchester, who was living at Taunton Castle. Though the old school remains, as we have seen, the great growth of the college called for a new home last century, and the school has now a great block of buildings half a mile away, with 75 acres of playing-fields, and a chapel looking out on a lovely garden with a memorial cross. The chapel has a valuable reredos. Other notable schools at Taunton are Huish's Grammar School, founded three centuries ago, and Queen's College, which began its career in the castle 100 years ago, but soon afterwards moved to well-equipped buildings near Trull village, looking across to Exmoor and the sea.

The people of Taunton have been wise enough to realise the glorious opportunity of making the castle the centre of their culture, and it is now the home of the Somerset Archaeological and Natural History Society. The very fine library has 26,000 volumes, mostly on Somerset, and is rich in works of antiquity. There are many important Somerset pictures, notably the Pigott, Tite, and Braikenridge collections. The museum is housed in the Great Hall and the new Wyndham Galleries, and among its possessions are extinct mammals of the Mendips, a notable collection of Somerset Bygones, remains from the lake villages and from Ham Hill, relics from Sedgemoor and the Monmouth Rebellion, local lace and needlework, pottery and tiles, pewter and brass, coins and medals, Somerset portraits, metal work and earthenware, Stone and Bronze Age and Roman antiquities, and birds, plants, and butterflies.

The town has three sets of almshouses: the grim red homes of Robert Gray in East Street, with their curious paired chimneys like sentinels and a coat-of-arms of 1635, as gaily painted as the founder's figure in St Mary's; the quaint thatched house of 1500 at East Reach, now no longer an almshouse, with an open corridor in front and the arms of Richard Bere, the abbot-builder of Glastonbury; and, newest of them all, pleasant blocks by a roadside lawn, an admirable bit of town planning.

But for its ancient tithe barn Taunton might possibly forget it ever had a priory; the barn is 600 years old, and has the points of three swords meeting in a boss between the mediaeval windows at the gable end. The barn is near the county cricket ground, one of the town's green spaces. Handsome iron gates lead us into another green space, Vivary Park.

On Taunton's outskirts at Wilton is a pretty little country church come to town (or rather the town has come to it) with a nave partly 500 years old, capitals on its west end columns 200 years older, and a south doorway 200 years younger. Five centuries of priests have passed through its chancel doorway, and a Taunton doctor of the 17th century, George Powell, has his arms with fiery suns in a 300-year-old window.

Tellisford. Out of our English chalice of beauty has come no fairer little place. It is thankful because all its men came back from the Great War (three went and three came home) but it must be thankful also for the beauty Nature and man have given to it.

We may dip down into one of its little hollows, and stand at a white bridge with lovely hills all round; or we may walk through primrose lanes in spring; or we may take the flagged path to the church, the long and narrow path between stone walls alive with white arabis and purple aubrietia, with a garden on one side and a farm on the other, and in front of us the most inviting pointed archway of the little church. It is a dream of beauty in the springtime, and the church is always lovely. On its wall remains the old mass dial.

We do not remember a more charming place in all our journeyings. The small arch of the porch has two orders of moulding and two lovely prim heads, a woman with a wimple, and a dignified man with a long beard. We come into a nave about six yards wide and nine yards long, plain with white walls, supporting the barrel roof with timbers centuries old, and an elegant arch into the chancel and another to the tower.

The chancel arch is about eight feet wide, and across it is an elegant oak screen with dainty tracery, and a lovely piece of oak-leaf cresting; the screen is new but the cresting is old, having been on the ancient reredos. It leads us into a chancel like a drawing-room, with a blue carpet, white walls, and a reredos in quiet red and gold with a beautiful frontal and curtains. The roof has black and white panelling. In the chancel is set a fascinating little sculpture from mediaeval England, the head of a 14th century village cross. A captivating group, it has the Madonna with a lily, St Catherine with a wheel, a figure of St Margaret, and the Crucifixion with Mary and John looking on.

The very charming pulpit is Jacobean, with the figures 1608 in the panels, one letter in each panel, hidden among the carved foliage. One of the nave windows has Jacob's ladder in it and another a Good Shepherd. The fine roof of the tower has still the rough old beams of the 15th century.

On the chancel wall is a stone to Henry Farewell, a rector who lived universally beloved and died lamented in 1708, but the rectors Tellisford remembers with affection are the Bakers. Father, son, and grandson, they were lords of the manor and rectors for three generations.

Templecombe. Where its old farm stands was the home of the Knights Templars, and their barns are still round the courtyard. In the garden is an archway and one or two old windows, all that is left of the chapel of the Templars. The church is mainly 15th century but has been much renewed and the north aisle is Victorian. The font with square bowl of Purbeck marble is *c.* 1200. The most striking feature is a large mediaeval painted wood panel showing the head of Christ, which was discovered some years ago in an out-house; it may have formed part of the roodloft parapet, or of an altar piece. Over all is a fine old wagon roof.

Thorne. Tucked away in a lane near Yeovil, it seems to have grown as naturally and daintily as its namesake in the hedges. We sat on a stone seat in the church porch and looked down on a row of old stone houses and a spreading fig tree. The small towerless church has been made new so often that only a 13th century doorway suggests its age. It has an oak pulpit of 1624, two carved chairs in the sanctuary, old altar rails, and an oak screen in memory of one who died in the Great War. There is an odd font like a garden urn. Stones from old Ilchester gaol have been used to make a rockery in the rectory garden, and the gaol bell hangs above the rector's roof.

Thorne St Margaret. It is a long, long climb to this small place, with its pleasant manor farm and a church made new last century, but still with its red sandstone Norman font. A brass inscription to John Worth cannot resist a play on his name and we read:

> *John Worth lies here, and John is grace*
> *And Worth doth virtue sound.*
> *His virtue praise hath left on Earth,*
> *His grace hath glory found.*

Thorn Falcon. Down a lonely lane men have tramped to a farm and a church for 500 years. Five heads of lions guard the doorway of the tower, in which still hangs a bell of Shakespeare's day. In this far-off little place is much splendid oak carving, and a 13th century font.

Thurlbear. Away from the village stand the rectory and the church, with a fine yew hedge between them. The nave has a double arcade of Norman arches and a plain round Norman font. Still ringing are four bells fashioned by Robert Norton, who was making bells in Exeter in the 15th century.

255

Thurloxton. The tiny mediaeval church is rich in carving, with a simple and beautiful 17th century screen, but combining in a rare fashion reading desk, prayer desk, and pulpit; for two book desks jut out from it, and in 1634 the pulpit, with its four striking crowned figures of Faith, Hope, Charity, and an unknown, was built into it. The Norman font has a quaint high cap matching the rest of this black woodwork, and black with years are two ancient doors, one cut in a single block from what must have been a mighty oak.

To Thurloxton in 1763 came the new curate from Ansford, none other than Parson Woodforde, whose famous diary has made him so many friends today. When he first came here he could find no lodging till invited to stay with the squire at 1s 1½d a day, horse, laundry, and all, which he did till the beginning of next year when he changed this curacy to go to Babcary.

Tickenham. The church exhibits work of all the mediaeval centuries, but it is predominantly 13th century; the fine tower with its stair turret crowned by an elegant spirelet is 15th century. Porch, font, and arcade of severe square piers are 13th century. The plain chancel arch is early Norman, with a window in the wall above it to give a view of the altar from a roodloft long since vanished; only the stairs remain.

There is a Jacobean oak pulpit, an altar table of the same age, and a curious mixture of two ancient stone altars. In mediaeval glass Our Lord appears on a green cross and the arms of the Berkeleys appear on shields, while below the windows are figures probably representing the Berkeleys themselves, though some say the two cross-legged knights and the grand lady are Roger FitzNicholas with his son Nicholas, and Wentylan, his son's first wife. It is a family group from the 13th century, the men with shields and swords, the lady richly gowned and elaborately coifed. Their descendants lived in the Court behind the church, a splendid example of a mediaeval house, with a great hall of *c.* 1400 and a fine collar beam roof.

Timberscombe. The fine manor house of Bickham, with a wing which was once a chapel, gives us a delightful picture as we come to it, but indeed the 15th century church has something lovely for us any time. It has one of those beautiful fan-vaulted screens that are the pride of scores of villages in Somerset; this one has long been disfigured by dull Victorian paint and is now rich and bright again. The font has been here all the time, and so also has the ancient door through which we come, its great planks strengthened by fine old ironwork. The shaft of the cross is 500 years old.

Timsbury. The great house next door is older than the church, and its gables are crowned with round balls.

The church was rebuilt in 1826 but still has some of its ancient possessions, including the font and a perfect Mass dial, now inside the tower. The handsome chancel was designed by Sir Gilbert Scott. The quatrefoiled parapet of the chancel has six lively gargoyles, and its windows have eight stone heads. There is also a fine old sanctuary lamp.

Tintinhull. On one side of the green is a 17th century house with mullioned windows; on the other is a fine old manor house with the church beside it. Tintinhull House is now in the care of the National Trust, and is open to the public during the summer. In the church is the portrait of an old parson in brass, only quarter-length yet seeming to have raised some doubts lest it should be too proud a thing for dear John Heth, who died in 1464, for the inscription has these words:

> *Be thou witness, O Christ, that this stone does not lie here that the body may be adorned, but that the spirit may be remembered.*

A strip of brass below is to a rector before him, John Stone.

The walls of the church are much as these rectors would see them, for they are 13th century, with an unusual stringcourse running round the inside and jutting out in one place to hold a vanished statue. Here is still the base of the old stone screen, with a piscina cut into it, and there is also a lovely double piscina in the chancel with stone shelves, 700 years old. The chancel windows are graceful with Norman pillared arches. The font is 15th century, the pulpit, carved with roses and thistles with a panelled back and canopy, is Jacobean.

A curious stone sundial is over the south porch, and in the churchyard stands a great block of stone like a gatepost. Cut in Latin on one side of it is, *Let us go into the house of God rejoicing*, and on the other, *Truly this is a holy place*. In an account of 1515 slipped into one of the church registers it is called the Stonyng Door, and we learn that it was set up here by a rector who was Prior of Montacute.

Tivington. It is one of the oddest places we have seen, and we understand that its church **has** been a school during its 500 years.

Now it is a church again, sharing its thatched roof with the cottage next door (the ancient priest's house), with a high chimney for a spire and a view from its windows for miles into the valley, over the moor, and away across the sea. The church bell is over the door, and inside, in an open fireplace, the sticks are laid ready for a cold Sunday evening. On the mantelpiece are sacred pictures, and on a windowsill a very tiny font. A door by the altar leads into the old priest's house which is now a cottage.

Tolland. It is a farm that we remember here, although the path by the stream brings us to a tiny church that we do not forget. It has a sundial which has been marking time 200 years, the old font and some mediaeval tiles, and a lancet in which St Christopher is bearing his precious burden across the stream.

It is the farmhouse that takes us back to history. To this house came James Turberville, the Bishop of Exeter who refused to take the Oath of Supremacy to Elizabeth I and was imprisoned for it, being then allowed to come to Tolland to spend the last years of his life. He is said to have spent them at what is called Gaulden Farm, but the house has been much altered since then. The principle feature of interest is the elaborate plaster work decoration in the hall.

Treborough. It has a remnant of an ancient past of which it seems to be dreaming as it stands solitary on the rough hill slopes of the Brendons, wild and lovely country. Once it had a hundred miners and their families for company; now the mine is deserted a mile away, a gaunt chimney and a broken track for a railway left for us to see. The railway climbed 1000 feet to bring coal from Watchet Harbour, but the enterprise was too costly and failed.

Even in Roman days men were trying to wrest from the Brendons the iron still hidden in these rocks, and the coins and the mining tools of Caesar's men have been picked up. Men have picked up also a prehistoric skeleton in a coffin made from five great slabs of stone, and it is good to know that the people of Treborough gave the remains a corner of their consecrated ground.

Their plain little church is whitewashed within and without. The 500-year-old font has angels under the bowl. There is a little mediaeval piscina on a pedestal, and a wooden pulpit older than the Reformation.

Close by is Leighland Chapel, which belonged to the beautiful

Cleeve Abbey and has been rebuilt, and down in a wood is a stream which falls 30 feet over a cliff of black slate.

Trull. We remember it for its magnificent mediaeval craftsmanship, for the church is full of dark carved oak, nearly all 15th century work. There is a splendid fan-vaulted roof screen, two small screens of delicate design, massive bench-ends, and one of the finest oak pulpits in England. The five saints on the pulpit are said to have been buried in the days before Elizabeth and so saved from the axe which spoiled some of the smaller figures above them; the five are St John, Pope Gregory, St Jerome, St Ambrose, and Augustine of Hippo. Angels hover over them, while in the buttresses between are many more tiny saints—for this is the church of All Saints.

Here and there among the bench-ends are delightful figures, once one behind the other as if marching to the altar, though this mediaeval procession has been broken up. The peasant who led it still marches along in his clumsy boots, carrying a cross almost as big as himself, but his followers are scattered. Here is a man bearing a candle, his trunk-hose showing below a short surplice. A man with a reliquary is on another pew, and then we come upon two choristers with books. One seat was made in 1510, some are Jacobean, and a high settle at the back of the church has the name of its maker, Simon Warman, with the date 1560.

The steps to the roodloft curve inside one of the pillars, and it seems to us that only the smallest boy could have climbed up to sing the songs of praise.

In the chancel windows is beautiful ancient glass, the oldest showing St Michael, St Margaret, and St George, all struggling with their dragons, while in the next window is a 500-year-old Crucifixion. There are also fine modern windows, one to the memory of Mrs Ewing, whose tales of *Jackanapes* and *Lob-Lie-by-the-Fire* delighted our childhood.

Ubley. The River Yeo flows by it, a little before it is captured to make a reservoir for Bristol, a great lake seen from many villages. The church has stood for five or six centuries, and we are charmed, as we come up to it, by the tiny-capped stair turret which vies with the spire for the place of honour. The turret is embattled and pinnacled like the great tower itself. It looks on to the old cross restored on the green, with small sculptures of the Crucifixion and Christ enthroned. The church has a handsome open parapet over the aisles, from one of which six hideous gargoyles look down. On the wall is the old mass dial.

Inside is a Norman font shaped like a cushion capital on a low pedestal. There is a chained copy of a book by Erasmus, a pulpit and an altar table of 1637 with panelling in the sanctuary to match.

Uphill. Here came the road from Old Sarum across the Mendips, carrying lead from the Roman mines to ships at the mouth of the Axe. Traces of the Roman camp are on the hill by the ruins of a church the Normans built and the English builders remade in the 15th century. The nave, reached by a Norman porch, is open to the sky, with a gravel floor. Two sundials are cut in the stone, one, with a Maltese cross, over another Norman doorway now blocked up, the other above a little window in the low Norman tower, with a curious gargoyle which has thee faces and possibly represents the Holy Trinity. From the top of this tower is a glorious view of the whole line of the coast down to Exmoor and Minehead, with the little heights of Brean Down and Brent Knoll nearest us, and the islands of Steep and Flat Holm halfway across the Channel towards the mountains of Wales.

The Norman font, with its seaweed decoration of a later period, has been taken down the hill to the new church, for only the tower and chancel of this old one are roofed over, to serve as a chapel for the dead.

The hill itself, a last spur of the Mendips, is being destroyed by quarrying, and already the famous bone cave has gone. It was probably a hyena den, being lined with bones of the animals which once roamed these hills—rhino, bear, bison, and boar.

Upton. It has an old tower in a field, a relic of its ancient shrine. The ash and the sycamore and the strangling ivy have bound it round, creeping up to the parapet with young life as if the tower itself were growing. We found a notice still in the tower telling us of the restoring of the church in 1793, but the seats have gone and the church has gone, and stones mark where the nave and chancel stood.

Here now the grass and nettles grow and the hens from the farm come scratching for food. The round Norman font lay all neglected when we called. The three old bells are in the new church—not ringing, for there is no tower.

Upton Noble. A Norman doorway with a little canopy set over it brings us into its church, and its children are still christened at the crude and rather curious font the Normans made. In the wall of the chapel is an ancient carving of the Crucifixion, and over the door is a perfectly delightful carving of the royal arms painted on oak. On the wall is the old mass dial.

Walton. Here in this village is a thatched rectory 500 years old, with transomed windows between buttresses, and in the church a rector older still, a stone figure from the 14th century, with a heart-case in his hands and a long-eared dog at his feet. His church, new when he was laid here and made new again last century, has ball-flower round the west window and the chancel arch, while convolvulus and a bird pecking grapes appear on the new stone corbels.

Among dyked fields at the foot of the Poldens is Sharpham Park, where Henry Fielding was born, and through whose door the last Abbot of Glastonbury, Richard Whiting, was dragged to his death within sight of the house. Whatever his crime (Henry VIII's commissioners accused him of holding back some small part of the abbey property) his death was decided on weeks before the trial, for Thomas Cromwell wrote in his diary of events to come: "The Abbot of Glastonbury to be tried at Glastonbury and executed there." However, it was worse than that. The weak and sickly old abbot was first sent to the Tower, then taken to Wells, then condemned to death, then dragged on a hurdle through Glastonbury and hung on Tor Hill. His head was stuck on his abbey gate, and other ghastly exhibits were sent to Wells, Bath, Ilchester, and Bridgwater.

The door by which we enter the church is almost covered with three great strappings of 12th or 13th century ironwork branching into leaves and flowers. They reach across the door and are truly delightful.

Walton-in-Gordano. One half of it has been caught in the suburbs of Clevedon, the other has escaped among the woods of the Gordano valley. Both have new churches and have divided between them what remains of the old one. Walton-in-the-valley has the 15th century font; Walton-in-the-suburb has the base of the tower and has patched up the old churchyard cross. On the crest of a hill sloping to the sea are the ruins of Walton Castle, an old place but not as old as it looks, for it was built in the 17th century in imitation of a mediaeval castle, its towers clustering round a citadel. The castle has embattled walls and a round tower at each of its eight corners.

Wambrook. In 1896 this village was transferred from Dorset to Somerset. The little mediaeval church has rounded doorways and a font of the 13th century, bench-ends carved 400 years ago, an Elizabethan chalice engraved with its price of 35s, and a gallery at the back for the ringers of three ancient bells.

Wanstrow. We come up a path bordered with old-world flowers, through the churchyard with its weeping ashes, to the trim 13th century church, which has been much renewed. On the wall of the nave is a tablet to John Yeoman who died in 1824 and who led the choir here for half a century, and next to it is a tablet to his son John.

Washford. With a little-known name, it has a great possession, a green courtyard with Old England still clinging round it, for here is the home of the farmer-monks of Cleeve Abbey. Farmers, gardeners, and makers of books they were, a little company of Cistercians who walked about this place 700 years ago, lived within these walls, slept in these dormitories, bowed down before this picture of Our Lord, looked up with admiration on these angels, walked on these tiles, sat on these seats, and lie to this day under this green turf.

They made parchment for their books from the skins of their sheep, and here are the rooms in which they worked and the fireplaces at which they dried the skin. They had one of the loveliest monasteries in Somerset, and though time has taken its great church away, except for a few of the tombs and the great foundations of the piers, it has left us an abbey with enough of its old grandeur to stir up visions of another world than ours.

Time was when all this glory was a farm, when the house of the monks housed cattle and sheep and carts. The great refectory, the dining-room of the monks, was used as a barn, and the ivy crept over the painted Crucifixion on the wall; we see the ivy-green all over it. Now it has all been saved for us by the public spirit of Mr Luttrell of Dunster Castle, and Cleeve Abbey is a lovely place again.

It is not a massive place like Fountains or Tintern, for it has lost its noble church, but it is a moving place for those who would wander for an hour in the footsteps of a little band of monks who came here about the year 1188, and stayed till our monasteries were destroyed by an imperious will.

We come to it over two bridges, through a gatehouse with guest rooms over it. Set in one gable is a niche with a Madonna, and on

262

the other is a canopied Crucifix. Very interesting are these two gables of the gatehouse, for under one is the name of the last abbot before the Dissolution, and under the other is a quaint Latin motto which means, let us say, *Gate open be to honest folk all free.*

Through the gateway we find ourselves on the green turf of the courtyard with the cloisters and the rooms about us in the square—the refectory and the dormitory, the common room and the sacristy, the workrooms, and the little penance chamber with a tiny window in which a seat has been cut for the watching monk in charge. In a passage are the lockers in which the monks would place their precious things, and just through the passage, outside the glorious windows of the dining-room where we may still see the ancient gargoyles on the buttresses, is the floor of the very first refectory in which the monks would eat their meals, the dining-room of the 12th century abbey before these 13th century buildings were set up. Here is one of the most thrilling little patches of England on which the rain falls down, for it is paved with 1000 mediaeval tiles with leopards and eagles and arms all over them. They are the arms of the benefactors of the monks in those old days.

The 15th century dining-room is over 50 feet by 20, with five great traceried windows on each side, except that one has been blocked up to form a fireplace. We come to it up stairs which sweep round like the marvellous steps to the chapter house at Wells Cathedral, and we are astonished as we come into this great room, for at one end the pale face of Christ looks down from the cross on the wall where the ivy has been stripped from it, and above it all is a magnificent roof, so hard that the death-watch beetle has not been able to get its teeth into it, and the timbers are as good as new. It is one of the best preserved roofs in England, every bit of it 15th century, its traceried beams arcaded and carved with leaves, borne by 21 angels and adorned with 50 bosses, one of them a gem with a bunch of grapes. At the east end red tiles from the church have been let in the floor.

Here is the great dormitory running along the whole side of the cloister, where each monk had a window so that he woke in the morning looking up to the hills. The windows, open to the sky, have seats cut out of the stone of the windowsills. It is here that we notice a curious thing, a skew window cut through the wall so that some monk from his bed could watch the lights on the altar to see that they did not go out. If they did go out he could run down an outside stairway out of the dormitory to attend to them. The dormitory has a barn-like roof with wood staples instead of nails. From the

263

dormitory a door led into the infirmary, which has gone, and this doorway is now left high up in the wall where the dormitory floor has been removed, and is remarkable for a very curious point that should be noticed. The doorway has one outer jamb and an inner one, with a socket in the centre showing that the door revolved on a pivot and did not hang on hinges. It would be quieter for the monks who were sick, but its interest for us today is not in its kindly thought, but in the fact that here was the ancestor of our revolving door.

Below us as we stand in the dormitory is the sacristy with a great rose window, the common room (with the doorway a farmer widened to let a bull in), and the chapter house, with a beautiful 13th century archway and wide low vaulting springing from the roof without a pillar, so beautifully made that it has never been restored or a single stone replaced. We come into it through a pointed doorway with charming windows on each side, each window with its lights divided by a beautiful mullion with a quatrefoil above it.

Watchet. From this small harbour set sail the Ancient Mariner. It was on a walk from Nether Stowey to Lynton that Coleridge arrived here with the Wordsworths, his mind simmering with the story. "And here," said he, "is where he shall set out on his fateful voyage."

Here, where today an occasional ship from Spain and Algiers puts in among the shorter-distance cargo boats, the Danes landed, and Watchet men fought them in a field still called Battle Gore. Another stranger to land is said to have been St Decuman, "floating in from Wales on a raft with a faithful cow, who gave him of her milk during the journey". Here he lived as a hermit till the natives struck off his head as he knelt in prayer. We see him in a niche on the tower.

The 15th century church above this miniature seaside town has a 600-year-old cross made new beside it, and a little portrait gallery in brass. The pulpit, with a magnificent sounding-board, is 500 years old; some of the bench-ends are 400. Angels support a roof of many carved bosses; other angels hold up a 15th century font that is used no more. There is a chest of 1699, ancient tiles before the altar, and a little glass which must be precious if it tells the truth about its age, for it is dated 1273.

The portrait gallery shows the Wyndhams, who lived at Orchard Wyndham and at Kentisford Farm near the church. A square 17th century pew carries their arms in a noble bit of carving, and some of their funeral armour hangs on the walls. Under a high canopy is the

Tudor tomb of John and his wife Elizabeth, with their portraits in brass. On another brass are two other Elizabethans, John and Florence Wyndham, and under their portraits is a dialogue between them, with Fate breaking into the conversation.

It is of this Florence Wyndham that a remarkable story is told, though we do not present it as true. It is of a thief who came to take away her jewels and gave her life instead. She had been laid here in her coffin, and the sexton, coveting her rings, broke open her coffin so roughly that it woke her from a trance. Back to her home she went, to give birth soon after to the son whose portrait is with his wife's on another brass.

The stone figures of two Wyndham brothers who died early in the 17th century kneel on gold-corded cushions. A brass of 1616 shows Edmund Wyndham, and a stone has an epitaph in this strain to his loyal son Hugh:

Here lies beneath this ragged stone
One more his prince's than his own,
Who in his martyred father's wars
Lost fortune, blood, gained nought but scars;
And, Earth affording no relief,
Has gone to Heaven to ease his grief.

Wayford. It looks through many mullioned windows across the Axe Valley into Dorset. We found its stone-walled pond pink with valerian flowers bending down to admire their reflections; and, warming itself in the sun among terraced gardens, stands an Elizabethan home with an arched porch such as is familiar under Italian skies. It was built *c.* 1600 by one of the Daubeneys, who carved on the escutcheon outside his fantastic badge of dragon's wings tied with a cord. Between house and church an enormous stone well stands in the courtyard. The church, with its tiny bell-turret, is mostly 13th century, a rough little place, and dark, for most of the windows are lancets under carved arches. Under a canopy is a double piscina on wooden pillars, and there is a 14th century font.

Weare. Because he had his portrait cut in brass and placed over his grave in the chancel John Bedbere is the best known man of this village. He was a 15th century merchant, and the artist has pictured him as he went about his business, with the big leather purse of those days fastened to his girdle.

The church in which he lies has a fine 15th century tower, with pinnacles and parapet, triple belfry windows, and a curious stairway. John Bedbere may have heard one of the bells, for it has a prayer to the Madonna and so must have been made before the Reformation. The splendid door, with 1755 on its latch, opens on to old oak pews with shapely ends, charming against the bare grey stone of the walls. The Norman font is scalloped beneath the bowl, there are fragments of 15th century glass, the chain of an old Bible is fixed to a lectern, and the roughly carved pulpit of 1617 has the stand for the preacher's hourglass on the wall. The altar table is a painted Jacobean chest with folding doors.

Wedmore. Somewhere near, perhaps at Mudgley, where massive walls have been unearthed, King Alfred had a palace, and to him here came Guthrum the Dane to sign the great Peace of Wedmore. A thousand years later, with another Peacemaker on our throne, the treaty was commemorated in the church in one sentence:

> *Alfred the King at Wedmore made peace:*
> *Death of Alfred 901—Edward the Seventh 1901.*

The church is one of the early ones made in the shape of a cross, the shallow buttresses to the chancel being Norman, the lofty tower 15th century. The south porch with its upper room is also 15th century, but the beautiful south doorway was made about 1200, and still has the original door on its hinges, decorated with ironwork of that time, many little tight coils on straps and hinges. The date 1677 is on it in studs with the initials of the churchwardens.

On the wall is a painted St Christopher carrying the Holy Child, a mermaid and ships about his feet, with the donor of the painting kneeling in a corner. A long conversation between Saint and Child is on a scroll, but is almost unreadable. Many quaint old corbel heads support the fine timber roofs, and one is built into the chancel wall. There is a stone altar, stone window seats, and a piscina curiously made in the corner of a windowsill. The font is 15th century, and there is an old studded ironbound chest with two great rings for lifting it. Some of the finest Jacobean carving in Somerset decorates the pulpit, with thistles and fleurs-de-lis.

Wedmore has on its church wall what is often said to be the last ancient brass portrait of an English soldier. It shows George Hodges wearing a buff coat, breeches, and jackboots, a long sword strapped to his side, a pike in his hand, and it tells us that his *better part was rapt into the best place* in 1630. Beside him is a brass engraved with the heart of his soldier ancestor Thomas Hodges, who received his last wound at the Siege of Antwerp in 1583 and died leaving three legacies: *his soul to the Lord Jesus, his body to be lodged in Flemish earth, his heart to be sent to his dear wife in England.* This delightful verse completes his epitaph:

> *Here lies his wounded heart, for whom*
> *One kingdom was too small a room;*
> *Two kingdoms therefore have thought good to part*
> *So stout a body and so brave a heart.*

Some time in the 11th century a man crept into this churchyard and buried his small store of coins in the safest place he knew, and now his savings are part of the treasure of the British Museum, for he never came back, and it was not till 800 years later that the pot of coins, all of the time of our Danish kings, was found beneath the 15th century churchyard cross.

There is another cross in the village, a beauty of the 14th century, though its canopied statues are sadly broken; and another wayside cross is in the hamlet of Stoughton.

Wellington. It has flourished for 1000 years. Alfred gave it to his children's tutor, but it was the conqueror of Napoleon who made it famous. He chose it for his title and bought land here with money given him by a grateful nation. Lying at the foot of the Blackdown Hills, and on the main road from Exeter to London, Wellington has grown up in the last 100 years into an industrial and intellectual town, with one of our famous public schools. It has ten green acres of parkland and garden, with a small lake fed from the stream running through the town; a children's playground at Rockwell Green, the outlying area with the red sandstone tower of a fine church as a landmark, and woollen mills whose work goes everywhere; in the Great War they received the biggest order for khaki ever given, a million and a half yards of it. Wellington School, founded in the 19th century, and well equipped for 20th century scientific education, is housed in a great group of buildings, of which the most notable is the chapel in memory of the boys who fell in the Great War. The chapel has fine craftsmanship in oak, much of it done in the school's own workshops and not unworthy of comparison with the work of our mediaeval craftsmen. The town is fortunate in having also an excellent school for girls, close to Blackdown Hills and in a lovely setting.

It is said that Wellington knew nothing of the town when he chose its name for his, and that only once did he visit the place, five years

267

after he had taken his title from it. His choice was perhaps a passing fancy, yet it made the name of Wellington famous, and the town repaid the compliment by building him a column 175 feet high, bayonet-shaped, on a spur of Blackdown. It was to be crowned with a figure of the Iron Duke and to be the centre of a group of cottages for Waterloo pensioners; but the scheme was too great for this small town, which found even the upkeep of the column, with its hundreds of steps, a big item out of its yearly budget, and has now handed it over to the National Trust.

The stately 15th century church, with a sturdy tower elegantly pinnacled, has 13th and 14th century work in its walls, and the east window is from the earliest days of tracery, 650 years old. Here they laid a Lord Chief Justice of England in Shakespeare's day, the man who sentenced to death the founder of the British Empire, Sir Walter Raleigh. He was Sir John Popham. We have only a glimpse of him, so high he lies in state, wearing his judge's red robes, his gold chain, and his square black cap. His wife is at his side and his arms are painted on a canopy set above him on eight black columns. Few men could have more sorrowing relatives about them, for a man and wife kneel at his head, another couple at his feet, 13 children are on his left, and 9 young women on his right a company of 26 people.

Sir John Popham was Speaker of the House of Commons and Lord Chief Justice, and he presided over two of the most famous trials in our history, those of Guy Fawkes and Sir Walter Raleigh. In Raleigh's trial he disgraced himself by allowing the infamous Coke to make savage attacks on Raleigh, Coke's language being so ferocious that at last the judge was bound to intervene and beg him to be "valiant on both sides".

Tucked away in a recess of the church wall is the stone figure of a man who was priest here over 600 years ago, with one of the earliest inscriptions ever written in English to tell that:

> *Richard Persone de Mere of Welintone Liggeth in grave. Jesu Christ*
> *Godes Sone grawnte him mercy.*

We can only guess at the last word, which is worn away. *Persone de Mere* stands for Parson of Mary, the name of this church. There is little more than a window left of the church he knew, for most of what we see is from the 15th century, when the very beautiful tower was raised and adorned with its clustered pinnacles, traceried windows, and queer gargoyles. It rises more than twice as high as the clerestoried nave.

A lovely stone reredos which we have seen in Taunton Museum

lay here for years, turned face downward to make paving stones for the sanctuary. Its many small figures in 14th century dress are worn and broken, but still the vivid picture of the Crucifixion stands out, with the jeering soldiers and the swooning figure of the Holy Mother; and round about, each in his small niche, stand the saints. There is an angel destroying St Catherine's wheel, and small fishes and a mermaid are swimming round the feet of St Christopher as he crosses the stream. Another bit of ancient carving is on a mullion of the south chapel window, a crucifix budding into five lilies. The piscina rests on four stone heads, a king, an ape, a monk, and a lady. The fine reading desk is made from a Jacobean bedstead, and there is a Jacobean chest. The pulpit, with its ancient panels, is raised on what was once part of the vaulting of the 15th century screen.

Wellow. Finely its church stands on a green bank, lifting up its eyes to the hills; it has been almost as we see it since the 14th century. Its tower is buttressed all the way up, there are two quaint faces on a window beside it, and over the doorway stands the patron saint, St Julian the fisherman.

The roof of the porch has lovely stone angels at the corners and two canopied niches with elaborately carved ceilings. The old door leading us into this stately place is panelled and traceried and has a colossal iron ring held by a hand, and it is curiously interesting for the wooden pegs which hold it together, which most of those who see them would swear to be iron nails. The old dial on the wall comes from the days before clocks.

It was Sir Walter Hungerford, one of the famous family we come upon at Farleigh Castle, who built this church 600 years ago, and he would recognise it today if he came. Here are the painted screens across the chapel and the chancel, both painted as in his day, one an elegant and perfectly charming piece of work, crowned with a carved cross Sir Walter would not recognise, for it was made by the village policeman. He would remember the roofs, especially the roof of the Hungerford Chapel, if he could squeeze himself behind the organ to get a peep of it. Sad it seems that the organ has been packed into the finest corner, where lies a lady of the Hungerfords under an Elizabethan canopy, a tomb richly carved and painted with an extraordinary figure of her in a ruff and a curious kind of bonnet. There is a battered tiny figure of a child below and two shrouded babes on toy tombs with most elegant little fronts. Above her is the painted ceiling in red and black and gold, borne on four stone angels, and in a corner is what is left of a carved and painted stone canopy. She lies under the east window, the walls of which have mediaeval paintings of the Twelve Apostles, fading away.

By this chapel lies the stone figure of a priest who was probably here before Sir Walter Hungerford built his church, a prim figure with a wig and a mysterious cross cut on his forehead.

The roofs are all magnificent, resting on 40 wood and stone angels with hundreds of bosses, and borne in the nave on superbly carved beams with spandrels. The roof of the chancel, barrel-shaped with a rich cornice and elaborate bosses, was given by a previous vicar in memory of his father, who was vicar before him; father and son preached here 75 years. The roofs of the nave look down on a majestic array of benches on which about 20 generations of Wellow folk have sat. There are over 50 of them, all 14th century with poppyheads and finely carved ends, and sturdy book-rests which seem to have been used for kneeling in mediaeval days. It is good to sit in them, for this is a light and noble place, aglow with bright windows. One is the War Memorial window with St Alban in silver armour, the Archangel Michael with a fiery sword and golden scales, and St Louis of France in a blue gown with golden fleurs-de-lis holding a crown of thorns. Below them are the badges of the 12 regiments to which belong the 20 men who did not come back from the Great War, two pairs of brothers among them.

The chancel has three windows rich in colour, with nine splendid figures. One is copied from a French cathedral window and has Moses, Aaron, and Melchizedek; another is a tribute to a 40 years chorister and has St Ambrose, Zacharias, and David with his golden harp; and the other has a blue Madonna with her mother in a green robe, and the aged Simeon holding the Child who is playing with a golden apple. The east window has Christ in sorrow and in glory, with eight saints. The font is older than this ancient church, for it was made seven centuries ago. There are two old chests and a table made from the canopy of a pulpit which has disappeared. There are carved peepholes by the beautiful chancel screen, and both doorways of the old roodloft are still here.

A little walk about two fields close by takes us far down the mists of time. One has four stones marking the place where the ruins of a Roman house lie hidden; the other at Stoney Littleton is an ancient tumulus into which we may go, a dark corner of the prehistoric world where tribal chiefs were laid in tombs like this. The farmer will let us have the key and we may walk inside, groping our way for about 100 feet through long low passages to small chambers made of flagstones. It is an eerie bit of the world of our unknown ancestors and is one of the ancient monuments looked after by the Ministry of Public Building and Works.

Wells. It lies within its ancient walls in the 20th century like a small mediaeval town, a matchless place. For twelve centuries there has been a church at Wells, since Ina, the Somerset-born king of the South of England long before Alfred, founded a shrine for his Saxon subjects. The Normans followed the Saxons, and a few Norman stones remain, but the cathedral as we see it was begun in the 12th and finished in the 13th century. It is not what it has been for

> *There is nothing so beautiful now*
> *As it used to be;*

but, though the stones of Wells may crumble, its glory will not pass away. It has been here 700 years and will stand 700 years more. It is unique as a cathedral group, the most complete example we have of what an ecclesiastical city was like in the days when the Church ruled the world.

Nearly all that is great in it lies by its walls—the cathedral like no other, the staircase leading to its noble chapter house, the Chain Bridge leading to the lovely Vicar's Close, the cloisters with the doorway through which bishops have walked to their moated palace for about 800 years, the great palace itself with the moat still flowing round its superb walls, the bishop's barn, the deanery, the Penniless Porch, all gathered round the famous green on which for generation after generation travellers have stood spellbound before the finest assembly of mediaeval sculpture in these islands.

The great front is nearly 150 feet across, and it was raised in tier after tier of sculpture, six lines running across, up and round the towers, crowned by a row of angels and another of apostles with Christ reigning over all. Many of the figures have gone and some are broken.

On each side rise the 14th century and 15th century towers, the northern tower showing Bishop Bubwith at prayer; he left money for it and built an almshouse in the town. The great towers stand majestically apart, independent and not encroaching on the nave, and behind them, rising superbly in the centre of this wonderful mass, is the noble tower set up by the earliest English builders as high as the roof and carried higher in the 14th century. We can climb to the top of it and see the valley in which this wondrous city stands.

271

There is no cathedral anywhere more interesting outside, and we walk round the walls enchanted by their beauty. The northern wall has one of the finest porches in England, lofty, with a vaulted roof, its walls arcaded, its spandrels filled with queer beasts, a stringcourse finished with dragons swallowing the end of the string and their tails twisting along the moulding.

A little farther along the northern wall rises the stone staircase which runs to the chapter house, to the bridge across the road, and then down into Vicar's Close—as charming a place as we have come upon, like a tiny mediaeval street surviving in the modern world, with 21 houses on each side, all with tall chimneys, leading to the little chapel at the end with the library over it. It is one of the delightful surprises of Wells, and has looked much as we see it for about 500 years. Bishop Ralph's chapel, built in the 14th century and made new in the 15th, has the original altar stone in the sanctuary, and the rough old screen has been preserved. There is 15th century glass with Bishop Bubwith's arms in it, and the ceiling of the library is also 15th century. Number 22 in the Close has been restored to its original 15th century proportions, and the Hall is a remarkable 14th century building with fine mediaeval furniture, rare old glass, brass and pewter, and ancient charters and books, including one of the 12th century.

Outside the Close, just through the Chain Bridge, is one of the loveliest windows in Wells, a delightful oriel which has been photographed thousands of times and has looked down on the comings and goings of Wells since the 15th century.

Between the road and the chapter house stands one of the almost hidden beauties of Wells, the charming 15th century Prebendal House nestling against this lovely mass of masonry, and approached by a beautiful porch.

Far away on the other side of it all is the old bishop's barn, a simple but stately structure 110 feet long, with immense buttresses.

The bishop's palace itself, a magnificent group started by Jocelin 700 years ago, is perhaps the rarest bishop's home now left in England, set in a great quadrangle surrounded by a magnificent wall, outside which the moat looks still as it has looked since the walls were built. Thrilling it is to walk along these walls and look about us, with the ruins of the great chamber now open to the roof, and nothing but the walls left of a great hall that was big enough for a marketplace. The bishop's chapel is still intact, with its vaulted roof and the fine foliage on its capitals.

It is true, no doubt, that all who come into the great nave of Wells are at first a little hurt by something like a gigantic figure eight, two massive inverted arches. There are three pairs of them facing the nave and the transepts, and they hold up the central tower. They are a unique device for averting the peril threatening the cathedral 600 years ago, and through all that time they have held up the great tower in the watery soil of Wells. There are those who are hurt by them; there are those who declare that they have a kind of beauty in themselves; and there are those who after a while get used to them and cease to look on them as an architect's freak, refusing to let them spoil the impression of one of the most remarkable interiors the genius of our English builders has ever set up. Remarkable it is from whatever angle we consider it—its general impressiveness, the richness of its decoration, the matchless carving of its capitals, its splendid tombs, its very precious glass, the wonderful peep through its forest of columns with the sunlight falling through its western windows, its unique set of misericords, its noble chapter house, or the marvellous stone stairway leading to it.

Between the last pair of the great piers on each side of the nave are set two tiny chantries, one to Bishop Bubwith and one to a treasurer of the cathedral with the curious name of Sugar, both 15th century men. The chantries face each other, and both are gems. We can sit in them and think of the wonder of this solemn place. They have six sides and fine tracery. In the Sugar Chantry the canopy of the altar is like lace, and there are angels with delicate wings and curly hair. Steps from this chantry lead to one of Somerset's four mediaeval stone pulpits. Two other chapels are in the south transept: those of St Martin and St Callixtus. In St Martin's lies Chancellor William Biconyll (one of the 47 ways of spelling his name). He lies in cassock and surplice, and the light falls on him through a window with magnificent modern figures of familiar heroes. In this small place is kept a book with the name of every Somerset man (11,275) killed in the Great War. Divided from St Martin's by a screen lies a figure on a nameless tomb in the chapel of St Callixtus. If it is nameless it is at least famous, for it has a series of panels with stately figures of three priests said to be matchless for their mediaeval vestments, set between two panels probably unique. In one of them is a delightful Madonna in a close-fitting kirtle with a mantle falling gracefully round her. She is holding up her hands as in surprise, probably at the small figure of Gabriel descending from above. In front of her is a pot with a lily. At the other end is a remarkable figure of the Eternal Father with his crucified Son. All five figures are the original work of 15th century craftsmen and are charming.

In the two chapels of the north transept (reached from the choir aisle) are two contrasting tombs, one an 18th century monument set up to Bishop Kidder, a piece of pompous monumental masonry, and the other the charming figure of a bishop of Shakespeare's day, John Still, looking lovely in a long red cloak. Every child should come to see him, for he wrote *Little Jack Horner*. Not far from Bishop Still is an exquisite carving of a lizard on a corbel. Under a canopy of three bays in the south transept lies one of the best sculptured figures in Wells, that of Bishop Marcia, who died just after the 14th century began. He lies on a cushion supported by beautiful heads of angels, and there are six heads along the front of the tomb.

Yet it is in the east end of Wells that its chief richness lies; we are not halfway through this wonder of 700 years. In the aisles round the choir sleep a long line of faithful bishops going back 900 years. The sculptures are 13th century, but the old bishops have been identified and their bones are in wooden boxes with stone casings, inside the tombs. In these aisles lie most of the famous bishops of Wells. One of the first engraved figures made in England is on a stone over Bishop Bytton, whose tomb was long supposed to be a cure for toothache; his coffin has been opened and his skeleton seen in perfect order, every bone in its right place, his teeth in fine condition after 600 years. Close by, within one of the most beautiful iron grilles in this country, lies a famous bishop who made an image of his own skeleton so that he could look at it; it is here under a wonderful canopy. Above lies Bishop Beckington as in life. Over his figure rises a beautifully painted canopy with a reredos of panels and tracery, and a miniature piscina. The top of it has a small vault of fan tracery and pendants; there are angels with finely wrought wings spreading over the arches, and traces of the original colour after nearly 500 years. Let into the reredos is a carved oak panel showing the Scourging, the Crucifixion, and the Road to Calvary. Lying with his face towards all this is the figure of the old bishop as he was in his glory, while under him is his skeleton. For 13 years he moved about this cathedral with this tomb in its place. The marvellous screen within which the bishop lies as in life and as in death is one of the treasures of Wells, and is probably matchless for its decoration with tiny faces. One shows the bishop himself in his mitre, apparently a portrait, and there is on one of the uprights a row of three faces unsurpassed by anything of the kind we have seen.

Next to the Beckington tomb is something finer still: a 19th century bishop with lion cubs at his feet. He is Lord Arthur Harvey, and the figure is by Thomas Brock, as beautiful as anything of mediaeval days, with stone flowing like fine linen. The alabaster figure of Bishop Harewell of the 15th century has two hares at his feet. On another tomb is the figure of Bishop Giso, appointed by Edward the Confessor and carrying on to William Rufus, a great conciliator in the Conqueror's day. There is an alabaster figure of Bishop Ralph in all the episcopal ornaments of the 14th century, and in a chapel of the north-east transept lies the rich alabaster tomb of Bishop Creyghton, who was in exile with Charles II and was made bishop by him on his return, in gratitude for which he gave the magnificent brass lectern in the nave. On it we read of his 15 years of exile with the king, and on the book-rest is the great Bible from which the bishop used to read. He would preach from the stone pulpit, for it was built in the reign of Henry VIII.

On the east wall of the chapel in which Bishop Creyghton lies is an ancient sculpture of the Ascension; it has traces of colour and is very charming for the upturned faces of the group of people looking on. In this chapel also is a figure of a chancellor of the cathedral who died 600 years ago, and not far away (near the ancient cope chest) lies the 14th century Dean Godelee. Hereabouts is a heavy carved frieze of acorns which has been rescued from the cowhouse of an old manor, and close by, in the north wall of the transept, is a canopied recess in which a 14th century stone figure is wearing away.

It is in the choir that we have what seems to us the loveliest peep of Wells, and it is fitting it should be so, for here is the oldest bit of the cathedral, the three western bays built at the very beginning of English building; they are 12th century. Here also are 60 of the finest misericords still left in England, the work of the original craftsmen of the cathedral. They show the usual variety of groups and scenes: a man riding backwards on a horse, an ape with a basket of fruit, a mermaid and a lion, dragons biting each other's tails, and a fox preaching to four geese, one asleep.

Below the magnificent Jesse window are seven niches with statues in them, all modern and all fine. Higher over the altar above this row of sculpture is one of the noblest Jesse windows in existence, a blaze of gold, with the figure of Jesse lying at the base as if meditating on that wondrous line of David that was to lead to Bethlehem. From his figure, as from the stem of the vine, comes the trunk of the tree with the Madonna and the Child both under canopies; Calvary is above; majestic figures in cloaks of red and green and gold stand about Jesse at the foot; and there is David with his harp and Solomon with the temple in his hand.

Standing here and looking beyond, through the columns behind the choir and into the lady chapel, we have perhaps the finest single view in Wells, like a rainbow of colour seen through a forest of columns. The richness and depths of the scene are not to be forgotten. It is from the windows of the lady chapel that the colour comes. They are filled with 14th century glass, much of it in mosaic fragments but all aglow with colour. There are 20,000 leaded fragments in four windows alone, and there are also among this fine old glass many quaint figures. They are in three eastern windows, which have figures of angels blowing trumpets, David and other patriarchs, the Madonna, Eve and the Serpent, Moses, and a number of bishops. There are about 50 of these extraordinary figures in all.

It is in the lady chapel and the choir that we find the best glass of Wells, but there is little anywhere that is poor. The clerestory windows have old figures of saints, one with St George in mail. The choir aisles and chapels have good glass of the 14th century, and there are figures of St Michael, Mary Magdalene, John the Baptist, and Paul teaching Timothy. There is beautiful glass also above the tabernacle work of the choir. The great west window of the nave has three long lancets, outer ones with 17th century glass, the middle one with glass renewed last century.

Among the things that are unique in Wells is one of worldwide fame, the chapter house, with its marvellous staircase and the Undercroft. The Undercroft, used in ancient times as a treasury, has still the heavy wooden doors that guarded its possessions. The inner doorway has beautiful hinges, and the outer door is studded with nails and has great bolts and a huge lock. In the doorway is a piscina with the carving of a dog gnawing a bone, and close by is a charming stone lantern projecting from the wall; it must have held a candle. Hanging from the ceiling of the Undercroft is a wooden canopy under which the pyx was hung before the altar 600 years ago. It is four feet high, divided in three storeys of open tracery, and has a crest of oak leaves.

Here we open a door and look up a staircase like no other in England. Somebody has said that parts of it are like a heap of windswept leaves, so curiously do the steps sweep this way and that, some leading to the chapter house, some up to the Chain Bridge over the street. In a window at the top of the staircase is a lovely small figure of a woman in a yellow dress and a grey cloak she has been wearing since 1320.

The chapter house is 13th century, a little younger than the stair

Wells: the gateway to the bishop's palace.

Wells: Vicar's Close.

Weston-Zoyland Church.

Yeovil Church.

way. It has a central shaft with 18 columns round and 30 ribs of vaulting, each with a carved boss at the end. There are eight great windows and 51 canopied seats round the walls, all crowned with faces in stone—kings, queens, monks, bishops, abbots, and wild-looking men, nearly all smiling. Everywhere the work of these 13th century craftsmen is small and exceeding rich. There are 150 tiny heads on pinnacles, about 800 acanthus leaves about the seats, thousands of ballflowers running round the windows and canopies, and about half-a-mile of small carving running everywhere.

He would never be forgiven by either young or old who omitted Jack Blandifer and his clock from the story of Wells. Jack sits high up in the triforium above the north transept as he has sat for about 500 years, kicking his heels every quarter of an hour through all these centuries to set two knights in armour striking the bells with their battleaxes outside the walls, and little mounted knights running round on horseback on the wall below him in the transept. It is one of the sights of Wells.

The old clock was marking time at the end of the 14th century, and it is to some craftsman in that far-back age that we must be thankful for whatever amusement or astonishment this marvellous mechanism gives us. Its mechanical parts have long since been renewed (though the old works are still going at South Kensington), and the figures can hardly be as they were, but for hundreds of years at most of the hours of the day a small group has stood watching this wonder work as the hours go by. The face of the dial is over six feet wide, set in a square frame, the spandrels filled with angels holding the Four Winds. The outer circle has 24 sections representing the hours, and the hand that points to them touches them with a golden sun. The second circle shows the minutes, and a small star moves round it. The third circle gives the days of the month and a crescent with a pointer shows the age of the moon. Above this dial is a little panelled tower round which four knights on horseback run both ways whenever Jack Blandifer kicks his feet on the point of the hour.

For those who, amid the great impressiveness of this mediaeval city, seek change or contrast in smaller things, there is a Wells with a jolly marketplace hemmed in by houses, shops, and inns. There is the splendid church of St Cuthbert which would be much visited in any ordinary town, if only for its fine tower and roof and its richly carved 15th century font cover, found in a stable and restored to the church; there is the town hall, which, though largely modern, has some interesting portraits (Charles II and his brother James,

K

Christi College at Cambridge; and by an odd coincidence a page torn out of it is bound up in another Saxon book in the same library.)

Williton. The village of white cottages is growing into a little town of red ones, and is still remembered as the place where an assassin was born in its manor house 800 years ago. He was Sir Reginald Fitzurse, leader of the four knights (three of them Somerset men) who slew Becket at an altar of his cathedral. After he had been months in hiding the pope absolved him if he would spend the rest of his life doing penance in the Holy Land, and he went, leaving half Williton to the Knights of St John and half to his brother Robert, who built here a chapel where men might pray daily for his wretched brother and for Becket's soul. Nothing is left of the chapel but a few stones in the walls of a new church, which has a bit of the old screen worked into a reading desk, an Elizabethan table, a tiny old chest, and a font of 1666 made of alabaster from the cliffs of Watchet.

In the churchyard is part of a 14th century cross. The historic house here is Orchard Wyndham, home for centuries of the great Somerset family, the Wyndhams. Parts of the house are 500 years old, but it was greatly altered in early Stuart times and again in the 18th century, when a fine staircase was built in the old courtyard. Among the great possessions of Orchard Wyndham is a grand pink marble fireplace which screens a Tudor mantel. On lead rainwater heads in the front of the house are the arms of Sir William Wyndham, War-Secretary and Chancellor of the Exchequer to Queen Anne.

Wincanton. The prettiest way into its steep streets is from Castle Cary, through Bratton Seymour, and across the River Cale, which gave the town its lovely old name of Wyndcaleton. But there is little of Wyndcaleton left, for a terrible fire in 1707 destroyed it. Perhaps the best thing it has to show us is the glimpse through an archway of the long courtyard of the Greyhound Inn, with roses, roses all the way.

Only in the church is anything of great interest. A carved stone thought to be mediaeval or earlier, and brought here for preservation, is built into a wall of the porch, and shows in relief an incident in the life of St Aloys, the blacksmith who became a bishop. He stands at his anvil with the detached leg of a horse in his hands, while the horse itself waits patiently on three legs. An attendant stands by, and another man is kneeling beside the bishop; horse, bishop, and men all headless.

The figure of another workman with his tools is in the churchyard. He is Nathaniel Ireson, a master builder and potter, who set up this statue of himself with his tools ranged proudly round the base. He died in 1772.

The church is really two in one, the second being a late 19th century rebuilding of a Georgian fabric. Only the 15th century tower is left from the ancient shrine.

Yet the town is old in story. The Romans settled here, and one of their pavements was found two miles away, near Sutton Marsh Court, a moated farm built out of a manor house in 1661. Many a part has it played in a history made up chiefly of battles. Here was shed the first blood in the Revolution of 1688, when the Prince of Orange, on his way from Torbay to London, met a party of king's men and put them to rout.

Winford. We walk under an arch of yews, through a lofty west door deeply splayed, into a church made new in 1796 except for its stately tower, and we read in great letters across the gallery that the church was built in 1796 and beautified in 1820. It has little of this beauty now.

There are fragments of old gravestones in the nave and the steps of the old cross in the churchyard.

Winscombe. It has Crook's Peak behind it, a vale in front, a charming village street, a spreading yew 18 feet round the trunk, and a 15th century church which adds to the picture the beauty of its tower, a pierced parapet, a roodstair turret, and great windows rich in mediaeval glass.

Anthony and his pig (with a bell round its neck) are in one of the windows, with six white and gold angels. The two friends who gave this window 500 years ago kneel below, the wife with her rosary, the husband with his purse. Saints and bishops are in more 15th century glass, and in a window of the 16th century St Peter appears three times in glowing orange and gold, with his staff, his keys, and a holy-water sprinkler. A host of winged wooden angels are round the new nave roof; a few old seats have carved ends, and a Norman font has marks where the lid was once locked.

We found a stone to a young man killed at Guadaloupe when leading an attack against this French island in 1794, and a stone coffin with a weighty lid.

A mile away is Sidcot, a hamlet well known beyond its bounds for its fine school, founded by the Friends in 1699.

Winsford. A book older than Chaucer's *Canterbury Tales* speaks of a stone 1200 feet up on Winsford Hill, and we found it here, with a name on its rough surface much chipped and worn but having enough left to suggest to us that it was raised to a kinsman of Caractacus, the dauntless Briton who was led in chains through the streets of Rome.

Winsford's fine mediaeval bridge has gone, but its pack-horse bridge with the pretty thatched inn next to it is left.

Winsford church was made new in Somerset's prosperous 15th century days, but the builders saved the Norman bowl of the font with its twisted arcade, and the 13th century lancet window in the chancel, where is another very charming square window of unusual design. Two other small windows are rare, for they are above the chancel arch where windows are seldom seen. Yet another window has a blue-robed Madonna with her Child in 15th century glass, golden stars around them. The 15th century builders also strengthened the massive ash door with straps of ironwork thought to come from Barlynch Abbey, now in ruins by the Exe.

The arcade arches lean outwards, and the tower arch reaches up to the fine barrel roof, one of its 18th century bells telling us that *Religion, Death, and Pleasure make me ring*. The pulpit and the carved altar rails are Jacobean. Painted on wood are the arms of James I, one of only a few of his in our churches.

Winsham. By having Winsham just on its side of the Dorset border, Somerset can boast of something no other county has. It looks nothing to the casual observer, just an old wooden board painted with a faded picture; yet it is considered a great treasure by those who know, for it is the painting which hung above the old roodloft.

Only a small group of churches has managed to keep these things, torn from their places in the first years of Protestant England; and Winsham's is unique, for, instead of being painted with the usual picture of the Last Judgment as a background for the carved figures of the Rood, this one is painted with the Crucifixion itself. It is very worn and faint now, but just discernible is the figure of Christ on the Cross between two thieves, and the figures of the two Marys, whose red robes are the only touches of colour left.

The 15th century screen above which the painting hung is very unusual and interesting in its design, and finely carved on both sides. Two winged angels hover above the cornices, and sprays of pomegranates decorate the panels at the base, where are two family badges, a stag and the falcon with a bundle of sticks.

The pulpit is splendid Jacobean work. The panelled font is 15th century. A wall-monument of 1639 to Robert Henley has a shrouded head rising from a tomb, with an angel sounding the last trump above him. There is a chalice of 1570, another cup of 1654; and the church has two more possessions from 1583, one a bell, and the other a copy of Foxe's *Book of Martyrs* with part of the old chain hanging from it. On the wall is a mass dial older than books or clocks.

Yet another curiosity is among the church papers: a book of Registers bound with pages from an illuminated manuscript of the *Golden Legend*. Thorncombe, over the border, has the same binding for one of its registers, and it is probable that the pages are small spoils from Forde Abbey.

Witham Friary. It takes us back (a little surprisingly, as it is all unlike a monk's countryside today) to the days when England rang with the news that Becket had been murdered, for here the king founded, as an act of contrition, the first monastery for Carthusian monks in England. The only Carthusian house now in this country is at Cowfold in Sussex, but here are the stones of Henry II's monastery, where Hugh of Lincoln was the prior. It has been refashioned, but we feel we are standing in the monastery as we come into the church. We half expect to see the monks walk into dinner, for, though it has an apse, it is all severe, rather like a refectory with the stone-vaulted roof running from end to end, springing from plain brackets between deeply splayed windows. It is late 12th century, and it is believed that St Hugh himself built it.

There are four fine windows to him, one showing him building his cathedral at Lincoln, one with the swan greeting him, one receiving the charter from the king. Very handsome the saint looks in his mitre and his white robes.

The most interesting window is filled with the 15th century glass which was set here during the Great War, brought from Burton Hall in Leicestershire by the Duke and Duchess of Somerset; in it are rich pinnacles, small medallions with heads of a king, a bishop, and a golden-haired woman, all set in a rich border of red and gold.

The roodstairs are still as they were before the Reformation, both doorways remaining. The Jacobean pulpit is charming with a overhanging crest of grape leaves; there are two old chests; and the 15th century font is back again after having had the curious adventure of being built into a tower which was pulled down.

Across the way from the church is the old dovecot of the monks, all unrecognisable now outside, for it has been a cottage and is now a reading room; but inside it are some of the nesting niches.

Withiel Florey. The grass-grown lanes to Withiel Florey are witness to the loneliness of its scattered farms. Through one farmyard a path leads to the church. It is 500 years old, but the font is Norman.

Withycombe. One of the hill villages of Somerset, it has a stream splashing past the cobbled pavement of its white cottages, which go climbing up till it is too steep for them. The village has a giant yew and a charming church.

The porch of the church is carried up to form a low battlemented tower, a good bit of 13th century work, though the archway and the massive door lean a little from each other as if weary of the years. The stoup for the holy water in the porch is still perfect.

It is the rich dark oak against the bare stone which provides the charm of the interior. The rood stairway remains, and the graceful screen of the mediaeval carvers, with one bay of their tracery removed to allow a certain stout parson to reach the 16th century pulpit more easily from his stall in the choir. Under a window lies the stone figure of a widow of 700 years ago with richly carved vases at her head and her feet, probably for candles; she may have been a Fitzurse from the manor house. Hidden in a wall recess is an unknown man from the Middle Ages; he has long hair and has been here since the 13th century. He wears a hat, and it is said to be one of the first hats to appear on a monument of this kind. Both these figures are holding heartcases, from which we may gather that they died elsewhere and only their hearts were brought home for burial.

The font with a band of cable moulding is Norman.

Withypool. The wind tears at the few thatched roofs of this small Exmoor village exposed to the storms driving over the hills around it. Rough lanes lead to it and rough is the country. On one side a ring of low stones 40 yards across marks some ancient rite, and beyond is Cow Castle Hill, its broken ramparts rising steeply out of a wild and rocky valley. Between this primitive fort and the village, Landacre Bridge spans the River Barle with five ancient ⸱rches. In a wood close by a few herons have their nests.

The church has a round Norman font, simply decorated with grooved lines, and an Elizabethan silver cup and cover. A cross cut deep in the stone of a tower buttress marks a spot anointed by the bishop perhaps 700 years ago.

Wiveliscombe. It has the shadowy memory of a Roman settlement and a British camp, but it has pulled down what was much nearer and should have been much dearer to it, its ancient church. Here, too, was a bishop's palace, but all that is left of it is an arch and a few windows.

There are two stately sculptured figures seeming not quite at home in the 1829 church, and the children of Wiveliscombe must love to see them, for they are Humphrey and Margery Wyndham who had the kindly thought 300 years ago of leaving ten shillings for every child who is regular and punctual all the year at school.

Wookey. It is famous among all who love Old England, for it has one of the oldest habitations in these islands, one of the most wonderful works of nature, a magnificent series of underground halls fashioned out by little drops of water falling for 10,000 centuries.

Young indeed seems all the rest compared with it, but Wookey church has come from our first and last great building centuries, and its font is 13th century. It has fragments of old glass in its window tracery, two fine old chairs, and an ancient cross carved with the Madonna and a Crucifixion. There is a heavy old door still on its hinges, and a small chest of 1689.

Two old houses of Wookey have in them something of the history of the church in ages past. Mellifont Abbey at the church gate, with a square embattled tower at the entrance, was built in the 18th century on the site of the 14th century rectory, and has some of its old stones. Court Farm with a 13th century doorway was the manor house of the Bishop of Wells.

It is nature's great temple at Wookey Hole that we come to see, one of the most remarkable caves in England, chiselled out of the Mendip rocks by four courses of water whose ways can still be traced. Except for an archway built so that we may see a lovely grotto, the cave has not been touched by man, but is as nature made it. We have seen nothing more impressive underground than the great caverns, the roofs sparkling with stalactites and the walls like coral.

Woolavington. It lies on the slopes of the little Polden Hills, overlooking the flat dykeland which stretches away to Burnham by the sea. The tower of its old windmill has been turned into a house, and most of the old buildings have gone, but there are one or two things of interest in the church. It has come down from Norman days, and part of the nave is as they built it. The chancel is 13th century, the tower 14th, and the font 15th. The porch has stone seats, and a fine old oak door with ornamental ironwork in its hinges, latch, and handle ring. The walls inside are of pleasing grey stone. The pulpit is made up from old carved panels rescued from an antique shop, it being believed that they originally came from the old home of Henry Fielding at Sharpham Park, which is at the other end of the Poldens. If so these panels would be in the house when the great novelist was born. We found lying on a windowsill the old stone head of a monk, which was dug up in a heap of rubbish in the rectory grounds at the end of last century. It appears to have come from an ancient tomb.

Woolley. We found it after riding about for miles on the hills that look down on Bath; it stands superbly on a ridge in that great valley to which we look down from one of the loveliest heights in Somerset, on the way from Bath to Gloucester. We must wind and wind and wind through a maze of the countryside if we would find Woolley as it is. There is just room to get a car between the hedges without hurting the grasshoppers if we would come to this gem among green fields, shining like a gem indeed on a sunny day when seen from Swainswick Lane, with the small church between two barns, low red roofs in front, and a little wooded hill about it.

Its odd square tower with a round arcaded bell-turret rises among elms and yews, and in front the green grass runs down. Behind is the great Down on which Sir Bevil Grenville fell leading his Cornishmen to victory; below is the home of Thirteen Heroes, a village like a T with the church at the bottom, down the little street with the water taps at the doors, little gardens in front, and the gate of a field which bids us go no farther.

It is as it should be, for here is Woolley's sacred shrine, one of the simplest and smallest and plainest churches in the land, yet a glorious place to Woolley even long ago, for a scrap of paper found in 1873 behind the pulpit says:

> *The ancient chapel being ready to fall down, Elizabeth Parker of Ravenfold, York, lady of the manor of Woolley, did order to be builded at her own charge this most glorious church in 1761.*

On the left of the altar is a tiny bracket of carved wood, and on the right an unusual wooden piscina. The east end is a simple apse, the plain walls are cream, and the roof is white. There is a simple font with oak leaves, rather like a vase, poppyheads looking very old fixed on to the bench-ends, oil lamps, plain glass, and a queer stone near the font with a childish picture of John Bigs.

Woolverton. The church has an attractive little tower, with a spire rising amid four pinnacles. The walls are so ancient that we found two sundials scratched on them, both with 24 hours quite clearly marked, and still another on a buttress, also with 24 lines for the hours.

The porch has a fine stone roof with six carved corbels supporting the ribs. The sturdy painted font is carved with Tudor roses. The neat pews have old panels of linenfold and one has a very fine piece of carving. The sanctuary has an old oak table and two chairs to match, and the altar has a Last Supper painted on a gold background of which a richer church would not need to be ashamed.

Wootton Courtenay. There is something for everyone here. Those who want peace may linger among lovely cottage gardens; those who want wind and heather and wild walking may climb 1770 feet to Exmoor's highest peak, the top of Dunkery Beacon. There the vast moor is spread out before us, and we can catch a glimpse on a fine day of the Malvern Hills 120 miles away, seeing into seven counties and as far as the Welsh coast.

Those who love old and curious things come to the church, now whitened so that the fine roof of the north aisle can be clearly seen, with some of the richest carved bosses in the West of England. The roof is 15th century and the bosses are deeply cut in the shapes of an eagle, a pelican, St George and the dragon, and other figures. On the pillars of the nave are delicate canopied niches, and there is a holy water stoup carved from a spiral column of stone 500 years ago. The font, looking new, is 15th century. In the chancel is a memorial to the first Bishop of Colombo, James Chapman, who was rector here for 15 years. In the aisle is an attractive painted wood reredos by Christopher Webb.

One of the windows has two angels guarding it outside from two fearful beasts crouching under the hood-mould.

Worle. It stands high among the hills near Weston-super-Mare, yet so sheltered that we found a palm growing by its church, which has a rare little show for a village, a row of carved misericords. On one is a dragon with a man squirming under its claws, and others originally pictured the seasons, but of these only January is left, a two-headed Janus looking back to the Old Year and forward to the New, clear-cut faces under a hood. All these are old, but those in the opposite row are modern. There is a stone seat under a handsome canopy, a piscina cut with an aumbry in the wall next to it. Another rarity is a beautiful 15th century stone pulpit. Leaves and rosettes run along the top and a vine curves round the bottom. In the porch is a tiny lancet cut by the Normans from a single stone; the doorway next to it is theirs, and also the base of the tower. A woman outside the west window tells us when this Norman church was changed to Gothic, for her horned headdress was the fashion in 1460. A queen and a bearded king are at the arch of an ornate doorway, and above them great gargoyles yawn.

The hill rising above the village is Worle Hill, where two stone ramparts and seven ditches mark an ancient camp with numerous hut circles in its keeping. There was a battle here in the days before such things were written down in books; we know of it from skeletons found with marks of their battle wounds.

Wraxhall. A dull world, as the poet says, if we cannot stand and stare, and we stood and stared at the blue line of the Mendips from the ridge above Wraxall, and then accepted the invitation of the seat round the village elm to sit and stare again, so lovely is the view. We noticed farther down the road a charming row of 19th century almshouses looking at it all.

We have the same fine view from the steps of the stately cross in the churchyard, where the turf is like a lawn and the graves are like flowerbeds. The cross (except for its head) is 15th century, like the glorious tower, which has a parapet niched for statues and a grand array of gargoyles.

A plain Norman arch on round pillars leads us into the church, and once again we stand and stare, this time at the interesting idea of a 14th century mason, who thought out the grouping which links together a pillar, a stone desk, and the font, an angel propping the desk against the pillar to hold up the service book for baptisms. Yet perhaps we stare most at the row of corbel heads under the fine timber roof, displaying like a mediaeval milliner the fashionable headdresses of 500 years ago. The chancel has a beautiful vaulted screen running right across the church. Fragments of the old screen are worked into it, and there is another rich screen and many traceried bench-ends branching into poppyheads, all the work of modern craftsmen.

In the chancel the painted stone figures of Sir Edmund Gorges (1512) and Lady Anne lie in state: he in armour with his head on a tilting helmet, a greyhound at his feet; she in a red gown trimmed with ermine and a black headdress edged with gold, and with her wedding ring on the middle finger of her right hand. She is lying on her husband's right to show her superior rank, her father being John Howard, 1st Duke of Norfolk, and she great-aunt to two queens, Anne Boleyn and Catherine Howard.

Wrington. Nature made it a fair place, in this lovely country of the Yeo, with a river and a vale and two lines of hills; and the 15th century left it fairer still, endowing it with a church crowned by one of Somerset's noblest towers. Every line of this tower seems to be striving upwards. It reaches 112 feet, with long double windows, and pinnacles everywhere—at each turreted corner, along the pierced parapet, and rising from the buttresses. Among the gargoyles are dragons and queer creatures, and we noticed one of a man strumming an accompaniment to his song. Panelling and fan-vaulting make the tower as charming inside as out, and on a shelf is a whole library of chained books. On the outside wall is the old mass dial from the days when the books were being read.

The light pours through clerestory windows into a nave rich with clustered pillars, carved capitals, and vaulting shafts reaching through a host of angel corbels up to the panels and bosses of the oak roof. Both aisles have grand roofs and the elaborate 15th century font has more angels.

The older chancel, in which lies a stone priest of 600 years ago, has an unusual five-light window, a beautiful stone reredos with tall pinnacled niches, animal heads above canopied niches in the buttresses designed by Sir Charles Barry in 1832, and a sanctus bellcot with a bell 400 years old.

Writhlington. The church was rebuilt in 1874 but incorporates much old material, mainly of the 13th and 14th centuries. The font with quatrefoils on its bowl is probably 14th century. There are three wall-monuments of three centuries. One is to a young lady of 1691 with the cherubs, skulls, and crossbones fashionable at the time; a white tablet is to George William Fairfax of Fowlton in Yorkshire, who died in 1787; and a third is to Ann Goldfinch, who was brought here in 1812 and lies under a painted stone with three lions and three cockerels on it.

Wyke Champflower. It is a perfect piece of Old England, mellowed by centuries and forgotten by time. The road brings us to a green and a company of elms, beeches, and chestnuts, not far from where the River Brue runs under a mediaeval bridge.

The manor house and the 17th century church are one, a lovely group in a garden. The tombstones have been taken up and made into a wall, over which peeps a chestnut, with all its white candles aglow when we called. The little battlemented turret has tiny pinnacles.

The old door brings us into a nave filled with box-pews, some so high that nobody can be seen sitting in them, every pew with a door on a fine metal hinge, and all with their own hat-pegs. Charming it all is in its great simplicity, and there is little else. But 14 painted shields look down from the cornice of the roof, heraldic medallions and fragments of old glass look out from the east window, and from wall to wall at the height of the roof stretches the great painting of the royal arms, the biggest we have seen, the only division between the nave and the chancel. The altar rails are Jacobean, and looking down on them is the wall-monument of Henry Southworth, who built and adorned this place in 1623 and died in 1625. His arms are bright, the black columns of his monument are neatly capitalled, and his perfectly charming cherubs are smiling as if conscious of the beauty of the shrine they guard.

The surprise of the little nave is its great stone pulpit, classical and worse for wear after 300 years, with flowers and scrolls in high relief, but a splendid possession from the 17th century, which has been here since the church was new. It is one of the few stone pulpits built between the Reformation and the Gothic revival.

Yarlington. Two curious stone heads look out from the tower buttresses of the church, which was mostly rebuilt in 1878 except for the 15th century tower. Here is a fine font with carvings of the 14th century on a still older bowl.

Yatton. Here we may climb the Saxon battlefield of Cadbury Hill at Christmas time and find a flowering thorn like Glastonbury's, or we may wander round Ham Farm with its ancient dovecot or about the old homes and almshouses of Yatton clustering round the church; but for us, when we come this way again, the beauty and glory and oldworldness of Yatton will wait, and we shall walk slowly through the churchyard, past the 15th century cross with its little canopied figures.

The church has been a house of glory for five centuries as we see it —and indeed for seven, for part of its structure is 13th century. The heavy piers by the central tower belong to that time, though the tower itself is 200 years younger. It has a truncated spire. The 15th century nave has pinnacles and pierced parapets; a glorious south porch with panelled front, canopied doorway, and vaulted roof; and a noble turreted west front with two worn statues in the niches, and God the Father with his Crucified Son above the great window.

The interior of the lofty nave, lit by a clerestory and a double lancet window over the chancel arch, has slender pilasters reaching to the roof, with a painted wooden angel and a stone head on each. Some are lovely women in fashionable headdresses, others are queer distorted faces, and looking at the preacher in the pulpit is one with great leaves branching out of the mouth. The tiny stone figure of St Margaret slaying a dragon stands on a corbel, and on a window-sill is one small bent figure, all that is left of Yatton's wonderful roodscreen with its 69 statues. Yatton men of this century carved the mediaeval-looking screen in the south aisle. At the back of the church stand two big wooden figures of Peter and Paul from the organ which has served in Bath Abbey and at Wells, and is still on duty here after more than 200 years.

The loveliest peep in the whole church is through a door cut askew in the chancel wall to where Sir John Newton and his wife lie on a recessed tomb, a pinnacle at their head, another at their feet, a row of canopied niches over them, and on the wall a relief of the Annunciation with a dove coming down from heaven. Sir John is in his armour with a wheatsheaf crest under his head, every detail perfect. His wife Isabel, who lies in a flowing cloak, built the beautiful south porch and this chapel with its panelled arches, rich canopies, a pillar piscina, and a pinnacled turret outside the great window. All this she raised to her husband's memory before she joined him in 1498. It was Sir John's father Richard who gave the splendid nave. His alabaster tomb, surrounded by figures, is near his son's, and his second wife, Emmota, lies by him, a dainty lady in a high-peaked cap. His head is also on the family crest of a wheatsheaf, but instead of armour he wears the red robes and cap of a judge, the wallet for his seal hanging at his side. Two dogs are at his feet, and a pet dog snuggles into the folds of his wife's robes.

Sir Richard shares his chapel with a man and a woman of the 14th century in wall recesses, the curly-haired man, with a long drooping moustache and beard, having flowers patterned on his belt. A woman's head appears in mediaeval glass above Sir John's tomb.

Yatton has in its keeping one of the oldest and finest bits of mediaeval embroidery in Somerset. For hundreds of years it lay in the chest with three locks, but now it is framed behind glass, two wide strips of blue velvet embroidered with saints and prophets in green and gold, all a little faded now, for they are part of two 15th century vestments for generations sewn together and used as a pall.

Yeovil. Every traveller in the West knows this busy little town, burned down 500 years ago, when happily its new church was rescued from the flames. Over 100 houses were burned down in 1449, but the church survived this great catastrophe and has become the Lantern of the West. Today the town is prosperous and spreading, with streets crowded on market days and 40 firms employing thousands of West Country folk in making gloves and other things. If we ask what these other things are any boy in the street will tell us that, for one thing, the first aeroplane to fly over Everest came from Yeovil's aircraft works.

So busy a town has given its people abundant green spaces for play and recreation, no less than 72 acres of them in nine recreation grounds, and one corner of exceeding beauty called Nine Springs. Here we find majestic beeches, shaded walks, water babbling and falling over rocks, and a lovely lake fed by nine springs. It is an enchanting spot.

Right in the heart of the town, in an oasis of peace and space, is the old church which was new when the fire destroyed the town, begun and finished in the greatest of our building ages, the 15th century. It is a stately building, 146 feet long with a tower soaring 90 feet high. Round the aisles runs a high balustraded parapet, and an unusual parapet of pierced panels runs round the western tower. On the eastern side of this tower a small iron cross is believed to mark the fact that Yeovil was exempted from taxation during a very hard period in its history. The nave and aisles are of one great height, and the soaring piers of the arcade, and the tremendous windows, give the interior an airy grace. The fine oak roofs have been made like new with their rich carving and painting. The grand font is 15th century. From those far-off days the church has preserved some notable possessions—a chained *Paraphrase of the Gospels* by Erasmus, with a note below it of the price paid for the book and the chain 400 years ago; a 17th century Bible; and three ancient keys now in a case by the south door. They were found in the hole for the beam which barred the door in those days. There are brass portraits on the wall showing Giles Penne and his wife dressed in the fashion of the early 16th century; they would see the Lenten veil drawn across the altar, and we may still see the old heads of a king and a queen, looking at each other across the chancel, which held up the veil before the Reformation. The life-like bust of Robert Phelips, showing him preaching to his people as he preached here for 40 years last century, is by Westmacott.

The treasure of the church is simplicity itself, so far from being proud that it may easily be overlooked. It is a brass lectern like a double desk, given 500 years ago by Brother Martin Forester, whose portrait is engraved on each side above a Latin inscription which says, *Come, make your petition from this place with humble prayers now, I pray, and may Brother Forester awake in the Blessed Life.* The lectern is supported on four crouching lions.

The church has a vaulted crypt into which we come through a grand little doorway with a pinnacled canopy; it was here that the builders started their great work about 1380, knowing nothing of the new ideas in architecture that would transform the plan of the church before the work was done.

Yeovil has given its 700-year-old churchyard cross to the Roman Catholic Church.

Attached to its admirable library Yeovil has a museum with a valuable collection of Roman remains drawn from an area rich in relics of the Roman occupation and of the local remains always so delightful to see in old country towns.

Yeovilton. It has a delightful walk across the fields to its nearest neighbour, with the sight of a waterfall and yellow lilies from one of the bridges over the Yeo. The 15th century church, with quaint porch windows, has fragments still in its walls of a Norman church destroyed by fire, with the marks of the fire which destroyed it. The piscina has a stone face carved on it, a wall-bracket has an animal's head, and there are two other stone heads on the walls. The font is 16th century. There is a little old glass in the east and west windows with the heraldry of Bishop Beckington and the letters R.S. and a swan for Richard Swan, the 15th century rector who helped to rebuild the church. The peace of this charming village has been shattered by the vast nearby Naval Air Station.

APPENDIX

Places of interest open to the public

(* Indicates National Trust Property)
(† Indicates property in the care of the Ministry of Public
Building and Works)

It is advisable for intending visitors to check times of opening as
these occasionally vary.

Axbridge: The Old Manor House, open May to September.
Barrington: *Barrington Court, open Wednesdays.
Bath: *Bath Assembly Rooms, open summer and winter weekdays.
Claverton: Claverton Manor, open April to September and all
Bank Holidays.
Clevedon: *Clevedon Court, open April to September.
Dunster: Dunster Castle, open June to September.
East Lambrook: East Lambrook Manor, open May to July, and
September.
Farleigh Hungerford: † Farleigh Castle, open all the year round.
Greenham: Cothay Manor, open May to September.
Kingsdon: *Lyte's Cary, open March to October.
Montacute: *Montacute House, open March to October.
Muchelney: † Muchelney Abbey, open all the year round.
Stoke-sub-Hamdon: *The Old Hall of the Priory, open April to
October.
Tintinhull: *Tintinhull House, open April to October.
Washford: † Cleeve Abbey, open all the year round.

SOMERSET TOWNS AND VILLAGES

In this key to our map of Somerset (which appears at the front of this volume) are all the towns and villages treated in this book. If a place is not on the map by name, its square is given here, so that the way to it is easily found, each square being five miles. One or two hamlets are with their neighbouring villages.

Abbots Leigh	L1
Aisholt	G6
Alford	M7
Aller	J7
Allerford	C5
Angersleigh	G8
Ansford	M6
Ash	K8
Ashbrittle	E8
Ashcott	K6
Ashill	H8
Ashington	L8
Athelney	J7
Axbridge	K4
Babcary	L7
Babington	N4
Backwell	L2
Badgworth	J4
Bagborough	G6
Baltonsborough	L6
Banwell	J3
Barrington	J8
Barrow Gurney	L2
Barton St David	L6
Barwick	L9
Batcombe	N6
Bath	O2
Bathampton	O2
Bathealton	F8
Batheaston	O2
Bathford	O2
Bawdrip	J6
Beckington	O4
Beer Crocombe	J8
Berkley	O4

Berrow	H4
Bickenhall	H8
Bicknoller	F6
Biddisham	J4
Bishop's Hull	G7
Bishop's Lydeard	G7
Bishopsworth	M2
Blackford	N7
Blagdon	L3
Bleadon	J3
Bossington	C4
Bradford	G8
Brean	H4
Brent Knoll	J4
Bridgwater	H6
Brislington	M2
Broadway	J9
Brockley	K2
Brompton Ralph	F6
Brompton Regis	D7
Broomfield	G7
Brushford	D7
Bruton	N6
Brympton	L9
Buckland Denham	O4
Buckland St Mary	H9
Burnett	N2
Burnham-on-Sea	H4
Burrington	K3
Burrow Bridge	J7
Bury	D7
Butcombe	L3
Butleigh	L6

Cameley	M3
Camerton	N3
Cannington	H6
Carhampton	E5
Castle Cary	M7
Catcott	J6
Chaffcombe	J9
Chapel Allerton	K4
Chard	J10
Charlcombe	O2
Charlinch	G6
Charlton Adam	L7
Charlton Horethorne	N8
Charlton Mackrell	L7
Charlton Musgrove	N7
Charterhouse-on-Mendip	L4
Cheddar	K4
Cheddon Fitzpaine	H7
Chedzoy	J6
Chelvey	K2
Chelwood	M3
Chesterblade	N5
Chew Magna	M3
Chew Stoke	L3
Chewton Mendip	M4
Chilcompton	M4
Chillington	J9
Chilthorne Domer	L8
Chilton Cantelo	M8

Chilton Trinity	H6
Chilton-upon-Polden	J6
Chinnock	K9
Chipstable	E7
Chiselborough	K9
Christon	J3
Churchill	K3
Churchstanton	G9
Clapton-in-Gordano	K1
Clatworthy	E7
Claverton	O2
Cleeve	K2
Clevedon	J2
Cloford	N5
Closworth	L9
Clutton	M3
Combe Down	O3
Combe Florey	F7
Combe Hay	O3
Combe St Nicholas	H9
Compton Bishop	J4
Compton Dando	M2
Compton Dundon	L6
Compton Martin	L3
Compton Pauncefoot	N7
Congresbury	K3
Corfe	G8
Corston	N2
Cossington	J5

Wincanton	N7	Withiel Florey	D6	Woolverton	O4	Wyke Champ-
Winford	L2	Withycombe	E5	Wootton		flower	N6
Winscombe	K3	Withypool	C6	Courtenay	D5	
Winsford	C6	Wiveliscombe	F7	Worle	J3	Yarlington	N7
Winsham	J10	Wookey	L5	Wraxall	L2	Yatton	K2
Witham Friary		Woolavington	J5	Wrington	K3	Yeovil	L9
	O5	Woolley	O2	Writhlington	N4	Yeovilton	L8